1968

ALSO BY RONALD FRASER

Blood of Spain

1968

A Student Generation in Revolt

Ronald Fraser

AND

Daniel Bertaux

Bret Eynon   Ronald Grele

Béatrix Le Wita   Danièle Linhart

Luisa Passerini   Jochen Staadt

Annemarie Tröger

Pantheon Books

NEW YORK

*Library of Congress
Cataloging-in-Publication Data*
1968: a student generation in revolt.
1. Student movements—History—20th
century.   2. College students—Political
activity—History— 20th century.   3.
Education, Higher—1965-   .
I. Fraser, Ronald, 1930-   .
LA186.A16   1988   378'.1981   87-46058
ISBN 0-394-54599-0
ISBN 0-679-73953-X (pbk.)

Contents

Acknowledgements

We wish to thank the more than 230 participants in six countries who shared their memories with us; without their help this book could not have been written. Regrettably, owing to the severe exigencies of space, many of those who talked to us do not finally figure in the book; their contributions were no less important for that and we would like to thank them particularly as follows.

Sally Alexander; Franco Aprà; Bill Ayers; Francesco Barbagallo; Rosalind van der Beek; Robert Bowen; John Bradbrook; John Conquest; Nesbit Crutchfield; Anna Davin; Rosalind Delmar; Luciano Del Sette; Robert Dent; Paola Di Cori; Vittorio Dini; Roberto Dionigi; Hal Draper; Gerold Ducke; David Edgar; Kay Eisenhower; Lorenzo Galli; Nadia Ghesini; Peter Gibbon; Juan Gonzales; Al Haber; Jacquelyn Hall; Olivia Harris; Geoffrey Hawthorn; Judith Herrin; Ray Hewitt; Paul Hirst; Harlon Joye; E. Ann Kaplan; Kasim Khan; Ilse Lenz; Bruce Levine; Charles Leinenweber; Randolph Lochmann; Cesare Marconi; Elizabeth Martinez; Mo Milner; Rosario Miticocchio; Iris Morales; Renato Musto; Ettore Pagani; Steve Palmer; Susan Penrose; Aidan Pettitt; Simone Reusch; Gitte Schäfer; Marino Sinibaldi; Ulrike Stein; Mariella Tagliero; Giuseppe Tibolla; Vittorio Vidotto; Nigel Willmott.

We also wish to thank Patrizia Guerra and the Instituto Cattaneo for having made available some Italian interviews. For the many millions of words transcribed, our thanks go to Vanessa Green, Lita Petrou, Marthe Zelter, Gabriele Dumdey, Annegret Fricke, Christel Macco, Ulrike Marski, Martin Rein, Gilla Schmitt and Lidia Sinchetto. Christine Colpin was responsible for coordinating the French interviewing programme in Paris, and Jeri Nunn, of the Columbia University Oral History Research Office, oversaw the American processing.

Finally, the author's personal thanks are extended to Jane Mills and Professor Fred Halliday for reading and making invaluable critical comments at different stages of the manuscript; and to Jeremy Lewis and Kate Horgan for their work on the final draft. Needless to say, neither they nor any of the participants who appear in the book itself are responsible for the final product or any errors of fact it may contain.

Preface

From Prague to Paris, London to Tokyo, San Francisco to Peking, student revolts erupted with unforeseeable suddenness in the 1960s to challenge the existing order of society – a challenge which in many places took them to the brink of radically changing history itself. Never before had such widespread rebellion by the young swept the world, threatening capitalist and socialist established orders alike.

In itself, there was nothing historically new about student rebellion: the last century, for example, saw students fighting alongside workers on the barricades of the 1848 revolutions. In this century, the Argentinian university revolt of 1918 won many of the campus rights which students in the industrialized West struggled for in 1968, while before and after World War II the role of students in the development of the Chinese and Cuban revolutions was particularly notable. What was surprising about the 1960s was the ubiquity of student revolt which broke out not only in the Third but Second and First Worlds also.

This book looks at that rebellion in six of the West's industrialized countries: the United States, West Germany, France, Italy, Britain and Northern Ireland. For it was in these parliamentary democracies, where for the best part of the twentieth century students had been a privileged elite, the bastion rather than the adversary of the established order, that the revolt came as the greatest shock. Even so, it must be noted that in the advanced West it was Japan rather than the other countries which led the way. By the late 1950s, Zengakuren (the All-Japan Federation of Student Self-Government Association) was a militant left-wing and anti-imperialist organization seeking alliances with sectors of the working class. In 1960, it spearheaded the struggle against the renewal of the Japan-U.S. Security pact, rallying 350,000 workers and students who invaded the ground of the parliament in a famous 'snake march' and staged a mass urination on the building's steps to show their contempt for parliament and the treaty. Pictures of Zengakuren students armed with helmets, shields and staves engaged in hand-to-hand combat with security forces in scenes resembling medieval jousts became well known in the late 1960s as Japanese students led anti-Vietnam War demonstrations.

The Vietnam War was, of course, one of the major factors that mobilized students in the U.S. and Western Europe. But it alone does not explain student rebelliousness. The aim of this book, which is based on the memories of over three hundred people who took part in the student movements, is to trace the roots of that rebellion; but it is also a study of a generation, for it is impossible to understand the 1960s without an awareness of what the 1950s represented for many of those who became student activists. Indeed, it is in opposition to the previous decade's cultural and political Cold War stasis that much of what happened in the following decade must be seen.

The 1960s, it must be remembered, represented a unique constellation of conditions in the history of the West. An unprecedented economic boom – in the thirteen years from the end of the Korean War in 1953 to 1966 and the Vietnam War, West Germany, France and Italy trebled, and the U.S. and Britain doubled, their gross national products; industrial wages rose two-fold in Western Europe and by one and a half times in the U.S. in the same period; and in all of these countries there was virtual full employment – nowhere were more than four per cent out of work by 1966. Added to this considerable material progress, was demographic growth: the post-war 'baby boom' (delayed only in West Germany and Italy by the effects of the war) resulted in a considerable increase in the number of teenagers in the population. At the same time, the capitalist system was itself changing, becoming increasingly corporate, and embarking on new technological advances which required a lower proportion of unskilled manual workers and a higher percentage of skilled and white-collar workers. This explained in part the dramatic growth in higher education, its expansion responding also to the demographic growth and pressure from those social classes whose children had traditionally been denied access to the university. It was, in short, one of these rare decades, repeated at most once or twice a century, when capitalism seemed to promise continuous progress, and previously unheard of social and economic possibilities were opening up.

In these very special conditions, it was hardly surprising that the post-war generation was also, in many ways, unique. Unlike their parents, the young who came of age in the 1960s had known neither the Depression of the 1930s nor World War II. The deferred gratifications that bourgeois society traditionally demanded of adolescents no longer seemed relevant at a time of relative prosperity; they did not have to 'play it safe' like their parents in order to ensure their future security: economically, socially, sexually, they could aspire to a new range and immediacy of experience. Thanks to a new youth culture, and a youth-centred market that went hand in hand with it, adolescents had for the first time the feeling of belonging to a specific age group with a place in society (though here, too, distinctions must be registered: in continental Europe and Northern Ireland the impact of the youth culture in the first half of the 1960s was far less than in the U.S. and Britain).

Aware of their social weight, valued by the free enterprise system as consumers, teenagers could, in full logic, demand no longer to be treated as 'citizens in suspense', disallowed to act as responsible for their own destinies – and by implication that of the society of which they were part. 'Young people were claiming the rights of citizenship, not acting in age-specific ways,' Michael Frisch, an American student at the time, observes. 'What we were saying was, my politics is not defined by the fact that I'm eighteen, it's defined by the fact that I have a view of the world, and I have every right and responsibility to act on that.'

The rights that they claimed and the causes around which they mobil-ized form the subject of this book. Here it is worth pointing to one more element that influenced the shape that student radicalization took: the failure of those political parties and organizations which had historically offered a critique of Western society to afford a radical vision which addressed itself to the contradictions of post-war liberal society. The Cold War, at home and abroad, welfare statism and growing material prosperity had contributed to locking these movements into the established post-war consensus. Moreover, in the East, the practice of Stalinism offered no viable alternative model to the majority of the labour movements in the West.

The burden of a radically different vision of society thus fell, by default one might say, on the shoulders of students – a transient sector of society, not a class, despite their own largely middle-class origins – with little or no apparent means to effect radical change. That they attempted it was therefore all the more astonishing. In some cases they had no models to fall back on; in others they were trying to rework Marxist and socialist models. In almost all cases they looked for inspiration to Third World liberation movements which, in challenging the orthodoxies of both East and West, appeared to be opening up a new political space. Starting from very different positions, the student movements progressively converged by the end of the decade. En route many of them at different times passed through similar phases. Among these were the attempt to expand the meaning of democracy by increasing people's control of their own lives; the notion of people's 'empowerment' by their direct action, which in turn radicalizes the individual; the concept of organization without leaders or led, in which active participation rather than formal membership was the overriding criterion; the search for a new political space and the theories to give it content; disillusionment with liberal or left parties; and a turn away from parliamentary politics. In short, a break with much that the Old Left stood for. But as the movements began more directly to challenge the ruling order and were met almost everywhere by an escalating and often violent counter-offensive, they sought in revolutionary Marxism and the mobilization of the working class and the oppressed strata of society the only means of overthrowing that order. The French May events, when de Gaulle's authoritarian regime was almost toppled by a general strike which followed student battles with a ferociously repressive police, and in the East the anti-Stalinist revolution ushered in by the Czech students – bloodlessly, until the Soviet Union determined otherwise by force of arms – served to reinforce for many the idea that revolution was on the historical agenda. Finally, then, the movements reverted to something much closer to the Old Left politics which, initially, they had rejected.

These differing but converging trajectories, seen through the memories of those who took part in them, form the core of this book, which in consequence is confined to the experiences of those who were students at some stage in the 1960s. At the same time, it considers the relationship between the student movements and those that followed, most notably the Women's Movement; but – and this must be stressed – it does not attempt to describe the history of any of these subsequent movements. Nor, indeed, does it describe in full the history of any single student movement; to do so would require a book for each. Many other aspects of that decade – the youth and counter-culture, for example, or political events – are described only in as far as they had a direct impact on the student movements themselves.

This book is the collaborative result of the work of nine oral historians. The first large-scale international oral history of its kind, it is also the first comparative study of the student movements in the six countries. Our point of departure was the belief that the student upheavals shared a sufficient number of characteristics to be thought of primarily as an international phenomenon; national specificities would take second place. In the broadest sense this remains true; but it must be pointed out that specific national conditions played a greater role than we originally assigned to them. Take, for example, the case of the Vietnam War. The attempt by the greatest economic and military power on earth to subjugate by every means – saturation bombing, massacre, defoliation – a small revolutionary Third World country radicalized tens of thousands of students internationally. But the forms of that radicalization and the particular responses varied because of the different conditions in each country and the way the war focussed students' attentions on the failings of their own societies. From the actual involvement of American universities in the war effort to the symbolic comparison of an authoritarian university regime to U.S. domination of a small country, the response was one of outrage, of drawing analogies between their own situation and the revolutionary Vietnamese struggle. But most of the actual events of 1968 stemmed from specific national circumstances which the war helped bring into perspective, as well as governments' response to protest.

Through protagonists' memories, we sought to recreate not only those events but, more importantly, their *meaning* to those who took part in them, the lived experience. The agenda we collectively set ourselves at the beginning placed as much emphasis on the comparative trajectories of individuals as on those of the movements. Due to the complexity of the latters' national specificities, this has regrettably proved impossible: the movements' developments, seen through participants' eyes, dominate here.

Memory, as is well known, is always conditioned by the events that have succeeded what is remembered. It is thus always 'fallible' if we expect it to reproduce exactly 'the thing as it was'. But what people felt (or, more accurately, what today they remember having felt), what they hoped to achieve as much as what they in fact achieved, what should have happened and what would have been better if it had not happened, constitute historical facts as much as the events themselves. At the same time, the omissions and repressions of memory are themselves significant. Some of the latter should be noted here. The utopianism expressed in the slogan 'We Want Everything', the joyful egalitarianism and the sheer folly that sometimes accompanied it, is rarely expressed; nor in many cases are the connections between personal and public life – one of the innovatory aspects of the movements. In concentrating on the local rather than the global, memory confirms the importance to each movement of its specific problems and struggles but ignores the inter-relationship between all the movements' struggles. Indeed, it must be admitted that despite our initial assumptions, this inter-relationship is not transparent (any more, perhaps, than are the inter-connections between the revolutionary uprisings of 1848). Certainly, in the 1960s the media played its part; so, too, did a number of common assumptions about the increasingly corporate and undemocratic nature of advanced capitalist society. There were also, of course, some contacts between activists in different countries; but nowhere can one see a direct causal link between the actions of one movement and another. What would seem rather to be the case is that movement activists borrowed, sometimes with considerable time lags, tactics and strategies from other movements that they felt would meet their local needs.

The absence of a collective assessment of what the movements achieved and what they failed to achieve – rendered ever more difficult by the established order's subsequent counter-offensive in the 1970s and 1980s – also appears to have made memory more problematic: for some, victories are better remembered than defeats; for others, personal defeats obscure the political victories which might otherwise have been seen to vindicate them. Indeed, much that seemed exhilarating, even triumphant, about the movements has been buried in memory by subsequent history. One of this book's major objectives is to contribute to this collective reassessment of the period.

The interviews in this book were conducted mainly between 1984 and 1985. They were based on an agenda of questions – though not a joint questionnaire – which we wished to pursue in each of the chronological stages of the movements' developments. Collaborators' drafts of each stage were sent to the author, rewritten and returned, revised by the collaborators and further rewritten – a process that extended over two years and included collective and bilateral consultations. A number of the national drafts run to close on the size of this book alone, but finally less than five per cent of the interview material gathered has, to our regret, found its way into these pages. The responsibility for the political and social description of each student movement belongs to the oral historians in the respective countries: the U.S., Bret Eynon and Ronald Grele; West Germany, Jochen Staadt and Annemarie Tröger; France, Daniel Bertaux, Béatrix Le Wita and Danièle Linhart; Italy, Luisa Passerini. Apart from my accountability for Britain and Northern Ireland, the selection of materials from all the countries, and the form and structure of the book, are my responsibility.

RONALD FRASER

Preface to the American edition
by Bret Eynon and Ronald Grele

When we were invited to participate in this work it was to collaborate in a comparative study of the student movements' development in the capitalist North Atlantic rim. That was, and has remained, the basic purpose of this book. At the same time, however, we left open the possibility that, should our publishers require it, additional national material might be added over and above that necessary for the comparative purposes we had in mind. This has been the case for this special U.S. edition which includes some 38 extra pages devoted to specifically American events.

The additional material amplifies two main areas covered in the general edition: the Student Nonviolent Coordinating Committee (SNCC) and the counter-culture. The former's importance in setting much of the American New Left's radical democratic agenda, and the interaction between the black and white American student movements, which provided a great part of the dynamic we sought to uncover, seemed ample justification for extending our discussion of the black student movement for an American audience. SNCC was in many ways unique to the U.S.; so, too, seemingly, in its different way was the counter-culture. Emerging first in the United States, it reached its apogee here in the 1960s, while in Western Europe (with the partial exception of Britain) its height came later. The American counter-culture was uniquely related to the other social movements of that decade, including the black movement, through its cultural program: rock 'n roll, the desire to reorganize the basis for personal relations, and the search for an alternative to the hegemonic personality of the white, middle-class businessman. To highlight the importance of the counter-culture and its institutions, we have added material which, for lack of space or questions of balance, does not appear in the general edition.

Finally, the events of the autumn of 1967 – a turning point for the American SDS – and the movement's brief resurgence after Kent State in May, 1970, have been expanded.

Despite these various additions, we must stress that we do not thereby attribute a more important role to the American movement than to the others, or intend to imply any alteration from that traced in the general edition in their respective causal relationships. While recognizing that the extra material inevitably produces a different overall emphasis, we have tried to maintain the thematic balance of the original text. We are solely responsible for this additional material, its selection, use, integration into the text and interpretation. Ronald Fraser's responsibility for the general edition does not extend to this added text.

The interviews collected for this work are, for the most part, the products of our collaboration. Most are now on deposit at the Columbia University Oral History Research Office where, eventually, they will be made available to others for alternative readings. A few, which were conducted by Bret Eynon between 1977 and 1981 for a study of the radical community in Ann Arbor, Michigan, remain in his possession. The interview with Michael Wallace was conducted by Alessandra Lorini, and that with Bettina Berch by Victor Smythe for a class at Columbia. Both are part of the Oral History Office Collection. In addition, Sarah Elbert graciously donated to us the interview conducted with her by Ann Klajment in 1976. It too is now on deposit at Columbia. In time we hope to collect transcripts of all of the interviews conducted in all six nations discussed in the book, and make them available for an extended study of this generation of activists.

We owe a special debt to the people we interviewed. They gave us their time, their consideration, and more than anything else, their good will. Oral history involves the subjects of a work in that work in a very unique way. Our book becomes their book; their memories, our memories. We can only hope that we have lived up to their expectations. As anyone familiar with the American student movement will note, we have included testimony from people with a wide variety of political positions. Everyone we spoke to knew that, for the most part, our views differed with theirs – both in the 1960s and now. Despite those differences, we have tried to look at them fairly and in context. They will judge our successes and failures, we hope, with the same patience and good will they showed us when we spoke to them.

In planning, researching and writing this book, we have made a special effort to focus on activist 'foot soldiers', both black and white, as well as more well-known national movement leaders. We believe the voices of local organizers and day-to-day activists provide a fresh perspective, one crucial to a full understanding of the history of the Sixties. It was the active commitment of hundreds of thousands of such people that drove forward the movements of the Sixties. But commitment was not without risk; possible consequences ranged from disrupted lives to severe beatings and, in some cases, death. It is to those who took the risks and made the commitment that this book is dedicated.

I

1968

Voices

My most vivid memory of May '68? The new-found ability for everyone to *speak* – to speak of anything with anyone. In that month of talking during May you learnt more than in the whole of your five years of studying. It was really another world – a dream world perhaps – but that's what I'll always remember: the need and the right for everyone to speak – *René Bourrigaud, student at the Ecole Supérieure d'Agriculture, Angers, France*

Freedom is the consciousness of our desires – French slogan

People were learning through doing things themselves, learning self-confidence. It was magic, there were all these kids from nice middle-class homes who'd never done or said anything and were now suddenly speaking. It was democracy of the public space in the market place, a discourse where nobody was privileged. If anything encapsulated what we were trying to do and why, it was that . . . – *Pete Latarche, leader of the university occupation at Hull, England, 1968*

It's a moment I shall never forget. Suddenly, spontaneously, barricades were being thrown up in the streets. People were building up the cobblestones because they wanted – many of them for the first time – to throw themselves into a *collective*, spontaneous activity. People were releasing all their repressed feelings, expressing them in a festive spirit. Thousands felt the need to communicate with each other, to love one another. That night has forever made me optimistic about history. Having lived through it, I can't ever say, 'It will never happen . . .' – *Dany Cohn-Bendit, student leader at Nanterre University, on the night of the Paris barricades, 10/11 May 1968*

The unthinkable happened! Everything I had ever dreamt of since childhood, knowing that it would never happen, now began to become real. People were saying, fuck hierarchy, authority, this society with its cold rational elitist logic! Fuck all the petty bosses and the mandarins at the top! Fuck this immutable society that refuses to consider the misery, poverty, inequality and injustice it creates, that divides people according to their origins and skills! Suddenly, the French were showing they understood that they had to refuse the state's authority because it was malevolent, evil, just as I'd always thought as a child. Suddenly they realized that they had to find a new sort of solidarity. And it was happening in front of my eyes. That was what May '68 meant to me! – *Nelly Finkielsztejn, student at Nanterre University, Paris*

For most of us the issue is not what's right and wrong. Most of us have a pretty clear sense of that. The issue is, what am I going to do? Am I going to do what's right, or am I going to do what's expedient? Because often to do what's right means you just get blown away, you know. So when somebody finds a way to do what is right and be effective at the same time, people just go OOOF! Because now they're liberated, now they can do what's right! – *John O'Neal, Student Nonviolent Coordinating Committee (SNCC) activist during the civil rights campaign in the American South*

My world had been very staid, very traditional, very frightened, very middle-class and respectable. And here I was doing these things that six months before I would have thought were just horrible. But I was in the midst of an enormous tide of people. There was so much constant collective reaffirmation of it. The ecstasy was stepping out of time, out of traditional personal time. The usual rules of the game in capitalist society had been set aside. It was phenomenally liberating . . . At the same time it was a political struggle. It wasn't just Columbia. There *was* a fucking war on in Vietnam, and the civil rights movement. These were profound forces that transcend that moment. 1968 just cracked the universe open for me. And the fact of getting involved meant that never again was I going to look at something outside with the kind of reflex condemnation or fear. Yes, it was the making of me – or the unmaking. – *Mike Wallace, occupation of Columbia University, New York, April 1968*

Hey Hey L. B. J.
How Many Kids Did You Kill Today? – *American anti-Vietnam War chant directed at President Lyndon B. Johnson*

We'd been brought up to believe in our hearts that America fought on the side of justice. The Second World War was very much ingrained in us, my father had volunteered. So, along with the absolute horror of the war in Vietnam, there was also a feeling of personal betrayal. I remember crying by myself late at night in my room listening to the reports of the war, the first reports of the bombing. Vietnam was the catalyst . . . – *John Levin, student leader at San Francisco State College*

I was outraged, what shocked me most was that a highly developed country, the super-modern American army, should fall on these Vietnamese peasants – fall on them like the conquistadores on South America, or the white settlers on the North American Indians. In my mind's eye, I always saw those bull-necked fat pigs – like in Georg Grosz's pictures – attacking the small, child-like Vietnamese. – *Michael von Engelhardt, German student*

The resistance of the Vietnamese people showed that it could be done – a fight back was possible. If poor peasants could do it well why not people in Western Europe? That was the importance of Vietnam, it destroyed the myth that we just had to hold on to what we had because the whole world could be blown up if the Americans were 'provoked'. The Vietnamese showed that if you were attacked you fought back, and then it depended on the internal balance of power whether you won or not. – *Tariq Ali, a British Vietnam Solidarity Campaign leader*

> We won't ask
> We won't demand
> We will take
> and occupy
> – *French slogan*

So we started to be political in a totally new way, making the connection between our student condition and the larger international issues. A low mark in mathematics could become the focal point of an occupation by students who linked the professor's arbitrary and authoritarian behaviour to the wider issues, like Vietnam. Acting on your immediate problems made you understand better the bigger issues. If it hadn't been for that, perhaps the latter would have remained alien, you'd have said 'OK, but what can *I* do?' – *Agnese Gatti, student at Trento Institute of Social Sciences, Italy*

Creating a confrontation with the university administration you could significantly expose the interlocking network of imperialism as it was played out on the campuses. You could prove that they were working hand-in-hand with the military and the CIA, and that ultimately, when you pushed them, they would call upon all the oppressive apparatus to defend their position from their own students. – *Jeff Jones, Students for a Democratic Society (SDS), New York regional organizer*

We Are The People Our Parents Warned Us Against
– *J. J. Jacobs, SDS, during the Columbia University occupation*

Those who are disgusted with the inhuman aspects of their society should DROP OUT of it and give themselves full time to making this world a more beautiful place with their every act. If all of us would stop spending our time and energy trying to save America from within and would instead unite in our own society to set an example, all of the really stupid things that are going on would be effectively pointed out to the rest of the people. – *John Sinclair, counter-culture leader, Detroit*

Everybody was terribly young and didn't know what was going on. One had a sort of megalomaniac attitude that by sheer protest and revolt things would be changed. It was true of the music, of the halucinogenics, of politics, it was true across the board – people threw themselves into activity without experience. The desire to do something became tremendously intense and the capacity to do it diminished by the very way one was rejecting the procedures by which things could be done. It led to all sorts of crazy ideas – *Anthony Barnett, sociology student, Leicester University, England*

Ho! Ho! Ho Chi Minh!
Dare to Struggle, Dare to Win!
– *American slogan*

There was a readiness for violence which came from an enormous anger, a rage. If it hadn't been so, we wouldn't have built barricades with other people's cars, without thinking for a moment to ask their owners. Wouldn't have overturned a bus as a matter of course and set fire to it. Yes, emotionally, we were out for war now, civil war . . . – *Barbara Brick, student at Munich University after the assassination attempt on the West German student leader Rudi Dutschke, in April 1968*

The CS gas made you vomit. But I believed you could vomit just as well going forward as back. I kept telling people, 'If you don't breathe through your nose, the gas won't do you any harm.' I may have even believed it myself for a time! But it was the kids who showed us the only thing that worked. With a bit of rag or blanket in their hand, they'd pounce on the cannisters the moment they landed and throw them back. It was unbelievable! And although it didn't stop them choking, at least it made the police choke as well. – *Bernadette McAliskey (née Devlin), Derry riots, Northern Ireland, August 1969*

Two cops came around the corner. They put their .327 Magnums up to my head and cocked the hammers. It was raining and I had my hands in my trench coat. We were armed at different times, but I wasn't armed then. They said, 'Take your hands out of your pockets real slow.' I was a goner if I did, I knew they'd say you were going for your gun. I couldn't make my hands come up. I kept telling them I didn't have one. What was racing through my mind was that it would be really stupid for the ruling class to do this right now, at the height of the strike. And then another part of my mind was saying that these two cops had probably never heard of the ruling class. They're just going to kill the straight-haired nigger, as the tactical squad called me. – *Hari Dillon, student at San Francisco State during the strike, November 1968–April 1969*

I began to realize what it was all about. The state had mobilized. It taught me two lessons. Students by themselves would never get anywhere. Secondly, that the contribution of student activism, intelligence, humour and organizational ability had to go into the workers' movement in some way. – *Paul Ginsborg, research fellow, Cambridge, England*

The duty of a revolutionary is to make the revolution. – *Widely adopted slogan of Che Guevara, the Cuban revolutionary leader*

One talked about revolution to begin with because the Vietnamese were having a revolution, or because the Cubans had a revolution. Then, by analogy, which may not have been that sound but was certainly strong polemically, people would pose the question: How do we think about the black movement in the U.S. in terms of revolutionary models? Is there a paradigm of the revolutionary society? Of the revolutionary personality? As the discussion got heated, people more and more started to think, Well, what would we be if we were revolutionaries? If we students became revolutionary? – *Carl Oglesby, former president, SDS*

In all extraordinary situations, and none is more extraordinary than a revolutionary situation, the world seems open all of a sudden. The traditional barriers between 'home' and 'abroad' break down to some degree. It's not only the revolutionary's 'extraordinary' state of mind, but the fact that the outside world changes. It becomes a matter of course to take part in unknown people's activities, whether at home or in a foreign country. Even normal, traditional people suddenly open their doors to strangers. That all this happened in 1968 and the following years indicates that there was at least a revolutionary climate if not a 'revolutionary situation'. – *Anna Pam, West German SDS*

You'd read about things like this happening in Russia in 1917. Now it was happening in our own streets. It was amazing! Here were barricades keeping the British army and police out of our streets, out of 'Free Belfast'. It wasn't as politically explosive as it could have been, but if you didn't make the best use of the occasion the first time – so what? You'd learn for the next time. – *Michael Farrell, People's Democracy student leader, on the uprising in Belfast, August 1969*

We had the idea that the social revolution had to start from daily life. Start from even the smallest unbearable aspects of daily life, like wearing a tie or make-up. Start to make our relationships of a different order to the existing one. Start to take things back into our hands, reappropriate what had been expropriated from us. The revolution must be a festival – the festival of the oppressed. – *Elsa Gili, researcher at Turin University*

2

Cold War

The Deadlocked 1950s

You had a stark choice, it was said. A choice between freedom and
tyranny – between the salt mines and Wall Street. That choice
meant renouncing the anti-fascist movement, the positive hope of
the Resistance, the radical populism of the war. Forget all that, it
was said, you had better go with capitalism with a human face than
fall into the Gulag. That was the dominant climate of the early
Fifties and people lived it like that – *Stuart Hall, student at Oxford in
the early 1950s*

Nothing, it seems, could stand more starkly distinct from the voices of
1968 than this vision of Western life in the early 1950s. These were the
years which, for the first time, saw a world frozen by the Cold War into two
antagonistic blocs, between East and West, between Russian-style Communism and American-style capitalism. A world which lived in unprecedented fear of nuclear extinction. The immediate post-war period had
killed off hopes that the West's wartime alliance with the Soviet Union
could lead to a new era of peace and social reform. The United States,
which had emerged virtually unscathed from the war, exerted its new role
as the world's leading military and economic power – a power devoted to
combating Communism, to maintaining the 'free world' firmly in the
capitalist camp. In this task it was assisted by the dominant classes of
Western Europe, whose power had been shaken, if not overturned, by the
war. In reconstructing or consolidating their bourgeois democracies, they
shared America's determination to defend their societies from all internal
and external threat.

Although post-war reconstruction fuelled an unprecedented economic boom which brought its own changes, the first half of the 1950s was marked by a political, ideological and cultural conformism. A virulent anti-Communism maintained and justified this climate. 'The grip of the Cold War was so great,' explained Hall, 'that to move a little bit left of centre was to be seen in danger of falling into the grasp of the Comintern, of becoming a subversive agent. If you had dangerous thoughts, you were clearly paid by Moscow. To be seen talking to a Communist was a straightforward way of getting your name on the lists of MI5 [British counter-intelligence].'

The effects of these convoluted political ideologies on those too young to comprehend them, yet old enough to face the reality of atomic warfare, can only be estimated. Jeff Jones, growing up in Southern California, recalled the effects of the bomb on his school life. 'In our elementary school we were taught that we lived in the greatest country in the world; a country that could do no wrong. Simultaneously, we went through the ritual of duck-and-cover. Twice a month the sirens and bells would ring and we would go to the farthest wall from the windows, cover our heads so that when the bomb exploded over Los Angeles we would survive. We would return to our seats thinking how terrible the Russians were for planning to do this to us, and thankful that there would be a chance to survive the attack. We are the first generation to live under the threat of the annihilation of the world.'

It was this general climate, then, which forms some of the earliest memories of those radical students who hoped to change the world in 1968. Without understanding the post-war period, it is difficult to comprehend what they sought to change and why.

As befitted its new world role, the United States was the epicentre of the anti-Communist campaign internationally and domestically. Pursuing policies begun under the Truman administration, Senator Joe McCarthy conducted domestic witch hunts in a wholesale attempt to discredit and destroy not only Communists but the left in general. So all-pervading was his campaign that few of the future radicals could escape it, as Bruce Franklin, then at high school in Brooklyn, remembered: 'I thought Joe McCarthy was right, there was this terrible Communist conspiracy. I thought we were in actual danger of nuclear attack, in danger of a Soviet invasion. We were exposed to doses of anti-Soviet and anti-Communist propaganda that were the heaviest until the 1980s. A young person who was concerned about political questions had far more chance of coming up as a militant anti-Communist than being involved in progressive social political activity or thought.'

In Detroit, where Robin Hood was banned from the public library for 'preaching Communist doctrine', Maurice Zeitlin, a student at the predominantly working-class Wayne State College, tried to organize a small action against the ban. 'Out of 28,000 students at the College, twenty-eight joined our picket line.'

So effective, indeed, was the anti-Communist campaign that future radicals grew up with little or no contact with a previous generation that had been radicalized by the Depression. 'We didn't know about the history of the left,' recalled Cathy Wilkerson, 'didn't know about Communist Internationals, about the history of the black left. I was a junior in college in the Sixties before I knew what people meant when they referred to the Thirties. We had no history . . .'

To those with a history, the sons and daughters of members or former members of the Communist Party, that history was mysterious and frightening. Steve Fraser, who was raised in a Jewish family on Long Island, remembered as a child 'my father taking the *Daily Worker*, and sticking it under the bed. They were supposed to sell the *Daily Worker* in Great Neck, Long Island! Believe me, they did not sell too many copies of the *Daily Worker* in Great Neck in the 1950s.' Rayna Rapp, also on Long Island, also from a Jewish family which belonged to the Party, also recalled the toll. 'I shouldn't call it paranoia. It was real fear. My parents were both minnows. They were not big fish. They were not underground, but friends of theirs were; and that was scary. They were scared in a way that I think you are when you lose your movement and feel that you have to do it as an individual. I remember terrible dreams, a muddling of World War II movies and bombing.'

Most young people in the United States, however, would not have come into contact with any left party during that time. Paul Buhle recalled his first meeting with members of the Communist Party when he was a student at the University of Wisconsin. 'The two regional leaders of the C P would come to Madison. They seemed so harmless, so pitiable. I think the Milwaukee C P was being funded by the F B I. It was a laughable operation.' 'You have to remember,' Free Speech Movement participant Michael Rossman noted, 'what we found when we met the Old Left. All that was left was the skin and bones. The flesh of what had been a movement was gone. Only the hard core remained, the true believers who had stayed through everything. The more spontaneous elements, the people who had made it a movement, were gone. It was not an attractive group.'

With the exception of Italy, the anti-Communist paranoia was perhaps somewhat less virulent in Western Europe. Nonetheless, American power exerted itself. In West Germany, the Communist party and its youth organization were outlawed in the Fifties. In France and Italy, where the Communist parties had played a leading role in the resistance to fascism, they were evicted by the ruling elite from the immediate post-war coalitions before the 1940s had ended. The reason in both cases was the same: American threats to exclude the two countries from the Marshall Plan which funded post-war West European reconstruction and ensured the continued existence of the free enterprise system. Similarly, the post-war British Labour government swung firmly into the American camp and was responsible for proposing the Western military alliance that became NATO.

Implacably opposed to Communism, the Catholic church played an active role in the anti-Communist campaign, and nowhere more so than in Italy. There it became a 'religious war' so bitter that it left deep scars which outlasted the Cold War itself. For many children, the war began in kindergarten, as Peppino Ortoleva, the son of an army officer, remembered: 'The nuns terrorized the children with stories. This is one I recall in particular. A Communist father had learned that his wife, who was a secret Catholic, had had their child baptized. In revenge, he put the child in the oven. When he opened it, he found the child kneeling, praying with clasped hands, "I forgive you, papa."'

'The devil will come and carry you off because your father is a Communist,' the nuns told Eliana Minicozzi at her school in a working-class neighbourhood in Rome. Torn between allegiance to her strongly Catholic bourgeois mother and her Communist working-class father, she took a decision at the age of thirteen. Going to the altar of the Sacred Heart, she spoke to it: 'I don't know whether you can accept this or not, but I prefer to love mankind rather than to love you – and I don't care what happens.' Thereafter, she started to help her father in his political work, selling the Communist party's newspaper, *L'Unità*.

In the war of rival social systems, capitalism was clearly presented as inherently superior to Soviet Communism. Social deprivation as the result of depressions like that of the 1930s would not recur, for capitalism, it was claimed, had reformed itself. Critical social analysis, Marxism, socialism – these were things of a past which had been transcended by the flow of capitalist history and material progress. Ideology was declared dead, yet nothing could have been more ideological than the intensely conservative consensus which was dominated by anti-utopian, reactionary theories of politics and human nature.

It was the conformism of Western societies, their 'boredom', which first springs to the mind of many future student activists. 'There was a pervasive feeling – certainly I shared it – that nothing was going on, America was a boring place,' recalled Mario Savio, of New York lower middle-class origins. 'A kind of boredom and apprehensiveness and foreboding. Behind the face of nothing ever happening was the fact that there were bombs, serious stuff, but it never impinged upon this apolitical consumer utopia. It was a time when a brand new laundry detergent was every bit as real and important as what President Eisenhower might be doing.'

Things were little better in Britain. 'There was a sense that the Labour government, which had done great things, had gone into the sands,' observed Anthony Barnett, the son of a Jewish businessman and Communist Party member at the time. 'The Fifties began with the Conservatives coming to power and the Queen's coronation. I wasn't an angry young man because I wasn't a young man, I was a boy – but I was angry. What about? About the complacency of the country. Everything I was angry about was symbolised by the Coronation. Here was all the old English upper-class crap coming back.'

The sense of stasis, deadlock, was shared in France and Italy; even family life seemed to offer no escape. 'No one talked in the family. There was a silence about anything that might have a political, social or cultural meaning,' remembered Bertrand Marie of his upper middle-class youth in France. 'Sexuality, even the body, was taboo. We never touched each other. I could almost say I was brought up as though we all lived in a hotel.'

'Life in a small provincial Italian town was suffocating. The only hope seemed to be to leave and never come back,' recalled Elsa Gili of her lower middle-class adolescence. 'We had to fight our families even for small things like going out in the evening, smoking, or meeting as a group of youngsters to discuss politics.'

It was perhaps in West Germany, however, that the reimposition of bourgeois conformism was to be most sharply felt because it came later. In the devastation of the immediate post-war years, children enjoyed a freedom they would hardly have known otherwise. Fathers – if they had returned from the war – were too busy scraping a living among the ruins, mothers too preoccupied with finding food to discipline their children. Millions of refugees from the East added to the chaos. Even solidly middle-class families, like Alfred Krovoza's, were affected: 'For us children it was wonderful. At home we had two families billeted on us, it was like being part of an extended family, there was always entertainment and excitement. Out in the streets it was just as fantastic. There were children of families whose home had been bombed, children of refugees from the East. A real mixture of classes.' But by the early Fifties all this came to an end. Krovoza's father became a civil servant, the billeted families moved out, and life returned to middle-class 'normality'. In contrast to the earlier years, he remembered the rest of the Fifties as being 'a time of intellectual deadness. I had these fantasies about hidden pockets of intellectual life somewhere around here, daydreams of a secret bohemian life, writers' groups – but obviously none of that existed.'

The fascist past hung heavily over West German youth. Confrontation with that past – usually through their fathers – was to become an important factor in forming future German student activists. Sometimes it was covered in silence, as in Suse Köhler's case. Her father returned from a Russian prisoner-of-war camp only in 1950, when she was seven: 'He looked pitiful when he came back. Every night we were woken by his screams and crying. I didn't know what happened to him during the war, but he was a complete stranger to me. My older sister and brother – we were all products of his home leaves during the war – rejected him, too. Everything was "verboten", he was totally rigid, suspicious, full of mistrust. I used to envy girls in my class whose fathers hadn't come back from the war. When I was ten or twelve I wanted to run away. Eventually, all three of us did.'

She was to discover only many years later that her father had been a member of a firing squad during the war.

Unlike Suse Köhler, Niels Kadritzke, a refugee from East Prussia, knew of his father's past and remembered two middle-ranking Nazi friends visiting him frequently to talk over the past. 'But, looking back, I think that more important than all this in my political formation was the fact that my father suddenly died in 1954. He was a very authoritarian man and suddenly he was gone. It was a very liberating feeling.' His feelings were confirmed when he visited school friends whose fathers were still alive. 'Mostly, they were totally authoritarian . . . Subconsciously, I must have felt that a family with a father is really something dreadful.'

Unlike West Germany, where the Allies condoned the continuation in office of former Nazis, the Communist regime in East Germany purged them. This was to have an important effect on the early politicization of a number of youth, like Bernd Rabehl, who later came to the West and played a leading role in the German student movement. For the purge created a virtual revolution in the school system where ninety per cent of the former teachers were replaced by secondary school students, young workers and artisans who encouraged discussion of the Nazi past.

'I really believed in the "anti-fascist democratic education",' Rabehl recalled. 'In elementary school I joined the Free German Youth [the Communist party's youth organization] and took part in many of their political activities. I was convinced that the German Democratic Republic [GDR] was the better Germany. When I was fifteen, in 1953, the Communist Party asked me to go on to high school. Only three to four per cent of working-class children were in secondary education, and the Party wanted more to go.'

The son of a cleaning woman who later became a typist, he agreed to continue his education which, as in both Germanies, had started late because of the post-war disruptions. Almost at the same time, there occurred the first of a number of events which brought home to him the realities of Russian-style Communism. On 17 June 1953, workers in East Berlin and other industrial centres rose in protest against the raising of work norms and shortages of food and consumer products. In Rathenow, the industrial town where Rabehl lived, he followed a demonstration of local workers carrying a red banner – 'it was the biggest demo Rathenow had ever seen' – and watched as a strike council was elected. 'Just then the secretary of the local Free German Youth yelled at the demonstrators to return to work. He was shouted down. Even as a Communist youth I knew the workers were right and that he was crazy.'

Soviet troops in combat uniform dispersed the demonstrators without firing in Rathenow; but elsewhere the rising, which lasted three days, was ferociously repressed by the Soviet army, and some fifty people, mostly in East Berlin, were killed.

Despite his sympathy with the workers, Rabehl continued to militate in the Communist youth. But three years after the East German rising, the repression by Soviet tanks of the Hungarian uprising of 1956 sharpened his criticism of Stalinism as he was experiencing it in his daily life. 'I followed the Hungarian events closely on the radio. I had the impression that it was the same as 17 June in the GDR – a struggle against rigidity, bureaucracy, the cult of personality or whatever words we used for it at the time.'

Seeing no future for himself, he left East Germany in 1960, a year before the regime built the Berlin Wall. 'The conditions in East Germany were so contradictory that they allowed no adjustment. As always, the conscious effort to adapt ends in non-adaptation. A rebellion of adjustment, I would call the Fifties in the German Democratic Republic.'

As in West Germany, the fascist legacy remained strong in Italy throughout the Fifties and beyond in state institutions and certain sectors of society. But its overall influence on those growing up in the Fifties appears less pervasive than in Germany. The Italian family, as a traditionally independent institution, showed considerable resistance to state intervention in its life; and fascism, moreover, had been met by popular armed struggle, even if mention of the Resistance, with its patrimony of rebellion and freedom, was to all intents and purposes silenced in the Fifties.

Romano Madera's father had been a fascist – 'a lukewarm one, like many people probably who, for opportunistic reasons, joined fascist mass organizations. At the end of the war, the partisans got him for "collaborating" and put him on trial. But the fascists were after him too for not having supported them to the end. And so he was acquitted.'

For other future Italian student activists, like Luigi Bobbio, anti-fascism was a continuation of a family tradition. His father had been a leading Resistance figure and Luigi inherited 'a sense of civic commitment, a feeling of always being alert to the dangers of a resurgent fascism. I saw anti-fascist demonstrations as an expression of a civic, civilized Italy in opposition to the fascists who were barbarians. And the Nazi example of extermination camps had a great influence on me . . .'

The Holocaust was inevitably present in the minds of many of the post-war generation. When Nelly Finkielsztejn, a French child of Polish-Jewish origins, discovered by chance at home a photograph of a little girl she took to be herself the whole horrifying world of the extermination camps was revealed to her. The photograph was the sole memento left to Nelly's mother of her entire Polish family, who had perished in the gas chambers.

'That little girl was my cousin. She was dead and I was here. It had a terrible effect on me. As I grew up, I began to feel that I was living in a hypocritical world that continued as though nothing of this had happened. I couldn't accept that adults who had so obviously failed at the most elementary level of humanity could give lessons to others, impose their discipline on the young. A discipline I associated with the Hitler Youth. The world couldn't go on like this, it was too disgusting a place. I wanted to be with people who felt the same as I, but I didn't yet know who they were.'

Through the first half of the 1950s the reigning conformism held on both sides of the Atlantic. It was a time when, as Sharon Gold, from an unpolitical white suburban Boston family, recalled, young American women of her background headed for Ivy League colleges and stable suburban marriages to doctors, lawyers and businessmen. 'If a young woman had any other thoughts in her mind, she was usually sent to a psychiatrist. I spent the first part of my life looking for something of meaning for my life, because I had made a decision at age six that the program was not for me. The most important word for me as a kid was "freedom". I didn't know what it meant, except that I wanted to get away.'

Family ties, traditionally looser in America than in Europe, became even looser in the 1950s as millions of American women joined the work force, and economic prosperity made cars, television, drive-in movies and the like more readily available. The loosening of ties was reinforced for most middle-class teenagers by plans to attend colleges away from home, and for which high school was seen as a preparation. The effect, as Mike Frisch noted, was to shift the focus of youth's moral universe away from the family. 'The major thing I was going through as a teenager was the definition of yourself and that came, at least initially, in terms of your peers.'

But the process of coming of age and rebelling against conformity involved not only separation from parents, but also from peers. His self-assertion from family came by listening to black gospel music; his separation from peers by the discovery, aged fifteen, of folk music. 'From that point in time I was kind of living in two worlds. I was still a happy high school kid involved in a lot, but there was always a part of me that had a reference outside, to kids with increasingly different values politically. A lot of it was involved with the early ban-the-bomb movement. So I was always aware that there was this kind of bohemian world that was not just the older beatniks, but kids who were growing up in this.'

McCarthyism left a gap in the radical political tradition; it was a cultural rebellion, spearheaded by the Beat poets' and writers' criticism of white middle-class America, that fertilized the ground for new forms of political dissent, for the eventual fusion of radical culture and politics in the 1960s.

In the previous decade, however, politics were rarely discussed either at home or at school. The ruling order's vision of social progress accompanying economic advance – juxtaposed with a deep pessimism that the social order was being undermined by some agent of evil like communism, organized crime, materialism – seemed to preclude it.

'In the fourth grade,' recalled Karen Duncanwood, who came from an apolitical working-class family in northern California, 'I won the American Legion Award for writing an essay on the flag. I don't think I was right-wing gung ho, but I was naively patriotic. I just didn't know anything else existed. And yet we were the family on the block with the least money. So I have a lot of memories of very subtle but strong feelings of being left out because I didn't have the right clothes or I couldn't do this or that.'

For some, like Paul Buhle, religious groups provided a certain sense of politics; but even this had its limits. 'For me, as for a number of other people, another kind of cutting edge was that our liberal religion seemed to promise all these things and then didn't deliver them. I became an officer of the Christian Youth Fellowship when I was fifteen. The directors made it immediately clear that it was a charity organization, more booties for the black kids and orphans at Christmas. I was just kind of outraged at this.'

In America as elsewhere, sexuality remained heavily repressed, an essential part of the Western conformity. As Gurney Norman, a student at the University of Kentucky, recalled, there was a sort of cold war between the sexes. 'The contest was to see how far you could go without going all the way. Everybody was committed to not going all the way. The struggle was to control your passions. The fact that you could go off in a car and kind of get half naked and pet for three or four hours, get aroused to some kind of incredible pitch and manage not to have sexual intercourse, says something about the times. Petting above the waist was considered wholesome, heavy petting was another matter. People who crossed over that threshold and developed a sexual relationship – a kind of mystique surrounded them. The more innocent looked at those couples with a certain awe, but also a little bit of judgement and disgust.'

Internalization of the prevailing sexual norms was reinforced by Catholicism in those countries like France and Italy where its ideological hold was strongest. Françoise Routhier, a seamstress's daughter in Lyons, renounced the Church and its norms when she was twelve. And having made her decision, she came to another conclusion: everything was now permissible. 'It was incredible! And that day I told myself: as soon as possible, I must get rid of my virginity. It took me four more years, however, to discover a method of not getting pregnant. When eventually I laid my hands on a book on the Ogino method, I studied it very carefully. Then when the right moment came, I went to fetch that boy. We made love behind the railway tracks, on a bed of ants. It was terrible! Afterwards I went to the swimming pool. And for three days and nights, through paranoid nightmares, I waited for my period. When it came I said, "Ouf! Now that problem is solved for a good number of years."'

The deadlocked society was experienced again – in Western Europe at least – by the stratified and discriminatory class nature of education. This was especially true for lower middle- and working-class children, as many future student radicals recall.

In France, where eighty per cent of the youth was of working-class or peasant origin, only the exceptionally bright could hope to get to a lycée, the high school dominated by the middle class – and then only on condition that a teacher could persuade the parents to allow their child to continue studying. As Routhier recalled, it was a 'total anomaly' for someone of her class to go on studying. But a passion for reading made her determined to continue her education: 'When I arrived at the best-known of the two girls' lycées in the city, I discovered another world. The school was for the daughters of very well-to-do families. I can still remember a girl whose father gave her 5,000 francs to buy a bunch of violets, and she kept the change. It struck me because 5,000 francs was what my mother fed all of us on for a fortnight.'

Upper middle-class children, like Hélène Goldet from a wealthy Parisian family, took their privileges for granted and thought everyone shared them. 'Talking with my high school friends I discovered a number of interesting phenomena. First, that a number of people made their own beds; second that there were some who didn't even have a maid, and last but not least, there were those who didn't have a weekend country house. As a result of these discoveries I went on to become a Communist.'

'It was hard for my mother to find the money to pay the tuition fees which the state-financed high schools still charged at that time,' recollected Ottfried Jensen in Germany. Since his father's death in a Russian prisoner-of-war camp, his mother – like seven million others who brought up children on their own – had to work to rear her family. 'In the morning at school, it was a middle-class world: a doctor's son on my left, a pastor's on my right, a lawyer's behind me. It was something I'd never known. When my mother bicycled to the school in her headscarf, she was treated like a poor dog because she was a single parent and working-class. She couldn't follow my homework any more, because she'd never learnt the stuff. In the afternoons, I went to work, as a messenger boy when I was eleven, later as a docker and in the holidays as a sailor.'

In Cremona, a small town in central Italy, Pedro Humbert, the son of a wholesaler in hides and skins and a housewife, experienced the class bias of school every day. 'The middle-class children sat in the front row of desks and competed to be the first to hand in their work to the teacher. After that they would help those sitting behind them, the poor, the "sons of Communists". One day, a boy from the back desks who was very intelligent threw the school books that the poor received free from the Municpal Assistance at the teacher – a socialist, who had been elected to the municipal administration.'

Humbert himself faced a critical and discriminatory decision after completing middle school at the age of fourteen. To aim for a university degree would require nine more years – five in high school, four at university – during which time he would earn nothing to help his two younger brothers. 'I went instead to the technical institute where after five years I would qualify as an accountant and be able to get a job.'

The class nature of state education was no less apparent in Britain, where wartime reforms had made free state secondary education and access to university available to all for the first time. Only those, however, who at the age of eleven passed an examination went to grammar schools which provided the main route to higher education; and few – six per cent of manual workers and ten per cent of clerical workers' children – had made it to university in the early 1960s, twenty years after the reforms were brought in.

Working-class children often felt discriminated against, as Rod Burgess, the son of a nightwatchman and a housewife, experienced at his grammar school. 'Very soon I knew there was something wrong. But I couldn't put my finger on it. It was only when I was fourteen or fifteen that I realized it was the way you talked, the way you looked, the clothes you wore, your table manners – and it gradually dawned on me that a lot of us who came from working-class backgrounds were being put down. The A and B streams [top divisions within a class] were full of middle-class people who had come from private elementary schools while those of us who were working-class were put into the bottom streams. We were the "yobbos" and most us stayed in the bottom stream.'

Although the British welfare state had done little or nothing to abolish class discrimination, it was offering opportunities to those whose parents had been deprived of them. Recognition of this was widespread among the youth who were its beneficiaries; however problematic family relationships might be, the welfare state provided a supportive alternative.

'I always think of myself as a child of 1945, when the welfare state was inaugurated, rather than of 1968,' David Widgery, from a lower middle-class family, commented. 'My parents were both Labour voters and strongly supported the welfare state. As a child I suffered from tuberculosis, polio and an eye disease. I spent a great deal of my youth in hospital. The fact that someone like me could get very good treatment which we obviously couldn't afford privately – and in another country wouldn't have had access to – made me very pro the welfare state.'

'I was very conscious of being working-class, poor working-class, though not starving – and of being very much supported by the welfare state,' recalled Bernadette McAliskey, better known by her maiden name of Devlin. 'Our way out, as for many Catholics of my class in Northern Ireland, was the availability of free education. If you could pass the exams you had the same right to an education as anyone else . . .' Dependence on the welfare state had its ambivalences, however, for the Catholic minority which was heavily repressed by the Northern Ireland Protestant regime, as she saw in her childhood. 'People despised the state but were dependent on it. I grew up with the idea that there was a certain morality in both fiddling the state and never being grateful to it. We were all basically brought up to bite the hand that fed us at every possible opportunity.'

First-hand knowledge of poverty, at a time of increasing material prosperity, could be a sharply radicalizing experience. The son of an elementary school director in Calabria, Southern Italy, Franco Piperno was from an early age struck by the peasant children's poverty. 'Simple things, like my bicycle, were for them an extraordinary object, a luxury. My family was not very wealthy, but the gap between my condition and that of my friends among the peasant children was huge, offensive. And what I found even more offensive was that the whole town, including my family, lived off the work of the peasants and at the same time despised them, treated them with contempt. And yet I knew, from being with them, that they were no different to me.'

Calabria was – and remains – one of the poorest regions of Southern Italy, almost totally dependent on agriculture. The north and centre, on the other hand, were relatively industrialized. During the Fifties, nearly one and a quarter million people migrated from the south to the large cities. To do so, they had not only to adopt new ways of life but learn to speak a new language – Italian – in place of their local dialects. Many of the later student radicals were the children of those who had migrated; and they felt discriminated against in their new environments while still keeping close links with their rural and impoverished origins.

Franco Russo had been able to join his parents, who had come to Rome from a village in the region of Naples when he was five, and had become concierges of an apartment block. With the job went a flat. His mother, who had previously been a baker, acted as concierge while his father continued to work as a carpenter.

'Although life in the village was much poorer – my grandparents with whom I lived until I could join my parents had no bathroom – there was, at least, little social discrimination. In Rome, as the son of a concierge [a post which under fascism was associated with police informers] I was made to feel at the bottom of a rigid social hierarchy. People would give me a tip when I opened the lift door. A girl more or less of my age would never say hello to me. I felt the discrimination so much that even today I won't say hello to some of those people who never greeted me as a child.'

The sense of inequality which class divisions fostered could equally affect upper middle-class children, as Hélène Goldet's discovery that her school mates had to make their own beds showed. She was not alone. Hilary Wainwright, who was at a private preparatory girls' school in Britain, often visited her grandparents' large estate. She would return puzzled. 'Why could they live there, why did I share it, too, when the friends I played with after school from the working-class estate near my home – who were tougher and gutsier than me and my school mates – didn't? And yet they were the same sort of people as me. Although I couldn't work it out, that experience of inequality became a basic ground point in later life. This system couldn't continue, there was no good reason for that sort of inequality.'

The hidden, subjective injuries of class, the recognition of the wider class societies in which they took place and the existence of class political parties, would lead many of the new generation of West European student radicals fairly directly into class politics. The same was not true of the United States. Here, while individual white youth could feel financially underprivileged, and others encounter poverty and be shocked, class inequalities were not a major radicalizing factor. Karen Duncanwood, for example, recalled feeling 'left out' of things because her parents had little money; and at high school she felt she was 'class-tracked into vocational training. I had to fight my high school counselor to get her to let me take algebra. It was double tracking in fact. I was a woman and I was working-class. Working-class women have no reason to take algebra.' But it was not class awareness which led to her radicalization; that came, as it did in the 1960s for many of her generation, from personal experience of racial discrimination in the Deep South. 'That's where I discovered injustice existed in this country that I believed was democratic. It made me angry, and more importantly, it made me want to fight.'

If the notion of class was, to say the least, vague, a number of factors could be inferred to explain it: the absence of a viable left, of mass political parties based on class; the real though uneven prosperity of the period; the constant media barrage describing the U.S. as a classless society; and the deeply held ideological precept accenting individual initiative and blame. Discrimination was thus not generally experienced as stemming from class inequality but, as Duncanwood has shown, from the institutionalized racism of the United States.

Taking the subway to and from his Quaker school in Brooklyn, Bruce Franklin recalled coming to certain stations where every black person, with rare exceptions, would get off the train and the car would magically become all white. 'It was a fact of social existence that I didn't think about a lot. But I did think of this as evidence that we lived in a segregated society. It seemed to me to manifest a kind of gross inequality in which black people lived. I think those opinions had a lot to do with things that were being raised at school. I had very strong feelings during that period about the oppression and exploitation of black people. It was one of the few areas of my thinking that was actually progressive, because on other issues I had really very reactionary ideas.'

Again and again, it will be seen that racism stands in for West European class in the consciousness of American student radicals. The civil rights struggle provided models for the white student movement, just as class domination in one form or another was the axis around which West European student movements developed. For people of color it is the starting point in the development of their consciousness. Terry Collins, later an activist at San Francisco State College, remembered the segregation of his early life in central Illinois. 'When we went to the movies we could only sit in the balconies, or we couldn't go to the swimming pool.' Bill Sales, in Philadelphia, recalled being excluded from *American*

Bandstand, one of the most popular teenage television dance shows. 'It was just a straight-up racist kind of thing. They wouldn't let us in. We were excluded from that.'

Charles Sherrod, who would become a leader of the Student Non-violent Coordinating Committee (SNCC) in 1960, grew up in the poorest area of Petersburg, Virginia, the oldest of five children in a fatherless family. 'When I was growing up to sit next to a white person was to ask for trouble. You didn't know what could happen. Sitting next to a white man was asking to get swung on, or maybe trouble with the police, or maybe jail. But sitting next to a white woman was much worse. Much worse. That meant death. That meant getting beat up real bad – serious injury.

'This stuff is deep. My grandmother used to tell me stories when I was a little boy. Stories about white people and what they'd do. She told me how my father had to flee his home county for protesting the killing of a black man, who was burned hanging from a tree, while his genitals were burning in another tree. Stories like that were part of my consciousness. That's what was passed down. Those kind of things don't just disappear.'

In a decade when a young black man, Emmett Till, was beaten to death in Mississippi for talking fresh to a white woman, such warnings were not to be ignored. Nor was racism confined to the South, as Hari Dillon, whose father was from India, and his mother half-Indian, half-Chicano, remembered: 'Growing up in central California, where there were many Chicanos around, I was just another Mexican "greaser" to most of the white kids who were racists and didn't know where India was. As a very young child, like in kindergarten or first grade, it was very very devastating. I didn't have the psychological equipment to really spit it back. I remember being very hurt.'

Racism, Dillon believed, had reinforced his awakening social con-sciousness; Emilio Zamora, a Chicano, felt the same. As well as racism, many Chicanos experienced a further discrimination: the mistreatment of migrant Mexican workers brought to the Southwest to harvest crops. Zamora's father had been one of these migrants.

'I remember once when I was young the farmer's wife drove up fast yelling to the workers that the INS [Immigration and Naturalization Service] was coming. We assumed the farmer had called the INS so as not to have to pay them because it was always happening. Anyway, they came in jeeps, and then airplanes flew above them and it was just – my mom called it an inferno. The poor men were running all over the place – grown men hiding, scared. They rounded them up. My mom almost fainted. She was hysterical. It made a strong impression on me. It just brought everything into focus.'

For whites, not surprisingly, racism was lived very differently: separation and distance are their dominant memories. Cathy Cade had gone to high school in Chicago, where the schools were integrated, before moving to Memphis, Tennessee, where they were not. She now rarely saw blacks of her own age, indeed rarely saw black people at all other than maids and gardeners: 'It's amazing how effective segregation can be. I really carry with me the experience of what it can do to you, because I had come there with other experiences, believing that while there are racial differences, black people are people. But after a while the stereotypes – those terrible things – started going through my mind. And I'd say, where are they coming from? But I didn't have anything to counter them with any more – a human being to relate to who would challenge them.'

In only one other country in this book was discrimination against a minority population as endemic in the Fifties: Northern Ireland. There, as in the American South, it was institutionalized discrimination – only against Catholics instead of blacks.

Of lower middle-class Catholic origins – his father was a bank clerk – Michael Farrell recalled the teachers at his Catholic grammar school telling pupils that 'there was no point in applying for the Northern Ireland Civil Service because, while you might get a job as a clerk, you would never progress beyond that. In the main, Catholics worked either in agriculture or were self-employed.'

To ensure its dominance over the Catholic minority, the ruling Protestant Ulster Unionist party resorted to flagrant electoral gerrymandering, a Special Powers Act that gave it sweeping powers of detention, and an exclusively Protestant paramilitary reserve force, the B Specials. The latter were called out in 1955, when the Irish Republican Army (IRA) launched its heaviest armed campaign against the Northern Irish government since the partition of Ireland in 1921.

'People were terrified of the B Specials,' Farrell recalled. 'If a crowd of eighteen-year-old Specials stopped a carload of Catholics of the same age coming home from a dance they'd make them get out, shove them about with their rifle butts and make them curse the Pope – there was a lot of that sort of thing.'

Institutionalized racism and discrimination at a time of so-called liberal progress was but one of the contradictions of post-war Western societies which would mobilize student protest. Peace through the threat of nuclear extinction; colonial wars at a time of decolonization; oppression and poverty – both material and spiritual – in the midst of consumerist abundance; and the failure of Social Democratic and Communist parties to point to a radical vision of the future in their political practice, were among the others. It would be around one or other of these contradictions that the first attempts to break through the deadlocked 1950s would occur; around one or more of them simultaneously that much of the student protest of the 1960s would mobilize.

Breaking the Deadlock

It was in that space where Stalinism ends and Social Democratic reformism begins that the British New Left began to emerge –
Stuart Hall, first editor of New Left Review, *London*

Just to say freedom is possible is the first step towards being free –
Charles Sherrod, first field secretary, Student Nonviolent Coordinating Committee (SNCC), USA

The first movements to challenge the reigning political stasis of the 1950s arose in Britain, France and the United States. They mobilized around some of the contradictions of Western society that have already been noted and also over those in the Soviet bloc. Russian tanks rolling into Budapest to put down the Hungarian uprising in 1956; Western imperialist adventures – Suez, in the same year – and colonial war in Algeria from 1954 on; the growing threat of nuclear annihilation, East and West; and institutionalized racism in the American South. Though the movements were not exclusively student-based, students played a role in their development or organized separately within them; and the lessons they learnt had an important impact on the events of the late Sixties.

In Britain, the Campaign for Nuclear Disarmament (CND) and the formation of the New Left started to fissure the political glacier in the second half of the 1950s. In its origins and aims, the New Left anticipated some of the conditions of the subsequent student movements, and it is worth looking briefly at its development. The New Left originated, as Stuart Hall, a West Indian student at Oxford, recalled, out of the crisis of the Soviet invasion of Hungary and the Anglo-French invasion of Suez, which occurred almost simultaneously.

'The Labour Party in Britain had been constantly telling us that reformed modern capitalism had renounced imperialism. The Stalinists claimed that an indivisible socialism extended from the borders of West Germany to China. It was perfectly clear from the events that neither was true. It was what Claude Bourdet, founder and editor of *France Observateur*, with whom we were in contact in Paris, was saying also. The name New Left was borrowed from his "Nouvelle Gauche" in fact.'

Seeking a political space on the left outside the confines of both Stalinism and Social Democracy, the New Left group, which originated in part from university circles, was given a further impulse by the defection from the British Communist Party after Hungary of a number of its leading intellectuals, the historian E. P. Thompson among them, who joined in defending its political aims: an independent socialism implacably hostile to Stalinism and irrevocably committed to criticising a Social Democratic reformism which maintained that, thanks to capitalist expansion, the social inequalities of the past had been resolved. It challenged, too, the prevailing view of what constituted politics.

'From the beginning we said that politics, seen as having to do principally with formal political parties, elections, getting the vote out, parliamentarianism, was ideological, confining,' Hall continued. 'We raised issues of personal life, the way people live, culture, which weren't considered the topics of politics on the left. We wanted to talk about the contradictions of this new kind of capitalist society in which people didn't have a language to express their private troubles, didn't realize that these troubles reflected political and social questions which could be generalized.'

These concerns – defining a new political space and, within it, new definitions of what constituted democratic politics – were to become dominant themes of most student movements at one stage or another of their trajectories.

The British New Left committed itself heavily to CND, the first mass protest organization in post-war Britain. The latter attracted large numbers of youth who saw in it a challenge to their deadlocked society. There was a 'kind of naive socialism' about the Aldermaston to London Easter marches which began in 1958, thought an engineering apprentice, Pete Latarche. 'Everybody mucked in, everybody suffered the same discomforts, everybody shared, supported everybody else. It was very good humoured, people sang, there were endless political discussions as you walked along in this great caravan. It was an emotional blast to be among so many like-minded people. This, I thought, was how a civilized society would behave towards its members.'

Latarche, who would later become national chairman of Youth CND, had been influenced by the 'Angry Young Men' movement of British playwrights, critics and writers who voiced a new language of protest in the second half of the 1950s. He was twenty; but many who joined CND were teenagers. And many more who were affected by the movement were even younger. David Widgery, who later became a student leader, lived in Slough on the Aldermaston route and remembered the marches from the age of twelve.

'Once a year the march passed through the streets with great clamour and glamour. People with battered top hats playing the cornet out of tune and girl art students with coloured stockings – the whole parade of infamy came through the town. It was terribly enticing. At school, we were told to beware of them, not to fraternize. There was a lot of quiet pandemonium about CND and these beatniks. It wasn't just that they were campaigning for nuclear disarmament, they were political in a different kind of way, into linking up with local and direct action groups. They were passionate, evangelical, calling upon you to do things now, to sit down, to stand up and be counted.'

For the young to wear a CND badge at school – often forbidden by the school authorities – became a symbol for every kind of outsider or political opponent. Another future student leader, David Triesman, was 'turned onto politics' by Youth CND. And when, in 1960, Bertrand Russell, the octogenerian philosopher, founded the Committee of 100, a breakaway group devoted to direct action and civil disobedience over the nuclear issue, its methods and tactics made a deep impact on a number of future British student radicals.

'The Committee was much more dynamic than anything else on offer politically,' Triesman observed. 'It was almost spectacular given the time and political climate. Russell was fantastically important. There was an old man articulating the necessity for dynamism in politics – it was a really attractive contradiction. I remember taking part in one of the Committee's mass sit-downs in Trafalgar Square. It was a very festive event. People were having a good time because they felt positively involved and emotionally engaged. The enjoyment had as much impact on your politics as the physical events that were taking place around you.'

The marked sense of personal involvement in the first post-war movements on both sides of the Atlantic would carry forward into the student rebellions of the late 1960s as one of their most characteristic traits.

Two events in the early 1960s heralded the decline of CND and with it that of the New Left. First, to the disillusionment of great numbers of CND supporters, especially the young, the Labour party machine fought a bitter and successful campaign to reverse CND's 'victory' at the 1960 party conference which had endorsed unilateral nuclear disarmament. Secondly, the Cuban missile crisis, precipitated in 1962 by the Soviet

Union's installation of missiles on the island and the American demand that they be removed, occasioned the gravest threat to world peace since 1945.

'We were faced with the stark fact that we could easily be blown up by the escalatory moves of the United States and the Soviet Union,' recalled Stuart Hall. 'It didn't matter if you had a mass movement or the votes – the whole thing could be decided in five minutes by whoever picked up the red phone and said, "We're going to bomb you out of the skies." We felt neutralized, impotent. As a result, both CND and the New Left lost confidence in winning a strategic victory.'

Despite this, however, CND's example had mobilizing effects in the U.S. and West Germany, among others; and in Britain its 'utopian aspirations for a qualitatively new society' made it, as David Fernbach recalled, 'an important ancestor of what was to come in the late Sixties'.

In France, the Algerian War, which began with a National Liberation uprising in November 1954, and lasted eight years, led to large-scale student mobilizations. It was France's second colonial war in a row; but unlike Indochina, from which the French were withdrawing, defeated, as the second struggle started, Algeria could not be justified by Cold War policies of 'containing communism'. The French Communist Party did not condemn the war from the start; and in 1956, a socialist prime minister extended the draft and ordered conscripts to Algeria while, at the same time, the French press revealed that systematic torture was being used by French troops.

'We had these pictures of Nazism, torture, the extermination camps fresh in our minds,' remembered Tiennot Grumbach. 'And then suddenly – French patriots, chauvinists that we were – we learned that France was torturing and killing people in Algeria. It was indefensible. We couldn't accept it. We rejected the war for moral reasons, went into politics because of a moral crisis.'

His introduction to politics was tough. 'Each time our Catholic circle tried to hand out a leaflet explaining our opposition to the war on religious and moral grounds, the extreme right, pro-war boys at my select Paris lycée beat us up. There was nothing for it but to set up an anti-fascist committee. We were only kids really when we started, I liked going to parties and having fun – but that didn't last long. Very rapidly we were plunged into politics. It was an absolute necessity to get involved on the Algerian side in order to put an end to the war. Soon we were completely into illegality. Our relationship to political life was akin to that of the Resistance during World War II: the same positions with regard to the police, the state, the judiciary. All of this radicalized us even more.'

It was an underground life which for some of the group involved hiding Algerian National Liberation Front (FLN) members and secretly transporting suitcases full of money collected from Algerian workers in Paris to Germany and Switzerland. For others, including Grunbach, there were illegal anti-war meetings to organize, proscribed books and leaflets to distribute, prohibited posters to stick up at night. 'We were totally involved in it, it was our life. At the same time it was an expression of the romantic side of youth.'

In 1958, the crisis provoked by the war resulted in Parliament calling on General de Gaulle to take power. He did so; but the war did not end. Instead, he ordered more troops to Algeria. Most of them were conscripts. Algeria was 'French soil' and would remain so.

The campaign against the war grew stronger; it was given additional momentum when, in 1960, the National Student Union (UNEF) came out in open opposition to the conflict. It organized prohibited rallies and on a few occasions attempted to block military trains carrying conscripts, many of them students, to Algeria. The war and French student mobilizations were closely watched by other West European student radicals. In West Germany, many members of the Socialist party's youth organization, SDS, as well as other youth organizations were active in supporting the FLN.

'Algeria was one of the first links in the imperialist chain to be broken,' Oskar Negt, a prominent SDS member, observed. 'We collected money privately to send to the FLN. Larger and larger sums. Everything had to be done clandestinely – it was highly dangerous work because the French secret services and right-wing extremist organizations operated freely in Germany, attacking people and organizations involved in supporting the Algerians. Each morning, Werner Thönnessen, a veteran SDSer, crawled under his car and examined the engine to make sure there wasn't a bomb in it.'

'The first demonstration in which I was beaten up by the police was for Algeria,' recalled Franco Russo, the concierge's son in Rome. 'Algeria – the Algerian liberation struggle – was a matter of passionate concern to us . . .'

Public opinion in France, as shown by increasingly large demonstrations, was beginning to turn against the war. In February 1962, eight people were killed as a mass of demonstrators tried to escape the police by fleeing into the Charonne métro station in Paris. Over 700,000 people marched in their funeral procession. The following month, a ceasefire brought the war to an end. Algeria became independent, and the student movement, which had mobilized tens of thousands, collapsed.

'We found ourselves without a cause,' recalled Roland Castro, who had virtually abandoned his architectural studies for clandestine FLN support work. 'At the beginning I'd seen very quickly that it was more important to fight against the war than to study. The French Socialist government's moral weakness and corruption over Algeria had only confirmed my idea that this was a rotten world. To support the FLN meant to me that I was doing what my father had not done – being part of the Resistance. But now that the war was over I returned to my studies.'

The Algerian revolution, the new society being built there, became an important pole of attraction for many student radicals. As Grumbach put it: 'We had been mobilized for so long, had invested all our energy into stopping the war, all our hopes into what Algeria would become after the war – a lay, democratic and fraternal country shaped in the image of our FLN friends. We knew we had to go there now to help. I planned to stay three days and remained two and a half years.'

He went with a supply of medicines for a hospital in Algiers. No one at the hospital could understand the labels on the boxes. '"Look", they said to me, "if you can't classify them for us you might as well take them back." So, though I wasn't a doctor, I stayed to sort out the medicines. People came to me for specific drugs and I dispensed them. It was quite surrealistic. At the same time, the people were wonderfully open, the sense of fraternity was so strong, that I can truthfully say that those were the best days of my life.'

As the British and French movements declined or came to an end, the first student movement which was to leave a characteristic mark on the 1960s was rising in the United States. This was the black Student Nonviolent Coordinating Committee (SNCC). Its struggle against institutionalized racism in the American South achieved notable victories for the civil rights movement and contributed in large part to the ending of legalized racial discrimination. At the same time, it blazed a trail which decisively influenced the white American student movement.

Because the black student movement charted terrain that others, in their specific national contexts, would also pass through, it is worth looking at in some detail. It is a story of youth inventing and re-inventing new forms of struggle, a story of courage.

On 1 February 1960, the modern American student movement made its first mark on history. In Greensboro, North Carolina, four black college students broke the deadlock of the 1950s with a simple direct action: a sit-in, at a local Woolworth's lunch counter, protesting segregation. When they were refused service they broke with tradition by remaining seated, demanding to be treated as full human beings.

Sitting calmly, many of them studying, dressed in their best Sunday clothes – the very embodiment of middle-class respectability – the students dramatized the irrationality of discrimination. At the same time, by occupying the lunch counter's stools day after day, they applied direct economic pressure on the management.

Within days of the first sit-in, hundreds of other students took similar actions at lunch counters around Greensboro. Spreading through a network of personal and institutional contacts, the movement grew and soon sit-ins were taking place throughout the nation. By the end of April more than 50,000 students had taken part in a sit-in. Hundreds suffered violence at the hands of white opponents, who punched them, threw hot coffee and other food at them, and ground cigarettes out on the backs of their necks. Thousands of students were arrested, but nothing could stop the tide of human energy. 'We had half the school down there with us,' recalled Charles Sherrod, then a theology student at Virginia Union University, of the Richmond, Virginia, sit-ins. 'The strategy was, as soon as we got arrested, the next group would go and sit down. I don't remember how many got arrested, maybe a hundred or more. We integrated half-a-dozen establishments in a few months. It was a great joy to be part of that. I saw a lot of kids grow up at the lunch counter.'

With the sit-ins, students began to play a major role in the civil rights movement. Black Americans had been struggling for equality and justice for generations, but during the 1950s their movement had developed new strengths. The migration of blacks from farms in the South to Northern cities, the rise of independence movements in Africa, and the NAACP's 1954 Supreme Court victory over legalized segregation of schools gave blacks new resources to draw upon. The victorious 1955–56 Montgomery, Alabama, bus boycott, which introduced the young Reverend Martin Luther King, Jr., to the struggle, was the first sign of what was to come. But it was the student sit-ins that made clear to all the potential for sweeping change.

The excitement of the sit-ins touched students throughout the country. At scores of Northern campuses students began actions in support of the campaign, such as pickets of chain stores, sit-ins of their own, or fund-raising for bail. For many, it was their first political activity. For Barbara Jacobs Haber, then a senior at Brandeis College in Boston, it was a 'big moment' in her life when a college speaker urged students to join the cause. 'As I sat in my seat listening to him speak, I was just throbbing with excitement. He said, "If anybody is interested in working on support pickets up here, come up." I could hardly wait until he finished. At the end I went up and said, "Me, me, me, me! Yes, yes, yes, yes!" It was one of those great moments of saying "Yes" that inside is totally transforming.'

John O'Neal, a student at Southern Illinois University, was also moved. 'For most of us – and I'm talking black and white now – the issue is not what's right and wrong. Most of us have a pretty clear sense of that. The issue is, what am I going to do? Am I going to do what's right, or am I going to do what's expedient? Because often to do what is right means that you just get blown away. So, when somebody finds a way to do what is right, and be effective at the same time, people just go *ooof*. Because now they're liberated, now they can do what's right. I don't think people like doing what's wrong. They don't enjoy it. It gives you a bad feeling – you feel bad about the world, about yourself; you feel like you're going deep into the mire, but you're impelled to do it. But when somebody figures out a way to say, "You don't have to do that, you *can* do what's right," it just galvanizes people.'

By the end of 1960 the first wave of student sit-ins began to subside, but the larger civil rights movement grew to become the most dynamic and important social movement of the 1960s. Across the nation, millions of black people rose up to demand the realization of the promise of equality. King and the 1963 March on Washington captured the nation's attention. But everyday black people, struggling in cities and small towns across the South, were the unsung heroes and heroines of the period. Acting with enormous courage and dignity, they overcame brutal sheriffs, snarling police attack dogs, and the midnight terror of the Ku Klux Klan. Young black men and women, many of them high school and college students, were in the front lines. As Sherrod recognized, they were not burdened by the 'legacy of fear and pain in the same way as their elders. They didn't have the burden to carry that the adults did.'

To keep the movement alive, Sherrod and other veterans of the sit-ins formed SNCC, a loose federation of local student groups. The founders, most of whom came from all-black Southern colleges, were convinced that students needed their own organization which they could shape according to their own aims, independently of adult organizations such as King's Southern Christian Leadership Conference (SCLC). The language of their founding statement, justifying their non-violent stance, was that of black Southern Protestantism, the product of generations of struggle. 'Non-violence as it grows from the Judeo-Christian tradition, seeks a social order of justice permeated by love ... Through non-violence, courage displaces fear. Love transcends hate. Acceptance dissipates prejudice; hope ends despair. Faith reconciles doubt. Mutual regards cancel enmity. Justice for all overthrows injustice. The redemptive community supercedes immoral social systems.'

This language obscured the radical nature of SNCC's aims which went far beyond desegregation, to demands for a society based upon equality, justice and freedom. By bringing blacks into the political system, SNCC believed that the structure of society could be changed. These demands were not going to be so easily met, as Sherrod came to recognize. 'When we jumped down here, we got a bigger fight than we thought! If I had known at the beginning that segregation was part of the total economic and political base of the international system, I would probably have been overwhelmed by the largeness of it.'

Without, in Sherrod's words, any working knowledge of past movements, without models, relying entirely on their own experience, he and others in SNCC developed a strategy that combined direct action, personal transformation, and community mobilization. 'I don't know where that strategy came from. Only our own successes and failures. When we demonstrated and were successful, the success itself would tell us, "Let's do it again." Some things I wasn't sure of, so I would act on them and in acting on them I would come up with a theory.'

Studies of SNCC which concentrate upon its Freedom Summer campaign of 1964 emphasize its interracial quality and its concentration on voter registration. But SNCC was always a primarily black organization. 'I understood SNCC to be an organization that whites could support, even join, but it was to be dominated by Southern blacks,' noted Martha Prescod Norman, a black woman who went South from Detroit to join SNCC at the age of seventeen. According to Norman, SNCC workers fought for integration not because they wanted to be 'just like whites', but rather because segregation was used to hold black people in a subordinate position in society. 'There is a difference between integration and assimilation. I never thought I was doing anything to assimilate into white culture – I'd had enough of that.'

SNCC used a variety of tactics and strategies. During the sit-ins SNCC workers used non-violent civil disobedience, or direct action, to challenge the segregation of public facilities. There were 'pray-ins' in segregated churches, 'swim-ins' in segregated recreational facilities and 'bowl-ins', at bowling alleys. From such efforts the emphasis shifted to community organization, voter registration, and eventually the creation of an independent black political party. The emphasis shifted over time and area, from project to project, depending on the needs of the community. In the spring of 1961 SNCC joined with the Congress of Racial Equality (CORE) in renewing its direct action campaign, this time organizing Freedom Riders – mixed groups of black and white, men and women, who rode on interstate buses through the South deliberately breaking the Jim Crow laws which segregated buses, waiting rooms and rest rooms. They were bombed and attacked by ugly white mobs in Alabama, but they did force a cautious Kennedy administration to enforce federal laws outlawing such segregation on interstate travel.

In November of that year Sherrod and a group of black students sat in at the bus station in Albany, Georgia. Their ejection by police started a massive struggle as the students decided that rather than pay bail and leave jail, they would remain and fill the jails until the whole system came to a grinding halt. 'We would be marching and singing, and Police Chief Pritchett would tell us if we came any further we'd be arrested,' recalled Rutha Harris, a student at Albany State College. 'We just kept on moving. After a while everyone was into it. We just filled the jails every night. They didn't have enough room in the Albany jail, so we filled the jails all around here. Filled 'em all.'

'It was by going to jail and fighting and holding out that we got most of what we got,' added her sister, McCree Harris. A deeply religious woman, she had prayed and 'something within' told her, 'if you're ever going to be free, you have to start somewhere and sometime. And now is the time.' As the black community threw itself into the struggle, she felt this was the 'realization of the true meaning of community.' Everyone pulling together with a spirit of love and togetherness. Beautiful. You'd wake up in the morning and – you know that song, "I woke up in the morning with my mind set on freedom"? That's how it was – fantastic. Unity can do things and we saw that work.'

The struggle in Albany went on for years, yet it eventually proved to be a victory for SNCC and a turning-point for the movement. 'What the Albany movement showed was that large numbers of adult Southern Negroes were ready to go to jail, and risk getting beaten up for civil rights,' explains Norman, who served as a volunteer in Albany. 'When you think about it, that's the basis for all the strategy of the civil rights movement from that point on; we can count on large numbers of adults to risk their lives and go to jail. What SNCC discovered was the strategy of a mass movement at that level of commitment. That was a big turning-point for the whole movement.'

At the same time, SNCC workers, led by Robert Moses, were developing their voter registration strategy in Mississippi. They saw that the political system could be a crucial tool for blacks to break the system of racism of the South. Using the tactics of community organization and mass mobilization, by 1964 voter registration would become SNCC's main strategy.

Across the South, SNCC workers doing community organizing and voter registration developed close ties with local residents. Leaving their colleges, and settling in isolated black communities, they came to rely upon the support of the local black churches which provided them with resources, links into the community, and a language of struggle against injustice. 'We were embraced by the community,' recalled Gloria House, who worked outside Selma, Alabama. 'There was a great deal of acceptance of us, affection for us, concern for our health and well-being. When we got up early to begin our canvassing, we knew that if food was being cooked anywhere, it was going to be shared with us.'

Day-to-day organizing also brought constant reminders of the harshness of black life in the South. Norman recalls being brought face-to-face for the first time with that reality. 'Daily canvassing involved visiting row after row of houses with no plumbing, and only overlapped sheets of paper to keep out the cold; speaking with men and women who worked hard, twelve hours a day, six days a week, to bring home $12.50; and seeing a level of untreated disease and injury unimaginable in America. Daily events were equally grim: floodings taking all from those with next to nothing, random police beatings of young black men, rapes of young black women. These were hard communities where almost every white man in a pick-up truck had a gun displayed in the rear window.'

Danger was also a constant element in the lives of the SNCC volunteers. Arrest and harassment by the police were a fact of daily life. SNCC workers were beaten, several were shot and killed. Norman recalled hiding

in a church while night-riders' bullets whistled outside. 'It was a dangerous period,' remembered House, who saw black men and women who
tried to vote thrown off of their rented farms and forced to live in tent cities.
'White people would go on night rides, and shoot into the tent communities, or shoot into the Freedom House where the organizers lived.' Her
most harrowing moment came after she and other SNCC workers,
including white seminarian Jonathan Daniels, were brought to an Alabama
jail, released into the night, and ambushed. Daniels died before her eyes.
This danger gave their lives a special intensity. 'There was a culture in
SNCC that was based upon a profound respect for human beings,'
explained Norman. 'Somehow, late at night, in kerosene-lit Freedom
Houses, traveling back roads in the black belt, doing jail terms, or through
hastily written letters, we shared with each other our most personal
thoughts.' House adds, 'I was very much in admiration of my co-workers. I
thought they were some of the finest people I ever met. They were living
without comfort, with very little money. But they had a sense of humor.
They laughed a lot. They liked each other, and they took care of business.
There was razzing and teasing, but there was more warmth than anything
else.'

SNCC developed an organizational structure built on the ideas of
community and consensus. 'We didn't have any high muckety-mucks in
SNCC,' according to Fay Bellamy, who worked in the Atlanta office.
'There was a striving for equality.' She recalled Bob Moses emphasizing
that leadership came from out there, in the community, from all sorts of
people. 'Everybody's a leader, and nobody's better than anyone else.
Period!' SNCC workers made a conscious attempt to break from the
hierarchical structure common to most organizations and institutions.
Some SNCC leaders, especially Sherrod, used terms drawn from their
Protestant heritage to argue that SNCC should strive to make itself the
model of the society they wished to create.

Beyond SNCC's unhierarchical, egalitarian structure, without leaders
or led, lay its vision of becoming a model of the 'beloved community' it
hoped to achieve; this, too, had its roots in the Southern black church and
the democratic strains of early American Protestantism, now combined
with Christian existentialism. 'One of Sherrod's notions,' recalled O'Neal,
was that 'whatever you seek to achieve as an end must be evidenced in the
process by which you seek to accomplish it. You can't say, the end justifies
the means. Sherrod's perception was right on!'

While much of the work was inspirational and dangerous, even more of it was drudgery. O'Neal, who worked in both Georgia and Mississippi, recalled that organizing usually involved more routine than excitement. 'The thing that impressed me most about that work, after becoming acclimated to it, was how pedestrian it was. Getting people to register to vote is a question of knocking on doors, talking to people, understanding what their interests and needs are. What their fears are. What their ambitions are. Finding arguments that may be effective. Getting a leaflet printed. Getting a flat tire fixed, having a car that will operate. Learning how to write a leaflet, how to get the word out that there's a meeting tonight, or next week. Just real pedestrian stuff. It's startling in its simplicity, but still the difficulty is great. The tendency with that kind of stuff, because it is so simple, and because of the boredom and dullness, is to overlook it and try to do something exciting. That's when mistakes are made, when people start substituting drama for the work.'

For the black students in SNCC the personal implications of what they were doing were clear. Their lives, and the lives of their families and friends, were limited by the injustice of racism. For white students, the situation was somewhat different. 'For me, individually, my involvement was never altruistic,' explained Casey Hayden, one the white students involved with SNCC from the start. 'I was never doing something for someone else. I saw that segregation was limiting me as much as it was my black friends. The movement was very existential for a while. It dealt very directly with who I was.'

For both blacks and whites, the overriding reason to be involved was the sense that what they were doing was going to have an impact, that it would change the path of history. Against all odds, hundreds of thousands of black people in the South were on the move. Social forces were in motion. Martha Norman recalled discussions with her co-workers about the implications of their victory over racism, and the sense that history was hanging in the balance. The future depended upon what took place at this moment. 'That's what a lot of young people understood in the Sixties. It was one of those times. That's when you stop everything, give up everything, and you go. Because if you don't, you might miss it.'

Freedom Summer

The excitement and daring spirit of SNCC extended beyond the South. For young people who became politically active in the 1960s, SNCC possessed a mythic quality. Predictably, they interpreted what they saw and heard in terms of their own situations. Bob and Jackie Hall, both of

whom were raised in religious Protestant homes, were reading existential-
ist authors such as Camus and Sartre at Southwestern University in
Memphis, Tennessee. The civil rights movement forced them to confront
the fact that 'segregation was evil'. 'The morality of it was so clear – who
was right and who was wrong,' noted Bob. 'Who had the dogs that were
biting people?'

Carlos Vasquez, a Chicano growing up in New Mexico, remembers
looking at the South from the outside. 'My image of the South was those
civil rights images, the dogs being put on people and the fire hoses. I
thought racism was wrong, and I thought if anyone had a right to protest it,
it was black people. They had been taken from their motherland, they'd
been sold as property, their families had been destroyed. The first
organization I ever joined was SNCC, not a Mexican organization.
Whenever politics came up, I identified myself as part of the black
movement, until I came to UCLA and started going to a Chicano group. I
was proud when my people began to fight back, especially taking direct
action. I thought that was just great.'

Marilyn Young, from a Jewish working-class family in Brooklyn, was a
Harvard graduate student and a young mother. She worked 'in a support
role, raising money, and protesting when people got beaten up'. She was
impressed, she recalled, with what a 'movement of ordinary people could
do. And there was a connection from a different end, a connection with my
past, my people, their ideals, and the way they had been constrained, and
the ways in which they had struggled and survived. So, there was a kind of
coming home as well.'

For young black people in the North, the implications of SNCC's
actions were especially powerful. Mike Hamlin, living in Detroit, who had
endured racism while a soldier in Korea, noted that the civil rights
movement 'reflected the rage that all of us had towards that system of
segregation and humiliation in the South. I was born in the South, and
when I got back from Korea, my feeling was that I would really like to go
back to the South and wipe out as many whites as I could. That feeling
was not unique to me. The civil rights movement intensified our
determination, our commitment, our do-or-die feeling.'

The sense that the movement forced one to reconsider one's own
actions, and one's own situation, was not limited to blacks or even other
minority groups. Frank Joyce, a steel-worker and part-time student at
Wayne State University in Detroit, recalled that the movement spoke to
the rebellious spirit of many young whites. 'At its simplest, most succinct

level, it was the civil rights movement that took the Rebels Without Causes and gave them a cause. Not them – us. There was a spirit of unrest in the late Fifties and early Sixties. There was the rebellion for the sake of rebellion aspect. Then Greensboro and the sit-ins and the Freedom Rides said we can take this energy and point it someplace useful. What we got from the civil rights movement was a cause, and a degree of defiance that made "rebels without causes" look like wimps by comparison. You could be a hot rodder, you could be James Dean, you could be whatever, but it was nothing compared to what it took to sit down at that lunch counter, or to ride that bus into Anniston, Alabama. This was courage. This was serious. This was worth doing. This appealed to my idealism, this gave me direction. That's the proton and the neutron of it.'

Sympathy and excitement moved these young Americans to look for ways to support the movement. Young helped raise money in Boston. Vasquez did likewise in Los Angeles. The Halls joined in demonstrations protesting the segregation of Memphis churches. Joyce and Hamlin in Detroit joined protests against segregated swimming facilities and discriminatory hiring practices on the part of local banks. New groups sprung up such as Boston's Emergency Public Integration Campaign (EPIC). Others were chapters of national groups such as: CORE, the Friends of SNCC, and the Northern Student Movement. But until 1965, the South was where the action was, and the Southern movement remained a mostly black movement.

There were a few Southern whites involved in SNCC, many of whom would soon form the Southern Student Organizing Committee to garner support for SNCC among white students. Among them was Sue Thrasher, a working-class college student from Scarritt College in Nashville who had been raised with strong attachments to the Methodist church. Her sense that 'things were wrong' in the South was dramatically reinforced in 1963 when she heard over her car radio that three black children had been killed in a white bombing of a Birmingham church. 'It just absolutely did me in. That to me was the moment when I thought to myself, this was done in the name of white Southern people, and this is supposed to represent me. Well, it doesn't represent what I think or what I believe! Those people aren't ever again going to be doing things like that on my behalf as a Southern woman.' With several other white students, and with the close support of SNCC workers, she helped form SSOC, which soon had chapters on many Southern campuses.

But the only large-scale white participation on a project developed by

SNCC was the Mississippi Freedom Summer of 1964. This dramatic change of policy met with serious doubts from many black SNCC workers. The plan was to induce as many as one thousand white students to work on voter registration in Mississippi, and force the federal government to intervene on behalf of blacks' constitutional rights. It marked a new phase in which the student movement was actively trying to put pressure on the state to bring change, and it was to have a profound effect on the American student movement.

SNCC's Bob Moses was the author of the plan, and it was tried on a small basis in 1963, with the aid of liberal activist Allard Lowenstein. Moses hoped to use the white students to draw national attention to the situation in Mississippi, the most recalcitrant of the Southern states, and force a confrontation between state and federal authorities. He also saw the effort as part of a long-term struggle to develop a home-grown freedom movement. With the aid of several liberal foundations, Moses prevailed in the debates within SNCC, and the word about Mississippi Freedom Summer began to spread through civil rights networks across the country.

The student volunteers were a mixed bunch, coming from all over the country. Steve Fraser was in his freshman year at the University of Wisconsin when he heard of the project. He came from a newly middle-class Jewish family. As a teenager, he had joined several demonstrations organized by CORE on Long Island. When he learned about the Mississippi Summer he was immediately interested. 'I knew instantly that's what I wanted to do. There was no doubt about it.' Mario Savio, a philosophy undergraduate at the University of California at Berkeley, had a similar reaction. Like Fraser, Savio had taken part in Northern demonstrations organized by CORE, and heard about the Mississippi Summer while in jail, after being arrested in a civil disobedience protest. Born in New York City's Lower East Side of a deeply religious Italian-American family, he had been attracted to the civil rights movement's moral seriousness. He saw the Mississippi Summer as his chance to act according to his highest moral aspirations. 'I only hoped that I would be good enough, that they would accept me,' he remembered.

Not everyone had previous civil rights experience. Karen Duncanwood, in her first year at San Francisco State College, had never taken part in a demonstration. She came from a conservative Scots-Irish family in rural Marin County, and had no direct contact with the movement until that spring of 1964. 'The civil rights project had a table out, and I walked by and sort of stuck my nose in the air and said, "Ugh, there's all those people that demonstrate. I don't want anything to do with them." Well, about the third day, my curiosity got the best of me. I wanted to find out why they were there. They had pictures of people getting beat up, and dogs sicced on them. I was reading the captions and I said, "Do people really get shot for trying to vote there?" And they said, "Oh yes." But I really didn't believe them. There was nothing in my experience that made me doubt that this country was perfect in terms of democratic political framework. They said they were having a summer project, trying to register people to vote, and they told me a little bit about it. Somehow during that couple of weeks, I came back to the table a couple of times. I had zilch political involvement before. I went to Mississippi Summer because I didn't believe what they said about it. I thought I'd go and find out.'

Together with several hundred other student volunteers, Savio, Fraser and Duncanwood traveled to Oxford, Ohio, for a week-long training session organized by SNCC. 'They scared us,' recalled Fraser. 'They told us that this was very dangerous, and we'd better not have any romantic ideas, or ideas that this was going to be a lark. My whole attitude changed. It made me much more sober and serious because people began to talk about their whole lives, and why they should be doing this. This was a big existential decision. It was a decision for personal freedom as well as social freedom. It had to be premised on an understanding of your whole past, all the limitations of your past. Why were you choosing to break with much of your past? Whether you should be doing that. Examining your motives. Having these long, excruciating internal inspections of yourself. I remember vividly, Moses and Mario Savio having this long discussion, talking in a way which was beyond me, and in a language that I didn't understand; a kind of existential leftism which had not been a part of my upbringing. I was more used to straight political language, and this sounded deep, and it moved me in some way.'

Savio's clearest memory revolves around the announcement early in the week that three young workers had disappeared. The three young men – Andrew Goodman, Michael Schwerner and James Chaney – were later found dead: the whites had been shot, and the black, Chaney, beaten to death. Announcing the disappearance, Moses called upon the volunteers to think carefully about their decision. Savio was deeply shaken. 'The night we heard about this we talked late into the night,' he recalled, 'as to whether we should go down. We were talking about the possibility that we might not come back alive . . . Think about it: for me, it was just two, three years from the first picket line I ever saw, in New York, to here I am in Oxford, Ohio, talking with a buddy I'd just met about the possibility that in the next few weeks we would be killed. We both decided we would do it, anyway.'

Duncanwood's sharpest memory is of meeting black people for the first time. 'I had literally not been within three feet of anybody non-white until the age of nineteen. It was that strong. I was completely naive. If I had any image of blacks at the time, it was the traditional image of "those poor blacks". Here were blacks who were educated, leading, in control, giving good leadership. Bob Moses was an impressive figure. It was during the time of participatory democracy, and so everybody said everything that was on their minds, and meetings took six, seven, and eight hours and were gut-wrenching. People would talk, have differences of opinion, say where they were coming from, and then Bob would say something. He'd start to speak, and within three minutes he would sum up exactly what had gone on. It was really amazing. There was nobody that I knew that didn't like him and respect him.'

After the training concluded, the volunteers headed for Mississippi. When Duncanwood's group arrived in Canton, they were met by a crowd of hostile whites. But before trouble could develop, a small, enthusiastic group of blacks whisked them away to one of the town's black churches.

'Soon, however, the police arrived, rounded us up and took us down to the station. They took our photographs and made us register as "guests of the Canton Police Department". Then they started telling us that we should go home, that the women would be raped by blacks, that the men would be beaten up, and that we weren't welcome, we should leave.' Duncanwood and her group were scared, but they all decided to stay.

In Jackson, Savio was assaulted in broad daylight on the streets by a group of white men armed with metal pipes. The church where Duncanwood taught black and movement history was bombed by the local police; and when she and other white students tried to worship in a white church one Sunday they were evicted by men wearing brass knuckles. But a sense of personal and collective power also characterized the campaign. Fraser was present at a meeting in a little grocery store owned by two old black brothers when the local police chief, accompanied by officers and dogs, tried to break it up.

'They did the standard number, they were there to scare the hell out of us, threatening to bust up the meeting. On previous occasions they might have succeeded. But someone – it might have been me, I don't know, I was almost moved to tears by it – someone began to sing. We continued the meeting by singing. And we outbluffed them. They retreated, went away. It was joyous, ecstatic. A victory over them, but also over our former selves, so to speak. We became something different as a community that night.'

Like most of the volunteers, Fraser experienced the warmth of the black community's support. He felt accepted as a member of the families which sheltered him, sharing their meals, their clothes, their possessions. His respect for people displaying incredible courage in the face of enormous hardships turned to love for them – 'for that set of human qualities that you'd never seen before. And I guess, it was a kind of falling in love with yourself because you were discovering that you could behave towards other people in ways that you had never before imagined. And so you felt a lot better about yourself.'

The warmth of the relationships did not mean, however, that black Mississippians easily overcame their fear of registering to vote – a fear bred by generations of white oppression and violence. Savio recalled accompanying an old, stooped farmer he had persuaded to register to the courthouse to fill out the form. When he saw him humiliated by the sheriff's wife who was in charge, he felt something in himself change.

'Until then I was still sort of an observer in a certain way . . . But here was somebody who, because of something I had done, was maybe risking his family and facing that kind of humiliation. The sheriff's wife made him eat shit before she finally gave him that form. He was afraid, but he stood his ground. That man's courage changed my life. You know, we used to sing about how we'll never turn back, ain't gonna turn around. That was the point at which it all became real for me. That is, I'd chosen sides for the rest of my life.'

Savio's success was rare, however. Of the roughly 17,000 black people who tried to register that summer, less than 1,600 succeeded. Most registrars found excuses to turn away black citizens or simply refused to allow them to register. To them Mississippi was, and would remain, a white man's state. Nor, despite widescale press coverage, did the campaign provoke the direct federal intervention by President Lyndon Johnson that the organizers had hoped for.

Duncanwood, who went to Mississippi a 'patriotic American' in her own words, was disillusioned by the summer's end. While she had learnt to expect no protection from the local police, she had expected something more from the federal government. 'Here people's lives were in danger, people were getting fire-bombed and shot and beat up, and the FBI knew exactly who was doing it. It was a real shock to realize that the federal government didn't give a hoot if you lived or died.'

But the campaign had one immediate effect: more than 80,000 blacks joined SNCC's Mississippi Freedom Democratic party (MFDP) which, at the Democratic national convention in Atlantic City in August 1964, challenged the all-white Mississippi delegates for their seats. When President Johnson and his running mate, long-time liberal Senator Hubert Humphrey, opposed the challenge and offered MFDP a token two seats, the new party refused and angrily withdrew from the convention.

Atlantic City was a turning point for SNCC, confirming for many in the organization that a black-white coalition had no future. The Mississippi Summer, with its image of white students organizing black communities, had in part contributed to this feeling among a number of blacks.

Even Sherrod, a firm advocate of allowing whites to work with SNCC, recalled the problems. 'Two organizers, a black and a white, knock on a door and a black person comes to the door. Who are they going to look at? The white. That's what our black kids couldn't stand. They couldn't take a white coming into their area – where they'd been for two years or all their life, where they'd worked and sacrificed, and it had taken you two years to get people to come to a meeting – and the white kid can come in and say something to the black people and they'll do it.'

Another cause of friction was sexual: there were angry mutterings among black women about the relations between black men and white women. 'Black men just couldn't leave those little white girls alone, white girls couldn't leave the black men alone,' recalled O'Neal. 'We were all young, bereft of parental supervision, and strong-willed human beings excited by the romance that we were involved with. So there was a lot of sex to it. Sometimes it got to be disturbing when there were meetings that were determined by who was fucking who.'

Many SNCC activists came to believe that black-white coalitions could only heighten the obstacles to black advancement. What was needed, they felt, was a national movement to mobilize all blacks, North and South. Only that could totally change American society. But to appeal to the rapidly growing Northern black slums with their unemployment, violence and black separatism preached by various Black Muslim groups, an angrier, nationalist language was necessary. SNCC's non-violence and appeals to the 'beloved community' had only a limited attraction in these ghettos, where heavy rioting or 'rebellions' erupted in 1964, 1965 and

1966. The rebellion in Watts, Los Angeles, in August 1965, revealed the rage and anger of America's black urban youth.

As SNCC confronted the problems of the Northern ghettos, its strategies in the South seemed amply vindicated. In March 1965, the civil rights movement reached its peak in massive demonstrations organized by Martin Luther King in Selma, Alabama, which prompted the newly elected Johnson administration and Congress to enact laws that were the death blow of legalized racial discrimination.

But the South was no model for the North, where it was not legalized segregation but unwritten institutional policies and economic handicaps that limited black opportunity. In the South, moreover, the liberal wing of the Democratic party had been prepared to make concessions in order to build a black base; the same was not true in the North where such concessions would threaten its power. SNCC struggled to find new strategies to deal with the North, with the liberal establishment and with the question of whether to accept whites in the organization at all, a problem exacerbated by the large number of whites who flocked to the organization after the Mississippi Summer.

Steve Fraser, the Mississippi Summer volunteer, noted the changed attitude to whites when he worked with SNCC the following year and visited the organization's headquarters in Atlanta. 'When we got down there, we realized things were changing between blacks and whites. It wasn't hostile, but it was real cool. We were really shut out of most discussions. It was a downer for me. And we knew it meant the end of something, that was quite clear.'

'I could see the blacks were right,' commented Michael Frisch, a Princeton graduate and a new SNCC recruit. 'Here they had been busting their asses for years on this thing. It was serious stuff, immensely complicated. And here were these white kids getting in on the last act, coming down wanting to sing "We Shall Overcome" . . .'

After two years of tumultuous debates and internal struggle over these questions, SNCC emerged in 1966 with a new slogan – 'Black Power' – and a new chairperson – Stokely Carmichael. A native New Yorker and a SNCC veteran, Carmichael's public declarations that the movement's demands for 'freedom' had achieved nothing and his call for Black Power had a galvanizing effect, especially in the Northern urban ghettos. For some long-standing SNCC activists, like Martha Norman, the Black Power slogan represented more a change in style than content. 'We were after Black Power in 1961. What else is trying to get people registered in

Mississippi about? Or trying to get them to form trade unions and cooperatives? We said then that we were bringing people together to create vehicles of power.'

But Gloria House, a Florida-born woman who was one of the SNCC faction pushing for Black Power, saw it as a definite rupture with the past. 'SNCC had been about the empowerment of black people, but the whole concept of empowerment had to do with integration of blacks into the mainstream. At a certain point, around 1965–66, there was an ideological change. There were certain revolutions and changes in Africa and Latin America, and some Afro-Americans were thinking about themselves differently. Malcolm X was insisting that there were other ways that we should think about ourselves. So, within SNCC there was a small but very strong and insistent faction that was saying, "No, we are not integrationist. That's not who we are, that's not what we want."'

SNCC's adoption of the Black Power slogan meant dropping the emphasis on non-violence, the exclusion of all whites (who were told that henceforth they should work against racism solely in their own community), and a shift from the strategy of trying to work through the white liberal establishment to the positions espoused by Malcolm X of relying on unified, self-confident, independent black communities. Malcolm X's belief that the oppressed would overthrow their oppressors, his increasing anti-imperialist stance and support for the Vietnamese liberation struggle, were radicalizing factors for many blacks; his assassination in 1965 deprived the movement of a crucial leader. For a time, some SNCC activists – in a move that would be repeated by the white movement later – turned to Marxism. But Carmichael, like many other SNCC activists, came out against class as a factor in the black struggle. 'The major enemy is not your brother, flesh of your flesh and blood of your blood,' Carmichael said. 'The major enemy is the honky [the white man] and his institutions of racism.'

Before SNCC's leadership could give content to the Black Power slogan, its notions were swept away in a whirlwind of hostile white media coverage. Instead, Black Power became a catch-all phrase covering everything from Afro hairstyles to promoting black businesses or violent revolution.

The effect of the media on loose democratic and 'leaderless' student movements was a constant phenomenon on both sides of the Atlantic in the 1960s. SNCC was but the first victim – abetted in part by Carmichael himself, who enjoyed the spotlight – of the media creation of 'leaders', whose public pronouncements had not always been agreed by their organizations. 'There was no organizational way to deal with people like that who were making scandalous and irresponsible remarks and offering strategies like "Burn Baby Burn",' recalled John O'Neal. 'Nobody knew what to do, and if they did, nobody would listen.'

As SNCC's rhetoric became more inflamed, it began also to confront the state in a new way. The FBI escalated its surveillance and infiltration, while President Johnson's Great Society programmes began to draw off energy and organizers that would have otherwise flowed into the movement. It was a carrot and stick strategy that would be used more than once on both sides of the Atlantic. SNCC's real problem, as O'Neal saw – and this, too, was one that most subsequent movements would face – was that 'the movement had gone past its own understanding of what to do. We, as the leadership, were no longer able to provide people with an orientation that would move them towards their objectives, that would satisfy their interests and needs.'

While SNCC struggled to find a new orientation, and urban riots grew in size and ferocity, new black groups emerged, most notably the Black Panther Party. Founded in 1966 by two Oakland, California, community college students, Bobby Seale and Huey P. Newton, the Panthers combined a Black Power rhetoric, inspired by Carmichael, with a Marxist-Leninist ideology and a militaristic structure. Although at first they saw themselves as allies of SNCC, which by now was in decline, they soon criticized it as a 'bourgeois, reformist organization'. Committed to organizing the black lumpenproletariat to revolutionary change in America, their support was limited primarily to angry ghetto youth; and at times they sank to little more than a radicalized street gang. But they received wide media coverage and, as will be seen in a later chapter, had a significant impact on both black and white student movements in the second half of the 1960s.

The black student movement's trajectory from non-violent civil rights to revolutionary engagement would be followed, through a series of twists and turns and with a time lag of usually a couple of years, by the white American movement. Early white U.S. activists cut their teeth on civil rights, and used language and organizational forms similar in many ways to SNCC's. Beginning from very different positions, West European movements passed through many of the same phases at different times in their own convergent trajectories. To understand how this happened, it is necessary to look briefly first at their very distinct starting points.

3

Shaping the Movements

Origins: 1960–1964

In the early 1960s, small numbers of student activists on both sides of the Atlantic formed groups or initiated movements that were to play key roles in the uprisings at the end of the decade. The contradictions of post-war capitalism, already noted, were largely responsible for their emergence, but their form and aims were shaped by their own cultural and political heritage. In West Germany, new interpretations of Marxism; in the United States, liberal radicalism and civil rights; in France, the attempt to reform the Communist party; in Italy, moves to expand the meaning of democracy – these were the origins of movements which, by the end of the decade, would appear very similar. And yet, underlying their diverse beginnings, many of these initial groups were searching, like the British New Left, for a political space beyond the confines of Social Democracy and Stalinism, a space in which to redefine the meaning of democracy.

The earliest and perhaps best known of these student movements of the Sixties were the two SDSs, the West German and American. As a rapid overview of their aims and positions will show, little appeared at first sight to link them other than the coincidence of sharing the same initials; but beneath their considerable divergences there also lay a number of interesting parallels.

The West German SDS

Until its expulsion in 1961, SDS (Sozialistische Deutsche Studentbund) was the student organization of the Social Democratic party. The reasons for the expulsion, which were to have unforeseen consequences for the late 1960s, were clear enough. As Oskar Negt put it, the student organization had been 'sharply critical' of the party's decision two years earlier to drop its vestigial allegiance to Marxism in an attempt to win over middle-class voters who had given the Christian Democrats victory in every general election since the war. The parent party, on the other hand, accused SDS of being open to 'Communist subversion' in supporting demands for talks with the East German regime – then not officially recognized by the West – on the question of the nuclear disarmament of both Germanies.

'All this was connected to a third reason – our conscious turn towards working-class politics which we felt was better represented by the trade unions than by the party. We had adopted then a rather orthodox Marxism which had died out in the party but which was still represented by a few active and influential people in the unions.'

SDS's 'turn to the left', in the relative terms of the parent party's swing to the right, had a number of other causes, among them nuclear disarmament. The deployment of American atomic weaponry on West German soil in the late 1950s provoked large-scale protests for the first time since the end of the war. Student Action Committees were formed on which SDS members like Jürgen Seifert played a leading part.

'Every week we produced a little paper which had one page of short and pointed analysis. The rest was made up of quotes from prominent clergymen and scientists about the nuclear issue,' recalled Seifert. 'We printed two to three thousand copies each time. And with such limited means we changed the political landscape of Münster where I was a postgraduate. Quite soon we had an SDS member on the Student Council's executive committee.'

Most leading SDSers, like Seifert, had no wish to be expelled from the parent party because, as he explained, 'there was no political space to the left of the Social Democratic party. Communism was discredited. And yet we were totally well-behaved about the expulsion, which took place without prior consultation. We didn't even try to force the party leadership to talk to us. We could have staged a sit-in at party headquarters, for example. Three hundred comrades waving their membership cards would have made a good newspaper picture! But it didn't even cross our minds. That type of politics didn't develop until much later.'

A small island in a sea of traditionally apolitical or right-wing students – only nine per cent of students were genuinely concerned with democratic processes, a Frankfurt University survey showed – the seven hundred or so members of the newly independent socialist organization seemed to be facing a bleak future. SDS was but one of a number of student organizations. What political space, what role, could it engage in? For a time, maintaining the traditional concept of socialist intellectuals supporting and educating the working class, its members worked within the trade unions. At the same time, as Michael Vester, who joined SDS in 1960, recalled, the organization was in contact with the British New Left. 'They weren't interested, like SDS, in creating a new theoretical line. After the immobility of the 1950s they wanted to stimulate the growth of a movement, linked into CND. Their book, *Out of Apathy*, a collection of essays by dissident socialists and communists, spoke directly to my experience of the Fifties. It was through them that we adopted the name "Neue Linke" [New Left] because their search for a space that was neither Communist nor Social Democratic seemed to point in the right direction. In fact, they seemed to have a closer connection to political reality than we in SDS.'

The search for a new 'theoretical line' continued, however. The introduction by Oskar Negt, a Frankfurt postgraduate student, of a weekly workshop-cum-seminar on Marxism was to have a significant impact on the organization's future course.

'It was the first fundamental and thorough study of Marxism within SDS,' recalled Negt. 'A whole generation of future SDS leaders passed through the study group which we ran for two or three years.' The example was soon copied until every SDS chapter had at least one such study group, which worked not only on Marxism, but unearthed old socialist and anarchist traditions and books critical of Social Democracy's past.

Many SDS members were, moreover, influenced by social and political philosophers – most notably Horkheimer, Adorno and Marcuse – associated with the Institute for Social Research, the so-called Frankfurt School, whose 'critical theory' combined Marxist and Freudian tools of analysis to uncover the connections between socio-economic exploitation and psychic oppression under advanced capitalism. In these SDS circles, concepts such as alienation, repression, exploitation, liberation, were as readily understood in their psycho-social and cultural aspects as in the politico-economic domaine to which Communist parties usually confined them. The critical posture of these philosophers towards Stalinism supported SDS's search for a new political and theoretical space. Continuing the involvement SDS had shown in the Algerian War, some study groups concentrated on Third World issues and imperialism.

'Although they struck me as being a sect because there were so few of them there,' recalled a non-SDSer, Niels Kadritzke at Tübingen University, 'they stood out as the only organization that raised Third World issues: the Algerian War, the Congo and South Africa. Their speakers were brilliant, people who wiped the floor with the other political student groups, especially the Christian Democratic organization. I realized then that, though they didn't behave in a radical activist manner, there seemed to be a correlation between intelligence and left political opinion.'

Until 1964, SDS effectively withdrew into its study groups in an attempt to 'reconstruct Marxist theory'. From this came a new critique of post-war capitalist society and a new political stance. Increasing capitalist rationalization and automation, SDS argued, required a more highly skilled technical and scientific workforce then ever before; blue collar workers would become increasingly redundant. This process, theorized also in a number of influential books by the Austro-French Marxist André Gorz, among others, would engender new social contradictions which the dominant classes would attempt to stifle by all the 'human engineering' means at their disposal. The task therefore of the 'critical' intelligentsia, among whom SDS counted itself, was to educate and politicize the 'objectively reactionary technical intelligentsia'.

This theory of capitalist development, which would emerge in various forms in other student movements throughout the Sixties, had direct repercussions on the university, since it was the latter that was mass-producing the professional and technical cadres required by contemporary capitalism. SDS's demands to democratize the university, which will be returned to in the following chapter, its attempt to form a new consciousness among students to prepare them to play an *active* role in the reforms that must come about, was one of the two issues that began to mobilize students in the first half of the Sixties.

The other was fascism. 'When *Das Argument* [a theoretical Berlin magazine around which SDS and non-SDS members gathered] reopened the discussion on the origins of fascism, seeing it as a phenomenon of capitalism, I saw that everything I had thought about history until then was wrong,' remembered Wolfgang Lefèvre, whose father had been a small timeserver in the Nazi era. 'Like many other Germans, my father had learnt his lesson well. "From now on we will be totally non-political. After all, we've never really been politically active" was his attitude. And I became in my teens what you might call a normal, stupid Christian-Democrat sort of citizen.'

Intending to become a Catholic priest, Lefèvre was studying philosophy in Berlin when he encountered *Das Argument* and the question of fascism. 'The latter made me realize how little I knew about what happened in

Germany before the Second World War or the working-class revolution after the First World War, or the revolutions of 1848. It was also my first encounter with Marx. I made a big effort then to catch up, to reach a minimum level of knowledge . . .' In the second half of the 1960s, he would become one of the major SDS leaders.

Summing up SDS in its study-group days until 1964, Oskar Negt observed that 'all of us were absolutely certain that we were working for the future, if only on a small scale. SDS was a small organization, but it was theoretically well grounded in Marxism. We were certain that our analysis of society was right and that our solidarity with Third World movements was correct.'

The American SDS

Students for a Democratic Society in 1960 was but one of a number of small groups on American campuses where political movement, after the stasis of the previous decade, was by now beginning to stir. Interest in the Cuban revolution, which initially appeared to be opening a new space between Cold War liberalism and Stalinism; support for the black student sit-ins in the South; demonstrations against the witch-hunting House Un-American Activities Committee, and hopes aroused by President Kennedy's election in 1960 were paired with, and to some extent nourished by, a student culture that was influenced by a growing bohemianism, in particular the Beats. If SDS rose to prominence among the competing white student groups it was almost for one reason alone: its immediate awareness of the civil rights issue and its rapid linkage with SNCC.

For over fifty years, the organization had been the student wing of the social-democratic League for Industrial Democracy, an anti-Communist reform group with close ties to organized labor. In 1959, in an attempt to revitalize the small student organization, it changed its name to Students for a Democratic Society and shifted its base from New York to the 'multiversity' of Michigan where a core of student radicals had formed. With great foresight, the new president, Al Haber, organized an SDS conference on civil rights before the first black student sit-ins and then hired his fellow-student, Tom Hayden, as field secretary to travel through the South with SNCC. One of the first whites to do so, Hayden's reports, and two arrests, brought SDS a new credibility among Northern student activists.

'SDS had the feel of something neat, new and dynamic. It seemed radical in a way that nothing else seemed radical,' remembered Jeremy Brecher, who joined in 1962. 'The left I had experienced before was preoccupied with respectability – they were so defensive. SDS seemed hip and bold. It didn't have that scared rabbit mentality. There was an enthusiasm for direct action, an attitude of defiance towards the establishment, and a constant looking for points where change could be stimulated and supported.'

The student organization's close links with SNCC were the first step to prominence (although veteran SNCC activists, like John O'Neal, were dubious about the connection: 'there was a general sense among people in SNCC that we did have responsibility for providing some kind of leadership to the white activists. But they weren't very good followers'). The qualitative leap came, however, when SDS translated SNCC's ideology into one capable of mobilizing white students, and in doing so rediscovered the radical democratic heritage of the United States itself. Invoking a moral vision of society that united individualism and community, self-cultivation and human 'brotherhood', the heritage was brought up to date in what is usually taken as SDS's founding charter, the Port Huron Statement of 1962:

A new left must transform modern complexity into issues that can be understood and felt close up by every human being. It must give form to the feelings of helplessness and indifference, so that people may see the political, social, and economic sources of their private troubles and organize to change society. In a time of supposed prosperity, moral complacency, and political manipulation, a new left cannot rely on only aching stomachs to be the engine force of social reform. The case for change, for alternatives that will involve uncomfortable personal efforts, must be argued as never before. The university is a relevant place for all of these activities.

In suggesting that students had a crucial and legitimate role in changing society, the young radicals looked beyond organized labor and the political parties as the agents of change. They saw in the upsurge of the black movement the 'most direct, visible and powerful challenge to the established power in America', and in the 'power of students and faculty united' a force for reform.

While proposing a host of *liberal* reforms to remedy America's ills, the

Statement called for *radical* means to attain them: 'participatory democracy', 'insurgencies' like the civil rights movement, the creation of grassroot movements. Participatory or direct democracy, in which all those involved participated with equal rights to speak and democratically to decide their course of action (as opposed to representative democracy, in which the elected have the privilege of speaking and the others the primary duty of selecting and electing them) was seen as both a means and an end. Experience in democratic movements would collectively change people's lives at the same time as they changed society into a political *and* economic system where they could participate meaningfully in the decisions that affected their lives. As with SNCC, the movement itself must prefigure the good society it hoped to create.

The ability to couch its demands for reforms in the liberal terms that students could understand, to address issues of everyday life, to envisage a movement as a community which was a democratic model for the future, and to see students as a force for change, gave the Port Huron Statement considerable appeal.

'I didn't have any sophisticated language to tell myself what was exciting about it, but I felt we were starting fresh and new,' recalled Barbara Haber, who helped write the statement. 'I came from a somewhat different place than most other people, because I had this socialist background. What was exciting to me was that we were talking in an American language about American experience. It was fresh. These people, collectively, this statement, seemed to be about my life. It was very exciting.'

'I read it from cover to cover and joined SDS in part on that basis,' recollected Jim Jacobs, a student from a Greek-American family at Harpur College. 'I remember reading it saying, "Wow, these people really analyzed how the student movement is connected to the civil rights movement." It seemed important that here were a group of people who were going to change the schools, and the whole system too.'

Jacobs, like many who joined SDS, was already active on his campus. To him, civil rights were important, but the main concern of his group of liberal friends were the issues of student life and student rights, such as living off campus, the ending of restrictive hours for women, and dress codes. 'We wanted to be treated as adults. We felt we were more mature than they gave us credit for. We were ready to do things and make decisions. We felt we took ourselves seriously, and they didn't.' On another level, he remembered, their goal was participatory democracy: the right of students to have a say in decision-making at the college. Though few Harpur students were radicals or activists, many could be drawn into campaigns on these issues. 'You could cut across ideological lines. We could go to meetings with the president of the school and say, "These are the things we want to change."'

Apart from acting on campus issues of concern to students, SDS mounted an attempt to use radical measures to effect political change in the ghettos of the North, where it hoped to emulate the issues of SNCC in the South. This campaign grew out of the experience of the SDS chapter at Swarthmore, a small Quaker liberal arts college near Philadelphia. Swarthmore students joined a group of blacks in Cambridge, Maryland, who were encountering fierce, often violent resistance in their efforts to integrate the community. Cathy Wilkerson, then a second-year student, was deeply affected by the action. 'If there was one event that changed my life, it was that trip to Cambridge.' The daughter of liberal Republican parents from Stamford, Connecticut, she recalled meetings in black churches, police dogs, and the courage of black organizers such as Gloria Richardson. 'It was a classic civil rights struggle, and it was big, heavy and intense.' At one point she was arrested along with a hundred others, mostly mothers, for picketing the local schools. It was an experience close to those of SNCC workers in the South. Buoyed by their experiences in Cambridge, Swarthmore SDS decided to try to build a community organization in nearby Chester, Pennsylvania. Wilkerson took responsibility for building a block association. 'I went from house to house and I got to know everybody on the block.'

She found most of the black people she met concerned with getting the city to service black neighborhoods in the same way white neighborhoods were serviced. 'The overwhelming goal was justice. There was injustice in the schools, there was injustice in the city administration, and you were out to fight it.' The people she met and worked with were friendly, if a bit puzzled over the students' motivations. The experience was ambivalent. Wilkerson affirmed that the students learned much about activism, and about the meaning of race and poverty in America, and even made some real contributions to the black struggle in Chester. But many students unthinkingly patronized 'poor black people' and ignored the existing leadership in the black community. 'I had this tremendous commitment to the people I worked with, which was good. But on the other hand I didn't understand about leadership and organization and the importance of black leadership in Chester. I was looking for leadership from the college chapter. I should have looked locally.'

In 1964, based on this model, SDS organized a series of Economic Research and Action Projects (ERAP) in a number of American cities such as Cleveland, Newark, Chicago and Boston. For the next two years, they remained the major focus of the organization's effort and resources. Their stated goal was to build an inter-racial coalition of the poor to seize political power in those cities.

Elaine Plaisance was born and raised around Richmond, Virginia. Her father was a Southerner and her mother a Canadian, and her family she describes as 'steeped in moral righteousness'. In 1964 she enrolled at Kalamazoo State College in Michigan. There she met SDS leader Rennie Davis, who recruited her to the Boston ERAP. Some of the decision to join was the result of 'his personal charisma, but I also liked the idea of community organization projects. What we did in Boston was, essentially, getting people their rights in the power structure via the welfare system, which was one of the most frequent targets. We worked organizing groups to go down to city hall. The issues were housing, rats and the food projects that were starting up at that time – food stamps or food donations. We got a positive response from the people in the community. I remember people just ready to do it. In retrospect it was rather poorly organized in that we were all white students who went into this multi-racial neighborhood. Being students we would never fit in. But what we were saying was correct, even if we weren't the right people to say it. I have a real sense of blacks and whites working quite well together, something you certainly don't hear about Boston.'

ERAP did not, however, have the hoped-for success in creating an inter-racial movement of the poor. Nonetheless it was an important moment in the history of SDS. As Carl Oglesby observed, 'the ERAP projects were a failure, except symbolically. Symbolically, it was great because it gave SDS a dimension, a sense of presence in the real world that it could never have if it was seen as operating exclusively in a campus context. It projected an image beyond the campus to the real world of poverty and racism and brutality. If we didn't organize community people, we nevertheless put maybe five hundred kids through a very advanced course in Sociology Today, as it is on the streets. So long as SDS looked at it as an attempt to save the poor, it was an abysmal failure. But maybe SDS's real purpose was to save the soul of the middle class, and in that respect it was one of the successes. But it was never defended in those terms.'

The differences between the German and American organizations were only too apparent, as Michael Vester noted when he went to the U.S. to study in 1961. As an official SDS representative, he contacted the American student organization and attended their conferences. 'You had the feeling that something was fermenting, about to move. It was exciting and I thought, if only we in the German SDS could get out of our theoretical objectivism we'd get into gear too! But when I got back to Germany and wrote two long articles in 1963 for *Neue Kritik* [the SDS theoretical magazine] on the American situation – the New Left, SNCC, a general analysis of the socio-economic situation – there was virtually no reaction. That would come only in 1965 when I wrote another article on "The Strategy of Direct Action".'

While Vester found a 'common wavelength' on which to communicate with American SDSers – the idiom of the British New Left – there was an evident communication gap across the Atlantic. SNCC's black Protestant language, SDS's moral vision of America, and their common emphasis on 'community' did not sit easily with young West European radicals. 'Community smacked of being "integrated" into the post-war consensus, when what was at stake was finding ways of criticizing and attacking it,' observed Richard Kuper, who had left South Africa because of apartheid to study in England. In consequence, the American movements of the early 1960s had little or no impact on their West European counterparts.

France: Working From Within the Communist Party

The Algerian War, which ended in 1962, radicalized great numbers of students; but the attempts by UNEF, the student union, to continue its mobilizations and direct them to specifically student demands did not catch on. Instead, those who wanted to continue in radical politics turned to the Communist Student Union (UEC). Despite the 1956 invasion of Hungary, and the defection of many intellectuals from the French Communist party, the Soviet Union was still widely seen by the French left-wing intelligentsia as a socialist nation which had resisted fascism and was appealing for peaceful coexistence. The United States, on the other hand, was perceived as the world centre of imperialism and military aggression – a vision which was given additional legitimacy by de Gaulle's strong anti-American stance and his rapprochement with the Soviet Union. The radicalized students attracted to the UEC in the hope of achieving socialism in France were well aware that the Communist party leadership was bureaucratic and immobile; but the UEC itself was relatively independent of the leadership and open to a wide range of political and cultural debates. Indeed, at the beginning of the decade it had fallen under the control of a group of young intellectuals whose ultimate aim was to democratize the Communist party. To do so, however, they had also secretly to criticize the Soviet Union.

'Their leader made it his job to get to know personally every UEC regional secretary,' recalled Françoise Routhier, the seamstress's daughter in Lyons. 'Once he had gained their confidence, he would tell them everything that the French Communist Party had hidden about its and the Soviet Union's past. Overawed, the secretaries would ask: "You mean it's true what the bourgeois press says?" "No, it's ten times worse ..." Convinced by his revelations, they would start to extend the network through their own region.'

Routhier remembered the day when the Lyons regional secretary took some of them aside to tell them the story. 'He was sweating like mad for fear that one of us would denounce him. I was enthralled by what he told us, it was like being initiated into a universal secret. And I thought, life is worth living to share a secret like that.'

There were others, such as Henri Weber, who were also trying to transform the UEC from within. Like a number of militant student activists in Paris, Weber, who would become one of the student leaders of the May events of 1968, came from the working-class and artisanal world of the Polish Jewish migration to France. During the Algerian War, he saw the French police beat up and arrest Algerians outside his high school. 'My parents had told me that the French police did the same to Jews during World War II. There was no question about it, the Algerian War was *le mal absolu*, total and undeniable evil.' He joined the Communist Party's youth organization; and at the Sorbonne, where he went to study sociology in 1962, he joined the UEC.

'My first impression of the organization was its amateurism. No one emptied the ashtrays or wastepaper baskets, the place was always left in complete disorder. It gave a very bad impression of the kind of society we wanted to build. In my first speech I argued against this lack of seriousness. It was as a result of this speech that Alain Krivine spotted me as someone of interest.'

Krivine was well-known as the former leader of the student struggles against the Algerian War; at the same time he was a secret member of the Trotskyist Fourth International. Weber met him again at an international youth camp in 1963 in newly-independent socialist Algeria. Krivine lent him some books which were a 'complete revelation. Isaac Deutscher's book on Stalin in particular. He didn't denounce Stalin from a humanist-liberal point of view, which I never found convincing. No. He explained Stalin's crimes as resulting from a specific type of society – a bureaucratic society with a new ruling stratum and its own logic of domination. The parallel with the French revolution was striking. During the latter, everybody believed they were moving towards a free, egalitarian, fraternal society, when in fact what was occurring was the creation of a new class society. Deutscher's analysis fitted in with my need to act, to fight – in contradistinction to the liberal point of view. I became a Trotskyist.'

Although there were only a few Fourth International Trotskyists in the UEC, they succeeded in winning control of the humanities chapters; this confirmed their belief that they could conquer from within whole sectors of the Communist Party. 'If we can do it in the UEC why not in the CGT [the largest workers' trade union, led by the Communist party] or even in the party itself?' Weber recalled thinking.

It was not to happen. Aware of the threat, the party bureaucracy expelled the Trotskyists in 1965 with the help of the UEC leaders and a newly formed pro-Chinese faction. The latter group formed around Robert Linhart, who discovered Maoism at the same international Algerian youth camp where Weber encountered Trotskyism. 'Of all the young intellectuals who went to Algeria,' recalled Tiennot Grumbach, who organized the camp, 'Linhart was the only one who really tried to understand what was happening. He did fieldwork in the cooperatives, ate with Algerians, lived with them, tried to help them. He had a very special talent in being able to build theories on the basis of *facts*. A clear understanding of reality. You don't talk about what you don't know, and you only know what you've done, experienced, verified.'

It was this pragmatic attitude which predisposed Linhart to Maoism. A student at the Ecole Normale Supérieure, which trained France's intellectual elite, Linhart there came under the influence of Louis Althusser, the Marxist philosopher. Soon he and a dozen other Ecole Normale students joined the UEC where they began expanding their Maoist network.

'Our line was that imperialism would not be defeated from within the metropolitan countries but by the struggles of the Third World. This stemmed from our experience of the victories in Algeria and Cuba and by the ongoing struggle of the Vietnamese. That was why we began to look to China which was, of course, the revolutionary leader of the Third World.

French society seemed to us to be too well-fed for anything to happen here.'

The start of the Great Proletarian Cultural Revolution in China in 1965 gave a boost to the Maoist line which was not tolerated for long by the Communist party; the Maoists were in turn expelled from the UEC in 1966.

After their expulsions both Trotskyists and Maoists set up their own organizations: the JCR (Jeunesse Communiste Révolutionnaire) for the former, the UJC-ml (Union des Jeunesses Communistes marxistes-léninistes) for the latter. It was these two organizations which were to spearhead most of the student mobilizations that preceded 1968. Both appeared pleased to have been expelled. 'Now we had our own organization, with three hundred members, experienced cadres, and our own newspaper,' Weber commented.

'For us it was a happy day,' Linhart recalled. 'Now we were able to engage in real political activity, started to recruit outside the university, in high schools, among young workers.'

Italy: Expanding Democratic Rights

Although the Italian Communist Party was a stronger political force than the French, the Italian student movement did not originate from it as in France. There were, for sure, attempts to democratize the party from within, as in France; but it was rather the highly undemocratic nature of the Italian university and the aims it served which led students to struggle for democratic rights. In the university, all power lay in the hands of a few professors, many of whom devoted more time to their professions and politics outside the university than to their teaching within it. In 1963, the first student occupations erupted in the architectural faculties of Turin and Milan in protest against the lack of democracy and the absence of concern for the social and political implications of architecture.

'One of our professors, who had his private plane, would keep us waiting for hours,' recalled Guido Morbelli, general secretary of the Turin architecture students' assembly. 'When finally we were admitted to God's presence, he blotted out our drawings with great strokes of his pencil. And what were these drawings? Plans for luxurious villas and great office blocks, never apartment housing for other social classes.'

The occupations lasted several weeks until the authorities, under pressure from local officials and members of parliament, agreed to set up a commission in which students could discuss with teaching staff how to implement their reforms. 'Young bourgeois that we were, we were leading a civic battle to make the faculty more useful to the community and country,' Morbelli commented. 'And we won! But in fact our victory turned into a tragicomedy, the political parties made capital out of our struggle, and our gains were quickly eroded. It wasn't until 1967–68 that our goals were again taken up – with more success this time.'

The failure of the governing Christian Democrat-Socialist coalition, regionally from the late 1950s and nationally from 1963, to carry out the bulk of its promised reforms led small groups of disaffected intellectuals to begin publishing a plethora of New Left-style journals. Critical of Communism, rejecting Social Democracy, they offered radical reinterpretations of Marxism and trenchant critiques of contemporary consumer society, often devoting their pages to cultural as much as to political criticism. Though these journals did not stem from the universities, they had an important influence on radical students, especially in Turin.

'It was through reading these journals' analysis of the working class that we realized that the problems of the university were not totally different from those of the labour movement,' recalled Luigi Bobbio at Turin University, who was close to the socialist left. 'We believed that the university had become a machine for producing the managers and technicians of capital that it needed in its new stage of rationalization and planning.'

The journals' critique, which was not unrelated to the West German SDS's analysis of contemporary capitalism, was based on the idea that the new stage of capitalism, with its need to regulate and expand the forces of production, required new means of ruling-class domination. Social, cultural, economic, even psychological control, had taken over from exploitation as the major forms of capitalist power. Public relations, industrial relations, the mass media, advertising, were among the new means of domination; economists, sociologists, psychologists, copywriters, as well as the mass of new scientists and technicians coming from the university, were its instruments.

'At the time, the only way forward seemed to be to contest this type of university training,' continued Bobbio. 'By insubordination, by making students aware of the processes by which they were being transformed into the instruments of capitalism, making them aware that, as students, they had the same right as workers to form a trade union. A mass, unitary organization, independent of the existing political parties.'

In the absence of an effective national student union, student representative councils elected annually or biennially at most universities and high schools were the major forum of student political activity. But the latter was directly linked to adult political parties. Coming from a long line of left-wing intellectuals – his father had been a leading Resistance figure – Bobbio saw in the student councils an important means of furthering democratic self-management by engaging the mass of students in a new form of politics: participatory democracy.

'We of the Turin UGI [a leftist student political organization] consistently put forward the idea of direct democracy. We were against any form of delegating one's power. Later, when I became general secretary of the university assembly, we allowed the council to die, and made the assembly, composed of all students who wanted to participate, the sovereign organ. I'm firmly convinced that these councils were a major antecedent, both in personal and general terms, of 1968.'

Similar struggles for democracy were going on elsewhere. At the Scuola Normale di Pisa, one of the few residential universities in Italy, Fiorella Farinelli and other women students were fighting to overcome sexual discrimination. 'We wanted to be treated equally with men. Women had to return to their college earlier at night than the men, and we had to go to the men's college for all our courses and meals except breakfast. We went to the director and said: "If we are considered inferior in these respects, then we must be considered inferior when it comes to our grades. In future, when it comes to our scholarship grades, they will have to be lower than those for men." We held an assembly attended by male and female students and a number of our teachers. The director offered us separate kitchen facilities. We refused. We wanted equal treatment. And we won!'

In a country which in the previous decade had been marked by the 'religious war' between Catholicism and Communism, it was perhaps surprising that religion should become a radicalizing influence on a number of future student activists. But again, it was an attempt to democratize the church through a non-conformist Catholic youth organization, Gioventù studentesca (GS), with its criticism of the church hierarchy and its openness to the poor, which was to play this role.

Romano Madera, the son of school teachers, liked the 'communitarian atmosphere' of GS. 'Every Sunday we went out to help the rural poor. In summer we spent a fortnight's holiday together and another fortnight in rural Calabria evangelizing and assisting the poor, like missionaries . . . Later, however, when GS maintained that charity and charity alone was all that could solve the problems of the Third World, I and a small group broke with them. Charity in a country like Brazil was absurd. Charity there meant to make the revolution. The Gospel and Revolution – the state had to be destroyed, reformism was impossible.'

The absence of nascent student movements in Britain and Northern Ireland in the early 1960s is the negative image of one of the reasons for their emergence elsewhere. In Britain, with the possibility of a Labour electoral victory in 1964, Social Democracy did not appear dead; in Northern Ireland, it seemed a distant dream.

Northern Ireland: A Score of Radicals

Few might have supposed in the early, or even in the mid-1960s that students at Queen's University, Belfast, would, in 1968, play a radical role in changing Northern Ireland's history. 'Out of four thousand students when I went there in 1962, only fifteen to twenty were interested in left politics,' recalled Michael Farrell, who was to become the undisputed leader of the student movement there in 1968. 'It was a parochial place. A lot of students lived at home and a great many were there to get their degree and a job.'

The small group of radicals, who were mainly Catholics, did not concern themselves with student issues nor, more surprisingly, with the problems of Protestant discrimination against Catholics. In a society where the sectarian divide was always present, Queen's formed a notable non-sectarian exception. Contact with large numbers of Protestants for the first time made it seem unlikely to Farrell, a Catholic, that they could be mobilized around specifically Catholic grievances. Instead, the radicals focused on class politics.

'It was at Queen's that I became interested in Marxism,' explained Farrell, who had left behind a Dublin seminary, and thoughts of studying for the priesthood, after a few months. 'On my first day our history lecturer – a very good Scots liberal – told us to read the *Communist Manifesto*, probably as a culture shock for kids from rural conservative Catholic or even Protestant backgrounds. I thought it was great – it explained everything.'

He made contact with a British Trotskyist group; but increasingly he became concerned about the Irish question, which he believed could only be solved by a socialist republic. In consequence, he joined the Northern Ireland Labour party and its Young Socialists and founded an all-Irish Labour Students' Organization, of which he was the first chair.

'But there was another influence which strongly shaped my political thinking: the American civil rights movement. It made a very deep impact on me and on a lot of Catholics in the North. I don't know how conscious I was of the parallels at the time, but by the mid-Sixties many Catholics felt that we were in the same boat as the black people. The fact that they were beginning to change things gave us confidence that we could do the same.'

More than in any other West European country, the American civil rights movement became the inspiration for Northern Irish student activism. But this did not become apparent till 1968; until then little moved the mass of Northern Irish students.

Britain: Waiting for Labour

After thirteen years of unbroken Conservative rule, the Labour Party returned to power in 1964. The belief that the electoral promises of the new Prime Minister, Harold Wilson, to 'modernize' the country would result in dramatic political and social change had led a large majority of student radicals into working for a Labour victory. As has been seen, the original New Left had to all intents collapsed two years earlier, and CND as a mass movement had declined. All hopes were now focused on Labour.

'I was imbued with the idea that a Labour government would produce some profound change in British politics,' recalled David Triesman, who had been active in Youth CND. 'The damned-up energy I had felt in society – and which retrospectively I'm not sure I was right about – would be reflected in a dynamic and progressive government, I thought then. It would sweep things to the left irrespective of the policies of those coming to power.'

Although disillusionment was not long in coming to many like Triesman, who saw the government 'slipping almost immediately into managerial politics', widespread disaffection did not come until 1966. Then it was sharp, and focused on the contradictions that impelled student movements forward elsewhere: racism in a colonial context, racism at home, and above all the Vietnam War.

What were to become full-fledged student movements in 1968 were, four years earlier, either little more than small groups of radical students or non-existent. Indeed, had it not been for a number of other factors – the economic and demographic boom, the creation of a youth market and culture, a continuing sense of political stasis in some countries – the conditions in which, later, the movements were to attract thousands of students might not have existed. For the new social possibilities being opened up in the 1960s – which were often in conflict with pre-existing social norms – generated their own forms of radical contestation of the established order.

The Boom Years:
New Cultures, 1960–1965

The teenage youth in the suburbs was a new phenomenon. They had everything they needed, the world was wide open to them. Their parents had worked their nuts or their tits off to provide for them in a fashion unique in modern-day history. If that hadn't existed, there wouldn't have been people who could just get up in the morning and say, fuck it! – *John Sinclair, counter-culture leader, Detroit*

The economic boom which had begun in the 1950s and reached its peak in the first half of the 1960s changed the landscape for the post-war generation. A hitherto unforeseen prosperity which, if still unevenly distributed, was more widely spread than at any time in the twentieth century, was accompanied by near full employment, availability of consumer goods that previously had been confined to the well-to-do and, for the young, access to money. 'It was the time when many families, like mine, began to change their way of life,' recalled Pierre Bringuier, a middle-class student in Paris. 'They bought washing machines, a TV, and a new car, moved into larger, more comfortable apartments and went to the country for weekends. It became normal to give children pocket money. Holidays abroad in the summer instead of visiting grandparents in the countryside. There was a shift from a work to a consumerist ethic, among the young at least. And youth itself came to have a value instead of being a handicap.'

It was a time – to cite a few indices of the new prosperity – when the number of cars in the West European countries doubled in the decade up to 1960 and doubled again (and sometimes more) by 1970. In the United States, where the economic boom began earlier, new car sales had already doubled by 1955 in comparison to the pre-war figure. Television sales saw a spectacular increase. From seven thousand television sets in the U.S. in 1946 to fifty million by 1960; from 300,000 in Britain to ten and a half million between 1950 and 1960. Mass tourism became a new phenomenon – by 1961 four million Britons were holidaying abroad, and by 1965 eleven million Italians were taking holidays where a decade earlier relatively few had done so. But one of the most impressive areas of growth was in education: in the U.S., the number of students at four-year colleges and universities had doubled by 1960 compared to pre-war; between 1960 and 1965, the number rose a further 70 per cent. The five and a half million students – 22 per cent of the country's youth of university age – easily outnumbered the nation's farmers by then. Between 1950 and 1964, France had trebled and West Germany had doubled their university student numbers; Britain and Italy showed smaller increases of 60 and 50 per cent respectively.

The reason, in part, for this massive increase was the post-war demographic boom. In Britain and France between 1946 and 1950 the birth rate increased by about 30 per cent compared to the last five pre-war years; in both these countries there were over 800,000 more teenagers in the population in 1963 than there had been ten years earlier. Although, largely as a result of the immediate post-war conditions, the 'baby boom' was delayed in West Germany and Italy until the mid-1950s, secondary educational reforms increased the number of teenagers staying on at school. In Italy, for example, their number nearly doubled in the decade to 1963. Staying longer at school prolonged adolescents' dependence at a time when (apart from Italy and West Germany) their social weight had increased. The gap between the two was to some extent filled by the creation of a youth market and culture. Although teenagers in Britain, to take one case, disposed of only some 5 per cent of total consumer spending per annum, that still totalled over £850 million in 1960; and with it they bought more than 40 per cent of record-players, nearly one-third of cosmetics and toiletries, 28 per cent of cinema admissions, and so on. Teenagers – even those still at school with only pocket money to spend – felt that their place in the world was being recognized in a new way.

'Suddenly there were whole shops catering for teenagers – clothes and record shops especially – and make-up and cosmetics designed just for young people,' recalled Elisabeth Tailor, who grew up in a London suburb. 'A lot of the people serving in the shops were young, too. As a teenager, it made you feel good, independent and at the same time part of a much wider group. At last we were being recognized; being a teenager wasn't something you had to be ashamed of any more.'

'Consumerism made possible new types of relationships and awoke people's fantasies and desires to break with old ways of life,' commented Laura Derossi who, as a sixteen-year-old in 1962, was at a private Italian school run by nuns. 'My first acts of rebellion were to go with a girl friend to an elegant Milan department store to buy cosmetics and dresses that would make us look older so that we could get in to movies forbidden to people under eighteen. This gave me and my girl friend a special type of friendship, a *generational* union, in place of the traditional family-based friendships, like my mother's. We changed everything, inherited nothing.'

The social space that was opened by market forces was simultaneously reappropriated by teenagers, especially in Britain and the United States, through their creation of a new youth culture. Epitomized by the early Beatles, this culture, with its particular idiom of music and clothes, expressed a feeling of belonging to a specific age group with interests that both set it apart from its elders and created a common world for its members. In a class-dominated country like Britain, it carried with it two other important connotations: youth's creativity, and the emergence of working- and lower middle-class youth as the originators of a new culture.

'When the Beatles started to write their own songs things changed,' noted a British student, Mick Gold. 'Young people were beginning to take over the process. Until then, pop music was thought of as something created by middle-aged men in Tin Pan Alley or Denmark Street in London. Now we felt that something was moving socially, the old order changing in a significant way. And to some extent, young people seemed in control of these changes. We realized, of course, that the youth culture was based on a consumer marketing boom. But still there was a euphoric, utopian atmosphere, an idealistic mood which came across in the music. Music operated as a sort of grapevine, spreading ideas around about political and social values.'

Rock 'n roll – 'rebel music', as more than one high school student at the time expressed it – had since the late 1950s often spoken directly to teenagers' feelings. Elvis Presley, Chuck Berry, Bill Haley . . . 'I remember Chuck Berry's song "School Days", about what a drag it is to be in school, and he just articulated stuff that we felt – how the teachers were uptight and not letting you express yourself,' recalled David Gilbert of his school days in Brookline, an affluent Boston suburb. 'Rock 'n roll was exciting, sexual, alive. It made me feel involved with black people because I could identify with the music, made me more open to the civil rights movement, I think.'

'Rock music became a whole new way of being. It expressed a basic aspiration to live our own life in a way that accorded with things that gave us pleasure,' observed David Fernbach who, as a teenager, set up a rock band with his brother in Britain. But this 'basic aspiration' was countered by another consideration. Despite the economic boom, the old values of hard work and a good education were usually seen by parents, who had gone through a world war and the Depression which had preceded it, as the main safeguards for their children's future security. Among the most marked by the hardships of the past, the West European lower middle and working classes were perhaps the most insistent on education as the way forward. 'Both my mother and father had had to work hard to avoid poverty and worse,' continued Fernbach, whose mother came from a London working-class background and whose father was a middle-class Jewish refugee from Nazi Germany. 'They wanted their children to get on in the world, not in terms of handing down large sums of money which they didn't have, but in educational terms. They were keen for me to study hard and get a good professional job. Throughout my teens, there was this conflict between what they wanted for me and doing my own thing here and now.'

There was nothing new about such generational conflict; what was new was that through the youth culture, and in particular the music, it was no longer lived in the silence of individual struggle as in the past but was communicated, across classes, nations and oceans to like-minded others. 'That was one reason why the music was so important,' observed Jeremy Brecher, an American SDSer. 'It was a way that people who were isolated in their areas culturally, who didn't have other people like them around, could be in a social milieu where there were a lot of other people like them. The feeling was similar to being involved in SDS. It was really exciting, had that sense of overcoming isolation.'

In fact, parents' concern about work and careers was very widely ignored: in societies of virtual full employment there were more jobs, full-time, part-time or casual, than ever before. 'We took for granted a sense of economic openings, what was then called "affluence",' recalled Todd Gitlin, of the American SDS. 'It was the cushion really for anything you might choose to do if you were a middle-class student.' 'A career? No, I wasn't interested,' remembered Rod Burgess, who came from a working-class background and 'dropped out' after getting his degree at the London School of Economics in 1966. 'We'd never known a recession. We thought at the time there were two options: either there was going to be continuous economic growth and it would be quite easy to live on the margins. Or, if there was a slump, there'd be a socialist revolution – in which case there was still no need to join the system. Part of the problem was that the Old Left never clearly explained to us that in a recession you get a swing to the right.'

Even in Britain, where a series of major financial crises followed the Labour electoral victory in 1964, the prospects of a recession still appeared remote to most people. Pop culture seemed dominant, 'Swinging London' – in a much publicized American journalist's phrase – effervesced; even the Establishment patronized the Beatles. The Rolling Stones, in consequence, came to be seen by many young people as a more authentic expression of their feelings. 'They were part of a high-definition rebellion which was breath-taking in its audacity at the time,' recalled David Widgery. 'The way they dressed, their long hair, their rather sophisticated take-on loutishness – and the way they got away with it on television – was fantastically bold. It had a real shock value.'

Part of the shock value was a potent male sexual aggressiveness – 'sexist, but at the same time expressing, as were other groups, changing views about sexuality which simply weren't being expressed anywhere else,' recalled David Triesman. It was the beginning of what came to be called the sexual 'revolution', which in turn was furthered by the advent of the contraceptive pill. In the Unites States, where the pill became fairly widely used by married women from 1965 on, many doctors would not prescribe it to unmarried women. Nonetheless, it can be assumed that a relatively high number of unmarried college women in larger cities where it was easier to find a sympathetic doctor did use the pill; and by the turn of the decade university health services dispensed it in the larger colleges. Something similar happened in Britain, where general practitioners and family planning clinics refused to prescribe the pill to unmarried women until 1969. 'There was no way we could get contraception until we went to university,' recalled Elisabeth Tailor. 'But in my first week at Kent in 1966, I remember we all went to the medical centre where they gave us the pill without any problem. They were desperate for us to finish our education without getting pregnant. At the same time, they were willing to treat us as adults. It was a real liberation to be in control of our own bodies!'

Continental students by and large were not as fortunate. With or without the pill, students' sexual attitudes often remained rather conventional in the first half of the decade; it was only the few who seemed willing to challenge them. The fact of taking a double room in a hotel during a left-wing Italian student conference made Laura Derossi and Luigi Bobbio, who were lovers, the butt of ribald jokes. 'We were the only man and woman to share a room – perhaps there were no other couples, I don't know,' recalled Bobbio. 'For us it was both pleasant and had a symbolic value, was a way of affirming something. The others couldn't accept it. At dinner they even gave us a small present, neatly tied with a ribbon – a packet of condoms.'

At Heidelberg University in West Germany, Tilla Siegel felt isolated and without many friends. Through SDS acquaintances she came into contact with the student organization which she viewed with some suspicion as being 'too radical' for her; the men, moreover, looked 'scruffy, and didn't care about dressing properly', but she continued to go to SDS functions. At one of these, a carnival, she 'hooked up with the SDS man who looked the most clean-cut and straight. I didn't sleep with him that night, only after we had met a couple of times. At that time I still wanted to marry. He probably sensed that, so he left me after a couple of months. He always stressed his need for freedom and I naturally thought I had to accept it, although I didn't like it.' As a result of the brief relationship, however, she was considered a *de facto* member of SDS and remained in the organization where, as will be seen, she later came to an understanding of 'the relationship between my personal liberation and politics'.

A sexual relationship also led fifteen-year-old Lily Métreaux to politics when, in 1963 and without the faintest thought of marriage, she became the lover of a young film-maker in Paris. The daughter of an impoverished mother and an army officer who were divorced, she was a rebellious student in a convent school when she met him. 'He said he was going to introduce me to a famous director with whom he was working to get me a part because I was very beautiful. Then he took me to his bedroom. The first thing he asked me was what I thought of the class struggle. I'd never heard the expression! I'll never forget it – I wanted so badly to give the right answer so that he'd fall in love with me. "No," I said, "I don't believe in it." I saw I'd got it wrong! He was a Trotskyist. To cut a long story short, through him I entered a world which completely changed my life, the world of the left-wing bourgeoisie. I'd never come across so many middle-class people as I did then on the left – and it was wonderful, through them I discovered that working-class people, the poor like us, were good and the bourgeoisie was bad!'

Sex, rock music and drink could on occasion be used to express a deliberate rebellion against middle-class norms. 'As a sixteen-year-old, my parents forbade me to go out alone with a boy, to ride on the back of a motor scooter, to drink, to go to a club where the Rolling Stones played,' recalled Elisabeth Tailor in London. 'So one night I deliberately broke every one of their norms. I went on the back of my boyfriend's scooter to the club, listened to the Stones and got drunk, and I fucked him in his house before going home. It wasn't just adolescent rebellion against being controlled, though that was part of it. There was something keener, fresher in the air. A sense that we were going to do things *our* way, and that there were a lot of us who rejected not just our individual parents but what their values represented socially.'

Apart from the youth culture, the impact of which was confined principally to Britain and the U.S., there were many other ways in which those who later became student activists began to develop a critical awareness of their societies: travel, the influence of school teachers and older family members, the patrimony of other cultures and literature, were among those most often recalled.

At the age of fourteen, and again two years later, Hilary Wainwright, a British student, accompanied her parents on holiday to Portugal. On the beach she met a radical Portuguese student. 'Through him I got an idea of the Salazar repression and also of an opposition growing up. Portugal seemed a mixture of incredible poverty – people barefoot and starving – and incredible wealth. A Third World peasant poverty and the riches of a Victorian ruling class. It made quite an impact on me, both in terms of oppression and of coming to see politics as concerning more than just Britain.'

Significantly, it was often through Third World examples that teachers attempted to make their high school pupils aware of social and economic oppression. As Angélique Pinto recalled in France, 'we had this teacher of Spanish who introduced us to the world of Latin American writers. Through them we discovered the poverty and oppression of the people there. It still brings tears to my eyes when I remember that teacher and what he helped to show us . . .' In other cases, the impact was more overtly radical. 'In my last year at school we had a devout Catholic philosophy teacher who was also a Marxist,' recalled Romano Madera in Italy. 'He taught us to read parts of *Capital* and told us about innovating tendencies within the Catholic church. But he also taught us much more than that. He taught us about life. He was married, had four children and was separated – he couldn't get divorced because it wasn't legalized until 1974. In short, a real life! The light had come to that damned school at last!'

Before she was even a teenager, Bernadette McAliskey was embued with radical Irish culture and was reciting it in a public talent competition in her Northern Irish home town. 'The Rebel' by Padraig Pearse, one of the martyrs of the 1916 Easter rising in Dublin against British rule, was among her winning selections:

> I say to the master of my people,
> "Beware the risen people who will
> Take what you would not give!"

'That's how the poem ends. A very powerful piece. I grew up with Pearse's work. We weren't much affected here by any of the 1960s cultures – ours was a very poor community where things became fashionable only after the fashion had gone out everywhere else.'

Among the literary influences most often cited internationally in the first part of the 1960s were Sartre and Camus, Kerouac, the Beat writer, the early writings of Marx, and Frantz Fanon. The latter, a theorist of the Algerian revolution, emphasized in particular the psychological oppression of the colonized and the subjective elements of rebellion and violence needed to overthrow that oppression. 'His book *The Wretched of the Earth* represented a sector of the world that probably even existed in our country, one to which we might even belong,' recalled Derossi. 'The colonized internalize the colonialist's violence and must free himself internally. In all our struggles there were important elements of self-liberation.'

Marx's early writings, which were then becoming more widely available in translation, were another important source of inspiration for many students. Their concept of socialist freedom as consisting not only in the social reappropriation of the economy but in the individual's power of decision over his or her own life as well as that of society, contrasted sharply with the Stalinist vision of Communism, as Richard Kuper in Britain recalled. 'The utopianism of those writings, the belief that the world could be totally different – at a time when the world seemed totally unchangeable – was a tremendous inspiration to me.' He joined the small, far-left International Socialists (IS), a breakaway a decade earlier from the Trotskyist movement. 'Until I came across IS I had been put off Marxism because of its Soviet connotations. Now I found a liberation revolutionary Marxist group which condemned Russia utterly as having nothing to do with the socialist freedoms we were discovering in Marx's early writings.'

The search for a left-wing intellectual tradition was especially acute in West Germany where, a generation earlier, Nazism had crushed the left. The void was in part filled by the Frankfurt School of social and political philosophers who returned from exile after the war and whose influence on the early SDS has already been seen; but there were other influential figures who, along with the Frankfurt School, began to have a widening impact among high school students in the first half of the decade. Ernst Bloch, the Marxist philosopher who left East Germany in the early 1960s, was one of these. Detlev Claussen met him at a discussion circle organized by a Protestant pastor. 'That was the best thing that ever happened there. I was about sixteen and I had just read one of Bloch's books with great difficulty. But then to be able to talk to him, to have him take you seriously, answer your questions – that's something that left a vivid impression on me for a long time.'

The new material prosperity itself helped to validate the challenge to the established order of another movement, the Situationist International, whose theories attracted numbers of future student activists in Western Europe. Founded in Paris in the late 1950s, the small Situationist group attacked from a revolutionary perspective every aspect of Western life and culture, including organized political parties. 'In the tradition of the Dada and Surrealist movements,' noted Dieter Kunzelmann, a West German Situationist, 'we were trying to achieve a radical rupture in the patterns of everyday life. We wanted to disrupt the clockwork mechanisms that regulate contemporary living by provoking people into thinking about the meaning of industrial society. Life, we maintained, must be the artistic product of the whole of society conceived in terms of human beings capable of communication and pleasure. For example, we had a vision of new cities with parks and labyrinths built to facilitate communication between people rather than to ensure that industrial production and traffic ran smoothly.'

This was only part of the vision, however; better known to most students was the relentless critique, elaborated by Guy Debord, the Situationists' main theoretician, of contemporary capitalism as 'the society of the spectacle'. As Donald Nicholson-Smith, a British member of the Paris group, explained, this crique saw capitalism as being based on 'the consumption of images as opposed to real things, that life had been reduced to a spectacle'. Claiming for itself a revolutionary heritage, the Situationist International maintained that the historical agent of change – the proleteriat – could no longer be considered the traditional working class but included almost everybody who was a wage or salary earner. While the main enemy remained capitalism in its latest form of 'the spectacle', Communist parties and trade unions which blocked off the revolutionary spontaneity of this new proletariat were to be excoriated. 'To some extent', continued Nicholson-Smith, 'we embraced the idea that the young had a privileged position in the struggle against the system because they weren't lumbered with the heritage of the past. One of the Situationist programmatic statements or slogans was, "Our ideas are in every-body's head and one day they'll come out." Basically, the Situationist International forecast 1968.'

Arguing that everyone was 'hypnotized by work and by comfort', the Situationists believed that the only way to revolution was to transform daily life, not through theoretical debate, but by passionate acts of subversion. Anyone who spoke of revolution without reference to the conditions of daily life was 'talking with the voice of the dead'.

'The idea that the social revolution had to start from daily life, start from even the smallest unbearable aspect, like wearing a tie or make-up, came to me largely from the Situationists,' remembered Elsa Gili, a Turin University research student. 'Start to make relationships of a different order to the existing one. Start to take things back into our own hands, reappropriate what had been expropriated from us. This couldn't be done through the structures of political parties. The revolution must be a festival – the festival of the oppressed.'

In the United States, the first signs of the counter-culture, which would emerge with full force in the second half of the 1960s to displace the youth culture, in the U.S. and Britain particularly, were now becoming visible. In 1963, Timothy Leary and a co-worker were expelled from the staff of Harvard University for experimenting with LSD on students, and Leary established himself on an estate in Millbrook, New York, as the guru of a cult of acid religionists. At the end of the following year, Ken Kesey, California novelist and bohemian who had visited Leary, held the first of his famous acid tests in San Francisco; and in Los Angeles the first underground newspaper, the *Free Press*, appeared. Drugs, LSD especially, were to play a significant part in the counter-culture.

Times of widespread radicalization are often heralded by a deep cultural ferment, and 1968 was no exception. The new cultural movements played an important role in shaping a wider society of dissent within which student movements could evolve. But the former were only a part – and even then an unevenly distributed part – of the conditions of student radicalization. Nationally and internationally things were changing. The Cuban missile crisis of 1962, which had seemed on the verge of precipitat-ing nuclear war, brought in its wake a positive gain: the first significant easing of the Cold War (of which the Nuclear Test Ban Treaty of 1963 and the establishment of a 'Hot Line' between Moscow and Washington were examples) and, for student radicals, the consequent opening up of potential political space as the glacial deadlock began to thaw. Significantly, nuclear disarmament no longer remained thereafter as one of the major focuses of protest.

Internally, too, Western societies were changing. In the United States, President Kennedy's election in 1960 represented a definitive break with the generation of wartime leaders like Eisenhower, his predecessor, and seemed to some young people – partly in response to his calls to their idealism – to prefigure a new politics. In a lesser vein, something of the kind could be said of Harold Wilson in Britain. Both put an end to long-ruling conservative administrations; both in the end failed to live up to their promises. Kennedy's failure to take rapid and decisive measures in support of the civil rights movement, his backing of the disastrous invasion of Cuba at the Bay of Pigs, and his gamble with nuclear war with the Soviet Union over the Cuban missile crisis, disabused many even before his assassination in 1963 ended whatever hopes might have remained. Nonetheless, his successor, Lyndon Johnson, launched his Great Society program which saw millions of dollars poured into increases in social security, housing, new educational and training programs. As a result of the continuing civil rights campaign, legislation to end discrimination in registration and voting was finally approved.

The first half of the 1960s represented the height of post-war American liberalism; but it was also its watershed. The dividing line was plainly drawn in 1965 with Johnson's escalation of the Vietnam War; but the roots of that division had been planted four years earlier by Kennedy's decision to increase America's military presence in South Vietnam. The second half of the 1960s was to be dominated by the consequences of that decision.

In Italy, also, there was hope of serious social and economic reform when a centre-left Christian Democratic-Socialist alliance came to power in 1962. These hopes were also rapidly dashed. 'I remember my father, who had always voted Socialist, expressing his disappointment after seeing "his" party in power,' recalled Elsa Gili in Turin. 'Almost none of the promised reforms were put into effect. The problems of the South, of the public health service, education, uncontrolled urban growth – nothing was really done. The centre-left preferred to increase public expenditure rather than really reduce privileges and make reforms. Combined with the fact that the Italian economic boom began to slacken from 1963, hopes among the young that reform was possible declined from the mid-1960s, leading to the idea that little could be expected from the state.'

In France and West Germany, where the old guard, de Gaulle and Konrad Adenauer, remained in power, not even the hope of such reform attempts appeared. France was experiencing its first real industrial take-off – financed in large part by the repatriation of capital from the former colonies and, after 1962, from Algeria – in which the state played a central role. This modernization, which benefited big business at the expense of salary and wage-earners, made constant appeals to young people who were hailed as the country's future. Those who refused to see their future as 'organization men' – something which French Catholic and intellectual culture had never propitiated – did not readily respond. For a brief time, a youth culture – the first Paris pop concert with French singers in 1963 attracted 100,000 youth, ten times the expected number – brought to some future activists the sense of sharing a common experience; but they soon turned away from it. Many of them felt – and their feeling was reinforced after de Gaulle won a second seven-year term in 1965 – a sense of political and social inertia. 'That's one of the reasons we moved to the left,' recalled André Liber, a high school student in the mid 1960s. 'Gaullism spoke endlessly of things that were totally foreign to us: national independence, the importance of an independent nuclear strike force, the role of the constitution – things that interested absolutely no one of my generation. And so we began to develop a certain nostalgia for the Resistance, the Algerian War – times when things were more clear-cut.'

Although Adenauer, West Germany's Chancellor since 1949, finally stepped down in 1963, the Christian Democrats continued in their uninterrupted post-war tenure of power. The country's 'economic miracle' produced a standard of living that was one of the highest in Western Europe; and yet, as in France, there was a sense of social and political stasis among many young people which was reinforced by 1965 when it became clear that the Social Democratic opposition would join the Christian Democrats in power, leaving the country without an effective parliamentary opposition.

The fascist past continued to hang in unspoken tension over the young. Until 1963, when he was fifteen, Detlev Claussen, for example, was unable to broach the past with his father, who had been a lawyer for the German navy during the war and had spent a year in a re-education camp after the war. 'Our teacher in civics read to us without comment Mitscherlich's book *Medizin ohne Menschlichkeit* [an account of concentration camp medical experiments], and I came home very upset and talked about it. Without explanation, my father responded by talking about the Communists after 1945. He simply refused to deal with the Nazi past. The East is now, the past is the past, he was saying in effect. I never heard him voice any concern about the past. I took that very badly, something broke between us, and later it led to a split between the rest of the family and my brother and me.'

In neither West Germany nor Italy did the youth culture particularly affect university students; in the former probably because they were generally older than in other countries; in the latter because activists were influenced by a left-wing culture with its strong Resistance heritage and a certain moralism. In Germany it was not until the mid-1960s that protest songs about political issues and everyday life, influenced by the Bob Dylan of the early 1960s, became popular among teenagers, reflecting a radicalization that by then was taking place at other levels also. In Italy, student activists continued to wear suits, ties and short hair until well into the second half of the decade.

Despite differing conditions in each of the countries, there was by the mid-1960s a growing sense among a minority of students that hope of reform, of a new politics, was illusory. Economic growth seemed assured; but growth for what? Celebrating the new social possibilities that the boom years were supposed to bring with them, which was the essential function of the youth culture, no longer seemed sufficient even in those countries where it had flowered.

It was on this backcloth that the students movements of the second half of the decade began to develop. But the most immediately decisive factor of student radicalization was, not surprisingly, the student condition itself. The formidable growth in student numbers marked the end of the university as the training ground of a small and privileged elite and the beginning of the era of mass higher education. It brought with it increasing numbers of first-generation university students whose familial expectations had not conditioned them for the routines of what, in Western Europe at least, remained very largely an elite, often authoritarian and indeed sometimes archaic university. In the United States, on the other hand, it was not the backward but the modern aspects of higher education, where corporate capitalism's needs – 'the university is being called upon to merge its activities with industry as never before,' wrote Clark Kerr, president of the 'multiversity' of Berkeley – were fashioning what was taught and how. Suspended in an undefined space between social origins and social destination, the 'free-floating' student intelligentsia found itself massed together for a number of years (minimally four in most countries for a first degree, although only three in Britain) in institutions where they were formally trained to develop a creative and critical intelligence in a narrowly defined discipline, but expected to question nothing else. Many of the new radicals were among the brightest, most dedicated students who demanded that higher education be more than this. The irrelevance to the problems they saw around them of much that was taught, the forms of teaching, the *in loco parentis* rules and regulations that treated them as non-adult, the over-crowded conditions, and ultimately the university's role in society became the focus of demands for radical change. The architectural students of Turin and Milan were the forerunners; but it was at Berkeley that the first mass explosion came in 1964.

The University: Berkeley and the Free Speech Movement

> The spirit of America was – and for many people is again – every
> man for himself. That's not what the spirit was in the civil rights
> movement. And it's not what the spirit was in Berkeley that fall –
> *Mario Savio, Free Speech Movement*

Flagship campus of the giant University of California system, Berkeley was considered a triumph of post-war America. A public 'multiversity' – not unlike Michigan, where S D S has its central core – Berkeley's low tuition fees opened it to all. With its 27,000 students, its scientists and engineers producing new technologies for industrial and military uses, and its social scientists serving government and business with vital social analyses, it symbolized for many the best in American society in the mid-1960s: democracy, achievement, equality of opportunity.

These were the very virtues which numbers of Berkeley students, including Mario Savio, had just found scandalously lacking in the American South during the Mississippi Freedom Summer under the auspices of S N C C. On their return, they were in no mood to have their democratic rights infringed on the campus itself. When, in September, the University banned political and civil rights groups from using a strip of land on the edge of the campus to set up their tables, hand out literature, solicit donations, the authorities met immediate resistance.

'It was that strip of land,' recalled Mario Savio, 'that brought me to Mississippi. Could I now forget Mississippi, I asked myself. Impossible. And it was impossible obviously for lots of other people.'

A coalition of the political groups, right and left, failed to persuade the University to revoke the ruling. When, on 1 October, university police tried to arrest a student who was working a table for the Congress of Racial Equality (C O R E), several hundred others spontaneously sat down and prevented the police car from taking him away. 'I was the first one to sit down – along with two hundred other people who say they were the first,' recalled Michael Rossman, a mathematics graduate student. 'And everyone's telling the truth. It was an act of spontaneous initiative.' Then Savio climbed onto the car. 'He spoke, but not as a leader giving directions,'

Rossman continued. 'He said it was wrong, we mustn't let the police take Jack [Weinberg] away. "We don't know what to do – let's talk about it." That was the first speech and that was the nature of the leadership – to give voice to the common consciousness.'

The group, which swelled from two hundred to a peak of more than three thousand, sat around the car for thirty hours, talking about the ideals of free speech in a democratic society, the importance of the civil rights movement, the role of public universities in modern society. 'I was twenty-four, almost twenty-five, and this was the first time I'd really heard a democratic public discussion in America,' Rossman continued. 'No one could even say it, because the words themselves had been so abused – "democracy", "Congress". It was like going to church for years, then watching God walk on Earth. You just realized, that's the meaning inside those dry terms. Here it is, it stalks among us, and nothing is changed yet everything is changed. So we were literally enraptured from that point on.'

As a result of the sit-down the university authorities agreed to release Weinberg and to reconsider the ban. But the coalition of student groups remained intact and named itself the Free Speech Movement (FSM). It was to find ways of applying the SNCC example to an American campus that were to bring Berkeley to a halt.

Despite the anti-Communist proscriptions of the Cold War, Berkeley had a relatively strong tradition of student politicization. In 1958, left-wing students founded a student political party, SLATE; and two years later, several hundred Berkeley students were arrested in San Francisco in the first large protests against the witch-hunting House Un-American Activities Committee. The civil rights movement, moreover, brought a new dynamism to the students. Berkeley CORE repeatedly mobilized hundreds of students to protest against local businesses which refused to employ blacks. 'What people were interested in was: how can we change the hiring practices of that particular business on that particular corner?' Savio recalled. 'And that was dangerous stuff. You can let people talk about Marxist utopias all they want. But how does that relate to anything? Maybe it did in Russia in 1905, but it didn't in America in 1964. But changing the hiring practices of that particular store – that was dynamite. Students increasingly were drawn into seeing their society as something they could alter.'

Drawing on this new sense of strength, FSM mounted a sustained campaign for repeal of the ban and for students' political rights in general. After six weeks of frustrating negotiations, the university authorities announced that they intended to punish Savio and other FSM leaders for the sit-in around the police car. The FSM called for a sit-in at Berkeley's Sproul Hall. Several thousand attended a rally on 2 December, and nearly one thousand marched into the Hall.

The FSM drew support from almost all areas of the campus. Graduates and undergraduates of every social class and political background – upper- to working-class, conservative to leftist – had coalesced in the new movement. Cultural rebels left over from the beatnik era and straight middle-class students aspiring to professional careers joined FSM. Each had their own reasons for joining, their own political aims: to advance the civil rights movement, to demand students' rights to a say in their own education, to defend civil liberties.

Brought up a fundamentalist Christian in a working-class home, Steve Hamilton became an FSM activist. 'I was touched by the demands of the civil rights movement and liked the idea that middle-class students were willing to fight for people at the bottom of society.'

For Steve and Pam Brier, on the other hand, the university itself was the central issue. 'We really did speak of Berkeley as a factory. Classes were immense, and you didn't feel that you could get near professors because they were this presence way up front on the lectern. If you were lucky, you were out there in the sea of a thousand faces. If not, you were in the next room looking at him on television.'

Both had hoped to find Berkeley an intellectual challenge; Steve had been deeply impressed that 'the children of the working class like me could go to a great place like Berkeley where the tuition then was $50 a term. It was really what public, democratic education was all about.' But the great 'multiversity', as its President Clark Kerr called it in his prediction that Berkeley was leading America into a bright new future, had not kept its promise. The Briers found the intellectual challenge instead in FSM. 'It was filled with excited discussion and intellectual growth,' Pam, who came from a 'marginally liberal family', recollected. 'I loved it, and the kind of pushing at what was right and wrong, defining what decent human values were all about, asking questions that I hadn't ever been asked to think about.'

'Politics and intellectual life were all wound together in that period,' continued Steve, whose father had been active in the British Communist Party before emigrating to California. 'There was constant confrontation with questions about what we were doing at the university – why are we here?'

Or, as Barbara Garson, an FSM activist, asked: 'Why should I work three months of the year supporting the farm workers' movement, and then turn around and spend nine months studying agribusiness at the Giannini Institute, learning how to grow square tomatoes and poison everybody? Many people were beginning to say: "I want to do something with my life. I don't want to be a sharply chiselled tool to be used for corporate profit."'

The fact that FSM could mobilize students from such different backgrounds and with such diverse aims reflected its leaders' ability to use democratic structure and language. 'The FSM was not run from above,' argued Michael Rossman. Executive committee meetings were often meetings of more than a hundred people of diverse viewpoints. 'We would meet in a circle, and when a decision had to be made, we would go around the room and people would say what they thought. The first criterion was, people had to be heard.' He remembered how different groups of students would simply decide that something needed doing and would take the initiative to go and do it. He was part of a group that decided to put together a history of student activism at Berkeley. Barbara Garson and others decided to put out a FSM newsletter to inform students on a daily basis what was being done and what actions had been proposed. Other groups took on other tasks. Then each group would send representatives to the Executive Committee meetings in order to coordinate their efforts. 'It was a collective of collectives,' Rossman noted.

'It was a very democratic thing' to Steve Hamilton, who served on the Executive Committee as representative of the University Church Council. He also recalled the big rallies where students in the crowd were invited to take the microphone and debate the direction of the movement: 'Day by day the leadership tried to stay in touch with what the students would support.'

'There was in the FSM a democratic ethos, which was very real, and I don't think people would have been so vocal or supportive without it', Steve Brier claimed. 'But I don't want to romanticize things too much. There was a lot of give and take, but there was definitely leadership. There were people with more experience, who had a larger vision, and they were accepted as leaders. How could it be different?' asked Brier. 'It's not something to apologize for or pretend didn't exist. It wasn't resented because the FSM had at the same time a very real democratic ethos, without which people wouldn't have been as vocal or supportive. I have nothing but the fondest memories of someone like Mario Savio, and always will.'

Indisputably a charismatic and important figure in the eyes of many FSM members, Savio himself strove to create a democratic movement modelled on SNCC as he had known it during the Mississippi Summer. His experience of the Catholic church, in which he had been brought up, and of the anti-Communism of the 1950s had already led him, he believed, to reject hierarchical, undemocratic forms of organization. 'We were all very conscious of not wanting to behave the way that we were told Communists behaved. I didn't know any Communists. But I knew we were talking about very manipulative people, who would control the masses. That was clearly bad. Whether the Communists actually did that, I didn't know. But it was a combination of accepting that this was clearly a bad thing and realizing that if we wanted people to listen to us, we'd better not be mistaken for this bad thing.'

His concept of leadership was also derived from SNCC. 'There the leader was on the same level as the people. The leader had more experience, but that didn't make him a different kind of person. And tomorrow *you* might be the leader. That was the model I tried to use at Berkeley.' But this concept of leadership was not shared by the media, whose need to personalize events, to report on the FSM's aims through a few quick and telling quotes, led journalists inevitably to concentrate on leaders as 'authorities'. 'Our decision-making was very collective, but that's not the way it was portrayed in the press, where there was hardly any notion of any decision-making process,' Savio recalled. 'We wanted to do things in a collective way, and then we were faced with this glare of publicity which focuses much more on one person than on others. If I'm the person the press is going to come to ask, then I'm representing the movement in a very special kind of sense. I'm the person who's going to get the thirty-second squib – or less, more like two seconds – on the tube. What I say becomes more important than it otherwise would, and how I say it becomes very important. So, inevitably that pushes you into, in a sense, manipulating your own image. After a while it's possible to become seduced by that image. It's like living in a house of mirrors. And that's not healthy.'

As Stokely Carmichael's case similarly illustrated, the conversion of the movements' leaders into media-created authorities threatened to separate them from the mass of the movement, to prejudice the very concept of participatory democracy. This was something that almost all student movements had to confront at one time or another. And yet without the media, the spread and impact of the movements would undoubtedly have been lessened. As Todd Gitlin, SDS president in 1963–64, recalled, 'in a way the development of the movement is so much involved with the media that you can't even perform the thought experiment of imagining what it would have been like without it. That was the water in which we were swimming.' Not only did it elevate leaders into 'celebrity status in which you either had to abdicate to get away from the pressure or pyramid your celebrity into some sort of media role', Gitlin continued, but it also 'inflated media rhetoric and movement militancy', 'accelerated time and heightened tensions between wings of the movement' and, because the media diffused the fact of the movement's existence, the latter came to be 'understood through some images and not others'.

These problems were to become even more acute later. 'In response, some people in the later 1960s sort of eschewed leadership,' Savio commented. 'I don't think that was realistic. I think you need to find a way between – we tried to find it in the FSM and I think we did pretty well. Despite what was happening, at least over that short span of time, we weren't seduced.' In great part this was no doubt due to the fact that his model of leadership went far beyond questions of actual leadership. 'For me, the civil rights movement was the loving community, people embracing each other, holding each other so they could withstand the force of the fire hose. So the movement was a means, but it was also an embodiment of the new community . . . That's what we'd seen and what we were part of, so we tried to do the same at Berkeley.'

It was with much of this fervour that one thousand students marched in to take over Sproul Hall to the strains of Joan Baez singing hymns and civil rights songs. 'We were really filled with that kind of idealism and naiveté about setting things right that characterized the mid-Sixties,' recalled Hamilton, who was acting as a monitor. 'There was a real ecstatic sense, you know, that we're moving and we're right and we're powerful.'

Once inside, the students took over four floors of the building. Some studied, others watched Charlie Chaplin films. Impromptu classes, a kind of alternative university, were organized. Several different religious services were held and a huge meal was prepared. The steering committee, Hamilton recalled, organized meetings in different parts of the building to 'inform people about what was going on, and to let them speak out about what they thought should happen'.

The occupation had meaning at two levels, Rossman thought. At one obvious level it showed that students were prepared to 'get beaten, arrested, everything, to bring the university to a grinding halt' in support of their demands. But at another, less immediately obvious, level lay a deeper reality: they were now occupying 'liberated territory. And in this new territory we were acting out, as fully as we could, a spontaneous collective experiment in recreating a sense of community, a reconstituted society, in our own style. It was an embryo, an embryonic image of everything we wanted to see in a good society.'

The experiment lasted only a short time. At about 3.30 in the morning after the sit-in began, the steering committee announced that the university administration was sending in the police. Those who wanted could leave, those who stayed were asked to be non-violent. The police entered the building in riot gear. They looked to Hamilton, who had decided to stay, 'very impressive with their helmets and sticks. I don't remember any real clashes like I saw a couple of years later. But they were pretty rough. A lot of people were arrested on the second or third floor – the cops just picked people up by their collars and pulled them down the stairs, letting them bounce along.'

What seemed a defeat was to turn into victory. On the morning after the eviction, the campus was occupied by police and National Guardsmen. 'It was like being in an Antonioni movie or a Kafka novel,' Pam Brier, who had not taken part in the occupation, recalled. 'There were cops stationed all over campus, with guns. And there were almost no students around. It had this eerie quality, like after a war, like being in an occupied country.'

The authorities' over-reaction proved, as it would time and again on both sides of the Atlantic, to be the student movement's best weapon. A student strike, led largely by the graduate teaching assistants, was overwhelmingly successful. The Berkeley faculty, which had tried to avoid taking sides, now voted by a large majority to support the basic FSM demands. A month later, the Chancellor, whose edict banning political activity on campus had given birth to the FSM, was fired. In the early spring, Mario Savio announced that, having fulfilled its aims, the FSM was disbanding. The first major confrontation on a Northern campus was over, and the student movement had won.

It had been in many respects a very American struggle to build a movement that could criticize American institutions and society on the basis of American values, that pressed America to live up to its highest ideals: democracy, community and even the prefiguration of the good society, which had been persistent themes in American history from as far back as the Puritans. This invocation of a national heritage – which has already been seen in the formations of both SNCC and SDS – helped to build the American movement by making radicalism less alien to students. Although SDS played no part in the Berkeley events and the Free Speech Movement disbanded, the latter's example would be widely followed by American students in the years to come.

But the FSM had more far-reaching significance for other movements as well. It gave voice to the feeling that the 'affluent' society was an unjust society; in rejecting the content and form of Old Left politics, it put new forms of organizing on the agenda: active participation without formal membership, no 'leaders', direct action to achieve the needed reforms. To the latter, with their strong 'moral' content, it added outrage at the way student life was controlled – both in its everyday aspects and in its ultimate aims.

'So for the first time the question becomes, what about us?' observed Michael Rossman of FSM. 'For the first time we took the conditions of our own lives, the institutionally determined conditions of our own lives, not as the base from which to address others' problems, but as the ground of our own oppression. When people began to make this sort of connection, the floodgates opened. And what came pouring out was an analysis of the system of higher education in this country, its social embedding, and a first table of remedial measures, reforms and experiments leading towards another kind of system.'

What this critique addressed was the role of higher education throughout the industrialized West. The new phase of capitalism, as Luigi Bobbio observed earlier in his comments on the origins of the Turin University student movement, required great numbers of highly trained professionals to manage it; simultaneously, the working and lower middle classes were demanding the right for their children to the university education that, pre-war, had been the exclusive preserve of a social elite. In Western Europe, with its strong class bias, they got only a little of what they were asking: rarely did more than six per cent of working-class teenagers reach higher education, a figure far below that in the United States.

Not surprisingly, perhaps, sociology students were often at the forefront of the new unrest. For sociology was widely seen as the key not only to understanding contemporary society but to transforming it. As Guido Viale, a Turin student, put it, 'the prevalent idea was that everything could be traced back to social relations. No problem, however mysterious – from God, consciousness, neurosis, to individual responsibility – could not, it was thought, be reduced to a discourse on society. In unveiling and explaining society, you discover the point from which you can start to transform it. That was certainly the idea in my head and in most other people's.'

But, like many other disciplines, academic sociology often disappointed student hopes. 'The teaching at LSE [London School of Economics] was either profoundly reactionary or incompetent,' recalled Richard Kuper, who had gone there in 1964 from Cambridge to do a doctorate in economic history. 'After a year I changed to sociology. That was no better. It was an intellectual backwater, an anecdotal sociology most of the time, very untheoretical even at an apologistic level. Even more appalling, it had nothing to say about why there was a war in Vietnam or about class conflict. What were they teaching that could say nothing about what was happening in the world?'

In Paris, Henri Weber, who was a sociology student at the Sorbonne, was adamant in his belief that 'if you want to understand the world, there's no better training than politics. It's much more to the point than academic pedagogy.'

The 'multiversity' of Berkeley was compared by some to a 'factory'; but the distant professor glimpsed at his lectern over hundreds of heads or on television was not necessarily brought any closer in a German university, where he entered the classroom flanked by assistants, who carried his briefcase, cleaned the blackboard and moved his chair into position. Once installed, the professor spoke *ex cathedra*, and brooked no criticism. The university belonged to the professors.

'The oligarchic self-administration of the traditional universities ruled by the professors,' wrote a West Berlin SDS working group in 1961, 'must be replaced by a democratic university constitution. This must ensure co-determination of teaching assistants and students in all committees. The student's position must be changed from a subordinate of the academic authorities to a citizen with equal rights.'

Attacking the university as 'catering to the demands of the ruling class,' the West Berlin SDS maintained that study was productive work and that students should be paid, a demand shared with the French student union, UNEF, and soon to be taken up by Italian students. Although university fees were low, the majority of West German students, like their French and Italian counterparts, had to finance their own studies, either through working or family support, and for some it could take many years to get their first degree. Most Continental students lived at home or in rented rooms; the British and American residential campus was virtually unknown. Universities like the Sorbonne in Paris were over-crowded, and there was little relationship between the degree courses and future job prospects; France's intellectual and technocratic elite was in any case trained separately in the Grandes Ecoles. At the Beaux Arts in Paris, France's leading architectural school, the atmosphere was 'archaic, corporativist and apolitical', in the words of Roland Castro, who had returned there to study after his time militating against the Algerian War. In a move that recalled the Turin and Milan architecture students' protests, Castro and a handful of others openly criticized their professors in 1966. 'We said publicly that the teaching was shit, our professors were useless, that we wanted to learn to build housing for people, not Greek- and Roman-style palaces. Quite unexpectedly, we got the support of a large majority of students and some teaching assistants. We began May 1968 in 1966 – it was the high point of my political life!'

In the United States and Britain the situation was different. In the latter, all university and college students were guaranteed a state grant which, if not handsome, allowed them to get by; and in the former, there was increasing federal and state funding of undergraduate and graduate students through low-interest loans and scholarships as a result of the National Defense Education Act of 1958. In neither was over-crowding so great, although in the U.S. classes were generally enormous and many students felt crowded. In Britain, eight new universities – sited as a rule in the countryside near small towns – were opened in the early 1960s; at the same time, however, a sharp, class-based demarcation continued in British higher education between the privileged university sector and a lower tier of polytechnics, teacher training colleges, art and business colleges.

While the Anglo-American residential campus eased some student problems it aggravated others because of *in loco parentis* rules and regulations. Sexual segregation, restrictive hours, dress codes, were among the targets of student complaint. 'I couldn't believe the rules about having to be in by midnight, about having to get excuse notes to go to London, about wearing gowns in the evening,' Kuper complained about Cambridge.

In West Germany, a Heidelberg psychologist reported in 1965 that 67 per cent of students were disappointed by their studies, 52 per cent felt incapacitated in their work by emotional problems, and 36 per cent felt nervous and depressed. 17 per cent – i.e. every seventh male and every fourth female student – were characterized by the report as 'really disturbed'.

But it was in Italy that the university situation reached its nadir. Unmodernized and decayed, short of teachers, classrooms and facilities of every sort, the universities were almost unable to cope with the flood of new students. Rigid curricula, professors reading lectures from manuals they had themselves written, lack of discussion, were the norm. As has already been seen, the universities were in the hands of a small number of professors whose power was so great that they were known collectively as 'barons'. These suffocating conditions had, finally, little reward for students: predictions of a rise in employment for university graduates failed to materialize and instead there was an actual decline.

Some of the misery of Italian student life was conveyed by Giuseppe Di Gennaro, the son of village elementary school teachers, who was studying electronic engineering at Naples University. 'The courses were rigidly determined from above, it was a very hard faculty. Books were rare and when we could lay our hands on them they were disgusting, full of mistakes. The rich students could buy other books, but for us the only way out was to take a tape-recorder into the classes. We recorded hours upon hours of lectures every day and then had to transcribe them at night. Ten years it took me to graduate!'

Di Gennaro considered himself privileged in one respect because he was able to share a flat with two other students from his home village. Most students from outside Naples had to rent a room in a family. But even this brought no relief to other aspects of his life. 'Every damned day we ate in the subterranean university refectory, every damned day pasta with the same sauce, a slice of meat. It was squalid. But we never thought of cooking for ourselves. We would have had to wash the dishes and that wasn't part of our culture at the time. We were all men – only men. That was another depressing thing: the total absence of women . . .'

The FSM experience did not have immediate repercussions among students in Western Europe, but it heralded many aspects of the student condition around which later protest would mobilize. In the United States, however, the Berkeley movement, like SNCC, opened up an arena of dissent that made students feel their right to protest. By pointing to the university as a constituent part of the ills of the wider society, it prepared the terrain for the type of actions that would shortly become widespread as the over-arching historical event of the decade – the Vietnam War – became the dominant mobilizing force.

Vietnam: 1965 – Spring 1967

1965 – that was the year for me of the connection between all this rhetoric of American values and what we were really doing. The connection between civil rights and the Vietnam War. Keeping down a large underbelly minority population at home and bombing back to the stone age a peasant population of another race and culture abroad – *Rayna Rapp, American SDS, University of Michigan*

There was the bombing and the relentlessness of the bombing – the headlines of the bombing, and I put a map of Vietnam on my wall. I think people now probably don't understand that, but it was just terrible. Everything that was progress was being used to destroy. Every day you opened the paper there were unknown tonnages going thousands of miles to pulverize peasants. My feelings were so strong that I feared the sense of my own violence – *Anthony Barnett, student at Leicester University, England*

I remember the first national left-wing student anti-Vietnam War demo in Florence. We had a poster we'd made, a skull on a blue background, with a quotation from Tacitus: *They made a desert and called it peace. – Fiorella Farinelli, student at Pisa University, Italy*

For years I'd had nightmares about the terrible bombing of Dresden at the end of the Second World War. I could see the houses burning still. And that's why I identified with the Vietnamese – the campaign against the war was a kind of working through my personal history – *Karin Kerner, student at the Free University, West Berlin*

Napalm, bombings, mass graves, executions – the fury of military and economic might against a small population of a different race – that was the Vietnam War for me. It was intolerable. That's why we went out into the streets chanting Ho! Ho! Ho Chi Minh! – *Nelly Finkielsztejn, student at Nanterre University, Paris*

Early in 1965, the United States escalated its military involvement in Vietnam, saturation bombing the North, and sending in the first combat troops in the South. By the summer, President Johnson was announcing that 125,000 American troops were being sent to South Vietnam and that the United States military draft was being doubled. The war that was to become the over-arching motif of mobilization in the advanced West, and to make the student generation aware of its collective existence, had begun.

Outrage at the flagrant denial of the West's self-proclaimed values swept thousands of new recruits into the small student groups. They brought with them a desire for action which would carry them forward to 1968 and beyond. Initiated and waged by the American liberal establishment, the war combined two of the most potent radicalizing elements of the previous decades – imperialist war and racism – and acted as a prism through which the flaws of Western societies suddenly stood out in sharp relief. Once again British and German Social Democracy, once again the French Communist Party, failed to provide the rallying call to which youth would massively respond. Instead, support for the Vietnamese revolution in its struggle against American imperialism swelled the ranks of those seeking radical solutions beyond the confines of traditional left politics in the West.

In the United States and West Germany, most notably, it was in the process of mobilizing around Vietnam that the two SDSs began to converge in their aims and methods. A turn to direct action, a more anarchist-style of politics, came to mark the German SDS alongside its commitment to Marxism; while the American SDS – or at least newly radicalized sectors of it – became increasingly influenced by Marxism and syndicalist strategies as they confronted the task of resisting an imperialist state. Both began to adopt a more openly confrontational politics as a result; but each, too, was marked by other specific influences that helped shape this new phase. Again it is necessary to look at their trajectories separately to understand how they began to converge.

The American SDS

In no other Western country did students have to face their own war machine and the threat of dying in the jungles of Vietnam. Bombings and mass murders, napalm and fragmentation grenades, torture cages and the returning dead – the horror of Vietnam taught lessons of modern war to an entire generation of American students. All were affected by it in one way or another – by the draft, by the anti-war movement or simply by living surrounded by news of the war.

as the first televised war and that made it very vivid,' remembered Levin, a Columbia student in 1965. 'We'd been brought up to believe in our hearts that America stood for fighting on the side of justice. World War II was ingrained in us – my father had volunteered. So there was this feeling of personal betrayal. And there was the absolute horror of it. I remember sitting by myself, crying, listening to the first reports of the bombings . . .'

'We lived with an incredible sense of anguish,' recalled Rayna Rapp. 'Every day you lived without stopping the war was another day of immorality on your part. People were dying every day, and unless we had a movement, they were going to go on dying. We had a sense that we were directly responsible for stopping it, for dismantling the war machine.'

The first surge of protest took place in the spring of 1965. With America's adult peace groups and leftist parties weakened or destroyed by the Fifties' witch-hunting, with liberals and labor leaders firmly integrated into the power structure, it was left to young faculty members close to SDS and students to take the lead. The initial protests, in the form of 'teach-ins', were organized by these junior academics and the first generation of New Leftists, who had been trained and inspired by the civil rights movement. The first of these teach-ins was at the University of Michigan, home of SDS's traditionally strongest chapter.

'I didn't really know much about the war, and I didn't understand this idea of protesting it, but I was curious,' recalled Susan Harding, a first-year Michigan undergraduate, and one of 3,000 students attending the all-night event at which faculty, students and experts discussed America's involvement in Vietnam. 'The idea that made the most difference to me was that the people we were fighting weren't foreign troops – Russian, Chinese or from somewhere else – but the people of the country who were trying to carry out a revolution. That changed my idea about the whole thing. And it changed my picture of America, too.'

The teach-in's success spurred more than a hundred such events on campuses across the country in the following two months. In the middle of this wave of activity came the first large national anti-war protest march in Washington, DC. Organized and planned by SDS from before the war's escalation, the call for the march read, in part: WHAT KIND OF AN AMERICA IS IT WHOSE RESPONSE TO POVERTY AND OPPRESSION IN VIETNAM IS NAPALM AND DE-FOLIATION? WHOSE RESPONSE TO POVERTY AND OPPRESSION IN MISSISSIPPI IS SILENCE?

Focusing the energy generated by the teach-ins, the march attracted more than 20,000 people, most of them under twenty-five, from all around the country. SDS leaders were surprised by the numbers. Speaking at the end of the demonstration, SDS president Paul Potter proposed a strategy based on the civil rights model for stopping the war and changing the institutions which had created it. 'The people of this country must create a massive social movement ... a movement that works not simply in Washington, but in communities and with the problems that face people throughout the society. What we must do is to build a democratic and human society in which human life and initiative are precious.'

This vision, instantly recognizable to SDS and FSM veterans, of the way to create the good society was not to serve, however. Decentralized movements of ordinary people addressing the problems of their everyday life, learning about community, personal empowerment and liberation, had proven a powerful force in the civil rights movement. But the war was of a different order. Desegregation in the South presented no threat to the ruling liberal establishment; indeed it could serve to give the Democratic Party's liberal wing a Southern base. Vietnam, on the other hand, represented the potential victory of Third World revolutions which, coming after the 'surprise' Cuban revolution, was a perceived threat to American hegemony on a world scale. The 'great conflict' between capitalism and communism was, and remains, the dominant struggle of the epoch. There could be no concessions here as there could be over civil rights. In its efforts to stop the war, the movement would have to confront the full force of an intransigent state.

But this would become clear only later. In the meanwhile, another reason made it difficult to recreate a civil rights-style movement: the black movement's low profile in the anti-war coalition. While SNCC published an anti-war statement in January 1966, its Black Power stance rejected a coalition with whites. 'We identified with the Vietnamese,' recalled Gloria House, a SNCC activist who was one of the statement's authors. 'We saw ourselves as black people, a nation within a nation, a people colonized, warred upon – and the Vietnamese were, too. So it made sense to say, "Stop this war!"'

But SNCC, while it set up a few draft counseling programs for young black men, did not generally focus organizational energy on the anti-war movement. Nor did the Black Panther Party. Though willing to enter coalitions with radical whites, it always concentrated on black-related issues. 'We will not fight and kill other people of color in the world who, like black people, are being victimized by the white racist government of America,' it declared in its 1966 founding statement. The party's appeal was largely to ghetto youth who had to face the draft and to black Vietnam veterans, whose familiarity with weapons and rage over their experience helped to shape Panther politics. Thus it was not so much the party's involvement in the anti-war movement as its militant politics, with their dosage of Marxist-Leninism, which were to have a continuing influence on white anti-war activists.

'Vietnam was important, but kind of remote,' recalled Bill Sales, a Pennsylvania student in the mid-1960s. 'The anti-war thing was what the whites were doing. Our thing was *here.*' Although black Americans in general were more likely to oppose the war than white Americans, their concern with domestic problems left the field open to white student activists who had for so long stood in the shadow of the black movement. And SDS's success at leading the first major national anti-war march made it the natural candidate to lead the student campaign.

The escalation of the war, the willingness of local SDS chapters to confront the issue and link Vietnam to campus discontents, such as decision-making in the university and university complicity, attracted tens of thousands of new recruits. As these new recruits were swept in, SDS's membership swelled from 2,500 before the march to ten times that number by October 1966. On campuses where the organization had been active, such as Michigan, this growth brought greater influence. 'We thought we owned the campus,' noted Rayna Rapp. 'There was a sense that it was our turf, that we were the rising tide of what was happening.' More importantly the movement, more loosely defined than a year previously, moved from the leading state universities and Ivy League colleges to less fashionable schools such as those in the South, or religious schools.

Gene Guerrero, the first president of the Southern Student Organizing Committee, recalled the change brought about by the war in the South. 'We began to work on teach-ins, and that began to happen around the South. We got involved in the whole anti-war movement, and began to work more closely with SDS.' SSOC itself moved from a conference-type organization modeled on SNCC to a membership organization modeled on SDS, and the two groups became one on many campuses. 'Those guys in SDS,' remembered Sue Thrasher, 'sort of adopted SSOC. They really helped us with organizational skills. The way they did things was the model that we used to do things, like the newsletter.'

Tom Gallagher was raised in a traditional Irish-Catholic working-class family in the Bronx in New York City. He attended St. Regis High School in that same borough, and while there became involved in various peace marches in New York City, partly through an interest in politics, partly through contact with the nascent Catholic peace movement. When he enrolled in Boston College as a freshman in 1965, he did so 'looking for the New Left'. 'To me SDS was magic. Those initials, there's always been something about those initials to me. It was, like, dangerous. You didn't know what you were getting yourself into because it was anything. You could be anything anywhere. There were people who were obviously mad in it, and there were people who were brilliant. And, if you're seventeen, that seemed the place to be.'

In October of his freshman year, he joined a demonstration against Hubert Humphrey. 'There were about hundred and fifty people, I was standing there watching for a while and it went by, and I thought, "Well, this is what I'm here for."' It was a small demonstration and they were harassed by 'this much larger crowd of normal BC types. Eventually we were saved by the mounted police. But that's what BC was like. After that my career was set. I always felt we had to do it that hard way. It was quite parochial when we started. There wasn't an SDS at that time. It started as a result of that demonstration. Then, it was not glamorous to be a radical. That first year it was not fashionable. You had to think pretty hard about what you were doing in this.'

These new recruits also changed the nature of the organization. The long domination by humanities and social science graduate students from leading public universities and private colleges in the East and Upper Midwest was now challenged by an influx of members from less prestigious schools. The latter, many of whom proudly called themselves the 'Prairie Power faction,' brought a new, less intellectual style to SDS. 'SDS was all very new to me,' remembered Sue Thrasher. 'I didn't understand it, and all of the Southern students came out of backgrounds more similar to mine than out of political backgrounds. When I met SDS people I thought they were from another planet. They were intellectuals. The people I ran around with didn't talk like that. They didn't analyze things. You acted on your gut instinct. You acted on intuition, and you acted on what you believed. To analyze things and talk about them like that was very strange.' Paul Buhle of Wisconsin, who was close to these prairie populists but represented a more mature Marxist grouping, observed that 'there were some real down home types among them. Hard-drinking

Texas types. As they said, you didn't want to crash out in a small room with a bunch of them after a party because they didn't take their boots off. That was their mentality.'

At the same time, Bob Ross, an SDS founding member, recalled, these new recruits brought 'an angry revulsion of the war with them, and an attempt to translate that into politics. Their spirit was different to people who came to the New Left through the civil rights movement.' 'The war threw us back into a traditional posture of protest rather than the new project of social re-creation,' commented Michael Rossman, the FSM activist. 'Fighting against the war absorbed tremendous amounts of energy, and it introduced us to despair. But we had no choice. That was what was on the historical table.'

The anger of the new recruits soon pushed SDS towards a more confrontational stance. As well as the horror of the war itself, there stood the threat of the draft. As the United States plunged deeper into Vietnam and draft calls began to mount, the security of student deferment disappeared. 'We lived under the shadow of the draft for three or four years, wondering what it would be like to go to prison,' recalled Pam Brier of the Berkeley FSM, who helped her husband, Steve, endure the situation. 'The draft had a lot to do with our frenetic political activity,' explained Steve, 'and everyone's impassioned hatred of Lyndon Johnson, since he was responsible for perpetuating it and this god-awful war.'

Draft resistance became a significant factor of the anti-war movement, spanning the entire Vietnam period. Activists recognized the draft board offices as potential organizing sites, places where recruits could be gathered and the war machine weakened. While many young men simply tried to avoid the draft through physical disabilities, real or feigned, occupational deferments and – in some cases – by going to Canada and Sweden, a small number decided to resist outright by refusing to cooperate in any way, hoping that others would follow their example. Some went to prison for it, but their example was emulated: more than half a million young men independently refused induction, contributing significantly to the weakening of the supply of manpower to the military. One of those who refused induction, though later, was Robbie Skeist, at the University of Chicago. He and a group of friends in the Chicago Area Draft Resistance Effort (CADRE) announced their decision publicly on campus in front of faculty and press and wrote to the head of the Selective Service System.

'We grilled each other until we finally felt our feelings were intense enough. We felt that if we weren't serious enough to be willing to take this kind of stand, we weren't serious about anything. There was the desire to make a dramatic impact on the political scene, and the desire to make a statement about who we were as people and what was important to us and what kind of lives we wanted to lead. That, for me, was one of the most appealing and unique aspects of the experience.'

Here there still echoed the emphasis on personal values characteristic of the early civil rights movement. But in many other respects, the 'old moralism', as David Gilbert put it, was no longer enough. One of the new generation of SDS activists who would transform the student movement, Gilbert was to turn to Marxism instead to understand the economic roots of the American power system and its foreign policy. It was a transformation from his liberal past.

The son of upper middle-class Jewish parents in Boston, he had been involved as a high school student in attempts to ease racial tension in the city. When he went to Columbia University in 1963, he was immediately struck by being at an elite university situated on the edge of Harlem, and in his second year there became involved in an off-campus tutorial program for Harlem children initiated by liberal students. 'Until then I didn't realize how bad the oppression was in this, the wealthiest country in the world. I saw the buildings, the houses without heat. Saw the police who seemed like an occupying army to me. Saw someone die in the family I worked with from a condition which, if he'd had decent medical care, would have been routine. These weren't abstract social issues but involved people with whom I had personal relations.'

When the first news of the American bombing of Vietnam was announced, the mother of the family he was tutoring, who had never heard of Vietnam, responded to his concern by saying: '"Oh, they're bombing people for no good reason, huh? Well, it must be colored people who live in Vietnam." Her remark really made a very powerful connection for me. I'd been aware of foreign policy, been aware of civil rights, but I didn't understand that there was a systematic racism, a structure. And things started to come together.'

By the time of the SDS anti-war march in Washington, he was beginning to think of himself as a socialist. 'Even though I was wary about certain examples, or what I had been taught about certain examples, I felt that the problems of the society could not be solved without some form of redistribution of wealth and power. More than just a redistribution of wealth, a question of community, people actually participating and shaping the direction of the community, as well as controlling the means of production. SDS seemed to combine a civil rights program, an anti-war program and a somewhat loose socialist philosophy.'

His first contact with SDS was at the Washington march. Earlier, he and friends had set up an Independent Committee on Vietnam at Columbia, and they organized a six hundred-strong delegation to the march. Nonetheless, he was concerned whether such efforts were enough. 'The march was a good feeling, it was drawing people together, there was some more vision and the hope that we could change things. Yet I kept saying, But is this going to stop the war? I never lost sight in the euphoria of that gathering that there was a basic goal involved. I realized that we were in an ongoing struggle.'

Joining SDS, he began systematically to examine American relations with the Third World, the nature of the economy, the State Department. 'I wanted to understand the economic roots of the power system, and I came to feel that the correct label was – imperialism.' He wrote the first SDS pamphlet on imperialism and began, along with others, to argue for their new position within SDS. 'By early 1967, some of us considered ourselves Marxists, and it was a position that we wanted to bring into SDS. We still rejected dogmatic Marxism and Stalinism. But we wanted to use that analysis because we felt the old moralism wasn't enough.'

The emergence of Marxist analysis and terminology in SDS was given increased impetus by the presence of Progressive Labor Party (PL) members in the organization from early 1966 on. A Maoist split from the American Communist Party, PL joined SDS when the latter dropped its constitutional clause prohibiting Communists from membership and because its own anti-war organizing had been relatively unsuccessful; energetic and militant, its members pushed SDS to take a hard-line anti-imperialist stance on the war.

Though most old guard SDSers accepted the idea that Vietnam was an imperialist war, many resisted Marxist terminology and analysis, as they had done from the early days. Radical democracy, the idea of forcing America to live up to its highest ideals, was their language. But Vietnam made their talk of America's heritage of freedom and democracy ring hollow. And some of the old guard saw that the civil rights model was inadequate to confront the intransigent state. Yet they could find nothing else. 'SDS found itself in front of this anti-war movement, and didn't know what to with it,' recalled Todd Gitlin, former SDS president. 'We didn't have a program, didn't know what to do. It was somehow bigger than us.'

The newly radicalized, like David Gilbert, felt that the old guard 'were in some sort of niche and didn't want to move out. Their main project at the time was ERAP [Economic Research and Action Project, which worked in the Northern slums]. I was flabbergasted that they were so laid back about Vietnam.' Soon the new recruits moved to take control. Carl Oglesby came to believe that 'you were not going to strike a blow against the war by organizing welfare mothers in Detroit. You only thought you were. If you really wanted to strike a blow against the war you would be working on campuses because it was the campuses that were generating the enormous heat, the enormous pressure, the enormous growth, and really shaping the politics. There was a student movement and it was growing. You didn't spend a nickel on it and it grew. It was like a weed, and the students just took it over.' Robert Gottlieb of the New York SDS, who had spent a year in Paris where he had been influenced by both the writings of Andre Gorz and the Situationist International, described the formation of the new coalition. 'In New York we were more and more influenced by new Marxist analysis, and saw the older SDSers as essentially a group of social democrats.' He saw the campuses as the crucial arenas for organizing the future 'new working class' of technocrats and administrators. 'Searching for allies we met Greg Calvert and the Prairie Power people who were coming to the same place from a different direction, from student power, and from a suspiciousness of the National Office. It was an uneven alliance but it was part of the emergence of the student movement on campuses.' At the Clear Lake SDS meeting of 1966 'the old guard just sort of withdrew.' As Buhle recalled, 'In retrospect we took a sectarian attitude. We were not too respectful, and they would just say, "OK it's your organization. Do whatever you want with it." We kind of snorted them off the stage as not being revolutionary enough. We were a new generation and we wanted new leadership, wanted a new movement.'

It was nearly eighteen months after the Washington march of April 1965 before the new radicals seized full control of SDS; the chance of becoming the national leadership of the anti-war movement had by then passed. Other groups, some nationwide, others local, had emerged, representing a range of liberal, religious and radical anti-war positions. At the national level, therefore, SDS defaulted on the initial leadership it had provided; but at the local level – arguably always more important than the national level in such a decentralized organization – SDS chapters led a stream of anti-war demonstrations, actions and protests of every sort.

The International Days of Protest in October 1965 were one of the actions in which local chapters participated. The initiative came not from SDS but from the Vietnam Day Committee (VDC), a Berkeley student organization which, since the spring, had led militant non-violent actions against the war, such as sitting down in front of trains carrying troops and material bound for Vietnam. As with SDS, the VDC brought forward new leaders, the most prominent of whom was Jerry Rubin, a twenty-seven-year-old former journalist and a newcomer to Berkeley. Quick with quotable phrases, he jumped into the movement and rapidly made a name for himself in the media as a self-declared student leader.

Helped by media publicity, the International Days of Protest were a success. While the VDC held a mass march to the Oakland Induction Center, from where they were turned away by the police, tens of thousands of demonstrators protested in cities across the United States. Although the national SDS leadership had nothing to do with it, fifty SDS chapters led local demonstrations.

In another action typical of local chapter activity, the University of Chicago SDS organized a massive campaign in the spring of 1966 against the administration's ranking by academic achievement of students for draft eligibility. Copying the model of the FSM, five hundred students took over the campus administration building. Participatory democracy again proved the means of giving the occupiers a new sense of community, all the more so as large numbers of students normally lived off campus. 'We'd have these huge open general meetings of as many as five hundred people, and we'd discuss things for hours,' recalled Carol Berland. 'If you raised your hand you could talk. What was communicated was respect for the people. There was a sort of leaderless unity.' Many faculty members were outraged by the occupation, remembered Heather Booth. 'One respected anthropologist came in and compared us to Nazi storm troopers. I thought, this guy is a jerk. He couldn't understand what we were doing, couldn't understand how history or culture happens. It was as if many of the faculty were having mental breakdowns.'

Despite the sit-in's immediate failure, it powered the way for success the following fall, and its example was to have important repercussions, for Chicago became the model for a whole range of actions on other campuses. Chapter activity, which was at the heart of SDS, was to some extent reinforced by a new, albeit transitory, emphasis by some of the new SDS leadership on student syndicalism. Chapters were encouraged to address whatever local campus issues would mobilize students to participate directly in decisions daily affecting their lives, and to push for 'student control' of university policies. The underlying goal was not so much to change the universities but, as Carl Davidson of the SDS leadership wrote, 'to develop radical consciousness' among students to stop the war, and to change the larger system that was responsible for it.

In practice, student syndicalism could mean anything from leading campaigns against repressive dormitory regulations to constructing 'free universities'; but many SDS chapters began to find in the university's 'complicity' in the war effort a potent force for mobilization. Campus-based military research, which they started to uncover, university cooperation with the draft, and open recruiting on campus for the military and war-related corporations made the university itself a readily accessible target for radicalized students.

In the course of these syndicalist and complicity campaigns a new, more confrontational style emerged. David Gilbert helped to organize a non-violent sit-in against the presence of the Naval Reserve Officers' Training Corps at Columbia. Cleared out by the police, he was thrown to the ground by three of them. 'In my mind, I said, it's like a game, they've won. We made our point. But when I was down they started to kick me. I saw this foot coming for my balls. I managed to roll and it hit my thigh. But that transformed it from a symbolic thing into being angry. I kept rolling and got up and went back to the door we were blocking, and everybody else came back, too. It became a big thing.'

But it didn't necessarily require police violence to stir activists to direct confrontation. Steve Fraser, who went from the Mississippi Summer to SDS and the Progressive Labor Party, took part in protests against recruiters from the Army Materials Command, at City College of New York, storming the offices where they were holding interviews. He later organized similar demonstrations against Dow Chemical, manufacturers of napalm. 'No one liked god-damned Dow Chemical, and once you had an organization willing to cross a certain threshold of action, people were ripe for it,' he commented.

'You had to be confrontational. I think that was the heart of why SDS was able to organize,' explained Cathy Wilkerson, editor of *New Left Notes*, the SDS national paper, who also worked as an SDS regional organizer. 'There was something about the wildness and craziness of SDS in those years which was why it was successful.' To start a chapter on a new campus, she recalled that she would stand in a place where students congregated with a little box of anti-war literature. 'And then I'd pick a verbal fight with somebody and start to yell. A crowd would collect. Then this enormous debate would happen and little groups would split off and everybody would be arguing. Afterwards people would come up and say, "I've been looking for some one to talk to about this stuff." So, out of crowd of three hundred you'd get fifteen people who were really interested. And you'd say, "Let's have a meeting." And you were off and running.'

While Vietnam changed S D S from one direction, the emergence of the new counter-culture changed it from another. The latter's first signs appeared in San Francisco's Haight-Ashbury district, where young people were living communally, dressing in flamboyant clothes, experimenting with such 'mind-expanding' drugs as L S D and marijuana, and generally having a good time. Living in relative poverty and chaos, sharing all they had with one another, these young men and women experimented with new ways of defining themselves, new ways of living together.

In early 1967 the rest of the country discovered the young 'hippies' of the Haight through the media. At first most of the coverage was quizzically positive. Hippies were good copy; they were young and attractive, colorful and outrageous. Magazines and television sent the images of pretty, long-haired teenagers speeding across the country. Drawn by such advertisements, thousands of runaway kids, curious tourists, and irresponsible thrill-seekers descended upon the Haight in the summer of 1967. The fragile hip community collapsed under the weight. But the culture it had modeled spread rapidly. Something vital had been touched in the younger generation. Long-haired hippies began appearing everywhere. Hip communities sprouted in large cities and university towns, wherever young people gathered. From 1967 on, the student movement was shaped in important ways by this emerging youthful counter-culture.

The counter-culture of the Sixties was not an entirely new phenomenon. Movements of cultural alienation, decrying society's spiritual corruption and cultural blandness, have a long history in America, as in the rest of the West. But the Sixties counter-culture did include elements of something new. The economic and demographic conditions of the Sixties allowed unprecedented numbers of young people to act on their alienation. When the Beat culture of the Fifties merged with the popular youth culture of the Sixties, the resulting counter-culture took on enormous social weight.

The counter-culture flowered in the mid-Sixties, when the baby-boom generation emerged into late adolescence. True children of the suburbs, lavished with the benefits of affluence, the baby-boomers could not fathom their Depression-born parents' desire for material and psychological security. They could not see the reason for playing it safe – sexually, socially, or financially. They could not comprehend why their parents were more concerned with house payments than with Vietnam, race riots, pollution, and the meaninglessness of middle-class life. The thought of growing up to be like their parents filled the young with horror. They were ripe for an alternative culture, a collective attempt to live differently.

The content of the counter-culture was a melange drawn from black culture and American Indian tradition, Eastern religions and American utopianism. Perhaps the most direct and important influence was the beatnik culture of the 1950s. Many Beat poets and writers became spokesmen for the counter-culture. It was no accident that hippies first appeared in the Beat capital of San Francisco, and spread quickest to cities with underground beatnik communities.

John Sinclair of Detroit was one of those beatniks who joined forces with the new hippies. Sinclair agrees that the two movements had much in common, but points out a signal difference in attitude. The Beats, he says, assumed that their rebellion against the sterility of American life would always appeal to only a tiny and beleaguered minority. There was little faith in broad social change, in the ability of large numbers to change their ways of living.

'We weren't interested in letting outsiders know what was going on in our homes and workshops,' recalls Sinclair of Detroit's small collection of Beat poets, artists, and jazz musicians. 'We knew how quickly outsiders could fuck us up. They were incapable of constructing tenable lifestyles for us or themselves.' Because they retained little hope of changing society at large, the Beats were content to remain outside the mainstream of the culture. 'All that we wanted was to do our thing and get away with it,' Sinclair explains.

Things changed in the mid-Sixties, however. A long-time user of marijuana, Sinclair began experimenting with LSD-25, or 'acid' in 1966. 'When beatniks started doing acid,' he recalls, 'it brought us out of the basement – the dark places, the underworld, the fringes of society. From being cynical and wanting to isolate yourself forever from the squares – one was suddenly filled with a messianic feeling of love and brotherhood.'

Under the powerful influence of LSD, Sinclair and other Beats opened themselves to the idea that large numbers of young people could be converted to the hip culture. And they saw some encouraging signs. 'When you saw the kids responding, that was the real impetus, beyond the LSD,' explains Sinclair. 'The LSD gave you the idea that it could be different, and when you saw the kids responding, that was the proof.'

By 1967, Sinclair was publicly identified with this new cultural force; the Detroit press labeled him 'the King of the Hippies'. From writing poetry and holding jazz workshops in hidden lofts, Sinclair shifted to organizing a gigantic 'love-in', and managing a popular rock 'n roll band. He organized a network of collectives calling itself 'TransLove Energies, Unlimited', which helped popularize the new hippie culture in the Detroit area. His new vision of individual and social transformation appeared in a column he wrote for a local 'underground' newspaper in March 1967:

> Those who are disgusted with the inhuman aspects of their society should DROP OUT of it and give themselves full time to making this world a more beautiful place with their every act. If all of us would stop spending our time and energy trying to save America from within and would instead unite in our own society to set an example for the rest of society, all of the really stupid things that are going on would be effectively pointed out to the rest of the people . . . These people need our help, brothers and sisters, but they don't know it, and won't let us talk to them. We can help them best by joining together in our community and holding our lives up to them as examples of what reality can do for you.

This vision appealed to young, middle-class Americans such as Genie Johnson. Born in 1950, the daughter of an Air Force colonel, Johnson grew up moving around from base to base, increasingly disaffected from the world of her parents. In her South Carolina high school she was 'a part-time greaser/beatnik,' she recalls. 'I used to wear black eyeshadow, a real big bouffant, a black leather jacket, and boots. At the same time, I was reading about Buddhism and reincarnation.' In 1967 she ran away from home with a boyfriend who was headed for Canada to avoid the draft; along the way, they stopped at Antioch College and did LSD. 'It changed my life,' states Johnson.

'I had every experience you can imagine,' she explains. 'We went out to the woods at Antioch and had this beautiful experience with nature. I fell in love with the world. I was just a true hippie. After that I wore tons of beads and moccasins, and let my hair grow, and never put on make-up again. I also had some scary experiences on that trip, where I was facing myself . . . looking at what I was coming out of. But most of all it came out being a good experience.'

After Antioch, Johnson and her boyfriend went on to Detroit, where he hoped to cross the border into Canada. They got lost and wound up wandering the streets, wondering what to do. Somehow they found their way to Sinclair's beatnik/hippie community center; after her boyfriend moved on, Genie stayed on at TransLove. 'There were lots of friendly people, lots of action,' Genie explains. 'The first floor was a storefront with a free store where people brought old clothes and you could get free clothes and free books.' Johnson threw herself into TransLove's activities – putting out poetry books, making beads and sandals to sell, building a psychedelic rock 'n roll ballroom called 'The Mystic Knights of the See Lodge'. 'It was something new happening,' she says. 'We wanted to build a community that wasn't based on all the bullshit. How to go about it was the question. At first it was just living together and trying to create an alternative economic thing, where we could live off of making our beads and having our music and all that.'

Music played a central part in this new life. A rock 'n roll band, the Motor City 5, lived as part of the TransLove commune; the proceeds from their concerts helped support the group. But rock 'n roll was more than economics: 'Our music reflected this whole movement of young people, and their dissatisfaction with American life, and their wanting to break away from it,' Johnson remembers. 'We wanted people to dance. That was a part of our whole thing, to get people moving again. Get the blood moving. Get people moving in harmony.'

The power and excitement of rock 'n roll music was probably the single most important factor in spreading the youthful counter-culture. In the short history of rock 'n roll, the Sixties represent a peak of creativity and vitality. Soul singers such as Aretha Franklin, Motown stars such as the Supremes and Marvin Gaye, and British groups such as the Beatles, the Rolling Stones and the Who all helped renew rock 'n roll's connection to its dynamic black roots. Folk musicians-turned-rockers such as Bob Dylan and Jerry Garcia brought new poetry and depth to a hard-driving idiom. Rebellious and sexy, witty and relevant, rock 'n roll became the voice of the emerging generation.

By the late Sixties, rock 'n roll symbolized the melding of a popular youth culture with an oppositional culture – it was social criticism you could dance to. The popularity of rock 'n roll fed the growth of the whole counter-cultural pastiche – long hair, sexual experimentation, free-form dancing, less rigid gender roles, psychedelic drugs, underground news-papers, interest in Eastern religions, etc. Some were convinced that the hip community could become a majority, could reshape society, could reshape history. Diverse counter-culture figures such as Sinclair, Beatle John Lennon, acid guru Timothy Leary and Yippie Abbie Hoffman agreed that if one projected a vision of a new age, a new way of life, young people would instinctively respond, and the world would change. The counter-culture carried forward the prefigurative theme of the New Left. Today Sinclair chuckles when he describes his approach as 'the clash between Flaming Youth and Stodgy Authority':

> We weren't interested in taking over administration buildings. We were interested in blowing people's minds, basically. Making them confront the idea that there was an alternative to the straight way of life.
>
> We never really felt very comfortable with the protest thing; we came from the point of view that said, 'It doesn't do any good to protest against these people. They're the ones that made it like this. When you go to them on a moral ground, you help perpetuate their phoney propaganda about themselves – that they are Christian, rational, reasonable, humanitarian. But in reality they aren't anything like that. That's all just bullshit.' So our idea was to expose how crazy and irrational and repressive they were and call for people who could make it be something different. In other words, 'Create an alternative way of life to this, yourself. They aren't going to do it, you've got to do it; we've got to do it.'

As Sinclair's comments suggest, the counter-culture and the student movement weren't coterminous. Sinclair and other counter-cultural figures felt that most student activists were too uptight, too negative, too power-oriented. Activists, for their part, criticized hippies as frivolous and naive about how to bring about change. Still, there was much overlap between the two.

'There was a continuum between politics and culture at every school,' explains Wisconsin student activist Paul Buhle. 'At one end there were these tight-assed people whom you suspected of being close to the Communist Party. At the other end you had a lot of burn-outs. Revolu-tionaries since yesterday. In between the flow was tremendous. It's important to stress how thin those barriers were.' Buhle remembers selling radical political publications to 'head shops' which carried underground comics, incense, posters and drug paraphernalia. And at a neighborhood cooperative grocery started by hippies, 'they had a huge poster on the wall, "Fight Imperialism! Eat Organic Food!" It was really sweet, and something you couldn't believe in unless you were nineteen years old.'

Early SDS activist Barbara Haber expresses the ambivalent feelings many activists had about the counter-culture. 'At its worst, the counter-culture was self-indulgent and trivial. At its best, it opened the left and, to a lesser extent, other elements of society, to important ideas about living, like the value of being, and the idea that a variety of lifestyles are OK. These are good values in and of themselves, regardless of whether or not they lead to revolution. Before the counter-culture, society was really dull and terrible; the choices were few and not meaningful.'

Some activists rejected the counter-culture entirely. 'I never believed that the best way to organize people was to get them stoned,' says Michigan SDSer Barry Bluestone. FSM and anti-war activist Steve Brier remembers that he was 'very negative towards the counter-culture. I saw it as a move away from politics, and I couldn't accept the considerations it raised.' Like Bluestone, Brier was particularly disturbed by the emphasis on drugs in the counter-culture. 'I saw a lot of people, our friends, who got screwed up in Haight-Ashbury because of drugs.'

Barbara Garson and her husband, Marvin, were among the founders of the San Francisco *Express Times*, a radical counter-cultural newspaper. But today Garson regrets having condoned drug use. 'Looking back on the whole of the Sixties, I would say that was my one real failure to speak up on what I knew. I wasn't sure, and I didn't want to look uptight. But I always hated drugs. I felt people were essentially experimenting with insanity. But I guess I couldn't say, then, "This is crazy". I felt like they were braver than I was.'

Others had fewer reservations. For them, experimentation with drugs was consistent with New Left attitudes towards social experimentation in general. Anti-war activist Joanne Stark suggests that the use of psychedelic drugs in the counter-culture reflected the attempt to open oneself to new ways of being. 'You trained yourself to accept an idea of life that was not linear, not rational, full of surprises, full of jeopardy. I think it was a part of a sense of disintegration, that it was good for life to disintegrate, that ordinary life had been a trap, a one-way conveyor belt, and that these drugs would open you to the delights of experience.'

FSM veteran Michael Rossman recalls that taking LSD made him feel 'as if I was here from Mars, seeing human relations and society with new eyes, actually seeing how strange they were . . .' Rossman says he 'gained a much deeper insight into the arbitrary nature, the constructed character of human society and culture. If we can say that the revolutionary fact is that this social order can be reconstructed, one must say that my revolutionary perceptions and faith were substantially deepened, because I came to see that this order was held by some very shaky things.'

Rossman feels that he and most other LSD users of the Sixties didn't fully understand the effects of the drug, however. Today he believes that LSD led him to overestimate how much could be changed, and how quickly, and contributed to the 'We Want the World and We Want It Now!' mentality which became increasingly common by the late Sixties. 'This attitude was not confined to politics alone,' he comments. 'It spilled over into the image of instant change in people's lives. But does the leopard change his spots, Jack? Not so rapidly or radically as everybody wanted to believe.'

A desire for personal transformation, or liberation, also shaped another element of the counter-culture – the sexual revolution. 'The biggest shift was in the idea of virginity,' recalled Mike Balter in California. 'When I was in high school and dating at the start of the Sixties, it was very important that girls remain virgins. To lose your virginity was a terrible thing, or so it was thought. Now no one wanted to be a virgin. Girls I was dating would make fun of them.'

'You became intimate with people very easily,' commented Devra Weber, another Los Angeles student. 'You were with large groups of people your own age, mostly single, who were all involved in intellectual work, and that's exciting all of itself. The attempts to be direct, where politeness was not the big issue, really getting at the truth behind matters, basically made people closer. And there was the music. The nights staying up and playing Bob Dylan, smoking pot, red lights on the lamps, and lots of people over talking, everyone sitting probably on a mattress because that's the one piece of furniture in the room except for a chair . . .'

'Our generation was the first that had the freedom to do sexual experimentation,' commented Cathy Wilkerson. 'The pill was crucial. For women the question was, here's a new form for communication that can be explored. We came from a variety of cultural and class backgrounds, none of which prepared us or had allowed us to think this was possible. All of a sudden it became physically possible. Right on to that! we said. Then Smash! Sexual exploration was not what the men were into. They were into sexual exploitation. We found men using it as a new form for possession and for power and manipulation.'

Despite its shortcomings, the counter-culture represented an enticing opportunity to break out of the isolation that has often afflicted the American left. Because of the counter-culture's growing popularity on American campuses, it came to define the context in which activists operated, the sea in which they would either sink or swim. Carl Oglesby argues that SDS was successful in part because it adapted to this new context.

'SDS people were into rock 'n roll, long hair, and dope,' he remembers. 'The damned socialist organizations couldn't stand that stuff, and they had no conception of the relationship between political and cultural rebellion. It was SDS's ability to cope with that, to relate both things, that made the difference. We could have been political in a conventional way, like the socialists, and would have remained a debating society. Or we could have been cultural and never formed a group. But our ability as a movement was our relevance to both sets of issues, to both sets of people. Our approach was always to bring the cultural and the political into the most intimate possible interplay.'

By 1968, there were many activists who had come to politics through the counter-culture. Mike Balter, who ended the Sixties a deeply committed political radical, was one of those who made such a journey. 'I first became a cultural radical, rebellious against institutions and culture. It wasn't so much a political outlook, although I think it led to a lot of my political outlook,' says Balter, who grew up in a conservative Los Angeles family. He remembers that the counter-culture gave him a way to express his dissatisfactions with his own life. 'Around 1965, post-Beatles, the hippies were beginning to come in. Alternative lifestyles. A lot of it was centered on relations with people. There was a lot of emphasis among my friends on trying to break down the artificial barriers between people. Sexual barriers, other kinds. There was something profound about it, trying to figure out why people have such a hard time getting together and being close to each other. A lot of what I'm saying is interpreting back from where I'm at now, but not totally. I think we really were aware of these things. There were a lot of superficial changes – how you dressed, how you wore your hair. And yet there was something that was not superficial – it really was about looking for different values.'

Balter's cultural explorations brought him into contact with political radicals who seemed to be similarly exploring new thoughts and values. He recalls a UCLA history professor, 'an anti-imperialist', who had students read William Appleman Williams and talked in class about 'Dylan and Phil Ochs, about the counter-culture and how it all tied into political things'. The politically-oriented people Balter met included an attractive anti-war activist, with whom he fell in love. Soon Balter was marching against the war and organizing UCLA's first SDS chapter.

Activist events took on a counter-cultural flavor. New York SDS organizer Jeff Jones remembers giving a recruiting speech at Fordham where he argued that 'making love was one of the most revolutionary things you could do in this society'. San Francisco State activists combined culture and politics with an orientation weekend that featured community organizing groups and the Grateful Dead. The SDS chapter at the University of Texas organized 'Gentle Thursdays', low-key be-ins designed to counter the macho, rah-rah atmosphere of 'Football Fridays'. They decorated a jet plane parked in front of the campus ROTC building with a banner proclaiming, 'Make Love, Not War', and invited all to join them in a festival. SDS veteran Jose Limon recalls: 'People were encouraged to show up at the West Mall and be frivolous, whether that meant picnicking or dancing or blowing bubbles. You were encouraged to bring live animals – puppy dogs and parakeets. There was a regular menagerie out there. And people would come in various forms of undress, and there was a lot of music, guitar playing. My strongest memory, though, is the bubbles. Everybody seemed to bring those little bubble-blowing things. The whole mall was full of those little bubbles floating around.'

Perhaps the most significant point of intersection between the radical movement and the counter-culture was the 'underground' newspaper, which mixed reports on local protests with rock 'n roll news, columns on drugs and Eastern philosophy, and colorful graphics full of flowing sexual imagery. According to participant/scholar Abe Peck, the first underground newspaper was the Los Angeles *Free Press*, which began publishing in 1964. By 1967 there were around twenty of these dissenting tabloids, and by the end of the decade, Peck estimates, there were as many as five hundred independent publications that fitted this mold.

The underground press soon became one of the most important factors in shaping movement thinking. Because of the movement's minimal organizational structure, the underground press came to serve as activists' channel of communication. Though this development helped the movement grow, it had some drawbacks. Rarely were underground newspapers responsible to any group or constituency. Increasingly, the ability to define the movement and its goals slipped away from movement leaders.

Peter Shapiro wrote for *Open Process*, an underground newspaper at San Francisco State. 'It had a format like the San Francisco *Oracle* – dizzy graphics, photos with poems superimposed. There was a lot of pornographic stuff,' Shapiro remembers. 'They let me write movie reviews, which I had always wanted to do. There was no discipline whatsoever on the writers. You could say anything that came into your head, and go on for five pages, and every word of it would be printed. Any editor who dared to suggest that it should be changed was a counter-revolutionary.

'These papers served an important role in holding the movement together, in the absence of any organization. The people who exerted the most leadership were the people with access to printing presses. It wasn't on the basis of their accountability to anybody or any kind of organizational backing, or even any kind of consistent political line. It was just who got published.'

The rising importance of underground newspapers and their editors as self-appointed movement leaders was only one of the changes the counter-culture brought to the movement. The increasing popularity of drugs meant that activists were more imaginative but less clearheaded. LSD, in particular, weakened activists' grip on reality and encouraged fantasies of instantaneous social transformation. The counter-culture also changed the appearance of the movement, ending the days when people demonstrated in jackets and ties. The movement took on an increasingly circus-like air. Language became less intellectual, less precise. Folk music and the gospel songs of the Freedom Singers were no longer heard at rallies – now it was the powerful drums and burning guitar chords of rock 'n roll.

In other ways, however, the counter-culture represented a variation on the themes common earlier in the history of the American New Left. The hippies' claim that love was the answer resembled SNCC's founding statement and the ideas of Martin Luther King. The counter-cultural concern with everyday life, with re-creating community, with finding new ways to live together, recalled the vision of the beloved community common in SNCC and the FSM. The idea that the personal was political, that personal liberation was an essential part of creating a new and better society, tied together the hippies and activists of the Sixties.

In the end, perhaps the most important change occasioned by the counter-culture was the gigantic boost it gave to the movement's self-confidence. The rapid spread of the counter-culture fed the sense that young people were on the move, doing something different, something important. Activists felt themselves a part of an enormous wave of energy that was shaking the foundations of the status quo. 'The music and the world it created helped give us the sense that we were defining the culture, and the whole society was following,' says Michael Frisch, an anti-war Princeton graduate student in 1966. 'We had this sense of growing power and growing inclusiveness, that sense of being part of a much larger circle.' For a moment, he says, 'you could really believe you were part of a whole generaton inheriting and changing the world.'

The West German SDS

In February 1966 the first large anti-war demonstration, organized by SDS in collaboration with the SPD and other youth organizations, mobilized 2,000 people in West Berlin. On its eve, SDS was shaken by a new form of activisim in its midst. Overnight, posters appeared in West Berlin and Munich denouncing the Christian Democratic Chancellor and the Bonn parliamentary parties of condoning murder in Vietnam: THERE IS ONLY ONE THING LEFT TO THE OPPRESSED: TO TAKE UP ARMS! FOR THEM THE FUTURE MEANS REVOLUTION!

The 'poster-action' was the work of a handful of activists influenced by a tiny counter-cultural movement called Subversive Aktion whose members had joined SDS. Their movement had nothing to do with the American counter-culture – the full impact of which would only be felt in 1968 – but with the Situationist International, whose radical critique of consumer capitalism was influential among some students. One of Subversive Aktion's founders, Dieter Kunzelmann, had been a Situationist and member of a Munich counter-cultural group, SPUR, in the early 1960s. A 'coffee house poet', he recalled one of SPUR's dicta: 'Marx based the revolution on science, we base it on fun and dance.' Under the growing influence of anarchism, Kunzelmann and others in SPUR began to think of forming a 'collective resistance' and of engaging in direct political action. Subversive Aktion was the outcome.

To two student refugees from East Germany, Rudi Dutschke and his friend Bernd Rabehl, who were students together at West Berlin's Free University, a number of Subversive Aktion's theories about Western society were appealing. In search of new political theories to replace the

Stalinism in which they had been brought up, and the West German Social Democratic party which refused to challenge the capitalist system in which they now lived, Subversive Aktion's theory of 'enlightenment by provocation' appeared a potentially mobilizing strategy. As Rabehl explained it, this meant actions which provoked the state into repressive counter-measures that would unmask its superficial benignancy and reveal its true oppressive class nature. But it also had another aim: of provoking SDS members into rejecting their organization's traditional forms of militancy which remained within the bounds of 'bourgeois legality'.

Rabehl felt attracted to anarchism at the time – 'or rather I felt myself an anarchist by temperament without really knowing what that meant . . .' SDS seemed to him to confine itself to legalistic political forms of protest, like organizing congresses in which the audience was addressed by 'famous' people, rather than engaging in actions, such as teach-ins, which would involve people directly. 'A younger generation, the same age as we, was disatisfied with the club-like character of SDS, with the intellectual airs the old guard put on.'

Despite these criticisms, SDS – in collaboration with other leftist groups, including Subversive Aktion – had revealed its potential militancy in late 1964 by taking to the streets of West Berlin alongside African students to protest against the official visit of Moise Tshombe, right-wing prime minister of the Congo (Zaire). Subversive Aktion saw this as the type of action SDS should be engaged in and joined the organization. Little over a year later, the 'poster-action' revealed that the groundswell for activisim had become so great that Dutschke and Rabehl were catapaulted into the SDS leadership.

Here, as in the United States, the old guard found themselves un-prepared. But unlike the American leaders, who were 'snorted' from the scene with relative ease, the West German leadership fought back by attempting to expel the 'poster-action' group. An SDS assembly was held to decide the matter.

'We didn't expect to convince the assembly of our positions,' remarked Rabehl. 'We argued that every revolutionary is obliged to go beyond the bounds of bourgeois law if that leads to raising the consciousness of the masses. To accept the legal system in power is to accept the power of the ruling classes. We argued that the Third World and its national liberation movements had taken over the classic role of the nineteenth-century proletariat. In the process of armed struggle, these movements had developed a new morality and ethic, new forms of society and government.

But they could only be victorious if open-minded people in the First World supported them, paralyzed their own system . . . We should interpret these examples in terms relevant for revolutionary change in the First World.'

Putting forward the idea that, as revolutionaries, they had to expand 'enlightenment by provocation' in order to awake the oppressed and suffering to the need for revolution, the new group made a radical departure from the former S D S position based on the working class as the main agent of revolutionary change. By a narrow majority, to Rabehl's surprise, the assembly voted not to expel the group. Henceforth, Dutschke, Rabehl and those associated with them began to play a leading role in S D S.

An important factor in this turn to activism related to the domestic political situation. In 1966, the Social Democratic opposition finally agreed to enter into a coalition with the governing Christian Democratic party. One of the reasons was to secure the passage through parliament of an Emergency Powers Act. This would give the government the right to bring in the armed forces in case of internal unrest and to force strikers back to work. These moves led to considerable disillusionment among politicized youth.

'They marked the real beginning of a student movement,' commented Jürgen Seifert, an old guard S D Ser. 'A parliamentary democracy without a real opposition led many youth to think that we were pretty close to an authoritarian state. The Emergency Laws gave people a concrete notion of what such an authoritarian state would mean. Hitler had assumed dictatorial powers in 1933 under a similar law after he became Chancellor with the help of conservative parties. The post-war constitution had consciously not provided for such Emergency Powers.'

The disillusionment was not confined to S D S members. Niels Kadritzke, a member of the Social Democratic party's student organization set up after S D S's expulsion, considered the Emergency Laws 'the decisive point in losing all faith' in the parent party. Chairman of the student executive committee of West Berlin's Free University at the time, he did not leave the party, however. 'If they wanted me out they'd have to expel me. I thought it was important to fight from within the party. Looking back, it was a completely foolish decision.'

A second factor which helped to open the way for the new 'anti-authoritarian' faction within S D S was the American movement's example. Mike Vester, whose earlier articles on the American movement in the German S D S journal had been ignored, wrote a new one, entitled

'The Strategy of Direct Action', which cited the examples of SNCC, America university occupations, the anti-nuclear movements and workers' wildcat strikes. 'Its publication in 1965 had a tremendous effect – it nearly ripped SDS apart!' he recalled. 'And that was because the whole atmosphere had changed.' The libertarian and anarchist traditions of the German workers' movement which, along with its Marxist heritage, had played an important role in the political formation of SDS before 1965 made many within it susceptible to the new ideas, he believed. 'In any case, it was time SDS got away from its "podium politics" in which the organization analyzed the overall situation and then looked for people to lead.'

The example of the explicitly anarchist Provo (short for Provocation) group which burst on the Dutch scene at the time also had an influence. Best remembered, probably, for introducing free communal transport in the shape of white bicycles to replace the ecological 'terror of the motorized bourgeoisie' in the streets of Amsterdam, the Provos also threw smoke bombs during the wedding of the Dutch Crown Princess to a German aristocrat.

The growing anti-authoritarian mood was seen when, in June 1966, 3,000 West Berlin students staged the first occupation and teach-ins at the Free University in protest against the authorities' refusal to allow them to meet in lecture rooms for political mobilizations such as the earlier Vietnam demonstration. Over the years there had been a number of protests at the university, but this was the first major left-wing one to mobilize into direct action a mass of politically unorganized students. 'The central issue,' declared the occupation, 'is no longer student working hours or longer vacations, but to overthrow the rule of the few and to realize democratic freedom in every part of society.'

Dutschke addressed the students, as Rabehl recalled. 'Until then, I'd felt that we were intellectually distanced from the mainstream. It had been like standing outside and watching yourself, thinking Good Lord! I thought people would burst out laughing when we turned up with our new ideas. But they didn't, they were carried away. Suddenly I saw that we were giving voice to a new mood, our ideas were becoming intellectually acceptable to masses of university students. Subversive Aktion had simply articulated something that was already present among young intellectuals, a mood or a feeling which spread very quickly. An avant-garde like us could be influential because the time was ripe . . .'

The anti-authoritarians' championship of direct democracy undoubtedly facilitated this change of mood; at the same time, the way in which a leading group could, unknown to the mass of students, use its position to produce the results it wanted was also evident to some, like Siegward Lönnendonker, an SDS member from the early 1960s. 'The messages of solidarity from various student councils and well-known individuals had all been asked for before the occupation began. But they were read out to the assembly as if they'd been sent spontaneously. In fact, the occupation's direct democracy included a number of well-planned dramatic techniques.'

As Lönnendonker also recalled, another sign of the changed mood was illustrated in a small but significant incident in West Berlin that summer. SDS and other organizations had been picketing a cinema showing a racist film about Africa. One evening they burst into the cinema: 'Every night we had stood outside the place, handing out leaflets – and nothing but nothing happened. But when they broke in and threw stink bombs, slashed the seats and shut the screen curtain – then it worked . . . Things couldn't go on in the old way, nothing was changed by us just talking. It was only through action that things could be made to happen.'

Anti-authoritarianism was given an added dimension when, on New Year's Day 1967, seven West Berlin SDSers – four men and three women – moved into an apartment together and founded Kommune 1. Dieter Kunzelmann, of Subversive Aktion was the guiding spirit behind the project. Kommune 1 rapidly became known for its provocative actions, the most notorious of which was turned by police ineptitude into a cause célèbre. The day before Hubert Humphrey, the American vice-president, arrived on an official visit to West Berlin in April 1967, police arrested a group of students, most of them Kommune 1 members, on charges of planning to assassinate him. Headlines in the popular press screamed that China had provided the bombs – bombs which, as the police were rapidly forced to admit, were plastic bags filled with flour and powder paint. Turning the media hysteria to their advantage, two Kommune members, one long-haired, the other with a wild beard, posed for press photographers looking like turn-of-the century anarchists: the revolutionary image penetrated to the furthest corners of the nation and into the minds of youth who saw in it the political expression of their own incipient feelings of revolt. For many of them, Kommune 1 was tangible proof that anti-authoritarianism was not just a political and strategic theory, but something that could be lived: the political and the personal could be combined.

The anti-authoritarian ideas began to make an increasing impact. When Kommune 1 reprinted *The Function of the Orgasm* and *Mass Psychology of Fascism* by Wilhelm Reich, the Austrian psychoanalyst and one-time Communist Party member, it stirred up intensive discussions in SDS on the connection between sexual liberation and political practice. (Reich's argument that sexual repression within authoritarian family structures, found only in patriarchal society, was the cause of the individual's alienation from her or his own nature, was to be influential in other West European movements also.) 'Discussing Reich and Freud among others in our SDS group was very important to me,' recalled Tilla Siegel who, after a brief relationship with an SDS man at Heidelberg University, found herself a member of the student organization which originally she had thought 'too radical' for her. 'Through them I began to understand the relationship between my personal liberation and politics. My sexual loneliness was only a symptom of my general isolation, you see. Brought up to control myself by rational thinking, I now discovered a rational legitimation for behaving differently – more aggressively to the outside world, dressing less properly, opening my mouth more consistently about things I wanted to see changed.'

Although Kommune 1 was soon expelled from SDS, to take part in direct action now became the litmus test of the 'true anti-authoritarian' SDS member, as Detlev Claussen, who was one of them, remembered. 'The central issue for us in 1966–67 was the Vietnam War. We anti-authoritarians tried to "get the masses behind us" through militant actions. "Provocative protest" was the key word – calculated breaking of the law. The American civil rights movement was clearly the experience we drew on. We looked to experiences in other countries we could use. And then there was Marcuse's "repressive tolerance". Somehow everything came together, and it turned our heads . . .'

As elsewhere, the linkage between Vietnam and the contradictions of their own society were beginning to be made by students in Germany. While the Vietnam War was a blatant example of domination by force and the Emergency laws were perceived as the threat of such, German students, like those in other countries, were increasingly aware of the other, more subtle forms of social and psychological domination that maintained the ruling order, as Herbert Marcuse, among others, was stressing. Marcuse, originally one of the so-called Frankfurt School of social and political philosophers who had remained in the U.S. after the war, was becoming popular among student activists, especially in

Germany. Himself now critical of the failure to translate critical theory into political practice, he addressed an SDS Vietnam Congress in 1966, and was the thinker who gave the most accessible expression to these new forms of domination. Human needs, he argued in a number of influential writings, were repressed and transformed by contemporary capitalism's creation of 'false needs' oriented towards the consumption of commodities; even 'permissiveness' was repressive because it did not lead to the realization of sexuality. Overall, this 'repressive tolerance', in which the influence of the mass media played its part, produced a passive, quiescent 'one-dimensional' man. Because socially marginalized groups like intellectuals, blacks and women had not been totally integrated into a system that was 'irrational as a whole', he vested in them the major potential for revolutionary change.

An irrational system – as the American counter-culture was forcibly saying – could not be appealed to rationally; peaceful protest was to remain within the bounds of bourgeois 'normality'. Vietnam offered students everywhere an exceptional field of action to go beyond these bounds; in Germany in particular the war proved that the American democratic model, which all young Germans had been taught to admire, was corrupt. And so, too, was their own society. The horror and brutality of the war, which awakened faint memories among some of the Second World War, fed into disillusionment with their own 'oppositionless' parliamentary democracy. Vietnam provided the moral justification for going beyond the bounds in order to awaken the public at large and to radicalize students taking part in actions; to this dissenting generation, the Vietnamese revolutionaries became the model, the people with whom it most closely identified.

The nascent student movements in Britain, France and Italy did not yet show signs of convergence towards the confrontational tactics of the two SDSs, although shortly they would take the same path. But they shared a number of points with the latter and among themselves. Vietnam was a powerful mobilizing factor in Britain and France; demands for democratizing the university in Italy had its counterpart among some British students; and the latter were increasingly influenced by Marxism, like their American counterparts. In all the movements, linkages began to be made between Vietnam and their own societies; and, in some of them, the linkages to students' own lives. As in the case of the two SDSs, it was also the specific conditions of those societies that shaped the movements.

Higher education in Italy, secondary education in France, which saw the beginning of a high school movement, were among these specific factors. In Britain, as in West Germany, it was the failure of Social Democracy that led to a new wave of radicalization among students.

Britain

> Where has Harold Wilson gone,
> Crawling to the Pentagon,
> When will they ever learn . . .

So sang a group of anti-Vietnam War demonstrators outside the U.S. embassy in London in 1965, expressing their disillusionment with the Labour government, under Wilson's premiership, which had come to office a year earlier. The Labour majority in parliament was so small that many were willing to suspend their disbelief about the new government's policies; but when Labour was re-elected in 1966 with a large majority, and there were no radical changes, disillusionment became rife. To Vietnam were added other, more specifically British causes: Rhodesia, racism, and the government's attack on striking workers.

For some, like Tariq Ali, who was among the demonstrators outside the American embassy, the conviction that social democracy was again about to fail came after the first Labour electoral victory. 'It was rapidly obvious that the City of London and the U.S. State Department were going to be running this government,' he recalled. 'The first sign was Vietnam. During his electoral campaign Wilson had said that Labour wouldn't back the Americans in Indochina. But as soon as the U.S. escalated the war, Wilson wholeheartedly backed them. For our generation that was crucial.'

Ali, a student activist in Pakistan before coming to Britain in 1963, was one of the main organizers of a teach-in on Vietnam at the Oxford Union, of which he was president, in the summer of 1965. 'To our surprise, the U.S. embassy said that Henry Cabot Lodge, who was shortly going to become American ambassador in Saigon, would fly in from the U.S. to speak. Then the Foreign Office announced that Michael Stewart, the British Foreign Secretary, would come. It became a big media event – and was totally manipulated by the BBC. A number of speakers demolished the Foreign Secretary's case, but they were barely represented on the edited TV programme. That was my first real education in how bourgeois democracy was manipulated by the establishment in Britain.'

For many, however, it was not Vietnam but Rhodesia which caused the initial disillusionment with the Labour government. In November 1965, the all-white colonial government of Rhodesia (later Zimbabwe), which had already imprisoned many black nationalist leaders, unilaterally declared its independence from Britain. The Labour government's refusal to intervene militarily incensed those who were already radicalized and helped to radicalize those who would later become student activists.

'The Labour government was quite prepared to send troops into Aden to crush the independence movement in 1965–66 which was supported by the majority of the Arab population,' noted Michael Thomas, a left-wing London University student who had worked for a Labour victory the previous year. 'They were not prepared to do anything to overthrow the minority racist and illegal government of Rhodesia under Ian Smith. That was a very important lesson to me about the nature of the British state.'

Two further racist measures – new laws largely curtailing black immigration and a decision to raise overseas students' fees, which hit particularly Third World students – further raised the temperature. Added to these, the Prime Minister launched a vicious attack on the seamen's union which had declared a strike; by the end of 1966, 'disillusionment with the Labour government was so great that you didn't label yourself a Labour party man,' commented Jack Straw, a left-Labour law student at Leeds. 'I carried on paying my subscriptions – I was one of the few who did – but it wasn't something you talked about in polite company. If there was a single incident which radicalized students against the government, it was the overseas student fees issue. It caused enormous disillusionment and for the first time it got students out on the streets. From 1966, the Labour Party as a formal institution was no longer relevant.'

Across the country 100,000 students took part in strikes, boycotts, marches, meetings and rallies to protest raising overseas students' fees. The day of action, early in 1967, was called by the newly-created Radical Student Alliance, a broad-left front organization. At the same time, radical and revolutionary students started to form socialist societies (commonly known as 'SocSocs') in many universities. The search for a new political space between social democracy as represented by the Labour government and Russian-style communism was again beginning. But it took a form very different from the original New Left in turning to past revolutionary Marxist theorists – Antonio Gramsci, Rosa Luxemburg, Lenin among them – for inspiration.

In some part, as in the United States, this turn was in reaction to what was seen as the original New Left's 'moralism'; but the appeal of Marxism to students in a country where, for the past thirty years, bourgeois intellectual life had been virtually closed to it, also had other causes, as David Triesman, an 'unaffiliated Maoist' at the time, noted: 'The entry into higher education of politically progressive people, many of whom had grown up in working-class communities, was among these. But then, too, there were a series of external events. Of these, the Vietnam War was probably the decisive one, for it jarred people into taking their socialism more seriously. For many, the war produced a whole series of knock-on effects in their political consciousness which took them right to the heart of their own society and its economic character. And that provided a seed bed in which quite a number of healthy plants grew.'

In the shadow of Vietnam, the Labour government's attitude toward Rhodesia and racism, and a massive financial crisis, the youth culture, exemplified by the early Beatles, began to wane. In 1965, a six-day London poetry festival, attended by American Beat poet Allen Ginsberg among others, marked the public emergence of a counter-culture, which left a deep imprint.

The following year the first underground paper, *IT* – combining 'art politics sexuality pop' – appeared. But, in its own words, it represented more of an 'inner-directed and permissive' movement than one of political protest as it 'slowly, carelessly constructed an alternative society'. Although more astringent voices could also be heard, such lack of concern with the directly political tended to sit heavily with some of the more orthodox student revolutionaries. 'Some International Socialists at LSE were very harsh about the whole hippie thing, were insensitive to a very important radicalizing feature of the movement,' recalled John Rose, an LSE sociology student who later became an IS student leader himself. 'But the more intelligent ones recognized that someone like me was exactly who they should be trying to recruit – I was part of a wider crowd, into dope smoking, personal liberation – because there was a connection between the hippie thing and student protest.'

While the counter-culture undoubtedly had an impact on student radicalization, particularly on those still in secondary education, its influence on the student movement itself was not as decisive as in the United States because the student political groups were less open to it. As important as the counter-culture, if not more so, for many radicalized students was the Chinese Cultural Revolution. 'Although it took us a long time to understand much about it except that it was a great upheaval, that in some ways it was against authority and the entrenching of a new system of privilege and power in post-revolutionary society, however successful or unsuccessful one might, in retrospect, see it, it had a great effect on us morally,' commented David Fernbach at L S E. He and others formed part of what was called a Maoist or Third World tendency within the L S E SocSoc.

The Radical Student Alliance, which had shown its mobilizing potential in the overseas students' fees issue, was unable to capitalize on its success, and collapsed after eighteen months. Its failure, paradigmatic of the belated attempts to form a broad-based student movement in Britain capable of containing different far-left organizations, was seen by David Triesman, one of RSA's founders, as the result in part of sectarian differences. 'The arguments between those who were Leninists or Trotskyists or libertarian anarchists – if one can break it down into these kinds of political tradition – finally became much more significant than the common ground.'

The far left, although very small, played a dominant role in the two attempts to create a specifically left-wing student organization in Britain. But there were other factors which sharply distinguished British students from their counterparts elsewhere. Unlike the Americans, they did not have to face their own war machine or the draft – indeed, Britain was unique in Western Europe for having abolished military conscription. Unlike Germany and Italy, they did not have the heritage of fascism to deal with, unlike France and Italy they did not have the patrimony of the Resistance to call on. They lacked the long tradition of Continental Marxism and anarchism, and a revolutionary working-class tradition to hark back to. The student activism of C N D and the New Left had been sunk by the Labour Party machine in the sands of the unilateral nuclear disarmament battle, leaving them no credible model of organization. Not least, their actual condition as students, with only three undergraduate years on state-funded grants, gave them a short, and relatively privileged, time at university compared to elsewhere.

It was thus mainly in the single-issue Vietnam Solidarity Campaign (V S C), originated in 1966 by a small Trotskyist group, and in university occupations that the 'common ground' of student activism was re-discovered.

Early in 1967, Tariq Ali went to North Vietnam as part of a fact-finding mission on behalf of the Vietnam War Crimes Tribunal, created by the

British philosopher Bertrand Russell. 'It was a searing experience. I'd never had any doubt that the U.S. was the main enemy, but now it was stamped on me for life. It wasn't demagogy when I said one should stay on there and fight. I didn't want to come back.'

Ali suggested to Premier Pham Van Dong that International Brigades should be formed to fight for the North. 'Pham Van Dong started walking towards me from the other end of the room. I got up. Then he embraced and kissed me on both cheeks. He said that it had been considered but, unlike the Spanish conflict of the Thirties, this war was being fought with the most technologically advanced weaponry and methods. Moreover, a call for volunteers from non-socialist countries might be taken as a slap in the face by the Chinese Communist Party. What was needed instead – and he stressed this many times – was a worldwide solidarity movement. "That is a task we cannot carry out here, but you can." We took these words to heart.'

On his return, he became one of the leaders of V S C, which many would see as the collective expression of Britain's movement, with its increasingly massive mobilizations in support of the Vietnamese liberation struggle from late 1967 to late 1968. But the 'common ground' was discovered in a smaller way in Britain's first occupation, which broke out in March 1967 at the L S E. Its origins lay in the School's appointment, after Rhodesia's unilateral declaration of independence from Britain, of a new director who had been the principal of University College, Rhodesia. But, in a near replay of Berkeley three years earlier, it was the authority's reaction, in suspending from the School two official student leaders for defying a ban on a protest meeting, which precipitated the sit-in. 'Students have no rights,' the existing director declared.

'We were outraged. It offended our deep-rooted liberal instincts about fair play, democracy, free speech and about what had happened to black students at University College,' John Rose remembered. 'And when we decided to occupy, it was like the revolution had started! I was just a typical student, like most of those sitting in. But we discovered what is meant by collective strength, we felt our power. I remember one of the I S [International Socialist] student leaders saying: "We are sitting in because we have to protest against starvation in the Third World." Clearly it had nothing to do with that – and yet somehow clearly it did. We were taking on the world, the political power structure, and we sensed that rebellion from below could change it. We were all agreed on that: students could start to change the world.'

It was one of those rare moments when an institution could be 'cracked wide open', Richard Kuper, one of the IS student leaders, believed. 'Right was on our side, we had the best arguments. There was this absurd arbitrary authority, and they couldn't answer us. In the face of that you called for more, for the occupation to continue. Upping the stakes was what politics was about then. You had nothing to lose.'

LSE's 3,000 students included a far larger number of postgraduate and foreign students than the average British university, and these foreign students played a considerable role. 'The radical American students definitely brought something of the FSM atmosphere with them,' recollected David Fernbach of the Third World Tendency. 'They were a very pleasant contrast to the IS types who were always trying to prove how proletarian they were. Although student politics only interested me in as far as they were anti-imperialist, I sat in with the rest. I felt it was a good thing.'

A theme that united the students, Kuper felt, was the occupation's attack on the hierarchical power and paternalism of the School's authorities. 'The single most important notion around on the left at the time was worker's control. The idea that people should be in control of their own destinies – whether this meant liberal democracy, radical democracy or socialist democracy – brought in a lot of people because we didn't have to clarify the term. Whatever you meant by control, it was clear we didn't have it.'

The aims of the occupation thus went far beyond its immediate causes to demand that the School should be 'democratized, opened up to student participation so that what people wanted to learn should be provided for,' in Kuper's words. 'Marxism was one such area. We wanted a genuinely pluralistic intellectual atmosphere. In putting forward such demands, I felt I was able to give expression to what a lot of people wanted to hear, there was a feeling of rapport, and that was very moving. You did what was right and it *was* right. Even in a moral sense, I don't baulk at the word any more, though I might have then. The fact that you were morally superior mattered, people were making a life choice at some level or another. The breaking up of the old world and the searching for a new had some apocalyptic element to it. And people made the choice because they were convinced emotionally as well as on the issues themselves.'

'The IS leaders were courageous, one step ahead of everyone in the debates,' recalled Rose. 'They raised their demands for action in an immensely plausible way, while making the general points connecting to the outside world as no one else was doing.' The connecting points included taking students to the picket lines of a hard-fought building workers' strike nearby. To an activist like David Triesman, who visited the occupation from Essex, where he was studying, the IS strategy was mistaken. 'To demand of these students, as IS did, that within literally a few days they move from inactivity to a revolutionary perspective which foreshadowed the overthrow of the state was short-sighted. I was unconvinced that they would remain active if they took that sort of battering, and I said so at the one or two meetings at which outsiders spoke.'

The occupation lasted nine days. Uncertain of how to continue it over the impending Easter holiday, a majority voted to bring it to an end without a victory, although a month later the two suspended students were re-instated. There would be no other university occupation for over a year. Unlike America and West Germany, the tardiness with which the student movement got under way in Britain and the relative narrowness of its base would never allow it to escape the shadow of the far-left groups. In this it was closer to the French student movement which, until late 1967, was dominated by the Trotskyist and Maoist organizations which had been expelled from the Communist Student Union. Both these far-left groups made the Vietnam War a central focus of their political activities.

France

'We believed,' recalled Henri Weber of the Trotskyist Jeunesse Communiste Révolutionnaire (JCR), 'that the future of the world revolution depended on the victory or defeat of the Vietnamese. After the "surprise" victory of the Cuban revolution, American imperialism was determined to block by every means, including massive military intervention, the revolutionary surge elsewhere. World revolution and counter-revolution were fighting it out in Vietnam. So it was the primordial duty of every revolutionary to ensure by every means possible the victory of the Vietnamese revolution.'

The fact that the French Communist Party was calling for peace in Vietnam, rather than outright victory for the revolution, added weight to the JCR's conviction of the need to organize a solidarity campaign. 'Vietnam provided an international rallying point,' Weber continued, 'a political common ground for left-wing militants everywhere. The Vietnamese drama was full of lessons. While the U.S. carried out its imperialist tasks with hypocritical and barbarous cynicism, the Soviet bureaucracy didn't hesitate for a moment to sacrifice the Vietnamese on the altar of peaceful coexistence. The workers and peasants of Vietnam, organized in the National Liberation Front, were meanwhile showing an incredulous world what revolutionary war could achieve.'

In opposition to the Trotskyists and to the French Communist Party, the Maoist UJC-ml created Vietnam base committees to organize solidarity. 'We wanted to support the Vietnamese revolution on the basis of its own principles,' explained Robert Linhart, the UJC-ml leader, 'and not on a pseudo-internationalist, but in fact Trotskyist, basis.' The Vietnam base committees mobilized several thousand youth in an organization that became considerably bigger than the UJC-ml itself; 'militarized' and prepared for street fighting, their militants were active in laying the ground for the 1968 May events in Paris, as will be seen in a subsequent chapter.

The most outstanding effect of the Vietnam War, however, was the way it sharpened the incipient radicalization of high school youth. This radicalization had started, as Maurice Najman, a Paris lycée student and Communist Youth member, explained, from the everyday grievances of high school students. 'We tried to develop a lycée movement around these grievances. Our first leaflets expressed these in a crude way: "We're pissed off!" "We want freedom of expression, freedom to meet, freedom to speak!" "We want to wear long hair, listen to music, be allowed to smoke!" In short, we were saying NO! to the BARRACKS-LYCEE.'

Lycée discipline had not changed for the past hundred years. Youth, however, had changed. They were fed up, especially, with gender segregation, something not confined to their unisex schools, for it existed even in the Communist Youth. Najman was one of those who fought to desegregate the organization. 'We won a crushing victory at our Congress in favour of admitting girls. Whereupon the Federation leaders intervened to say that the vote was meaningless because the girls – who of course weren't there – had not expressed their opinion on the matter. They buried the issue! But after that, a number of us Communist Youth members in different Paris lycées started to contact each other, and we decided to set up our own high school Vietnam committees. The first was in my school, the lycée Jacques Decour, in April 1967. Our slogan was: "Peace through victory". As a result of all this, I got kicked out of the Communist Youth, and a lot of the students at my school followed me out of the organization.'

Najman became a Trotskyist. He joined a group whose main thesis appeared 'luminous' to him. 'This was: the era of the working-class movement based on the theory and practice of Bolshevism is *finished*. Now it is necessary to pass on to something else, workers' self-management.'

This led him and his group to the idea of creating lycée action groups. 'The fact that scores of high school students were mobilizing around Vietnam was creating a problem in the school system. Just as we were discussing our plan, a J C R student was kicked out of his lycée for wearing long hair. Not very long, in fact, but at the time it seemed very long. The J C R-led Lycée Vietnam committees called a demonstration in front of his school in protest. There were nearly three hundred of us and we were dispersed by the cops. Not long after, another student burnt an American flag in the courtyard of his lycée and was expelled. Again we took up the battle over freedom of expression in the schools.'

These battles, spearheaded by Vietnam committees, brought closer the realization of lycée action groups. When, at the end of the 1967 school year, teachers staged a strike for a few days, Najman and other students at his school set up a support group in which each class was represented. 'We met in a café opposite the school. When the strike ended, I told the others on the support group that it was a shame to dissolve. And out of that came the idea of the Comité d'Action Lycéen [C A L].'

The C A L were at the forefront of the widespread struggles and occupations of high schools in May 1968. 'Only a dozen or so were in existence by April, but in May there were hundreds all over France!' Najman, who remained active in the high school movement after he went to university, recalled.

One important way in which students demonstrated their opposition to the Vietnam war was by responding to unrest in the American army itself and helping G Is in Europe to desert. Carried out especially by French and West German students, who organized escape routes and sheltered deserters, their work started in 1967 and continued for many years after.

In Paris, Anne Querrien, at Nanterre University, sheltered an American S D Ser who, with the help of a French network, had escaped the court martial trying him for deserting the army. Of anarchist leanings, she found the treatment he was accorded by French Marxists presumptuous. 'Every day these Marxists came to my place to give him political lessons in order to raise his level of consciousness. Political lessons, can you imagine! And I acted as interpreter. He was a very nice guy who, after the 1968 May events, went to Canada. From there, he wrote to me, saying, "Fortunately, the May events got me out of the deeper and deeper paranoid trip I was on . . ."'

In West Germany, Detlev Claussen, vice-chairman of the Frankfurt SDS, was one of those involved in GI work, providing deserters with money and organizing escape routes. 'There were quite a lot of them because Frankfurt is a major U.S. military base. We were very serious about our work and checked out each potential deserter in long individual talks to find out if they could put up with a life in exile. We warned them about what to expect: an alien culture and language, long, cold winters etc. The organizing of escape routes and finding people abroad to look after the deserters was pretty rudimentary in 1967. We did it partly through the SDS national office's international contacts, partly through private connections. We'd know someone in Sweden, for example, and ask them to take care of the deserters. We had absolutely no contact with American organizations doing GI work. In 1967, I went to France to organize stopover places because the German-Danish border had become too dangerous and the French borders were still open.

'Through my GI work I learned the criteria of real political work: the unpretentious day-to-day organizing without any "grand gestures", done without telling anyone, carried out only for its own sake. It formed me in a way, satisfied me that I was doing something concrete that was also right.'

Italy

Italian student reaction to Vietnam was no less sharp than in other countries, but it took place in a different political context. To begin with, the Communist Party played an active role in fostering a broad front anti-war movement; secondly, Vietnam was but the latest in a long line of anti-imperialist issues which had mobilized students in a country where, due to the influence of a mass Communist Party, anti-Americanism had been strong since the war; and lastly, radicalized students felt that their struggle to democratize the university was intimately linked to the wider struggles outside. Nonetheless, Vietnam qualitatively changed this overall context, as will be seen.

Officially, the Communist Party called for a 'free' Vietnam. But, as Peppino Ortoleva, then a pro-Chinese Turin student, recalled, both rank-and-file and Communist Party leaders said 'a "red" Vietnam was the slogan they had in their hearts. "We call for a 'free' Vietnam so that they can be free to choose to be red!" Well, you could criticize their slogans, but in fact you couldn't accuse them of not fighting for Vietnam. You could disagree politically with them, but at the same time you went to the demonstrations they called on Vietnam. Anyone who wanted to do something in terms of political opposition in this country had to take the Party into account because of its mass base.'

Demonstrations that took over Turin streets and squares to protest on international issues were already commonplace events for most radical students. 'We had been mobilizing on anti-imperialist issues and events in other countries for a long time,' remembered Laura Derossi. 'Algeria, the revolt of the American blacks, Cuba, the Congo – and now Vietnam. But Vietnam couldn't be separated from the liberation struggles in Africa, the general issue of imperialism. We always shouted "Giap! Giap! Ho Chi Minh!" on our Vietnam demos, but we also shouted "Lumumba!" and held up posters of Che Guevara and Frantz Fanon.' Nevertheless, as she observed, 'Vietnam did have a particular influence on politicized youth: it gave them a sense of the possibility of revolution, a Third World revolution, a creative form of politics different from what we knew here.'

In the first three months of 1967, a wave of occupations hit Italian universities and colleges on a scale unprecedented hitherto on either side of the Atlantic. Turin, Pisa, Naples, Trento, were only some of those affected. Common to all was the demand to democratize the university. The most famous of the occupations was that of La Sapienza, a building of Pisa University, where the occupying students produced a statement in the form of theses. Among other things, these stated that the university belonged to the students and that the student assembly should become the 'sovereign body'. The old style of student representation based on political party affiliation should be replaced by direct democracy and a mass student organization, like a working-class trade union. 'The student is a worker and, as long as he is productive, has the right to a salary,' one thesis proclaimed, echoing demands made in France and West Germany. Students who did not produce should leave the university. 'The right to study is a specific case of the right to work.'

But it was not only the right to study, but the right to determine *what* was studied, that had begun to agitate students in Italy as elsewhere. The rigid curricula of Italian higher education was now being challenged. At Trento, the Institute of Social Sciences offered the only possibility in Italy of studying sociology – the great hope of many students in the 1960s – but even then no specific degree in sociology was awarded. Students occupied the Institute for eighteen days in early 1966 in an ultimately successful struggle to win the right to such a degree.

'We believed that sociology would help us found a critique of society, of the family, of the values, organization and content of education,' recalled Agnese Gatti, a Trento student. 'It was essential for us to be able to criticize society, establish a *critical* society. From this came the idea of a critical university, of critical study. So, in every subject matter, the demand was that courses be made relevant to society, that we be given a greater wealth of information from a wider range of viewpoints. The textbooks we had were too traditional, too local, too narrow.'

The necessity of a social critique was reinforced for many students by the appearance of a book by a Catholic priest which movingly illustrated the discriminatory class nature of state schools. Using the words of the rural pupils at the 'people's school' he had set up to challenge the system, Lorenzo Milani's *Lettera a una professoressa* showed how state education privileged the children of educated families and discriminated against the poor; the book called on students and teachers who wanted to fight for justice to oppose this system. 'That book was decisive for us, the only real text that inspired the Turin student movement,' recollected Guido Viale, a Turin student leader. 'In exceptionally simple, clear language it went straight to the point about the state's system of discrimination against children of the lower classes.'

The struggle to democratize the university, institutionally and educationally, would feed into the events of 1968 and later. Increasingly, although not yet decisively, liberation struggles in the rest of the world, Vietnam included, were seen by students as part of their own struggle in the university. 'We understood that there was a link between our specific condition as students and our political activity in wider movements,' commented Gatti. 'We felt we were as much the subjects of history as others, we stressed the importance of transforming the self, of creating the "new man".'

The death of a left-wing student, Paulo Rossi, in a clash with fascist students at Rome University in the spring of 1966, had been clear proof of the persistence and strength of fascism there. Demonstrations and occupations took place in Rome as in many other universities in protest. 'At the Rome student assemblies,' recalled Piero Bernocchi, an engineering student who was not openly political at the time, 'I learnt that you could start from Vietnam and explain Rossi's death as a reaction by fascists who felt the ground was slipping from under their feet. I'd had two violent clashes with fascists at the university. I didn't see them in ideological or political terms. To me they were sons of bitches who assaulted me because I wore my hair long – something that wasn't common among university students then – to express my sense of freedom. But they were the same people who pushed Rossi to his death.'

The wave of occupations in the spring of 1967 expressed a growing determination to open up the university, and the representative student bodies within it, to new forms of democracy. But the struggles themselves were still being waged in the old way, under the aegis of political party representation among students. 'It was still a thing of the head,' Luigi Bobbio recalled of the Turin occupation, 'still organized as in the past, still under the illusion that we were fighting against the capitalist moderniz-ation being introduced by a centre-left technocracy. And yet I lived that period of 1966–67 convinced that there was a continuous growth, that something was going to emerge from it. The international situation contributed to the feeling – the world was moving in the same direction: Cuba, the Chinese Cultural Revolution, the black movement in the U.S., Vietnam. All of these fitted into the general scene, were part of the picture. And in 1966, when *Quaderni Piacentini* published a series of articles on the Berkeley F S M, that was fundamental. Everything was ready.'

4

Opening Rounds

First Confrontations: June–December 1967

> It's not hard to tell when something's a movement and when it
> isn't. It's like looking at somebody and knowing they're in love. It's
> connected with the things that are most vital to their life objectives
> and their sense of themselves. They say, we'll throw ourselves into
> it because, if we do, this is going to happen, that is going to happen,
> something is going to happen – *Jeremy Brecher, American SDS*

Although it was not then perhaps apparent, the first rounds of 1968 were
fought out between June and December 1967, as students confronted
growing and sometimes brutal reaction from the forces of law and order. It
began, ominously, with the fatal shooting of a student in West Berlin on 2
June. Black and white students had been murdered in the American
South, but nothing like this had happened in the parliamentary democracies of post-war Western Europe. Four months later, the first 1968-style
confrontation with police forces in the United States was sparked off by
Vietnam; almost concurrently, the Italian student movement erupted in a
new wave of university occupations that were countered by police repression. These events foretold where the burden of the future struggle
lay; student organizations which had been growing in strength and
militancy were now turning into *movements* that would have to confront
state repression.

In West Germany, the killing of the student Benno Ohnesorg during
demonstrations against the Shah of Iran's official visit to West Berlin
marked the transformation. Unprecedented state security measures had
been taken to protect the Shah and his wife: many Iranian students were
temporarily 'exiled' from Munich, highways were closed and extra police

forces mobilized. Apart from throwing eggs and – the police alleged – some stones from across the street when the Shah attended the opera, the thousand or so West Berlin demonstrators were not violent; the police, however, were. They beat up the demonstrators and, when some tried to escape into a house, ran in after them; Ohnesorg was shot in the head there by a plainclothes policeman.

The demonstrations had not been organized by SDS, which at the time was moving a campaign against the recent colonels' mounting putsch in Greece, but by the Iranian Confederation of Students and members of Kommune 1, which had been recently expelled from SDS. But SDS members participated, as did many students, like Ohnesorg, who were not political activists but were beginning to take an interest in student politics; his fatal shooting shook the post-war West German consensus – both the West Berlin senator for international affairs and the head of the police resigned, followed two months later by the mayor – and set the student world alight.

'You woke up the morning after his shooting on 2 June and people you'd never seen before were suddenly "there", on your side. It was an experience that had never happened before,' recalled Detlev Claussen, the anti-authoritarian SDSer at Frankfurt University. 'It's from then on that you can really talk about a *movement* in West Germany as opposed to the history of SDS as an organization. It was euphoric.'

'In Berlin these events sent us into a crazy "high",' recalled Wolfgang Lefèvre, one of the anti-authoritarian leaders. 'First the shooting and then the resignations – it looked as if the Berlin Senate [the city's political administration] was about to fall. The latter was enough to make any of us jubilant. And it was a "high" that carried us through to 1968.'

In protest against the shooting, thousands of hitherto unpoliticized students took to the streets chanting – in a moment of historical outrage that evoked a repressed past – 'Students are the Jews of today!' 'Yes, we now felt ourselves members of a persecuted community,' recalled Siegward Lönnendoncker, a West Berlin SDSer. '"What happened to Ohnesorg could happen to any of us," people said. And then something happened that had never happened before. In place of the abstract notion of solidarity that the SDS comrades had conjured up previously, there was now real solidarity.'

The impact of the killing spread far beyond the normal SDS confines. Barbara Köster, who was part of the fashionable set in Munich, was living with a rich young man at the time. 'We both considered ourselves students.

And then it's Sunday and he goes out and gets rolls and comes back and says, "They've shot a student to death." A fuse blows in my head and I say, "They can't do that, can't kill our people! We've got to do something right away!" We rushed out without breakfast to look for SDS and couldn't find them, so we went instead to the Liberal Students Union and joined immediately. Then there was a huge rally and demonstration. I went with real drive, thinking, now something's going to happen. And what happened? A series of these typical, really dull leftist speeches! Yeah! So I climbed up on a rubbish bin and made a speech, saying it can't go on like this, we've got to do something now! Really spontaneous, quite unpolitical . . .'

The situation was further inflamed when, in West Berlin, all demonstrations were banned for a fortnight – proof in many students' eyes that democratic procedures could be suspended at will – and by the fact that the policeman responsible for the shooting was still on duty while a prominent member of Kommune 1 was in jail on charges of stone-throwing during the anti-Shah demonstration.

The outrage spread beyond universities and high schools to young workers and apprentices. Michael Köhler, working as a dishwasher in Berlin, watched the funeral procession leaving the city for Hannover, Ohnesorg's home town. 'I think that was the real turning point for me. I had seen Rudi Dutschke on TV and I was very impressed by what was happening. Later I phoned SDS from a public call box and asked, very naively, if non-students could join. After a lot of palaver, they told me to "drop in some time". I sneaked round there once, and then I got scared and didn't go in.'

Dutschke's appearance on television was the first time that the German student movement had been able to argue its positions to a large audience on the media; at the same time, it catapulted him into the limelight as the 'leader' of the movement. At an SDS rally after the funeral in Hannover, Dutschke analyzed the political situation in which police could shoot a demonstrator, the role of liberation movements and of the intelligentsia. 'But then,' as his friend Bernd Rabehl, who was present, recalled, 'like a jazz musician improvising, he got carried away by the sound of his own voice and said that we had to defy police bans on demonstrations, organize actions in the coming days. But he didn't justify this tactic by any political or theoretical analysis. Habermas saw this and leapt on the point . . .'

Professor Jürgen Habermas, a second generation Critical Theorist of the Frankfurt School, responded to Dutschke's call by accusing him and

SDS of promoting left fascism. What kind of a political theory was it, he asked, that simply proposed 'action' as a way forward? To challenge state power in that way was to run the risk of graver violence than had already been done. And that had, precisely, been the course pursued by Mussolini and Hitler before 1923.

'I was shocked at that moment when he called our movement left fascist,' Rabehl continued. 'How could anyone say that? Basically, he was saying that the murdered were themselves the murderers. But, as I came to see, he was pointing to something: our lack of political analysis. From his position as a distanced political scientist, he had hit on something that was correct.'

The outcome of Habermas's intervention, however, was to bring the old guard SDSers, who supported Dutschke in the controversy, closer to the new anti-authoritarians. More importantly, the mobilizations furthered the feeling that the left was becoming a mass movement for the first time since it had been crushed by fascism a generation before. SDS, moreover, had shown itself as the only left-wing student organization with cadres sufficiently experienced to deal with an emergency. But whether they knew what to do about the future was a different matter, as Rabehl remembered. 'An expression of our helplessness was a meeting of the most important people in the West Berlin SDS with older SDS comrades after the June events. Instead of getting down to a programmatic discussion, we played soccer. I think that says a lot: we knew that we needed to do something urgently but we were so dried out, so exhausted that we chose to play soccer.'

Nonetheless, a campaign against former Nazis, especially judges still in office, was mounted during the summer. 'We must organize an uprising against Nazi teachers, prosecutors and judges,' proclaimed a leaflet distributed during the trial of the Kommune 1 member. But the summer also brought a fairly recurrent phenomenon in student movements: dispersal, the seeming disappearance of the movement altogether, as students went on vacation. In the national SDS office, Detlev Claussen was depressed that, so soon after the June events, the mass of students who had rallied to SDS had vanished; so, too, had many SDS cadres. 'There we were, alone in the office, students gone, SDS people gone, only us with our revolution which didn't happen because the masses had gone. On top of that, we had to listen to the mild irony of old gentlemen like Hans Maier [a literary historian who was one of SDS's admired figures] saying: "What kind of revolution is this which stops short in the summer vacations?"'

The situation was not, however, quite so bleak, for when Herbert Marcuse visited Berlin in July, he spoke to audiences of 3,000 or more students on four consecutive nights. On the second, he addressed himself to the question of what the student movements were fighting for, and the response of the state. Stressing that the movements were opposing both the majority of the population and a 'well-functioning' society, which did not normally resort to open terror, he added that they were also opposing 'the omnipresent pressure of the system which, more and more inhumanly, degrades and turns everything into a commodity through its repressive and destructive productivity.' Such a system, however, was not immune; it was already having to fight, even if the opposition came only from the intelligentsia. 'And though we may see that opposition cannot help, we have to continue to struggle if we want to be able to work and be happy, because within the existing system neither is possible.'

Claussen, who heard Marcuse speak, felt that he had reinforced the anti-authoritarians' position. So, too, did Karin Kerner, a West Berlin student, who was impressed that someone from the older generation should be encouraging them. 'But over and above that, he appealed to us because we had a strong need for idols, fathers, intellectual guides,' she added. 'Some of ours had died in concentration camps, others in Stalin's prisoner-of-war camps. We knew little history, had no tradition, needed to search for our forebears.'

In the autumn, when students reassembled, the movement's impetus was suddenly regained: SDS was overwhelmed with new members. 'We'd barely overcome our disappointment at the summer low,' Claussen recalled, 'when masses of people started joining. I remember a meeting when two hundred people became members. SDS grew tenfold in just a short time. It was terrible! A sort of hierarchy developed. I'd been a member only a year and now I was one of the "old boys" – especially in my own eyes.'

Anna Pam, who had been out of West Germany for over a year, was amazed to see the transformation on her return to West Berlin that autumn. 'I remembered the SDS centre, a war-wrecked building on the fashionable Kurfürstendamm, as a sort of badly-managed foster home for those who couldn't adapt to the type of society created by West Germany's economic miracle. Now it looked more like a train station without a proper timetable. When I raised the question of organization with old comrades they looked at me as though I were a Social Democrat – which was the worst thing one could be called. "The revolutionary masses will develop their own forms of organization, our role is to mobilize them," they said.'

The new mood affecting activists in some universities was expressed by Holger Klotzbach. Having founded an SDS chapter in 1966 at the theological seminary where he had gone with the intention of becoming a Protestant pastor, he was carried away by the student movement and went to Tübingen University. 'There I barely saw the inside of a lecture hall unless it was to disrupt the class. It was a full time job being a student revolutionary! Snotty as brats, we'd go into the classrooms: "The shitty Americans are continuing their fucking war and you're still sitting here. You'd better get out to such and such a demo!" You had to be careful not to let it get to a vote because most students were still under their professor's influence. The liberal profs were the most dangerous in this respect. And you had to avoid so-called "rational" debate with the teachers because it always ended up in a purely academic exercise. In any case, I had nothing to offer theoretically, I'd barely read any Marx! But I was rational, conscious and had the best arguments: every egg was a better argument than a twenty-five hour academic debate! It was the determination with which you stood up for something that convinced people. Through 'rational' debate you wouldn't have broken through the old irrational authority structures. After a while you were looked on as a liberation hero simply because you were daring and insolent.'

There were also stirrings amongst army conscripts. After eight weeks' training, Ottfried Jensen decided to try to declare himself a conscientious objector. 'It suddenly dawned on me that my old man had gone in for this sort of shit,' he recalled of his SS father who had died in a Russian prisoner-of-war camp. At that time, the student movement had barely impinged on him. Of working-class origin, he had worked his way through high school in the Fifties, but had not continued into higher education. 'At the time I was trying to get out of the army, the headlines were full of the "wild jerks of Berlin" and our sergeants called us the same bad names . . . In the end, it only took a couple of months for the army to throw us out. We were part of the first wave of conscientious objectors and they didn't want us to contaminate the other conscripts. And having learnt what was going on in the student movement, I decided to go to Berlin to study political science.'

By the autumn of 1967 SDS had become virtually unmanageable. To try to deal with the situation, the Berlin organization was restructured around four major "project groups", each of which was sub-divided into study groups. 'Every SDS member was supposed to be in a study group to ensure that new members were educated, politicized and organized,' Bernd Rabehl explained. 'The study groups were to elect delegates for an all-Berlin SDS Council. In fact, however, the project groups became the kernels of political factions whose differences were never thrashed out in discussion.'

To some extent these groups became a power base for the different student leaders. And here there arose a problem which has already been seen in the U.S.: the role played by the media in the creation of leaders and the failure of movements to deal with it organizationally. Though Dutschke was not the only one affected, his case was in many ways paradigmatic, especially after an influential television interview in 1967. 'Although he dominated the subject matter very skillfully on television, we were furious because he put forth a number of programmatic ideas which we had not discussed internally,' recalled Rabehl. 'As a result, a sort of charismatic or populist type of mass democracy came into being in SDS where people simply hung on his words, agreed with them and discussed nothing.'

'It was SDS's great mistake not to have reorganized itself at the height of its influence to ensure that its leading members had to justify their actions,' agreed Oskar Negt, a veteran SDSer. 'Instead, you had these completely uncontrollable charismatic leaders. A Mr Dutschke would arrive at the train station and announce. "Now we are going to do this," or equally – because he had that power – "No, we're not going to do that." Each time the crowd went along with him. His and the other leaders' ideas were invented on the spur of the moment. These sort of moments can be spellbinding, I know, and there's no way that individuals alone can break that spell. It can only be kept under control organizationally. But these leaders never had to justify themselves to the SDS membership. I tried several times to start a debate about reducing the gap between the organizational and populist sides, but it fell on deaf ears. Instead, the mistakes and defeats were worked out by these leaders getting up at the next mass meeting and saying, "Well, comrades, we made a mistake, we'll have to prepare better in future – by the way, tomorrow we are going to occupy such and such an institute."'

This charismatic style of leadership was by no means the sole responsibility of the media, nor confined to SDS. Niels Kadritzke, a leader of the Social Democratic student organization SHB, felt 'flattered' when the prominent magazine *Der Spiegel* featured him as one of the most important West German student leaders, though he was well aware that the magazine was unjustifiably trying to give importance to his organization's moderate role in order to counterbalance the dynamism of SDS. 'And yet I was pleased – and not only that, from then on I tried to live up to and assume the role which had been ascribed to me. After a time, I even believed it myself.' This self-deceptive process was reinforced by a whirlwind of speaking tours as high schools, adult education centres and other institutions started to invite movement leaders, whose names they had seen in the press, to talk about 'what students want'. 'Suddenly you found yourself on platforms with local and national celebrities, whose names you'd only seen in the paper, and discovered how easy it was to out-argue them, how helpless they seemed in direct confrontation. It gave you a feeling of power and self-esteem you'd never experienced before. Then the publishers started chasing you, asking you to write something, or if you were too busy, at least to edit a book . . .'

After a journalist who had interviewed him passed on to Dutschke an offer from Coca-Cola to pay him one thousand marks a month for putting a Coca-Cola bottle beside the microphone each time he spoke, Dutschke rang up Rabehl. '"I've made a mistake, these pigs want to buy me," he said, and he asked for an internal discussion on the matter. He realized that the media were using him, instead of him using them.' But the major victim was not Dutschke but SDS's participatory democracy which, as a mass of new members flooded in, found neither the will power nor the organizational means of making their own leaders accountable to the demands of the majority.

The German SDS's massive increase in members was more than replicated by its American counterpart which, in the two years to the fall of 1967, had grown three-fold to 30,000 members. But 'the movement' itself now encompassed millions of people, ranging from revolutionary blacks in the Black Panther Party to high school students with long hair, the youth groups of left-wing sects to followers of LSD guru Timothy Leary, Quaker peace activists and Roman Catholic radicals to New York and San Francisco hippies.

Vietnam was the main issue; demonstrations in New York and San Francisco the previous spring had mobilized nearly 300,000 people; student radicals in New York City had staged the first collective draft card burning; 20,000 liberal activists had gone door-to-door during a 'Vietnam summer' campaign, talking to their neighbours about the war; students on a number of campuses had demonstrated against their universities' secret military research and willingness to rank male students for the draft; vigils, teach-ins and protests had taken place nation-wide.

'I remember the sense of triumph we had,' recalled Carol Williamson about New York City's huge Spring Mobilization. Then a high school student, now a doctor, she contrasts her memory of that march with one held in upstate New York in the early days of the movement. 'Back then a few dozen marchers straggled along dusty roads going from one small town to another. People kept coming out of the bars along the way – really angry, red faced people. It was really striking how much people hated us.' By 1967 this feeling had changed. At the spring Mobe in New York, 'there was this incredible sense that, "this is it! Now people are with us. *We* are what's happening now!"' It was, 'like your ideal of how a movement should work – it starts out small with a few people who are ahead of their time, and eventually the whole country sees that you're right.'

Others were less optimistic. Bruce Franklin of Stanford noted the emergence of a disturbing pattern. At Stanford, with its 20,000 students for example, the first SDS meeting of the new academic year would draw one hundred and fifty to two hundred people; thereafter, meetings would dwindle until only a hard core of between fifteen and twenty-five people was left. 'These people would work their tails off, very discouraged, and the media would be saying "the movement's gone." Then, typically, in the spring, the government would do something especially outrageous, and all the patient work of this very small corps of people would show its results. And there would be a massive outpouring, and thousands of people would be fervent for, predictably, a very brief period of time.'

Meanwhile, President Johnson made it apparent that, no matter how many protests took place, he would continue to wage war in Vietnam. The growth of the anti-war movement seemed increasingly to some as a Pyrrhic victory. By the fall of 1967, a small but significant section of the white student movement was dissatisfied with peaceful protest and ready to try out new tactics. 'Stop the Draft Week' and the March on the Pentagon – the latter called, in fact, by the moderate Mobilization Committee and criticized by an SDS National Convention as the sort of demonstration that had no effect on American policy in Vietnam – became the occasions for these new confrontational tactics.

'There was no point any longer to going out for a Sunday afternoon and applauding a thousand different speakers saying the same thing,' recalled a Berkeley activist, Frank Bardacke. 'Everyone knew the war was the shits.

We didn't have to educate anybody anymore.' He and a fellow-group of activists planned 'Stop the Draft Week', a series of militant demonstrations to be held the week before the Pentagon march. 'Our idea was highly influenced by the Black Power people,' Bardacke continued. 'Plus, it happened right after the summer of Detroit and Newark [where massive ghetto rebellions had had to be quelled by the National Guard and paratroopers] so there was a real revolutionary impetus. The idea was, we were going to threaten chaos in the country, and by threating chaos we were going to stop the war in Vietnam.'

A new organization, the Resistance, was at the head of Stop the Draft Week. Its original organizers and program merged passivist concerns about the draft with a call for more militant actions against the war. 'It was a spirited group, both militant and moralistic, advocating confrontational tactics, including people burning their draft cards, refusing to be inducted, going to prison if necessary,' recalled Steve Hamilton, the former FSM activist who had subsequently joined the Maoist Progressive Labour Party but left when he saw it turning to more traditional working-class organizing. By the time of Stop the Draft Week, the Resistance had spread to dozens of cities and towns, each of which was left free to decide its own objectives and type of demonstration. Two actions in particular captured the nation's headlines: Oakland and Madison.

> To end the war, it is necessary to comprehend its true nature, to understand the extent to which major institutions such as this university and Dow Chemical are committed to its continuation . . . We must move from protest to resistance. Before, we talked. Now we must act. We must stop what we oppose.

So read an SDS leaflet protesting against recruiting by Dow Chemical, manufacturer of napalm, on the University of Wisconsin campus at Madison, a radical stronghold. On 16 October, SDS members handed out leaflets; the following day they led several hundred people into the University's 'Commerce' Building, where the Dow recruiter was scheduled to hold interviews. The campus police were called to move them. Paul Buhle, a graduate student member of SDS, recalled, 'To a man, to a woman, we said, "We're not going to leave. You can't scare us."' The campus police then called in the city police of Madison. Heavily armed, dressed in riot gear, they assembled outside the building. With little warning they moved into the building's lobby where the protesters stood massed in tight ranks.

'The police tried to push their way in, and were pushed back,' recounted Buhle. There was a moment, he claimed, of terror. 'The police were pushing in, and we were pushing back, you were picked up off your feet and couldn't control your own movement, and you thought, "Oh shit, I'm going to die." Or, "I'm going to lose my glasses." Whatever. Something will happen. I can't control it. I can't control it.' Then the police smashed in the doors and began to drag students out of the building through the glass. Between the glass and the clubs of the police, student blood was soon spattered all over. At first the students absorbed the blows but then began to move. 'The police allowed us to escape out of a rear door,' Buhle recalled. 'But instead of running away, which maybe they thought we would do, we circled around to the front of the building. By the time we got there, there were a thousand other students there.' The crowd, many of whom never considered themselves radical, was furious at the beatings they witnessed. 'The second the cops started clubbing heads, the entire situation changed dramatically – emotionally, psychologically, politically, sociologically,' says Buhle. 'Very suddenly, fraternity boys, athletes, all sorts of normal people who were just going to classes, people who were a little ambivalent about the war but who would never go to a demonstration, were unbelievably outraged and were eager to wade into the crowd and sock the jaw of a cop.'

To Maurice Zeitlin, then on the faculty at Wisconsin and close to the students, the irony and paradox of the moment was that the seasoned activists were not in the forefront. 'The most adventuristic kids were clearly the Wisconsin-born kids. The rage, the outrage, the sense of horror of the war enveloping them, and the simultaneous sense of being double-crossed – having been taught what America was and then discovering it isn't – all of this sudden burst from naivety to consciousness was what brought those kids to go up flagpoles, take down American flags, burn them, smash store windows.'

The police began to tear gas the students, but the clouds of stinging gas only made the crowd angrier. 'Tear gas was pretty easy to deal with,' according to Buhle. 'You take your jacket off, pick it up and throw it back at them.' As the crowd grew larger and began to outnumber the police, students challenged them: shouting, throwing rocks. 'We would move forward. They would move at us. We would move back. They would single out one person and keep moving at them. Sometimes we blocked them successfully. Sometimes we let the person disappear into the crowd. The cop would go into the crowd and take his chances. There was,' says Buhle, 'a strange aura of excitement. There was in that terrifying moment an aura of tremendous romantic upsurge. I wouldn't call it erotic but somehow you were in a new relation with all kinds of people immediately around you, men and women. It was an epiphanic moment. And it was so exciting that you lost your fear. You had this feeling that you had to go back. Maybe because you were so angry about the war. Maybe because you would have missed the most important, exciting moment in your life if you didn't.'

The clashes lasted throughout the day, and were followed by a general strike among the students. 'There was a reservoir of shock,' claims Buhle, 'the classic American radical's shock of recognition: "O God! Everything they told me was a lie." That happened to 4,000 people in one afternoon.' After several weeks of strikes the students won some concessions, and a temporary ban on Dow recruitment. While it lasted, thousands of students challenged the University and the police with boycotts, rallies, sit-ins. These students, according to Buhle, were the true new leftists. 'They were made in that moment of the uprising of the students, and they bore the unique stamp of that radical generation. It wasn't just a matter of protest, but now the campus could actually be taken over, and could become a center for calling the empire to a halt; a center, one center, for re-creating the whole society, or laying out a model for a whole new society.' Such actions at Madison, at Stanford, at Berkeley, at the University of Washington, at CCNY were crucial in moving the movement to a new stage. 'Had not the kids at Wisconsin sat in and done things that I thought were outrageous,' claims Zeitlin, 'taken over classrooms, shouted at professors, interrupted lectures – all those things I was opposed to, and still am, for civil libertarian reasons as well as tactical reasons, these major events would not have taken place. Those students who did those things, knew what they were doing because that's what swept people in. It was the excitement. It was the glamour. It was the romance. It was finally and ultimately the real confrontation that took place. Had those campus disruptions not taken place across America, had we gone on merely having teach-ins, I don't think it would have mattered.'

On the same day that Wisconsin students were battling in Madison, California students attempting to block the Oakland Induction Center were being attacked by hundreds of police. Clubbing people as they fell, the police also used mace, a newly developed chemical that temporarily blinded its victims. The level of violence was astounding. 'That morning was a key event in my life and the lives of many people I know,' Stanford activist Bruce Franklin remembered, 'I can still hear the sound of clubs hitting their heads. It sounded like the smashing of watermelons. I saw the police coming in there in a flying wedge and knew what was going to happen,' recalled Peter Shapiro, then a student at San Francisco State College. 'The most violent act I had ever committed was whipping the dog on the rear when she wet the carpet.' Being caught in the police attack was shocking. 'You know, if you're a nice respectable law-abiding white kid, it's very terrifying to see policemen armed to the teeth coming at you with every intention of putting you in the hospital.'

The chaos of blood, screaming, and mace reigned for nearly an hour. But soon, those not caught directly in the police attack began to retreat. Most headed home, but a few tried to salvage the day by disrupting traffic in nearby intersections on the theory that this might stop the buses from leaving the Center. 'People moved away from the main scene,' recalled Franklin, 'and quite spontaneously started blocking intersections and were very much surprised at how much this disorganized and confused the police. People would take an intersection and when the police came people would run away and go to another intersection. It was very different from sitting down and getting your head clubbed by the police. Before there was such a terrible feeling of impotence because people were being clubbed. But now, you felt you could do something.'

In the immediate aftermath of 'Bloody Tuesday', as it came to be called, activists were confused as to how to continue the struggle. 'We were scared,' recalled Steve Hamilton, one of the Resistance leaders. 'We'd done a lot, but at the same time a lot of people had been hurt and arrested, and it could get even more out of hand.' It took two days – one of impotent picketing at the Center, the other of large campus rallies to discuss what should be done – before the momentum built up again. On Friday morning, 10,000 people returned to the scene of the battle, ready to draw on their experience of three days earlier. Shapiro was one of those preparing to put to use new tactics.

'This time, instead of standing there and getting beaten up when the police came, people put up barricades. They'd push cars into the intersections and let the air out of the tires. They pulled trash cans into the streets. And the police would have to pick their way through the barricades. And when the police drove you back, you'd pull back about half a block and throw up a barricade and then move on and try to get to another intersection before the cops did.'

Bruce Franklin and others had also developed new tactics. They had bought a pile of plywood and made hundreds of shields which they distributed to the demonstrators. The ability to defend themselves changed the whole tone of the demonstration, he recalled. 'This cop was right near me, clubbing people, with this really ferocious expression, and I'm thinking, am I really going to use this shield? So he swings at my head. I put up my shield. The club hits it. And I'm thinking that this cop is going to get enraged and pull his gun, or God knows what. Instead, he just kind of crumples. Trying to put this all together, one couldn't help relate that to the scene of the police clubbing people in the street on Tuesday. And it was clear that their sadism was fed by our non-resistance, and that even this primitive form of resistance changed all that.'

With their new tactics, the demonstrators blocked off the Induction Center for several hours, creating total chaos in downtown Oakland. After they pulled back they celebrated what they felt was a stunning triumph. 'It was a qualitative leap forward,' Shapiro thought, while for Bardacke there was the sense that 'We finally had ourselves a white riot . . . We had the streets. When it came to street battles now, we felt real confident – and with good reason.'

The following day, 21 October, between seventy and one hundred thousand people gathered for the March on the Pentagon in the largest anti-war demonstration Washington had yet seen. Recognizing the growing restlessness in the movement, the organizers had hired Jerry Rubin, Berkeley activist, to help organize the event. His response had been to arrange for Beat poet Allen Ginsberg and a rock band to lead the crowd in a mass ritual designed to 'levitate' the Pentagon; at the same time he and the Mobilization Committee arranged for a public turning in of draft cards and suggested the possibility of civil disobedience in front of the Pentagon. There was, in consequence, a large number of groups among the protesters – seasoned peace activists, liberals, SDSers and other young radicals, and for the first time a sizeable contingent of hippies – but little agreement about the march's objectives. Nothing, in the end, happened according to a comprehensive plan.

From the crowd milling around in a parking lot by the Pentagon where the march had reached, a group of several hundred, led by New York City SDSers, suddenly broke through the police lines and charged towards the Pentagon doors. A few made it inside and were immediately beaten and arrested. The rest sat down in front of the doors. Others from the main body of the march came to support them, swelling their numbers to several thousand. 'Join Us! Join Us!' they chanted to the soldiers surrounding them, while some demonstrators placed flowers in their rifle barrels. Scores of young men, defying the Pentagon officials watching from inside the building, pulled out their draft cards and set fire to them.

As night fell, thousands of demonstrators decided to stay. They built fires with placards to stay warm. In the middle of the night military police began arresting them, beating some badly in the process. 'They would take one line of people away, and another would take their place, and it went on like that all night, till the sun came up,' Jeff Jones, a New York S D S organizer who was among those who had made the initial charge, recalled. 'That's where I saw state power being exercised for the first time,' remembered Richard Eagan, a student actor from a non-political background. 'Not like on television or something in the movies, but happening four rows in front of thousands of people just like me. I couldn't believe it! For the first time in my life, I had a sense of solidarity with people who believed in something. I knew the war had to stop, at that point I was ready to put myself on the line.'

In the morning most of those who were still sitting in decided they had made their point and marched away in a body. For Jones, who was one of them, it had been an 'exciting, powerful, intense' experience; but he was glad it hadn't turned into an Oakland-style mobile battle. 'It was more effective as a piece of political drama. A set piece. We were here, the cops were there. We were demonstrating for profound political issues. And the cops were using violence to stop us.'

In all, 683 people were arrested – the largest number of any anti-war protest up to that time. Undoubtedly, however, the majority of those who had taken part in the march remained unconvinced by the 'confrontational' tactics used. Demonstrators for the first time were carrying wet handkerchiefs in case of tear gas, and many were deliberately goading the police. Paula Koepke, a Michigan student on her first Washington march, was upset: 'That wasn't my idea of what should go on – if you had a march it was as a show of strength, and it wasn't like a football game or a fight. All that cop-baiting activity was ridiculous, I thought. People taunting them, calling them ugly names, seeing if they could get them to react, like they wanted the police to hit them and then make a scene, you know. It might have been necessary to create that kind of uproar and violence to really make things happen, but I couldn't believe in it personally. And I'm not sure it was necessary.'

Nothing, however, was going to stop the new-found mobile militancy. A month later, a demonstration called by the New York peace movement to protest against the presence of Secretary of State Dean Rusk, one of the war's architects, at the prestigious Foreign Policy Association's annual dinner, rapidly escalated into mobile confrontation when some SDSers threw bags of cows' blood at the police. As in Oakland and Madison, the protesters moved away from the police who began to beat people indiscriminately; but instead of disappearing, they blocked intersections with trash cans, harassed police and the limousines of the wealthy and powerful members of the Foreign Policy Association, many of whom had to get out and walk, and generally created chaos.

It was the implementation of a new strategy designed, like that of the SDS anti-authoritarians in Germany, to reveal the violence of the state. Although never embraced by the majority of anti-war activists, the street fighting style attracted a substantial following – a following large enough eventually to dominate, with the help of the media, the public image of the movement as a whole. Street fighting had the appeal of the new, the cachet of black militancy and the urban rebellion, as Frank Bardacke's comment on Oakland that 'we finally had ourselves a white riot' revealed; but it corresponded also to a critical moment in the movement's development. Participatory democracy and community organizing, which had served so well in many earlier local campaigns, were proving of limited use in challenging the federal government on foreign and military policy. Like the black students before them, white student activists began to think of new strategies for confronting state power.

'It was like when the riot in Watts happened,' commented Paul Buhle, recalling the feeling at Madison after the riot. 'I remember a poem in the *Guardian* saying "Next time, next time it may be Armageddon". And the feeling was the same, as the war escalated and we got crazier and crazier. The feeling was, "Boy! That Dow demonstration really shook the shit out of the campus! What's going to happen next time? So far it's gotten bigger and bigger. It'll have to get even bigger. What's going to happen next time?"'

Only weeks after the Pentagon march, the Italian universities exploded again. It was the start of a five-month long struggle which virtually brought the university system to a halt. In Turin, a new theory of activism changed the nature of the struggle from that of the past. Before looking at this new wave of Italian militancy, it is worth pausing to consider not only the new Turin theory but others being worked out by radicalized students to explain their movements' aims. In one form or another, all of these now put forward goals that would radically alter existing society.

Before these goals could be clearly defined, however, left-wing student leaders, formed in their earlier struggles against the contradictions of advanced capitalism, had first to answer a question: where, in a class society, did students fit? Both Italians and Americans now answered with a new definition of the proletariat.

In Italy, the argument ran, advanced capitalism had permeated through to and *dominated* all layers of society that were functional to its ends. Domination, not only exploitation, was the key to defining the proletariat which, in consequence, was much larger than assumed by traditional Marxist theory. The proletariat could now be seen to extend to all dominated social strata, from intellectual workers, including students, to the unemployed; but it was not an undifferentiated proletariat, for it was composed of these many different strata. Within the proletariat as thus conceived, it was equally possible to speak of a students' condition as it was of a workers' condition – though the two were not analogous.

'My main idea, then,' recalled Guido Viale, the Turin student and major proponent of the new theory, 'was that the revolt against the student condition could be the mainspring of a far-reaching social and cultural movement. A movement which could establish links with non-university youth and the working class on an equal footing. We didn't adopt a paternalistic attitude towards the working class, or believe we were "going to the people". No. We wanted to have our own autonomous positions which the working class, still obviously the most important social class, could respect. Our theory proposed that students themselves were legitimate bearers of revolutionary aspirations.'

The idea that revolt could spring from the student *condition* – 'dig where you stand' – was, in the context of the Italian university, to have particularly dynamic results. The American attempt to expand the definition of the proletariat, which bore resonances of the early West German SDS analysis of contemporary capitalism, also had an important impact in turning the American university into a site of struggle.

The new working-class theory in the U.S. put forward the idea that technocrats, engineers and other essential service workers were a class in and of themselves, but a class which, like the working class, shared a lack of control over the means of production. They were a 'new proletariat' which was being churned out by the university for jobs where, although they did not suffer privation, their labour was alienated, their leisure repressed and they experienced a poverty of spirit. Bob Gottlieb, a graduate of the New School who had studied in Paris and been in contact with the Situationist International, was one of the authors of the new theory. As he recalled, its purpose was to 'go beyond the narrow Marxian notion of class which gave a privileged position to industrial workers.

'We were seeking to keep the structure of Marxian analysis, but also to legitimize the student movement. It was answering the criticisms made of the student movement that it was a secondary phenomena to the working-class movement. This was looking at the students as primary. It fit in with what was going on because by that time it was obvious that students were emerging as the central group in the New Left.'

Today's students were tomorrow's workers; a radicalized student would become a radicalized worker, the American theory maintained. Thus the focus of radical activity should be the campus. Students could transform universities from mechanisms of social control into arenas for producing a radical new working class. The theory slotted into the syndicalism of the new SDS activists, and was crucial in redirecting the organization back to the campus, in merging students' personal concerns with an attack on the nature of the university. At a time when the latter's complicity in the draft and the war effort were becoming ever more plain, this was vital in developing the anti-war movement.

The most vocal opponents of the new working-class theorists in the U.S. were the members of Progressive Labor (Maoist). Hewing to a more traditional Marxist line, and critical of the lack of analysis of imperialism in such theories, their tactic was not to organize on campuses but to send students to work in factories in an attempt to raise an anti-imperialist consciousness among workers. In 1967 and 1968 they sponsored summer 'work-ins', which many in PL recall with a certain fondness. To Deborah Levenson, who worked in Boston, 'those experiences are just unforgettable for me, because there is a reality about America that has to do with working in a factory. You see that people are poor, that they work very hard, that it is tiring, that it takes all of your time, that you can't do much else. Harvard kids did this, Boston University kids did this. And they flipped out. I don't think that many people were successful about talking to people about the war in Vietnam, or about racism, but they were somewhat successful. And that was important.'

There were also moments of comic relief. Steve Fraser, then at City University of New York, was hired as a cutter in a garment factory. 'I saw it advertised in a newspaper, a cutter. I didn't know what a cutter was.

Otherwise I never would have had the temerity to apply for such a job. I showed up for the job. I'm twenty years old. The guy says, "You're a cutter?" I said, "Yes. I know how to cut. I've done it." It was a little sweatshop so the guy wasn't too inquisitive. He brings me into the factory. The next thing I know there's this sixteen-layer-high pile of fabric, and a pattern is laid across the fabric, and I've got an electric machine in my hands. Somebody switches on the motor and the machine goes wild. It cut the fabric into shreads. I couldn't control it. The guy stood there aghast, in disbelief that this was happening. He was astonished by my chutzpah. I was a kid from Great Neck, and middle-class. I didn't know from nothing about this kind of thing.' The experience did, however, bring Fraser into contact with working-class people and their attitudes toward the war. 'There was a *kind* of anti-war sentiment. It was a kind of cynicism about the intentions of government and elites generally. A sense that no matter what's happening we're going to get screwed. It wasn't worked out, but a sense of the big boys are running the show, and we're cannon fodder.'

Though differing in their premises, both Italian and American theories gave a revolutionary perspective to student struggle against the university and around the student condition. In other countries, like Britain and France, the far-left groups which played an important role among students perceived the situation differently. For example, the group which attracted the most student support in Britain, the International Socialists (IS), might agree that the future of most students lay in the working class, albeit as white-collar workers. The 'undoubted divisions' between unskilled, skilled, clerical, professional and other workers, they stressed at the time, were *not* class divisions. But it was not students as such but the working class which was the agent of revolutionary change. As Richard Kuper, one of the IS leaders at LSE, observed: 'Even though I was very involved in student politics, even though IS did take the student issue seriously despite the fact that some members were anti-student, we spent all our time politically saying that the real struggle lay outside. The student struggle was important insofar as we mobilized people through it for that other struggle.'

This position was strenuously contested by other British students. A group around *New Left Review*, for example, argued that students were the 'weakest link' in society and could 'severely restrict the ruling class's field of action' by struggling to overthrow bourgeois ideological hegemony. Students were the weakest link, as Michael Thomas, an independent Marxist, explained, because they were between home and employment.

'With the development of critical strands in sociology, philosophy, economics etc. they could counter bourgeois ideology and break down the
hold of society. Within the university, challenging course content, introducing Marx, Engels, Lenin, Mao, Guevara, was more important to me
than democratizing the university. Finally, students were particularly open
to internationalist politics, both in learning from and organizing solidarity
with other countries.'

In general, however, British students did not follow either an American
syndicalist approach or concentrate, like an important sector of the Italian
movement, on the student condition. Nor did the two leading French
far-left groups. On a visit to China in the summer of 1967, the leaders of
the Maoist UJC-ml were persuaded by the Communist Party leaders that
the French proletariat was potentially revolutionary, and that they had to
learn from their own working class.

'Mao said, there are three categories of intellectuals: those who look at
the flowers sitting on horseback, those who dismount to look at the flowers,
and those who make the flowers grow,' Robert Linhart, the UJC-ml
leader, explained. His group took Mao's saying to mean that they should
work politically and manually on the land with farmers. That summer and
the following they carried out their new policy, calling it the Long March.
'To look at the flowers was already better than staying at home,' Linhart
continued. 'But, as we also decided, dismounting and leaving the horse in
the stable to go into the factories was even better.' A small number of
UJC-ml students followed the new turn to become factory workers (a
strategy which the American Maoist Progressive Labor also pursued). But
the French Maoist group did not expect a student movement to ignite the
revolution; this would come, they maintained, from the working class
itself, especially now that over half a million workers, many of them young,
were unemployed.

In contrast, the French JCR, following the positions of the Trotskyist
Fourth International, theorized the student movement as an 'alternative
vanguard'. 'When the working-class movement is unable to play a vanguard role,' explained Henri Weber, the JCR leader, 'because of trade
union bureaucracy, established routines, conservatism, then other groups
come to express social opposition. This was the case with the students.
Half a million people concentrated in enormous university complexes –
people who were profoundly discontented – constituted an important
oppositional force. And that's exactly what happened: the student movement played a role of a vanguard, and triggered the worker's movement in

May '68. Our predictions that indefinite economic growth would not continue, that wage earners and the salariat were now more numerous, more educated, and more demanding than ever before, that they would react when the downturn came and large-scale social conflicts would erupt – those predictions came true. I must admit we were surprised when it happened, though! Are we dreaming? we asked each other. We ought to have put more trust in what we've been writing, we thought!'

Arguably the best known of the German SDS anti-authoritarians' concepts was the 'Long March through the Institutions', which Rudi Dutschke put forward in early 1968. This proposed that the students' task was to

> deepen the contradictions already existing at different levels of society (in high schools, vocational training schools, universities, stagnating branches of industry etc.) . . . in order to break sections and factions from the repressive institutional totality and win them over to the revolutionary anti-authoritarian camp. The Long March through the institutions means making subversive use of the contradictions and possibilities inside and outside of the complex state-society machine in order – in the course of a lengthy process – to destroy it.

In general, however, as Bernd Rabehl recognized, the anti-authoritarians produced practically no theoretical work – 'and the little we wrote up was because a bourgeois publisher was breathing down our necks for a book, *Rebellion der Studenten*, edited by Dutschke . . . We had no concrete political plan for the future, no clear concept of Germany. We saw ourselves as agitators, travelling round – every God-forsaken university had teach-ins by now – as a sort of SDS circus, talking about the revolution and "What does SDS want?" Socialism – hell knows what else we talked about!' (The extent of the audience for these ideas can be judged by the fact that *Rebellion der Studenten* went through eight printings and sold 170,000 copies in four months after its publication in May 1968.)

In the whirlwind which shortly embroiled the movements, many of the new theories were blown away. The political space in which they might have served was compressed by the escalation of events, by confrontation and the state's counter-offensive. What was clear in this period, however, was that students in a number of countries were beginning to feel themselves as a collective, a feeling which was concretely expressed by their determination to take up their own education. The movement to set up 'free' universities began in the United States and was boosted by the experience of the Berkeley FSM, when students organized spontaneous seminars to teach themselves what they wanted to know. Largely under the impetus of SDS local chapters, students elsewhere followed the example in an attempt to show what a radical, non-establishment education could be like, and to teach courses not available on the official curriculum.

One of the most extensive and successful free universities was at Stanford in Palo Alto, California. It combined the counter-cultural movement which had grown up around novelist Ken Keasey and his 'Merry Pranksters', the pacifist community centered on Joan Baez and her husband David Harris, and Marxist activists such as Bruce Franklin and the members of the Mid-Peninsula Red Guard. The Free University at one time had over one thousand members. Each contributed ten dollars every three months to pay for the few salaries needed, and to print its newsletter and catalog. Courses were offered on the Human Potential Movement, the book of Dao, second hand clothing, Maoist theory, movement history, Reichian theories of psychology and body painting – which Gurney Norman describes as a class 'where everyone got naked and they rubbed paint all over one another.' Anyone who wanted to offer a course simply listed it in the catalog, 'and whoever was interested showed up.'

It was, Norman noted, 'against Stanford. It was a reaction to Stanford. It certainly was no alternative. In a way it was complementary. But it was essentially anti-intellectual; certainly anti-bureaucratic, and anti-heirarchical. It was a way of saying that we want to have experiences and lines of inquiry that we don't have to be sanctioned to study. There was a rebel consciousness that held it all together.' By the end of 1966, there were fifteen of these 'free' universities – free also because as a rule anyone could attend, and there were no grades or exams – and several hundred grew up in the following years.

Influenced in part by the FSM example, the West German SDS created a 'Critical University' which opened with fifty courses in West Berlin in the autumn of 1967. The concept, originated by an old-guard SDSer who had spent time in the United States, was intended to educate and integrate the large numbers of dissatisfied students who were moving towards left politics. The three main areas of study concerned subjects of direct relevance to students' political activities, like Third World liberation movements and the Emergency Power laws in Germany; the conditions and implications of social research, including university reform; and a critique of the theoretical and ideological foundations of established university disciplines by the study of psychoanalysis, Marxism, social medicine – which had been traditionally excluded from German universities.

'Truly revolutionary courses worked well if they had a rather concrete political goal,' recalled Anna Pam. 'But to revolutionize theory was practically impossible in those hectic times.' Despite such problems, however, the Critical University became a model for many others in Germany and abroad, notably in Italy and France.

The first of the new wave of Italian occupations occurred at the Private Catholic University of Milan in November 1967. It arose directly out of student conditions, notably an increase in university fees; but it rapidly turned into a demand to reform the university itself which effectively shut down teaching for the rest of the year. Shortly afterwards, in protest against financial speculation involved in the building of new faculties outside the city, Turin students took over the Humanities faculty, the Palazzo Campana, in the centre of town. Immediately, the occupation turned into a radical critique of the university and the student condition, along the lines of Guido Viale's new theory. 'We were influenced also by the Situationist International positions,' recalled Viale. 'Assemblies analysed in detail the forms of oppression students suffered personally, academically and culturally in their lives at university.

'Most wonderful of all was to hear students talking about their experiences,' Viale continued. 'The real discovery of the occupation, which had started for rather banal reasons, was that students *found a voice*, spoke out for the first time about authoritarianism and cultural emptiness at the university, began to live daily life differently. The themes that the group of us had been working on since the summer were visibly being expanded in front of our eyes. Best of all were the confrontations with professors when students told them to their face what they thought about them.'

The time of airing grievances was soon replaced by more concrete activities: the setting up of a free university. 'We were enthused by the idea of the counter-university,' recalled Luigi Bobbio, another of the leaders, 'and very much influenced by the anti-authoritarian West German movement and its concept of direct action. That meant simply that "instead of asking we act. We are not a movement that exists to bargain, we exist to act." So we stopped asking for university reform and did it ourselves. We built the free university with the slogan, "We study what we want to." That was how we interpreted the slogan of student power. The Berkeley FSM had been a struggle not against the university, but a struggle for free speech, the right to speak, to meet. Very concrete things. In contrast to our earlier occupation we had found our voice now, an authentic voice that started from lived experience.'

The free university offered courses on the philosophy of science, pedagogics of dissent, psychoanalysis and social repression, Vietnam, imperialism and social development in Latin America, and social struggle in 1960s Europe. In the context of a university where, for example, any developments in psychology after 1879 were not taught, to be able to study Freud was a real innovation. 'We invited Musatti [the founder of Freudian analysis in Italy] to talk to us,' recalled Anna Trautteur, 'and read his works. We studied Marcuse's *Eros and Civilization* and the *Diary of a Schizophrenic* by an anonymous Viennese. We were all on the Freud-Marcuse line.'

The Turin occupation unleashed a wave of similiar takeovers through-out Italy. Within a fortnight, a third of all universities were in a state of turmoil and a dozen had been occupied, including Naples. Giuseppe Di Gennaro, the electronic engineering student who was forced to tape-record lectures because he couldn't afford books, was one of those who launched the engineering faculty occupation in Naples.

'We were in the middle of national student representative elections when suddenly we saw on TV that something big was exploding in universities all over Italy. Two totally distinct things: elections about which no one cared and these other, stratospheric events on TV in which students are finally attacking their professors. It seemed we ought to call an assembly! We'd heard that that's what they did in the North, though we had no such tradition at all! So we called one and seven hundred people turned up. As soon as it started two or three of us got up and began to vent all our hatred of the professors. Then a series of people went to the microphone and all of them said that things weren't going well in the faculty but we ought to try to right them. I got up: "No, things are going really badly," I said, "everything in Italy shows us that. We must raise ourselves to the level of the others . . ." As I was launching into a strong attack on our teachers, the dean grabs the microphone from my hand. I grab it back. There's an uproar! Terrific applause! The dean went scarlet and lost his head!'

His resolution calling for an occupation was narrowly defeated. Another assembly was called and this time 2,500 students showed up. 'There was a unanimous decision to occupy. We took over everything – buildings, laboratories, institutes, everything, including the computer. The occupation lasted sixty-four days, something quite exceptional for an engineering faculty. The first twenty days were of absolute happiness, and I'm not exaggerating, for the five hundred of us in the occupation. Everything was organized with great precision, people who had never attended an assembly before now stayed until late at night. All decisions taken by the faculty council had to be approved by the student assembly.'

Here, as in Milan and Turin, direct democracy was now at work. The student assembly was the sovereign body. The students began to study – 'with an engineer's seriousness – Marx and the revolutionary classics in a scientific and systematic way. To relax, they played football in the faculty hall. 'It was a crazy thing to do, we could have smashed ourselves to death on the columns but it was such fun, so liberating!' Di Gennaro remembered. 'It was marvellous becoming friends with people I'd never known before, discussing not only the occupation but my life, their lives. Ferocious discussions conducted like mathematical exercises. What is friendship? After half an hour we reached an acceptable definition. All right, if this is what friendship is, can you really call yourself Fernando's friend? Yesterday you did this, this and this, what sort of a friend are you? We all got gastritis, but we kept up this ruthless analysis for the whole occupation – and for many years afterwards.'

Although the students' unity began to falter after the first three weeks, the occupation continued. There, as in Turin, students refused to vacate their 'liberated zones' for the Christmas holidays. 'People were having too good a time to leave,' remembered Luigi Bobbio at Turin. 'Hundreds stayed in order to do what they wanted. The documents we put out at the time, which were both aggressive and funny, naively exalted and childlike, show how good it felt to stay at the university without the professors.'

After Christmas police dislodged the occupiers from the Palazzo Campana in Turin, only to find them firmly re-occupying two days later. Again the police ejected them. As the new term started, hundreds of students roamed the different faculties scattered throughout the city. 'It was a great experience,' remembered Laura Derossi, 'we interrupted lessons in many of them. No professor could teach at the University any longer without our permission. If they tried, they were interrupted by these hordes of barbarians who erupted into the classrooms with megaphones, explaining the reasons for their intervention. The democratic professors were traumatized, to the point of saying that our actions were like those of the fascists, that political intervention in the cultural sphere was typical of fascism. But nobody could restrain us any longer. The police would arrive, we'd resist passively, they'd throw us out, close down the building and we'd move elsewhere, to the trade union offices or another faculty.'

The accusation of 'fascist tactics' was turned back on the accusers in Italy by referring to a common heritage of freedom. When Luigi Bobbio interrupted a lecture that was taking place only thanks to the protection of a strong police force, he shouted, 'This isn't a lecture, you can't teach in an unfree situation threatened by armed force!' He was immediately seized by a policeman, Laura Derossi remembered, and badly manhandled down the stairs. 'I threw myself in front of the police jeep that was about to take him off, but my friends dragged me away.'

Police tactics became tougher as students were evicted from their occupied buildings; at Pisa University, the occupation was cleared out three times, and demonstrating students assaulted by police; other universities went on strike in solidarity with their fellow-students. Trento declared a permanent occupation; only Rome, important for being the largest university and strategically situated in the capital, had not 'moved' by the end of the year; but before 1968 was five weeks old, Roman students also launched themselves into the offensive.

Although in Britain no university had followed the example of the LSE occupation the previous March, by the autumn many students were beginning to feel that the situation was changing. 'I felt something really big was happening,' recalled Martin Jacques, a Manchester University student who had just been elected to the Communist Party's National Executive. 'Suddenly there was a New Left emerging which was not defined by the old traditions or the old issues – it was thinking in a new way and bringing in people who had all these new ideas. In the past I'd been the initiator, now I felt I had to stand back and learn.'

The changing mood was heralded at the Congress on the Dialectics of Liberation in the summer, a blend of the political and the counter-cultural such as had not been seen in Britain before. Organized by R. D. Laing and three fellow-psychiatrists, the two-week Congress saw leading French, American and British left intellectuals – among them Lucien Goldmann, Herbert Marcuse, Laing himself – address audiences of several thousand in an atmosphere that included happenings, drugs, and 'freak-outs'.

The Congress, nonetheless, was devoted mainly to the political rather than to the counter-cultural, as Robin Blackburn, a former student of, and then lecturer at, LSE observed. 'It represented a definite shift to politics compared to events like the counter-cultural poetry festival a couple of years earlier. It was already closer to the political spirit of the late Sixties. A shift away from the CND nuclear pacifist orientation to an attitude which identified strongly with the more revolutionary wing of the Third World countries and with revolutionary movements in the Third World itself.'

Among the speakers, Marcuse, on his return from encouraging the anti-authoritarians in Berlin, left an indelible impression on many in the audience. 'He was brilliant, so delicate and fragile and precise,' David Widgery remembered. 'It was the authentic voice of a recovered Marxism, a lineage that was being reconnected. It was astonishing. There he was – and other middle-aged and quite old people – saying what I actually felt. It was very important to see those one or two figures who stood up not just in solidarity but with a welcome on their faces for us. We felt very isolated – marginal, crazy, an embarrassment to our parents and the authorities – and then we'd see old Marcuse beaming out at his audience as though we were his spiritual children.'

Like most radicalized British students at the time, Widgery was similarly impressed by R. D. Laing, who argued in a number of influential books that adaptation to existing capitalist norms was nothing more than adapting to 'a world gone mad'. 'He was the guru – though no one likes to admit it today – because he put the subjective revolt in an allegedly political framework,' Widgery continued. 'He and others associated with him demonstrated that the "normality" we'd had beaten and taught and learnt into us – family life, being a man, being a woman, being sane – was an excruciatingly artificial construct.'

That summer, Widgery went to the United States. Three years earlier, as a sixteen-year-old, he had been expelled from his grammar school for using the word 'contraceptive' in an unofficial school magazine. Until then the school had tolerated his membership of CND, his long hair, his general rebelliousness, because he was of university calibre. Now, his father, a commercial draftsman, marched him off to work in the local Brylcream factory. There, as at school, music formed a large part of his life.

'The black musicians of America were aristocrats and heroes to me. We'd sit around talking about who played fourth trumpet in Duke Ellington's orchestra and who had the most authentic reproduction of Chicago rhythm and blues sounds. It was all part of a cult – slightly flip, slightly hip . . . And then, one day, my girl friend's father, a middle-class

Communist from the 1930s, produced a pile of old Stalin and Lenin pamphlets from a cupboard. I was terribly interested. Part of the attraction was that they were even more obscure than Chicago rhythm and blues.'

He joined the Young Communist League, then the Young Socialists, the Labour Party's youth organization, which was to all intents and purposes controlled by Trotskyists. 'There were some very formidable people among them, people who saw class politics as their life, and history as the struggle of classes – and they were internationalists. I began to read Victor Serge's novels, Brecht's plays, Mayakovski's poetry. It was a process of discovering the richness of the Bolshevik tradition, of discovering that it had expressed itself in other revolutionary forms in other parts of Europe.'

It was, however, to visit 'the land of opportunity, the land of jazz and the blues' that he went to America. He was immediately overwhelmed by the poverty and violence he saw, North and South. In the deep South he met a group of SNCC organizers with whom he became involved. 'They talked about self-organization, how the black people possessed a culture and how resilient it was, how you couldn't import Northern politics. Their views made a big impression on me. And I can still remember the sound of skulls being cracked as policemen's batons bashed on the heads of black ministers when they were kneeling praying. This wasn't like the stick you got for sitting down in Trafalgar Square – this was the real thing.'

He visited Cuba. 'In Havana I remember having the stupidity to say to a Cuban at one point, "Don't you think guns are a bit . . . well, violent?" I wasn't a revolutionary, just a tourist who still thought of himself as a sort of lefty pacifist who liked jazz. The Cuban just walked us into the student union headquarters and showed us thirty-six pictures of past union officials who had been gunned down by Batista. That was it, you didn't say anything after that.'

Back in the United States, it was the concentration on Vietnam that hit him hardest. When he visited SDS headquarters in Chicago, en route to trying to find a blues club, and saw a poster which said: 'No Vietnamese ever called me a nigger', he felt a deep change in himself. 'That's when things started moving in my mind – from a CND-oriented, non-conformist pacifist, who thought himself a bit hip, into something more serious. Vietnam, the intensity of American racism and the seriousness of the black movement really woke me up. I went back to England determined to stop pissing around.'

On his return, Widgery joined International Socialism, the far-left group, and went to medical school where he soon emerged as an IS student leader. The new militancy which he expressed was reflected in the first Vietnam demonstration called by the Vietnam Solidarity Campaign (VS C) in London in October 1967, after a request from the Resistance in Berkeley for international support. 'That's when we saw that things were changing,' recalled Tariq Ali of VSC. 'Ten thousand people turned up – we'd never imagined that would happen, it was VSC's first demonstration. We weren't calling for "peace" in Vietnam, like the Communist Party, we were calling for victory to the NLF. The mood was very, very militant and the cops were totally taken by surprise. We almost made it into the American embassy – we were on the steps, outside the glass windows with our NLF flags before they got us back. If we'd wanted to, if it had been planned, we could have got in. But I'm glad we didn't because the guards inside were armed.'

It was the beginning of the Vietnam mobilizations which, in 1968, would become increasingly massive and – on one occasion at least – directly confrontational.

The autumn, and the beginning of the new academic year, saw French students mobilizing in large numbers for the first time. The issue, as in Italy, was directly concerned with the student condition: word had gone round of the government's plan to make degree courses more difficult. It was at Nanterre, a new university on the outskirts of Paris, that the agitation was the most notable. Hurriedly built on disused army land – and still under construction in the mid-Sixties – Nanterre was designed to accommodate a part of the swelling student population. Its first drab concrete buildings were barely finished in 1964 when the first two thousand students moved in; three years later, six times the number were studying there. The campus itself was separated by a high wall from the largest *bidonville* or slum in France, inhabited mainly by North African migrants, and a permanent reminder of the 'affluent' society's underbelly. Lacking many facilities, the university had little to offer those students who lived on campus; in 1966, anarchists and Trotskyists attempted unsuccessfully to desegregate the women's dormitories and the police were called in. Moreover, there were constant battles between extreme right law students and left-wing humanities students.

In November 1967, a strike started by sociology students spread rapidly to the whole university. The main reason was that career opportunities for students were becoming scarcer because of a downturn in the economy.

The strike spread to other universities, including the Sorbonne. The student union, UNEF, called a delegates' conference from various universities. 'Although I wasn't an elected delegate, I went to the conference,' Dany Cohn-Bendit, a sociology student at Nanterre, recalled. 'I was amazed by the atmosphere. The UNEF bureaucrats would call on a delegate to speak with the microphone for five minutes, but most of the time they were having whispered discussions and nothing was happening. Several times I asked permission to speak, saying that I had been fighting fascists for the whole year at Nanterre and it gave me the right to speak, but each time they turned me down because I wasn't elected. Finally, I realized I could speak *without* the microphone, so I went up front and told them the students weren't interested in the kind of issues UNEF was raising, and that they should focus instead on the problems of students' everyday life.'

'Nobody knew this funny red-haired man,' remembered Anne Querrien, one of the official delegates at the conference. 'He spoke with a great sense of humour, was very witty. He predicted that within a year the whole university system would be on strike, and everyone laughed. But I thought he was absolutely fantastic and to the point.'

Even Cohn-Bendit could not imagine that he himself would be a key figure in fulfilling his prediction. He was, as Querrien observed, remarkable for his joyful lack of respect for any kind of authority – something that came to him almost from birth, he believed. The second son of German Jewish parents – his father was a lawyer who had been forced to emigrate to France for defending Communists when Hitler came to power – he was born, as he put it, the 'child of liberty'. 'When the war broke out, the French put my father in a sort of camp as a German. He escaped and went into hiding with my mother in south-west France. When the Allies landed in Normandy in June 1944, they thought, "Freedom at last!" and I was conceived. I was born nine months later, *l'enfant de la liberté . . .*'

Shortly after the war, his parents split up and his father returned to Germany. Both children stayed in Paris with their mother. 'My brother Gabriel, who was nine years older and had been born in France like me, influenced me a lot. He was in the French Communist party and left in 1956 [the year of the Russian repression of the Hungarian uprising]. He then became a Trotskyist, then a critic of Trotskyism through the small group Socialisme ou Barbarie, and finally came to anarchism. I went through the whole trajectory with him. That's why it never crossed my mind to join the Communist Party or any Trotskyist or Leninist group. At nineteen, I was already into anarchism. But of a non-violent sort, a type of radical reformism.'

He had spent his last years of secondary education in a progressive boarding school in Germany, which he liked; it was during this time that he chose German nationality because children of Jewish parentage were not liable to military service there. But in fact, as he said, he didn't give 'a damn about nationality' and, both his parents having died, returned to Paris to go to university. 'I wanted to do something useful, like becoming a planner in education, planning for children, but I gave it up when I couldn't keep up with the mathematics, so I registered at Nanterre to study sociology. I went because I had friends there whom I had met in an anarchist summer camp in Italy.'

There he soon made himself known by interrupting the professors and starting debates. 'Look, in high school I hadn't been able to listen passively for an hour, so why should things be different at university . . . At UNEF meetings, we anarchists wanted everyone to participate, not just the leaders, the bureaucrats. We liked being provocative, making fun of all authority, including the leftist groups – especially the Maoists who took themselves so seriously. We liked to have fun ourselves, basically. I remember one evening we had nothing to do. "Where shall we go? To the movies? No, let's go to a *real* show instead." The [Maoist] UJC-ml was having a meeting about China, and the orthodox pro-Chinese Communist Party announced it was sending its activists to disrupt it. Every time someone from the UJC-ml started to speak, he was howled down by the others. They'd even brought whistles. Then the orthodox people started chanting, "Marx! Engels! Lenin! Stalin!" And the others, "Marx! Engels! Lenin! With Us!" "Sta-lin! Sta-lin! Sta-lin!", the first lot shouted, giving the clenched fist salute. "No! Stalin, No! Stalin is finished!" the UJC-ml lot shouted back. It was hilarious, we almost died of laughing that night.'

By the Christmas holiday, the strike at Nanterre was over. But the campus was still restless. For this reason, the Education Minister chose the first day of term, when he hoped not many students would be present, to inaugurate a new sports complex and swimming pool. Surrounded by his officials, the minister had just finished his formal address when, out of the handful of people present, he saw an unknown student approach, holding a cigarette and asking him for a light. 'It was a sudden impulse,' Cohn-Bendit remembered. 'An hour before we didn't even know he was coming. He gave me a light. Then I said to him, "Monsieur le Ministre, you've published a report on youth problems which is ridiculous. You don't mention any of the real problems – for instance, there's not a single word on sexuality in it. What about that?"

'"Young man," he answered, "if you've got problems about that, may I suggest that you take a dip in the swimming pool?" That reminded me of the Nazis' emphasis on sport and cleanliness, so I gave him a mocking Nazi salute.'

Confusion ensued; some cheered, while the minister, surrounded by officials, withdrew. The incident was widely reported in the press; learning that Cohn-Bendit was not French, the minister's office took steps to have him expelled from France. In retaliation, Nanterre students began to take photographs of plainclothes policemen on the campus and to plaster the walls with their pictures. It was the beginning of the agitation that would lead to the creation of new political group at Nanterre – a group that came to play a key role in the start of the French May events of 1968.

By the end of 1967, radicalized students on both sides of the Atlantic were making the connections between their own lives and their societies, between their societies and Vietnam. Increasingly the movements were beginning to influence one another. 'Direct action' tactics, the development of alternative institutions like the free or critical university movement, the search for new theories to give a political coherence to their movements, marked the start of a certain convergence. In each country, it seemed, radical students took what was useful to them from the experiences and tactics of other movements. Thus, the German SDS 'discovered' the black civil rights struggles, FSM and the free university movement at a time when they could put their examples to use; similarly, Turin students found in the anti-authoritarian German SDS, the Berlin 'Critical University' and FSM models that could serve them in their new phase of struggle.

The many other student struggles being waged around the world at the time also had their repercussions. These – in Japan, Spain, Turkey, Chile, China, Czechoslovakia, and other countries – fall outside the scope of this book; but they gave students on both sides of the Atlantic a sense that they were part of an international movement, that they were the wave of history. At the same time, the murder of Che Guevara, the Cuban revolutionary hero, in 1967, created a new international revolutionary icon. He had given up all his official posts in Cuba to fight for revolutionary causes elsewhere, broken with Russian Communism, and attempted to initiate a revolution in Bolivia as a 'second front' to aid the Vietnamese. Finally, arms in hand, he had died fighting the Bolivian military dictatorship. His life exemplified for many the dedicated revolutionary activist who was prepared to put his ideas into practice. On posters and walls, his picture henceforth became an identificatory symbol to student militants.

Above everything, the movements' readiness to pursue confrontational tactics was the decisive factor. 'Direct action' was a response to their feelings that 'rational' discourse had no purchase on their societies, would not, above all, bring to an end an 'irrational' war. These tactics were bound, sooner or later, to run the student movements up against the state's repressive forces which, as events in Germany, Italy and the United States showed, were prepared to pre-empt or crush the perceived threat to the status quo. The stage was being set for the major confrontations of 1968.

Upping the Stakes: January–April 1968

The year began in an astonishing fashion. On 20 January, the Vietnamese National Liberation Front suddenly unfurled its Tet offensive which revealed to an awed and amazed world the vulnerability of the American war machine; almost simultaneously, American financial power was threatened by the strains of the war: a 'gold crisis' undermined the dollar and there were serious fears that the West's post-war financial system might collapse. When, on 31 March, President Johnson announced that he would not stand for re-election because of the growing opposition to the war, and when Martin Luther King, the black civil rights leader and, later, Robert Kennedy, who was seeking the Democratic presidential nomination, were assassinated, the American political system, or at least its normal method of functioning, appeared to be breaking down. Politically, militarily, economically, America was in crisis due to Vietnam and the gathering strength of the anti-war movement.

The manifest vulnerability of the American system brought renewed determination to student and anti-war movements on both sides of the Atlantic. America's weakness could only weaken the capitalist regimes of Western Europe and increase the leverage of student protest, it seemed: in Belgium, university demonstrations overthrew the government at the start of the year. Moreover, the crisis was not confined to the West. Regimes in the Eastern bloc were also being challenged. Students in Poland demonstrated against the Gomulka regime, setting in train a process that would lead to its downfall two years later after working-class riots. In Czechoslovakia, where student protests had already helped the reforming Alexander Dubcek to the leadership of the Communist Party, President Novotny was forced to resign after eleven years in power. The vestiges of Stalinism, it appeared, were there being swept aside peacefully for the first time in the East.

It was without doubt the Vietnamese Tet offensive which had the most dramatic political and inspirational impact on the student world everywhere. After years of being told that an American victory was just around the corner, here was the United States military machine reeling under a Third World peasant army's offensive. 'In that amazing week,' Michael

Thomas in London remembered, 'the NLF managed to infiltrate and fight its way into Saigon and Hue and a great number of other towns. The offensive completely destroyed the political image and confidence of the U.S. It was a shattering blow for the U.S. globally – the most important event of 1968 because it changed the course of history, whereas the next most important event, the Soviet invasion of Czechoslovakia in August, prevented it from changing. In any historical perspective, the events of Vietnam and Czechoslovakia were more important than the student upheavals.'

The 'revolutionary' implications of the offensive were not lost on students. 'It was a world-shaking event that allowed me to imagine what the Russian revolution must have meant for people with socialist ideals,' recalled Peter Tautfest in West Berlin, who at the time did not particularly share those ideals. 'There, next to the American embassy in Saigon the battle was raging from house to house, the NLF's flag was flying over Hue. It was said that students were mainly holding the city. There was no doubt now – the world revolution was dawning . . .'

Whatever the later arguments about the military effectiveness of the Tet offensive, which was finally beaten off by American forces, the initial Vietnamese success significantly raised the temperature of the student movements. This was reflected in the International Vietnam Congress, organized by the German SDS in collaboration with Social Democratic and left-liberal youth groups, which opened in West Berlin a fortnight after the offensive started. The aim of the Congress was to show outright solidarity with the 'victorious' Vietnamese and, 'as a matter of revolutionary practice', to provide a forum for the international movement. American, European and Third World left-wing student groups, including a number struggling clandestinely against dictatorships, were invited; so, too, were deserters' groups and Russian and East German students – the latter two groups not finally attending. It was an emotional event, saluted by telegrams of solidarity from leading left intellectuals on both sides of the Atlantic.

Before the Congress even began, the demonstration planned to conclude it was banned by the West Berlin authorities. There had been trouble only a few days earlier when students threw stones at the sales offices of the right-wing German Springer Press empire which was violently opposed to the student movement. Planned to end in West Berlin's American sector, the demonstration – or certain sections of it – was secretly preparing to storm the U.S. McNear barracks. 'Dutschke had heard from a deserters' group that black GIs would mutiny as soon as the demonstration approached,' recalled Bernd Rabehl, the SDS leader, who was resolutely opposed to this 'adventurist' plan. 'Whether the deserters had reliable information was open to question for a start. But I think also that this piece of exaggerated radicalism was an attempt to show off in front of the Italians and French. There had been talks about it with them beforehand apparently and they had agreed to take part. They certainly turned up in Berlin with helmets, batons, bicycle chains and God knows what else.'

The ban heightened tension in an already tense city as students arrived for the Congress. The excitement at the possibility of defying the ban turned into a sense of triumph when the SDS's lawyer, Horst Mahler, won a last-minute court decision revoking it. The Congress opened in an atmosphere of enthusiasm and militancy on 17 February. Even those like Niels Kadritzke, leader of the much more cautious Social-Democratic student organization SHB, was affected by it. 'Although I couldn't share the SDS people's revolutionary optimism, everybody was carried away by the euphoria, including myself. The international participation at the Congress, the mass demonstration – all this was a completely new dimension which swept one along.'

The Congress hall was dominated by a huge Vietnamese NLF banner and Che Guevara's slogan, 'The duty of a revolutionary is to make the revolution'. Barbara Köster, still in the course of radicalization which had begun with the shooting of the student Ohnesorg the previous year, walked around the hall, taking in the atmosphere. She was excited by it. The big debates on the Vietnamese revolution, the anti-imperialist, anti-capitalist struggle in the advanced West, Latin America and the Vietnamese revolution, were above her head, she recalled. So, too, was the vibrant speech by Hans-Jürgen Krahl, the leading Frankfurt SDS anti-authoritarian, demanding that an international campaign be launched to destroy NATO – a demand which was overwhelmingly approved in the concluding session. 'But the atmosphere was thrilling. I liked this whirling, milling crowd of people. I'd been in England and totally identified with rock music – the Rolling Stones had been my politicization. The atmosphere was a bit like that.'

The daughter of a lawyer and a housewife in Minden, a medium-sized town, Köster had been attracted by the SDS anti-authoritarians for some time. They were the polar opposite of the men she had known until then. 'I lived with this rich guy in Munich, part of the smart set. The men spent their time buying, consuming. I'd spend hours in a boutique with them when a new collection of suits came in. They'd ring each other up and all of them would come to the shop to try the things on. Then we'd go off to a certain coffee house in the Leopoldstrasse [the principal Munich shopping street] and they'd drink whisky and talk about cars. After that it was swimming or a round of golf.'

In the fall of 1967, she decided to transfer from Munich to Frankfurt University; there she attended all the courses by the social and political philosophers of Critical Theory which SDS members frequented. 'I didn't understand a word of what was being said, I hadn't read a line of Marx, but I didn't dare say, Damn it, I don't understand. I was fascinated by the SDSers. I could see that they looked at things differently, had a personal-political motivation I couldn't grasp. But though I wanted to, I didn't dare contact them. I started going to the student cafeteria, which was something totally new for me because before I'd always eaten in restaurants, and looked for a table next to theirs. It wasn't only their intellectual standard but their odd manners which fascinated me. They had dirty fingernails, they didn't stand up when a woman came to their table, didn't help a woman on with her coat. They seemed vaguely interested in me as a woman but there was a barrier between us because I came from this smart set.'

Persevering with the seminars she made one or two contacts among the SDSers. 'I saw that they read a lot. One of them told me he always travelled by streetcar because it gave him ten more minutes to read. I walked to classes so as not to put on weight! So I started reading ten hours a day and said to myself, one day you'll get it. But when I went back to my boyfriend in Munich on weekends, full of enthusiasm about what we were doing, I could never explain why we were doing it. Although I went to all the teach-ins, I didn't really understand what SDS wanted. And to tell you the truth, I still don't today!'

In Berlin, she was preparing for the final Vietnam Congress demonstration when someone thrust a placard into her hand. 'It was of an elderly lady. I didn't want to carry round this picture of a fearful-looking old granny so I exchanged it for one of a good-looking young man. I really didn't know who Rosa Luxemburg and Che Guevara were. But I kept his name in mind. And then the demonstration began.'

'Twenty thousand people marching with red flags in what was the capital of the cold war! Phenomenal, absolutely phenomenal!' recalled Tariq Ali, the British VSC leader, who was one of the official speakers.

'As we marched through the old quarters you felt that the old revolutionary movement was being revived, that history was being re-made.' 'It was there that I first really felt what you could call the spirit of '68,' remarked another of the British contingent, Robin Blackburn. 'It gave me a quite extraordinary sense of a new political climate. All round the city there were little knots of people talking to the demonstrators, asking, "What are you doing this for? You're Communists, you're helping the Communists" – but at the same time willing to listen. It was very inspiring, not a spectacle but a real political event, quite unlike any demo I'd been on before.'

Dany Cohn-Bendit, who was part of the French delegation, was impressed by the broad political mobilization of students. 'That didn't exist in France yet. We had mobilizations against the Vietnam War but none which included university issues. We learnt this from Germany. Their idea of the critical university impressed me. So we invited Karl D. Wolf [national S D S chairman that year] to come to Paris to talk.'

'We are a small radical minority!' chanted the German demonstrators, in an ironic reprise of the media attacks on them. The French and Italian contingents made a great impact on other demonstrators. 'The French impressed me enormously,' Köster recalled. 'They had stationed themselves in a side street and moved at the double with militant precision to take their place in the demonstration.' 'Arms linked, they kept up their *Ho-Ho-Ho Chi Minh!* chants throughout,' Blackburn remembered. 'The demo was communicating a totally new impulse . . .' 'And then the Italian contingent shouting *Che-Che-Che Guevara!* . . . And at the end some black G Is came onto the podium and started singing, "We ain't gonna go to Vietnam, 'cos Vietnam is where I am. Hell no, we ain't gonna go!" The audience went absolutely crazy,' Ali recalled.

The plan, unknown to all but a small S D S group, to storm the barracks had been called off at the very last minute. Already warned by police officers that orders had been given to shoot, Rabehl attended emergency meetings during the Congress with the Protestant bishop. The warnings were repeated: the American military police were under orders to shoot. 'Finally, during the demonstration – but not before,' Rabehl recalled, 'Rudi agreed to call it off. But it wasn't Klaus Meschkat [an old-guard S D Ser] or I who convinced him, it was the bishop.'

Three days after the Berlin demonstration, the city administration, political parties (including the Social Democrats) and major trade unions called for a counter-demonstration. Eighty thousand Berliners, according to police estimates, turned out. Workers and civil servants were given the afternoon off to attend. There were ugly scenes: a female student was knocked to the ground, and a student who looked like Dutschke was assailed by a group chanting 'Lynch him! Hang him!' Thirty five people were injured; nobody had been hurt in the student demonstration. West Berlin was in a state of near civil war.

In the weeks immediately following the Berlin Congress, sections of the West European movements began to turn from protest to resistance. A willingness to fight the police was a sign of the change on both sides of the Atlantic. In Rome, London and Paris street battles occurred, culminating at Easter in the worst riots in forty years in West Germany.

In the Italian capital, unprepared and unarmed, students found themselves engaged in a bitter, five-hour battle with police on 1 March that proved a turning point for the Italian movement. A month earlier, Rome University had joined the wave of occupations, which had been sweeping Italy since the previous autumn, and up to 10,000 students took over their faculties under the nose of the government; it was a move that the political class could no longer ignore.

The occupation was, however, different from the Turin movement, for it did not start from the student condition, and sought immediately to extend the movement outside the university. 'There were many politicized cadres at the University already,' Franco Russo, a Fourth International Trotskyist who was one of the undisputed leaders there, recalled, 'and we took up the issue of anti-imperialism from the start. Vietnam was studied on a mass basis. True, we had our counter-courses, our interruptions of classes, our incursions into the examination rooms where we listened to students being examined [all exams are oral in Italy] and intervened in the discussion over marks to be awarded.'

But the major objectives were the world beyond the university; students organized commissions to investigate the problems of the outlying and underprivileged areas of Rome and to mobilize building workers. They had to fight off fascists and resist police when the usual round of evictions and re-occupations took place. There was, as usual, a sense of liberation at having made the university their own – a sense of liberation heightened for Russo by operating outside the confines of a political party.

'For the first time, we were acting within a real movement rather than through a political party. People organized without anyone dictating the political line. It meant for the first time being the subject of your own political activity. You had to take decisions on the spot – about the police, the government, the comrades who had been arrested. As a leader you had to participate personally all the time: in demonstrations, assemblies, writing, interrupting classes. That was the real impact of 1968.'

On 1 March, Rome students decided to reoccupy the Valle Giulia architectural faculty from which they'd been locked out and to protest against the violence of the previous day's eviction from the faculty of letters, as Franco Piperno, one of the Rome student leaders, recalled.

'We were determined to get back into the architecture faculty. We weren't going to do any one harm or injury in our attempt, but we had tomatoes and eggs to throw at the police if they tried to stop us. There weren't more than two thousand of us. Before we even got into the park [in which the faculty is sited] police in jeeps charged us. There was a moment's panic and dispersal. And then something happened that none of us on the preparatory committee, who had tried to foresee everything, could have imagined. The students fought back. The police found themselves caught in a hail of stones . . .'

'It was the first time we hadn't retreated in front of the police, the first time we took the initiative and advanced on them,' recalled Piero Bernocchi, an engineering student leader. 'It gave us a sense of strength, of doing what we hadn't been able to do before. We were profoundly convinced that we were right to be doing it. We ripped up the wooden park benches and used the planks as clubs.'

'People were prising up the ancient paving stones as weapons, jeeps were set on fire and overturned on their occupants,' Piperno continued. 'The battle went on for five or six hours. We'd thought the police would try to stop us re-occupying, but not that they'd use jeeps and tear gas grenades which they aimed directly at us . . .'

When it was over one hundred and fifty policeman and as many students had been injured. Rome appeared in a state of siege, with police sirens wailing and policemen hunting down students in the streets. The media were already reporting that six, seven, eight thousand students had attacked the police. Noting the sudden change from protest to overt resistance, Piperno observed that the explosion had been 'accumulating strength for months' as students suffered police repression and offered only passive resistance in return. Now there was outrage at the stepping up of police violence. Added to which was the implicit anti-fascist connotation of the students' struggle in taking on a police force unreformed since the fascist era.

'It was a very significant experience in the student movement's and opposition's formation,' Piperno commented. 'The fact that the students fought back contributed to a change in the relationship between police and mass demonstrations. And psychologically it was important that an unarmed demonstration confronting a large police force could take the faculty.'

In the six months from the autumn of 1967 to the following spring, the Italian movement developed into the first 1968-style wave of student struggle in Western Europe. The battle of Rome marked a decisive build-up of the state's counter-offensive against the university occupations which continued to sweep the country. In Pisa, a massive sit-in was attacked by the police, resulting in fifty people wounded and seven arrests. In Milan, whose three universities had thrown their weight into the struggle by the end of February, students trying to reoccupy the Catholic University were charged by police. By the middle of March 1968, 488 Turin students were facing police charges and thirteen arrest warrants had been served on the leaders, some of whom went underground. Laura Derossi, the only woman among them, felt the changes that were affecting both herself and the movement: 'It was already the beginning of the end. Being in hiding awoke all my weaknesses; I was anxious, slept badly, needed consolation. Something had changed. Repression, then and later, made me very fearful.' The daughter of a self-made entrepreneur and housewife, she had until then felt that the Turin movement enjoyed a 'festival-like' quality. 'Even if we resorted to violence, we had no hatred, no rancour, no desire to destroy. We had ideas, things we wanted, we were convinced that our actions to achieve these were right.'

Educated at private Catholic schools, coming from a well-to-do family, she had, from the age of sixteen, begun to rebel in small ways against her background. 'I was brought up at home in a very moralistic atmosphere and had a strict education. I was expected to make a very good marriage, and went to all the parties and dances given by my middle- and upper middle-class friends. At the same time my father, who was a liberal, and my older brother were very influential in making me want to read and learn. It was a family which put great emphasis on culture. Until I was sixteen, though, I believed I was in love with Jesus Christ.'

At seventeen she fell in love with a young Communist, joined the party and became an activist. Most of her friends were expelled as Trotskyists but she felt she had to remain in it because it was 'the party of the workers, of the people'. By now also she was beginning to find in herself this 'very strong will not to create families like those of our parents. I would have stood any torture rather than end up in a monogamous family with children and a job.'

At university she threw herself into student politics and, alongside Luigi Bobbio and Guido Viale, became a well-known leader. The two men had gone underground at the same time as she – the only woman student to be threatened with arrest. Advised to emerge and face trial, all three did so; but while the men were taken into custody she was told that, as a woman, she would be allowed to remain free. 'Before that, in the movement, I had never had the sense of being different, of enjoying fewer rights, being allowed to do less things. I made a terrible scene, showed them that I was so determined that in the end they sent me to jail. But from that moment on I never again felt equal, never!'

After their release from jail, where they spent a week, she and Bobbio married. 'We went to live in an apartment that was a sort of commune, but things had changed. The period of invention, creativity, novelty, wonder, amazement, joy, amusement, change, of happy collective living, was over. I have the memory before that of something like a festival, a play, in which we were deeply motivated, had a great certainty of our rights and needs, a great self-awareness.'

The sense of 'festival' that accompanied a sense of self-liberation was one of the features of the Italian movement in this period. Tired of organizing demonstrations when their leaders were jailed, Turin students took to the streets in a different way. 'We started what we called, I don't know why, the Nōh theatre,' Peppino Ortoleva recalled. 'Once I stood on one side of the main street dressed as a bourgeois in tie, jacket and waistcoat. And on the other side, my friend Andrea called out loudly, "Viale has been arrested!" And I: "Who's Viale?" "A student," came the reply. "A student – ah, the usual rogue!" People would stop in astonishment. It was great fun, enormously liberating.'

In Rome, a small group of students, hostile to the occupation strategy of sending students out to mobilize the working class, employed pranks to unmask the 'repressive spirit' of the left groups. 'On one occasion we brought sheep into the university,' recalled Marco Rostan. 'When the police arrived to clear out the occupation, we walked through the police lines pretending we were shepherds and carrying the sheep.' Known as the 'birds' for their habit of 'roosting' in trees, the group's most notorious exploit was to 'camp' on the dome of a famous seventeenth-century Roman church to demonstrate, among other things, that students took over buildings both for the fun of it and because they had no other place for themselves.

The differences between the Turin and Rome wings of the movement were significant. The former's concentration on an anti-authoritarian struggle within the university and the latter's emphasis on carrying the struggle outside to mobilize the working class appeared somewhat para-doxical, given that Rome was a mainly bureaucratic, white-collar city, while Turin had a large working class centred on the Fiat automobile works. There was little understanding between the two wings. Luigi Bobbio, the Turin leader, was angered by the incomprehension he met in Rome.

'We explained to the people there the importance of our struggle against the professors, university rituals, an authoritarian and manipulative cul-ture. "But that's all rubbish," they said. "Professors aren't important, sure, you can do it, but we must fight against capitalism, make links with the working class." I told them Rome was a city of civil servants, those were the people they should be talking to, but they didn't give a damn. In Turin, we argued that perhaps the working class was more important than us, but our individual voices were as valid as workers' because ours were the voices of liberation. We had a heightened sense of our selves, of the fact that what was at stake was *our* liberation. And we always felt that our liberation must be won by our self-activity.'

In Britain, where the police were kept on a closer rein than elsewhere, and post-war demonstrations had been generally peaceful, there seemed less likelihood of violence. Indeed, police traditionally marched alongside a demonstration both to maintain order and to prevent trouble from counter-demonstrators. There was considerable public shock then when on 17 March violent confrontations with the police broke out during the largest Vietnam demonstration London had yet seen.

It was the second demonstration to be called by the Vietnam Solidarity Campaign (VSC) under its slogan 'Victory to the NLF'. Tariq Ali, the VSC leader, was amazed when he saw the number of demonstrators filling Trafalgar Square. 'Twenty thousand people – the bulk of them university, polytechnic and school students, with a small layer of young workers. The whole of Oxford Street was a sea of red and National Liberation Front flags as the demo marched towards the American embassy chanting "Ho! Ho! Ho Chi Minh! The NLF is going to win!"'

'It was one of the happiest moments of my life,' remembered Rachel

Dyne, an LSE student. 'We took over the whole street as though we could do what we liked, it echoed to the chanting. I felt we were a real force, part of an international movement that could change the course of events on a worldwide scale.'

'The demonstrators didn't do what the police told them, didn't march in neat little categories and territories like on the CND Aldermaston march. That had become so shepherded,' David Widgery remarked, 'that it was like a sheep-dog trial, but this was a pouring onto the streets. Just as the Vietnam War was different in scale, culture and intensity, so VSC had to be different tactically from CND and other movements. VSC was using the weapons of Americanism – the theatricality, the masks. And it pulled in a lot of non-student cultural dissidents.'

Among the latter was Mick Jagger of the Rolling Stones. His song 'Street Fighting Man' was written after the demonstration. 'And there was also a large West Berlin SDS contingent on the march who were put out that no plans existed to seize the embassy,' Ali remembered. 'We had discussed it, but accepted that we couldn't do it. The demonstration was to show our hostility to the Labour government and the Americans in the most effective way possible.'

As the demonstration moved into Grosvenor Square, with the embassy on one side, the police lines broke and the gardens in the centre were suddenly found to be open terrain. Seeing the opening, hundreds of people swarmed in and ran towards the embassy. Widgery couldn't believe his eyes. 'Instead of doing the English thing of nudging the police a couple of times and then moving on, people were actually pushing through the police and running for the embassy steps . . .' Among them was Dave Clark of Manchester University. He had only one thing in mind: to get to the embassy and burn it to the ground. But before he could do so, there were more police lines to break through. As a mounted policeman charged at him, he and another student pulled the horse to the ground.

'We'd worked out in advance how it could be done. There were theories around that lion's dung would scare police horses, and there was even an expedition planned to the Manchester zoo to get some. But I and a bloke from Sheffield University planned that as the horse charged, one of us on each side would grab the reins and pull down. In retrospect it was a crazy thing to do because the horse was just as likely to trample you to death. After we'd done it, the police went absolutely barmy, and I took a real beating from their fists, knees and boots. Fortunately for me, a large group of people behind me saw what was happening and pulled me back. We'd planned beforehand if anyone got attacked by the police, the rest of us would rescue them. Still, it was quite an experience being beaten by the English police.'

During the couple of hours that the fighting continued, police hurled back smoke bombs thrown by demonstrators, dragged people away by their hair and badly beat a number. Some student demonstrators, like David Smith, of Lancaster University, were alarmed by the violence. 'I remember thinking, thank God I'm not in the middle of that! I was a middle-class lad, and suddenly the police were attacking people with great ferocity. There was blood and I thought it was very scary – but there was also something very exciting about it, a sense of bridges being burnt, a Rubicon crossed.'

By the standards then prevailing, a dramatic change in both demonstrators' and police attitudes had taken place. Widgery helped to carry away a friend with blood flowing from a scalp wound; shortly afterwards he met some French students. '"If only we French were like you English in Grosvenor Square," they said. "Well, we're pretty tough in London, you know," I answered. And that was little more than a month before the May events in Paris and they were fighting against riot police, tear gas, and putting up barricades!'

From the New Year on there had been an increasing number of illegal anti-war demonstrations in Paris which the police dispersed by force. André Liber, a lycée student activist of the Maoist UJC-ml, recalled that his organization copied the system of secondary rendezvous used by the Algerian War resisters. 'In each group there was only one person who knew which metro station we were going to. And when we arrived, there was another person waiting who knew where the demonstration was really to be held. It was fun to organize. The police never knew until the last minute where we would strike. That's how we managed to lob Molotov cocktails through the windows of the South Vietnamese embassy one day.'

Confrontations not only with the police but with extreme right-wing groups over Vietnam were becoming more frequent. 'We learnt karate with left-wing lycée teachers to defend ourselves from the fascists,' Liber continued. 'Fighting them became a major thing in our lives. When they held a meeting to support the puppet South Vietnamese regime we decided to attack it and bought workers' hard hats. But we found the meeting was protected by heavy lines of Gardes Mobiles [militarized police corps] with their helmets and truncheons. I and all my friends were in the front line facing them. Suddenly one of us gave the order to charge. It was the first time this had ever happened. The Gardes Mobiles were stunned, they'd never seen anything like it. We charged, but they were a lot stronger than us and we got a beating!'

The Maoists fled but regrouped down the street where they were attacked by municipal police. 'These we could handle better! There was a pile of paving stones handy nearby and we used them. The police only had plastic shields which split when the cobbles hit them,' Liber added. From then on every rally ended in a violent confrontation with police. 'We would form a defensive line behind which our comrades could retreat. The cops charged the line. It was frightening, but we were as impressive as they with our helmets and clubs, and so I guess they were as frightened of us as we of them. We were exactly like the police, stupid and disciplined. In these conditions, it's quite easy to fight them.'

The Trotskyist JCR was also organizing Vietnam demonstrations in Paris. On 20 March, one of these ended with windows in the American Express offices being shattered. Six Nanterre students were arrested the following day *in their homes*: a previous rumour that the university Chancellor kept a 'black list' of activists now seemed confirmed. A general assembly of students was called on 22 March and voted for Dany Cohn-Bendit's proposal to occupy the administrative high-rise. It was the first occupation of a French university.

'Being very cautious as always, I proposed that we occupy the bottom floor only,' Cohn-Bendit remembered. 'There were a couple of hundred cops on the campus, and there had been a small fight. It was Duteuil [a radical French anarchist and close friend of Cohn-Bendit] who insisted that we go to the Chancellor's office at the top of the high-rise to look for the black lists. Somebody had made duplicate keys of his office. It was one of our principles to try to open locked doors, either real or imaginary, whether in buildings, institutions or in the mind.'

Once in the Chancellor's office, the one hundred and fifty students held an assembly. The 'extremists' wanted to wreck the office but were headed off by the JCR and Cohn-Bendit. A quick search for the 'black lists' proved unsuccessful; the question now became what to do next. Cohn-Bendit organized the discussion; he impressed Prisca Bachelet, who had never met him before. 'He had a totally democratic, personal style, and a remarkable sense of humour. During the discussion I had an idea and I went up to him so that he could pass it on to the assembly. "Go on, tell it to us all yourself," he said. I'd never experienced anything like that before in leftist groups – there it was only the leaders who spoke.'

From the assembly came the proposal, put forward by Cohn-Bendit and the JCR, to organize an anti-imperialist day at Nanterre for the following Friday, 29 March. 'The JCR wanted a large meeting. I was more for discussions in small groups, combined with occupations,' Cohn-Bendit recalled. '"If there are twenty of us, we'll occupy a classroom. If we're one hundred, several classrooms. If we're five hundred, a whole building. And if we're a thousand . . ." The idea of occupying came to us from America and Germany.

'My proposal won the day. After the night-long occupation we left, having decided to write a leaflet explaining why we had occupied and calling for the anti-imperialist day. A dozen of us from different groups went off to get it printed. But who was to sign it? As we disagreed among ourselves on many issues we couldn't sign on behalf of our organizations. So we decided instead to sign it, "Le mouvement du 22 mars".'

Given the sectarianism of the French student movement to date, the 22 March Movement was a new phenomenon. It was made up of students divided by their different political beliefs but united by a common will to act, and a pact that all decisions would be taken by general assemblies. Without formal leaders, without common theoretical positions, the new movement was to play a key role in the May events that were shortly to rock France and astonish the world.

As the tide of militancy rose, so too did the counter-forces working to stop it. In the United States, leading anti-war activists – including Dr Benjamin Spock, the famed 'baby care' writer and pediatrician – were indicted for conspiring to aid young men to avoid the draft; and many anti-subversive agencies dormant since the witch-hunting 1950s were resurrected to crush the movement, the Black Panther Party in particular. Only later would it be confirmed that the Johnson administration and the FBI had initiated a special counterintelligence program – COINTELPRO – systematically to disrupt and infiltrate the movement.

The counter-forces did not operate exclusively within the government. One assassination – that of Martin Luther King – and the attempted assassination of Rudi Dutschke by a neo-fascist in the streets of Berlin – were pivotal events in April. In the United States, riots and rebellions broke out in 167 cities and on innumerable campuses in response to the King slaying. 'Harlem was on fire, all hell was breaking loose,' recalled Bill

Sales, a leader of the Student Afro-American Society at Columbia University, bordering on Harlem. 'The people took to the streets, police were running around cracking heads, fires were blazing. It was the first time I'd seen such social disruption where there was a real life-and-death situation.' Although Sales, who was influenced by the Black Power movement, did not support King's non-violence and moderation, he was shocked by his assassination. 'But in Harlem I saw people were really hurt in the gut by it. They weren't intellectuals like we were, arguing that his line was wrong, that he was an apologist for the system. They may not have agreed with him but they were outraged that he had been shot.'

For the first time in several years, black and white students marched together in demonstrations to protest the killing. Two black students had already been fatally shot and forty others wounded by the South Carolina National Guard when they protested against segregated bowling facilities; and several bombings of campus buildings, notably those of the Reserve Officer Training Corps, had occurred. Starting the previous autumn with Stop the Draft Week and the Pentagon march, the move from protest to open resistance was encouraging, as Steve Hamilton noted, 'the more revolutionary elements within the anti-war movement. The more limited, reform-minded elements and pacifists were being pushed to the sidelines.'

Students in West Germany had just staged demonstrations over the King assassination when Dutschke was critically wounded by his would-be assassin, a twenty-three-year-old house painter. The student leader was sitting on his bicycle waiting for a chemist to open to buy medicine for his three-month-old son when the painter approached and asked if he were Dutschke. Drawing a revolver, he fired three shots, one of which hit Dutschke in the head; the latter staggered fifty metres and collapsed. (Though paralyzed, he recovered the ability to speak; after two years, he was able to resume his studies, going to Cambridge until the British Conservative government refused him permission to remain in England; eleven years after the assassination attempt he died of the brain damage that had been inflicted.)

Dutschke's critical wounding sparked off a virtual student insurrection in West Germany and the heaviest street fighting since the Weimar Republic forty years earlier. Two people were killed, four hundred injured, some of them seriously, and one thousand arrested in the five days of battle over Easter. The main targets of the insurrection were the Springer Press buildings. For months the right-wing press empire had been vilifying the student movement. An incendiary headline in one of its mass-circulation papers the previous February proclaimed: 'Stop the Young Reds' Terror Now – Don't Leave All the Dirty Work to the Police and Their Water Cannons.' It was an incitement, students felt, to actions like Dutschke's shooting.

In major West German cities, 60,000 people blockaded Springer buildings. 'There was a readiness for violence now which came from an enormous rage,' recalled Barbara Brick, of the Munich SDS. 'We were out for war now, civil war. If it hadn't been so, we wouldn't have built barricades with other people's cars, without thinking for a moment to ask their owners. Wouldn't have overturned a bus as a matter of course and set fire to it. Yes, emotionally we declared war, at first primarily on the media which killed people by its defamations and slanders.'

Bernd Rabehl, whose long friendship with Dutschke had earlier become strained, now felt guilty that he and others had not done more to protect him. 'We knew there had been threats on his life. I had seen his car surrounded by a dozen taxis whose drivers wanted to beat him up during the International Vietnam Congress. We should have protected him as any political leader in this society has to be protected, protected him in spite of – no, rather because of – the chaotic personal life he had to lead due to all the threats. His American wife was pregnant and scared, and she wanted to leave, he couldn't take care of her or their son, and he felt guilty about it because that was what he really wanted to do, he could never finish an article because he couldn't live in his apartment on account of the threats and couldn't get hold of the books he needed . . . But instead of helping him with his private life, we were preoccupied with our own quarrels, we joked about his personal life – perhaps because all of our own lives were in such disarray. Relationships which had been stable for years were falling apart, a chaos of attitudes and behaviour was taking over. In the process part of one's own identity was lost . . .'

At a mass meeting a few hours after the assassination attempt, Rabehl called for the Springer offices in West Berlin to be stormed. 'I didn't hesitate for a second, I felt that I simply owed it to Rudi. The Springer campaign had already been prepared, we had an objective, an analysis, facts and figures ready to hand for teach-ins. Now one could really "agitate" . . . The events made us realize clearly that we had an historic role to play. Our adversaries were taking us seriously, attacking us. The student movement had become a mass movement, had a long-term political perspective. As everyone came to realize this, we began to make more serious attempts to draw up a programme, to come to grips, for instance, with the labour movement.'

Some fifty West Berlin students broke through police cordons and got into the Springer headquarters; but then withdrew to avoid violent clashes with workers and employees inside. But outside they seized newspaper trucks and set fire to them. The battle went on through the night, with police bringing in water cannon to fight off the demonstrators. Even harder battles were to be fought in Frankfurt and Munich. But it was less the heavy street fighting than the mass of new recruits who had joined the students that was significant.

'Suddenly great numbers of young workers showed up. That was the big change,' Detlev Claussen remarked, 'it was no longer a student movement. I think a lot of these youths were more interested in fighting the police than in the political content of the demonstrations, but they were there. You couldn't talk about a student movement now, it was the Extra-Parliamentary Opposition, the only real opposition in this country. And that's how we understood it at the time.'

One of the new working-class recruits was Michael Köhler, who had wanted to join SDS after the shooting of the student Ohnesorg the year before. A locksmith by trade, he was working as a servant in a hotel on the outskirts of Berlin at the time. 'As soon as I heard the news of Dutschke's shooting, I took off my apron. "I have to go to the city immediately!" The two women who ran the hotel warned me, but they really didn't understand what was going on inside me. I joined the demonstration heading for the Springer headquarters. I'd had no experience of demonstrations. When I saw the newspaper trucks going up in flames I thought it was great, not in the sense – well yes, in the sense that something was being destroyed. Some people were throwing things. I didn't. I was just there, demonstrating my outrage.'

The Extra-Parliamentary Opposition's first target was the media. 'Action Committees of Workers, Pupils and Students' printed their own daily papers in an attempt to combat media bias; and in West Berlin they demanded an hour a day to put their case on the publicly financed and controlled radio and TV network as well as seats on their supervisory boards.

The Easter events mobilized not only working-class youth but brought into the Extra-Parliamentary Opposition a wave of mainly unpoliticized middle-class youth and even an occasional right-wing sympathizer like Michael von Engelhardt. Brought up in early youth by his middle-class

Nazi grandfather, for whom Hitler's SS still remained a 'national elite', Engelhardt had, until 1967, despised student protest for its 'meekness'. But on the second day of demonstrations in Frankfurt, his home town, he turned out. 'I had an incredible emotional feeling of being part of this mass of people, the power relations had been reversed. We broke through the police lines to get to the city hall, and the police attacked. That clarified things for me. The Easter events were the beginning of my political life.'

Dany Cohn-Bendit, who was in Frankfurt for personal reasons, was not unduly impressed by the combativeness of German students. 'When, for instance, a contingent of mounted police charged us demonstrators, I stood there and was about to throw a bicycle between the horses' legs because I felt the police were attacking me. I assumed the others would do the same. But suddenly I realized I was totally alone. In France, by contrast, violent clashes with police and right-wing groups were a matter of course, although the mass mobilization I was witnessing in Germany hadn't taken place there yet. But there was a large gap between the verbal militancy and the reality in the German streets.'

'I remember this red-haired boy, open-mouthed, during the Springer actions,' Detlev Claussen recalled. '"We'll do this in Paris, too!" he said, and told us a bit about the 22 March Movement. And we thought, Well, he's just a young lad, but he'll do all right. A month later the whole world knew about him. How he grew in that month, it was unbelievable! Put someone in a specific historical situation and they become completely different people. I saw it happen a lot then, but never so spectacularly as in his case.'

In Hanover, Beate Schmidt, SDS member, was among those who, after blocking off the Springer building, was arrested and thrown into jail. 'We quickly found out how to create the maximum disturbance, banging on the heating pipes and singing the "Internationale". The prison was in an uproar all night.' When she and the others were released in the morning, they were welcomed outside the prison by old Communist Party members and former left-wing concentration camp inmates – but not by fellow SDSers. The lack of personal solidarity, which had left Dutschke vulnerable, was symptomatic of the movement's failure to take care of its own members at a human level – a failure that was repeated when Schmidt and four others were facing trial. 'SDS offered us only the barest of advice and had no defence strategy at all. The SDSers were fine when it came to "spectacular" actions on behalf of the defendants, but they didn't want to bother themselves with any of the shitwork in between. The people who really helped was a group of women – girlfriends and wives of SDSers but not members themselves – who got together to form a legal aid group, while I took on the responsibility for organizing our defence.'

While for many of those in the movement political involvement appeared to justify a divorce from direct concern with the personal problems of fellow-members – a phenomenon confined not solely to West Germany – the fatal injuries to a press photographer and a student during the street fighting in Munich led to a major debate in the Extra-Parliamentary Opposition. The uncertainty about which side was responsible for the deaths added to the tensions which were finally resolved by the decision encapsulated in the slogan: 'Violence against things – yes; violence against people – no.' But the violence stemmed more from the police than from the movement. 'We'd talk to the policemen, be friendly,' recalled Barbara Brick in Munich. 'And they'd talk back. But the moment they got the order to attack, it was as if a film came over their eyes. You could see it. You'd still be talking and they'd club you. Once the order came to stop they'd start talking again. It was just foolish, I began to think, to fight people who could turn themselves into automatons. Street fighting as a strategy came to seem more and more absurd to me.'

Other students, however, began to discuss how they could fight the police more effectively. A week's vain struggle led them to consider new forms of fighting back, among them organized underground struggle which, in a few minds, started to become more than a theoretical consideration.

Dutschke's attempted assassination provoked solidarity demonstrations in New York, Berkeley, Toronto, London, Paris, Rome, Milan, Belgrade and Prague among many other cities. It was the first time that an event affecting a student movement in one country led to student protests internationally.

In Paris, the German SDS students contacted the leftist groups. As Cohn-Bendit recalled, 'both the UJC-ml Maoists and the JCR Trotskyists wanted the demo but weren't on speaking terms, so they couldn't possibly organize it together. The 22 March Movement became the go-between. We had to arrange different rendezvous so that, as we marched, the JCR could join us at one and the UJC-ml at another, later one. They both arrived in full marching order, protected by their own teams of marshals. In the Place de l'Odéon we held a meeting and it was the first time I talked with a loudspeaker. That's what put me on the map.'

In London, Tariq Ali immediately rang up all the leading Vietnam Solidarity Campaign members. 'It was Easter and there was a big CND march. "We must have a big VSC banner and megaphones and try to take the whole march to the *Daily Mirror* building [site of the Springer offices in London]," I said. And that's what we did. A large crowd broke away from the march and demonstrated outside the building. The *Mirror* offered us a whole page the following week to explain why we were protesting, and published it.'

It was on the other side of the Atlantic, however, that one of the bitterest clashes occurred. 'We called a demonstration outside the Springer offices at Rockefeller Center,' recalled Jeff Jones, the SDS regional organizer who had been at the Pentagon. 'I was in a karate class with the Mother-fuckers [a self-defined anarchist counter-cultural New York street gang] and that morning we left the class, went to a bar and fortified ourselves with some beer. Meanwhile people marched from Columbia to meet us. And that demonstration was very militant, it turned into a street fight. I think there were eight felony and fourteen misdemeanour arrests. There were beatings on both sides. The militancy generated there, I've always main-tained, carried over to a week later when they occupied Columbia. It was the same people and the momentum was building.'

The Columbia rebellion, which began on 23 April, arose out of the many contradictions affecting the prestigious Ivy League university in New York. War-related research work, slum-landlordism, racism on campus and off – the latter most notably in the university's attempt to usurp a neighbouring Harlem public park to build a gym – were among the most prominent of these. The occupation also revealed how far the American movement had travelled in the four years since the Berkeley FSM, the factions into which it was splitting, the emergence of an SDS leadership committed to revolution and, more generally, the elan of '68'.

It was the gym issue which was to bring black students to play a leading role in the Columbia events. To be built on public land, the gym would exclude Harlem residents. But at first, as Bill Sales of the Student Afro-American Society (SAS), recalled, he and other black students at Columbia did not see the racism involved. 'We went down there one time and said, "Look, man, this line of stopping the gym is wrong. You can't stop Columbia from building it. The fix is in. But you can get an equal share." We didn't realize that we were saying, separate but equal. They looked at us and said, "No. The gym is not going to be built, and that's it."

And that's when we began to see that, because we thought we knew so much, we had missed the point altogether. We began to develop a better appreciation that "ordinary folks", as we saw them, are much closer in their guts to what's really happening than we were.'

Sales came from a Northern black family; his father, a college graduate, had worked for most of his life as a skilled laborer. A good student, Sales had never doubted that he would go to an Ivy League college. First at the University of Pennsylvania, where he was one of seventeen blacks in a student population of seventeen thousand, he went on to Columbia to study international relations. As a Northerner, he had never identified with SNCC, had found its idea of 'redemptive suffering' unpalatable; his memories of the civil rights movement were rather of 'the violence and the murders' in the deep South. 'We missed the human drama, had no real understanding of the profundity of what had happened in the South since Reconstruction. Our general orientation to the Southern movement was that those folks didn't know what they were doing. They needed to bust some heads. We were chauvinistic, aggressively militant when it wasn't dangerous to be so. We were elitist. Just about everything one could do wrong we did.'

At Columbia, he came closer to Malcolm X's views and identified with Black Power, read Frantz Fanon and began study classes with other SAS members in Marxism – Mao in particular – black history and culture. By 1968, a sense of impending crisis started to make itself felt.

'There's this tremendous ferment. You get up in the morning and you look for the demonstration. You look for the protest. You look for something to be different before nightfall. It was natural. John Coltrane [the black jazz musician] died in 1967 at age thirty-nine. Malcolm X was killed. Che Guevara dies. King dies. It all fit together.' At the same time, he and other black radicals would have nothing to do with their white counterparts. 'We were so angry at the time we didn't want to hear anything from anyone who was white. The style of SDS put us off, not the goals of demonstrations which we always supported but the lack of seriousness. "These crazy white boys." When we moved it was serious. No one could say, "These kids aren't dressed right" or "They're acting crazy".'

It was a surprise move, then, when SAS students joined the rally on 23 April called by SDS which led to the Columbia rebellion. The gym was but one of the issues. Threatened suspension of SDS activists over their protests at Columbia's links with war-related research, and the university's ban on indoor demonstrations were others. 'But SDS was going to challenge the disciplinary rulings that day and the "jocks" were going to be there,' Sales explained. 'We went to kick ass. But there were thousands of people there, the radical forces were in the majority.'

The radical forces were unsure what to do, however. After marching to the administrative offices and finding the doors locked, they made for the gym site where they started to tear down the fences; but when police arrived rapidly and fist fights broke out, SDS leader Mark Rudd called on the protesters to return to the main quad where the rally had started. There they listened to more speeches. At the end of his speech, Sales said: 'What are white people going to do? It looks like today you're here to take care of business. Do I need to say more?'

The students made off for the undergraduate administrative center in Hamilton Hall which was open, locked the dean in his office, and occupied the building. 'Then we set up an integrated steering committee,' Sales recalled. 'But SDS was confused. It was going through its participatory democracy thing. Decisions were being made and reversed every fifteen minutes. We said, "Man, we can't deal with this madness. These people are crazy. They've got to go." So we told them, "If you want to do something that's relevant, grab as many other buildings as you can. But you guys got to leave. This is ours."'

Participatory democracy had been rebuffed; at 4 a.m. the white students left and took over the administrative offices in the Low Library; the next day they seized the mathematics building, and school of architecture in Avery Hall, and Fayerweather, which housed the social sciences and history departments. The occupation lasted eight days. The Hamilton students contacted the black community for support and supplies; fearing a Harlem riot if the black students were evicted, the administration did nothing to dislodge the whites either.

As the students set about organizing their small spaces of liberated territory, the vast changes in both the black and white student movements since the days of SNCC and the Berkeley Free Speech Movement were revealed. No longer was there any over-arching concept of the beloved community or of participatory democracy. The pressure of the war, the need to find new strategies for confronting state power and changing society, had created many disparate and conflicting visions of what role the student movement should play. Some of these visions, which had their counterparts in SDS at large, were reflected in the Columbia SDS chapter: the 'Praxis-Action' group which supported the new working-class theory of students; the 'Action Faction', led by Mark Rudd, which urged escalation of confrontational tactics to raise students' radicalism; the (Maoist) Progressive Labor (PL) whose strategy of building a student-worker alliance led it to deprecate hippie lifestyles or any actions that might alienate the working class; and counter-cultural forces which urged the values of personal liberation.

Like a topographical map, these and the many other tendencies within the movement could be seen positioned in the different buildings that had been occupied. The Low Library became the center for the activities of the more political SDS members, PL included, who spent much of their time systematically examining the university's files. Mathematics was for off-campus 'crazies', the Motherfuckers among them; Fayerweather mixed counter-cultural types, graduates, liberals and some heavy student politicos; while the blacks kept Hamilton. Their styles accorded with their different visions of the struggle.

'Mathematics was a bastion of militancy, a liberated zone,' recalled Jeff Jones, the SDS regional organizer, who had joined the other off-campus occupiers. 'We elected a government, put a lot of energy into trying to figure out what building we would seize next. The assumption was that we would just keep seizing buildings till we had the whole thing. It was the culture of total resistance to society.' Out of Mathematics came some of the early lore and many of the future members, among them Jones, of Weatherman, the section of SDS which went into clandestine armed struggle in 1970.

Fayerweather, on the other hand, offered spontaneity, visions of personal and social liberation, films, concerts, endless political arguments, votes and re-votes. 'The political discussions were like nothing I'd ever heard before,' recalled Richard Eagan. 'It was like blowing away these cobwebs from the dark corners of the attic of the past, and having the world make perfect sense to me.' In one of the high points, the political and the personal were brought together in 'the wedding in the revolution'. Eagan and Andrea Boroff were approached with the idea of getting married.

'It was seen as a statement of unity and a way to hold the building,' Boroff recalled. 'Since we were already planning to get married, we said, "OK. What the hell!" It was as simple as that. They found the campus chaplain and he climbed in a window. Somebody got me a pair of white jeans and a white sweater, and I got all loaded up with jewelry that anybody in the place had. Somebody got Richard a Nehru jacket, a Black Power pin and a bunch of beads. A woman whose name I never found out handed me this ring. "Here," she said, "it's my grandmother's, I want you to have it." We went out on the balcony and the chaplain proclaimed us children of the new age. They had somehow gotten three hundred candles into the place. There were flowers. There was cake. They took us out and marched us around campus with people banging on pots and pans. It was sheer madness. Someone had keys to some faculty office and they gave us a honeymoon suite.'

In Hamilton, the black students had 'everything organized, under control,' Sales remembered. 'The place had to be spotless, no bullshit wildness. It was systematic, almost regimented. That helped people with their fears. We trained for possible police attack, students were drilled on what to do in case of tear gassing. We had bricks but no guns. The decisions were made by what I would later recognize as democratic centralism. We would discuss every position for hours, but once we took that position that was it. Everybody held to it. Only certain people talked to the press. We knew how to do press conferences. We had four people up front talking and eighty behind – everybody glaring.'

When, after a week, negotiations failed to end the occupation, the university president called in the police to retake the buildings. Each responded in much the way that it had organized its occupation. Maintaining their discipline to the end, the black students marched out of the open building in drill formation to waiting vans; and the police were disciplined. But at Low and Fayerweather, where passive resistance was adopted, and in Mathematics, where the occupiers blocked the door with furniture, the police beat and dragged the students out. Then police plainclothesmen swept through the campus, striking indiscriminately at all students, up to two hundred of whom were injured. It was this last police charge that swung almost the whole of the university community to the side of the students. As at Berkeley four years earlier, a strike of academics and students began the next day, bringing the university to a halt; in its place, and with the help of sympathetic faculty members, the movement created its own university within the shell of the old.

'It was exhilarating, there was suddenly a tremendous explosion of opportunities for learning,' recalled Bob Hall, a graduate student. 'You could talk about issues like Vietnam and the role of higher education. Faculty people were being drawn into debate with graduate and undergraduate students. That's where the barriers and hierarchies just fell apart. It was a much richer experience.'

But this vision of a reformed university was not the one that concerned the increasingly revolution-oriented SDS militants, like Jeff Jones, for whom the strike was a 'political weapon'. It had to be permanent, had to be extended to other campuses in order to force the state to send in troops and weaken the war effort in Vietnam. 'Creating a confrontation with the university administration, you could significantly expose the interlocking network of imperialism as it was played out on campuses. You could prove that they were working hand-in-hand with the military and the CIA and that ultimately, when you pushed them, they would call upon all the oppressive apparatus to defend their position from their own students. That was SDS's most militant and far-reaching period.'

Although more students were now prepared to battle with the police, the gap between those who wanted to further the strike and the SDS 'Action Faction' which was concerned with escalating the confrontation opened up space for a third force. Despite further campus confrontation with the police, the Action Faction lost its leadership of the strike movement to this new liberal force, Students for a Restructured University, which – with a $40,000 grant from the Ford Foundation – came to represent the majority student concern for university reform. The month-long strike was brought to an end.

The same gap between the increasingly revolutionary positions of the SDS leadership and the mass of students was seen when one million students all over the country staged the largest student strike in history. The 'Ten Days of Protest' against the war, called by SDS itself but conducted almost exclusively *outside* the organization, were overwhelmingly peaceful and orderly. Coinciding with the Columbia strike, they demonstrated that, while the student movement was continuing to grow, the mass of students still appeared to opt for traditional forms of action, including electoral politics, to stop the war.

Nonetheless, it was the revolutionaries who were going to make most of the running in the next two years. SDS had travelled a distance that was bringing it closer to the West European movements. In fact, the French May events, which broke out during the Columbia strike, sustained the SDS revolutionaries in their hopes. 'Heady days!' remembered Jeff Jones. 'Tie in Columbia with what was happening in Paris, where it appeared that the government might actually fall and there might be a new left revolution . . .'

The Columbia strike was soon overshadowed by events in Europe, especially in Paris that May. To students like Mike Wallace the news from Paris was electrifying. 'Holy shit! Look what we set off,' he recalled himself saying. 'The sense that we were plugged into an international explosion was breathtaking.' In many minds Paris and Columbia became forever linked. To Steve Fraser, then moving toward the Labor Committee and its theory of the mass strike derived from Rosa Luxemburg, 'the Columbia strike was the embryo. For a while it set up a dual institution, a new kind of university with different loyalties, different allegiances, which did not pay attention to the old structures of authority. Of course, Paris was just that. Paris was the bigger, better macro-historic example. Paris was the confirmation. The moment had arrived. We were now entering a period like 1905. Paris is the mass strike on a society-wide level. It was changing the whole balance of power in the world.'

Hari Dillon, then a member of P L, saw Paris as critical. 'The reality of a national strike started by students but spreading to the working class had a huge impact ideologically in this country. When it appeared that the French Communist Party sold out the 1968 uprising, that boosted the prestige of the pro-China Marxist-Leninists.' To Bruce Franklin, it was the interrelatedness of the events of 1968 that was so striking. 'Even for the sake of analysis they are intimately interwoven. Tet, the upheavals of April, the next wave that came in May and April, the victories of McCarthy and Kennedy in the primaries. And then the growing awareness that the financial underpinning of the empire was questionable. This is, after all, the point in history when the price of gold broke. May '68 in France was a manifestation of weakness of U.S. imperialism and the growing strength of the revolutionary forces. In the U.S. people saw the French rebellion as inspirational. It was that demonstration in support of the rebellion in France which led to the first actual street fighting in Berkeley and the first trashing. In the back of people's minds was Stop the Draft Week, and the street fighting didn't just last one night. It went on for several nights. In form, things didn't seem so far apart.'

The moment was euphoric. When asked seventeen years later what he thought was going to happen, Paul Buhle replied, 'I thought I would be head of the party school in the New Left international that would grow out of S D S. If people wearing Levis and wanting to dance to rock 'n roll was some kind of a sea change, then this was the next sign of that change. It was massive. It was widespread. In S D S we had some contacts with these other student movements – the German S D S, the Japanese Zengakuren, the French students. We knew they were the same as us, and that they too were on the cutting edge of history. We assumed there would be something like a new international. Obviously it was so incredibly unworkable as to be loony to think of it. But on the other hand that was one direction things could go. The popularity of the Beatles and the Rolling Stones and Dylan, and whatever, gave you the idea that there was no way to predict how a revolution could take place, but you were a part of a mighty and unstoppable human surge.'

5

The Movements Challenge
the Established Order

The French May, 1968

The 'May events' in France, watched with awe and fascination on both sides of the Atlantic, were the apogee of the student 1968 and all it represented. Here was a student movement that had barely existed in force six months before, taking on and shaking a seemingly secure and authoritarian regime. Here were students catalysing the largest general strike in French history at a time when, even on the left, it was widely held that the working classes were so firmly integrated into capitalist society that no sudden cataclysm could occur. Here was a challenge to the social order which fitted no preconceived pattern and that burst on the world without warning.

Given what was to come, it all started in a small enough way. On 2 May, an ultra right-wing commando attacked a student union office at the Sorbonne in Paris. It was part of a continuing fight between right- and left-wing students that had become more bitter in recent months. The same day, leaflets circulated saying that right-wingers were going to 'exterminate the leftist vermin' at Nanterre. Left-wing students there called on Maoist militants trained in street fighting to help them protect the university. Two to three hundred of these Maoist students, with helmets, clubs, catapults and ball-bearings, took up position early in the morning of 3 May. Robert Linhart, the UJC-ml leader, was there.

'We put down oil so that enemy vehicles would skid, broke down the barbed wire fence that separated the university from the shanty town so that immigrant workers could come to help us in case of battle, organized students in self-defence groups – but no fascist dared show his face that day.'

Looking out of his window on that early morning, the dean of the Faculty of Letters was reported to have said that he thought 'a foreign army' was occupying his university, and closed Nanterre *sine die*. UNEF, the students' union, called a meeting at the Sorbonne the same day to protest the right-wing threats. Nanterre activists attended. 'It was a ridiculous meeting,' Dany Cohn-Bendit recalled, 'there were barely two hundred of us, the leaders and activists of the groups but nobody else.' After the meeting, rumours circulated that the right-wingers were marching on the Sorbonne. Student marshals were posted on guard at the entrances, a few table legs were torn off as weapons and a sit-in organized. Called in by a panicky Chancellor, the police arrived.

'They surrounded the building,' Cohn-Bendit remembered, 'and we agreed that they should check our identity cards and then let us go. But in fact they only let the women go. They shoved the men into police vans and started taking us down the Boulevard Saint-Michel.'

Calling in the police to the Sorbonne was an extraordinary move; even during the height of the mobilizations against the Algerian War the police had never dared venture into the Sorbonne, which remained firmly student 'territory'; moreover, the Chancellor's action infringed all notions of the university's traditional independence, its freedom of expression and critical thinking.

It was a serious mistake on the government's part; but the consequences were even more extraordinary. As the police vans drove off, they were spontaneously attacked by students; Hélène Goldet, one of those allowed to leave the Sorbonne, was among them.

'It was great! Who started it, I don't know, nobody knows to this day. People just didn't like seeing that huge column of black police vans carting off those who'd been arrested. They ripped up the iron gratings from around the trees on the pavement to block the vans, threw everything they could lay their hands on at them, burnt newspapers to prevent the motorcycle police getting through. It was a great battle, a festival! I felt happy. The violence was restoring to the student movement what it had lost since the end of the Algerian War.'

Inside the vans nobody knew what was happening. Maurice Najman, the high school leader who had gone by chance to the Sorbonne that day and been arrested, was amazed as bottles, ashtrays and mustard pots taken from cafés rained against his van. 'I kept thinking, how's this possible? All the student leaders felt the same. Who was organizing the battle if they were all in the vans? "Are these your people?" the leaders asked each other. "No . . ."'

The students' spontaneous reaction – aroused, as eleswhere, by an 'outrageous' governmental action – took the police as much by surprise as the student leaders. The former set about beating up everyone they could lay hands on, including many innocent passers-by; the newspapers the next day were full of vivid reports of their brutality. Immediately a considerable sector of public opinion swung behind the students.

This was only the beginning. The students now had a cause – to free the Sorbonne and four youths who were immediately sentenced to prison for their part in the attack on the police vans. The student leaders, who were released the day after their arrest, met and called for a strike and demonstration the following Monday, 6 May, outside the Sorbonne; the university teachers' union supported the move. But when students tried to respond to the call, they found the university area totally blocked by police. Soon they were milling by the thousand on the Boulevard Saint-Michel, the main thoroughfare through the Latin Quarter.

By now it was not just university but lycée students who were involved. The politicization in the Paris high schools of the previous two years, the creation of the Comités d'Action Lycéens (CAL), was bearing its fruit. Lily Métreaux, who was in her last year of Catholic high school, was one of the newly radicalized. 'I had begun to acquire a real culture, Marxism, to understand what was at stake in Vietnam, to take on responsibilities although I was still very young . . . Well, one morning my young brother comes running home, out of breath, with his little satchel, saying: "Come quick, there's a demonstration!" So instead of going to school I followed him and we found ourselves on the Boulevard Saint-Michel in the middle of this huge demo. How can I describe it? A fabulous happiness, a tremendous joy! I recognized a lot of friends from the Vietnam committees, we kissed. And then I see myself, holding hands with my brother, shouting, laughing, going through the streets with the demo. It was May '68!'

Who, if anyone, was going to lead this outpouring which assembled outside the new Science Faculty on the left bank? The demonstrators listened for a while to the far-left leaders expounding their strategies: the Maoist UJC-ml's proposal to make for the working-class suburbs to mobilize workers because they alone had the strength; the Trotskyist

JCR's answer that the German and Italian movements had shown the way, to fight first on your own ground was the best possibility of mobilizing active support . . . Restless at hearing these arguments repeated, attracted as though by a magnet to the Sorbonne, the students started making towards it. They were blocked by heavy police forces. JCR leaders, who had to run to catch up, diverted them across the river to the right bank instead where, for a couple of hours, the demonstration meandered, gathering support from bystanders. But the pressure to get back to the left bank and the Sorbonne built up.

'We'd been walking for six hours without food by then,' recalled Henri Weber, the JCR leader. 'So, after recrossing the river, it was on empty bellies and weak legs that we reached the first and huge police road-block. Police coaches across the avenue, three rows of CRS [Compagnie Républicaine de Sécurité, a highly-trained riot-control police force]. The road-block in the next street was smaller. As we made our way towards it police fired tear gas grenades and attacked us with truncheons. We retreated, started to organize. People dragged cars across the street to make a road-block, others "borrowed" hard-hats from a neighbouring construction site. Still others handed out lemon juice which was supposed to help against tear gas. The whole shapeless crowd transformed itself into an active, self-organizing ant hill. Everybody seemed to find something to do. And then the clear ring of steel as cobblestones were prised up . . .'

As the CRS moved forward the students moved forward too and met them with a hail of cobbles. The police buckled under the attack, then fled in disarray. Unprotected by riot shields, many of their men were left injured on the ground. For the next two hours the students rained cobbles on each police attack, fighting them off.

Stimulated by their audacity, the students scattered to make for Denfert-Rochereau, a large square a mile or so from the Sorbonne, where they had called a solidarity demonstration. Between twenty-five and thirty thousand people marched from the square towards the Sorbonne. Never before had the French student movement mobilized so many people.

The march was brought to a halt by a hail of tear gas grenades. But there was no retreat. Again, the demonstrators transformed themselves into a self-organizing column; tearing up cobbles from streets way behind the 'front line', long chains of young men and women passed them to the fighters at the front. Hurling cobbles at the police, most of these were fighting not just the CRS but what they represented: repressive authority in all its forms, 'years of humiliation and oppression in my Catholic school.

In fighting the police,' Lily Métreaux felt, 'it was the nuns I was trying to kill.'

Amidst the all-pervasive smell of tear gas, the battle continued until 10 p.m., when the police finally dispersed the demonstrators, savagely beating those they could lay their hands on and leaving many unconscious and bleeding in the streets. The police claimed 487 casualties among their men; no one knew the number of injured students since many refused to go to hospital. It had been a ferocious street battle which aroused considerable emotion throughout France.

The students had not succeeded in recapturing the Sorbonne; but their courage had won them a political victory. The brutality displayed by the police served to isolate the Gaullist regime in the eyes of a large proportion of the population. In this, 6 May showed both how exceptional the battle had been and how exceptional France under de Gaulle was. Large and militant as the movements had become in the U.S., West Germany and Italy, they had not mobilized so large a proportion of the population into rejecting the regime itself. Only in Northern Ireland would a small and sudden student movement five months after Paris precipitate something similar. The reason in both countries lay in the exceptional nature of these authoritarian states.

Normally it is relatively easy for the governments of advanced bourgeois democracies to isolate and blacken those, like the Paris students, who take to the streets and fight the forces of law and order. The media, if not the government itself, denounce the 'men of violence' in the name of democracy. But in France, as in Northern Ireland, things were different: it was the government which for many years had resorted to violence to maintain its 'democratic' order. In France, the brutality of the CRS was only too well known to workers who had carried on long strikes in the 1960s, to peasants and small wine-growers demonstrating against low prices for their crops. Moreover, the CRS was only the most visibly oppressive force of a regime whose authoritarian and arbitrary nature had come to be increasingly resented. A resentment suffered in silence until, by their very action in attacking the police, the students shattered the silence, expressing openly what many had unspokenly felt.

An opinion poll two days after the battle reported that four-fifths of Parisians supported the students. It was clear from this that large sectors of the middle class – including students' parents – were behind them. The government was unmoved; the police remained in the Sorbonne. The leaders of the different political student groups, of UNEF and the university teachers' union, decided to call a demonstration every day until the Sorbonne was liberated and the four youths arrested had been released.

The first demonstration was large and peaceful – 45,000 people swarmed up the Champs Elysées in a sea of red and black flags and sang the 'Internationale' over the grave of the Unknown Soldier at the Arc de Triomphe, one of de Gaulle's most revered monuments. UNEF and university teachers' union leaders, Sauvageot and Geismar, respectively, believed that they could start negotiating from a position of strength. The next day they gave the government a sign of goodwill, allowing Young Communists and hardline Trotskyist students of the Fédération des Etudiants Révolutionnaires (FER) – both of whom argued that to fight the police was to play into the latter's hands – to persuade demonstrators to go home. Cohn-Bendit, who had been giving an interview to the BBC, arrived soon afterwards to find people crying. 'At first I thought there had been a battle with tear gas. But no, they were crying out of frustration. Geismar, Sauvageot and the whole gang had tried to make a deal behind their backs. But the police were still in the Sorbonne.'

He returned to a meeting of the 22 March Movement. 'Physically we were all very tired. But psychically we were electrified by what was at stake, which was to get rid once and for all of uncontrolled "leaders" who decided things behind our backs. We had to fight now for the movement's *autonomy*. 22 March hadn't been active enough in this respect. We had to find ways for people to meet and speak up and decide together what *they* wanted to do. And if they felt like moving into a head-on confrontation with the police, so be it! We would help the movement express its collective will and side with it.'

His arguments rallied the one hundred or so 22 March students from Nanterre who were present. From the start of the events they had met nightly in a small Paris apartment, at the suggestion of Anne Querrien, a 22 March member, who had seen that the Nanterre group might otherwise collapse. The women cooked, cared for the injured, bought food, prepared banners. 'We felt – and I still think – that by taking care of these material aspects we were being fully political. The men were making the speeches, but we made sure everything worked. At times like that it's worth being a woman, you know.'

At 2 a.m. Geismar, whom a friend had fetched, arrived exhausted and shattered. 'We accused him of betraying the movement,' recollected

Cohn-Bendit. 'He burst into tears. "You're right, I've betrayed the students, I've been a damn fool!" "Crying won't help," we said, "let's call for a new demo."'

'So there we go again! We started writing a leaflet,' Querrien continued. 'I had developed a special skill which was to write a leaflet under the guidance of an assembly. I would read back a few sentences and they would say, "No, that expression isn't right, let's put it this way . . ." and through this feedback we achieved a very efficient kind of collective writing. It was 5 a.m. when we finished the leaflet.'

After only three hours sleep, but feeling 'great', Cohn-Bendit presented the other student leaders with the fruits of the 22 March Movement's night-long meeting. '"Here you are, we're calling a rally at Denfert-Rochereau tomorrow at 6 p.m. We've printed 100,000 leaflets" – I was bluffing, there was no way we could have managed that – "and called a press conference. Either you join or you quit." Geismar was in favour, Sauvageot hesitated, the FER was against. But the JCR came out in support. So the leaflets got printed.'

This rally on Friday 10 May was to lead to the bitterest battle of all: the night of the barricades. But the previous evening, the movement received an important political filip. A large international meeting in Paris of the Trotskyist Fourth International, to which the JCR belonged, was opened at Cohn-Bendit's request to the movement. The meeting was very important, in Henri Weber's view, 'because it matured the movement politically. Listening to the speeches by student delegates from Germany, Italy, Spain, Belgium and Holland, the Paris students became aware of the international dimension of their struggle.'

Cohn-Bendit told the meeting that no single leader, no single group could claim for itself the leadership of this movement which would have to find its own voice, its own goals.

The next morning, 10 May, saw thousands of high school students roaming the capital, pulling one school after another out on strike. Lily Métreaux was among them. 'I felt our time had come at last. There was a sort of magic island coming out of nowhere, and it was us, the young ones, who were pulling it out. I was with my young brother and his high school friends. They were all in tenth grade, I was in twelfth [final year]. My brother's best friend, Nicolas, and I fell in love, became lovers. And on that famous Friday, 10 May, I helped them bring out their school on strike, going from classroom to classroom. All the kids ran into the streets . . .'

For some, this 'magic island' had no exact parameters or specificity, its appearance couldn't be explained. 'Like everyone else, I was in the streets shouting, "Free our comrades!"' recalled Brigitte Ballet, a UJC-ml member, 'and then I went home to find some friends of my parents there who asked me to explain what exactly we were asking for, what we wanted. I was absolutely incapable of explaining, I couldn't say that I didn't even know who these comrades were, couldn't say that I wanted to demonstrate for the sake of demonstrating. The fact was that to anyone who asked rationally enough "What do you want?" I had no answer at all. I left the room, I was a teenager.'

Many perhaps felt the same but lacked the honesty to admit it. And yet, on the other hand, it was the refusal to articulate demands that fell within 'rational' bourgeois discourse that characterized much of the movement because the latter was felt precisely to be a protest against the rationality that permitted a regime like de Gaulle's to exist.

That evening 20,000 people crowded into Denfert-Rochereau. The student leaders climbed onto the statue of the lion in the centre: they were in a quandary about what to do. In Weber's view, 'it had to be something new, instead of attacking the police once again. But what? Attack the prison where the four youths were being held? Hopeless. Try to take the Town Hall as the people had done during the Paris Commune in 1871? Not very easy. Make for the TV station? It was heavily guarded – and *who* could speak in the name of the whole movement?'

Something had to be done. True to his principles, Cohn-Bendit tried to turn the rally into a general assembly; but even he had to admit that direct democracy had met its limits. 'There were 20,000 of us, and from the top of the lion I was proposing that we decide collectively where to go. It couldn't work. The prison wasn't far off and some people started marching towards it. Then the whole crowd followed.'

The prison was not protected by police forces. The demonstrators cheered when inmates waved handkerchiefs through the barred windows, sang the 'Internationale', and went on. There was no leadership; Cohn-Bendit had made all the groups' delegates agree previously that there would be no marshals, no 'bureaucratic leadership'. The demonstrators could decide where they wanted to go. Nonetheless, UNEF tried to bring in its marshals. Cohn-Bendit went to the head of the march. 'I climbed onto a bench with my loudhailer and shouted for as long as the demonstrators were marching by: "There are no marshals and no leaders today! Nobody is responsible for you! *You* are responsible for yourselves, each row of you responsible for itself! *You* are the marshals!" People were really surprised . . .'

The demonstration circled around the Latin Quarter before reaching a square not far from the Sorbonne. By now it was 9 p.m. Weber saw that the police were leaving only one route open – back to Denfert-Rochereau. 'There was no way we were going back to where we'd started from. But we still didn't know what to do. We – the leaders of the various groups – got together, there on the pavement, surrounded by the crowd and by a lot of people who insisted on giving us their advice . . .'

The pressure on them now was tremendous; they had to find a way forward. But with the crowd all around they could hardly hear each other talk, let alone think. Some people linked arms to make a large circle around them, keeping the demonstrators at a distance. From the leaders' huddle there emerged a new tactic. 'Cohn-Bendit suggested it,' recalled Weber. 'We were to occupy the whole of the Latin Quarter around the police lines and organize small discussion groups. We'd stay the whole night if necessary and the next day until our demands were met. "We will not attack the police, but if they attack us we shall retaliate."'

As the leaders dispersed through the crowd to explain the decision, they were met again and again by the same question: how do we retaliate if they attack us? 'With cobblestones', came the answer. Not to be caught by surprise, the crowd split up immediately into small groups and began to pile up stacks of cobbles. Communist students tried to dissuade them; the whole thing was a provocation, they said. No one listened; the demonstrators were happy to have something concrete to do. Then, as the piles of stones grew, Weber saw something new.

'It was a real stroke of genius. People were beginning to make the piles into barricades. Militarily speaking, it was probably silly. But politically, it was exactly the thing to do. The image of barricades in French history is associated with all the heroic moments of popular uprisings: 1830, 1848, the Paris Commune. The barricade is a symbol, the defense of the poor, of the workers against the armies of the kings and reactionaries.'

There was euphoria as barricades began to spring up everywhere in joyous confusion. Some faced one way, others another: ten were built one behind the other in the Rue Gay-Lussac alone. There was no central plan, just the need to *do* something – something that echoed to a long revolutionary tradition. Cohn-Bendit pitched in with the rest. 'Then someone came up with a map on which he'd marked all the places where barricades were going up. "Go back," I said, "and tell them to leave room to retreat." I could see that if the first barricade were taken, the second as likely as not was going to stop people escaping. I went to the front line to cool out a group of toughs who wanted to attack the police straight away. Three of them came back with me. "We're going to stay with you in case you need protection." From then on, every time anyone came up just to look at me, they'd say, "Leave him alone, he has important things to do."

'I toured the whole area. Residents were at their windows, offering us food and milk. The atmosphere was fantastic. It's a moment I shall never forget. People were building up the cobblestones into barricades because they wanted – many of them for the first time – to throw themselves into a *collective*, spontaneous activity. People were releasing all their repressed feelings, expressing them in a festive spirit. Thousands felt the need to communicate with each other, to love one another. That night has forever made me optimistic about history. Having lived through it, I can't ever say, "It will never happen" . . .'

Radio reporters were on the spot, transmitting live news of the events all over France; demonstrators with transistor radios kept them tuned in and, through the feedback, felt they were participating in the making of history.

The government was now caught in a trap: if it ordered the CRS to attack it would be cast once again in the role of a maleficent force and rally large sectors of the population against it. But to give in would be a sign of weakness which might encourage those same sectors to emulate the students' successful 'direct action'. It tried to steer an uneasy course between the two by having the Chancellor of the Sorbonne announce that he was prepared to meet student delegates. Then there began an extra-ordinary negotiation conducted over a radio link and broadcast live between Geismar and the Sorbonne's Vice-Chancellor. Geismar demanded that the four youths be freed as a prior condition of negotiations – a demand the demonstrators at Denfert-Rochereau had insisted on. The Vice-Chancellor responded that this was not in his power to grant, but that he would contact the Minister of the Interior and call back. Geismar said that the minister could communicate his answer to the students over the radio, and asked people in apartments in the Latin Quarter to put transistors on their windowsills. Nearly an hour later, the Vice-Chancellor called to say that he could not go beyond his original offer. Geismar responded: 'We have put forward our positions publicly, in front of the people who are all listening. If the government is not prepared to assume its responsibility in the matter, then it is the people who will have to. That *is* clear to us.'

The negotiations were cut off. Direct confrontation seemed now almost inevitable. A chance meeting with one of his Nanterre sociology professors, who asked Cohn-Bendit to accompany him to a meeting with the Sorbonne Chancellor – but did not tell the latter the student leader was coming – gave Cohn-Bendit a last-minute opportunity of trying to prevent a bloodbath. 'That night I knew I was the only one who could cross the police lines without being thought a traitor.' As he went through the lines the police recognized him. 'I've *never* seen such hatred on anyone's face. They were also frightened, I think. You could hear the sound of the crowd, the barricades being built all around. It had been going on for several hours by now.'

At last he found himself facing the Chancellor. '"What do you want me to do?" he asked. "It's very simple," I said. "Get the police out, re-open the Sorbonne. I'll find three or four bands and that'll be it. A festival. Nothing else will happen. People will dance and drink and be happy." Then the phone rang in the next room. He went out. When he came back he said, "Are you Cohn-Bendit?" "Yes." He returned to the other room and the phone. Then he came back again and, very sadly, said: "I am sorry, there is nothing I can do", and left the room.'

The Minister of the Interior had told the Chancellor not to negotiate with Cohn-Bendit: the government would not negotiate with the forces in the street, with a leader who was not a duly elected representative. A small group of ministers met to impose order by force. There were those, it appears, who wanted to order the police to shoot; a dose of moderation at least prevailed.

At 2 a.m. students saw the CRS putting their gas masks on in preparation for the attack. The barricades were still held by thousands of people. Hearing the news, youths had swarmed in from the working-class suburbs to lend a hand. Behind the barricades people turned on the water hydrants to douse the tear gas grenades and put scarves round their mouths. And then they heard the police order to attack . . .

The savage night of battle that followed was heard all over France. Radio reporters covered it live. The exploding plop of tear gas grenades, the vicious, brutal shouts of the riot police as they stormed barricades, the thud of exploding car petrol tanks, the groans of wounded students being carted off to ambulances – it was in everyone's front room. A well-known former soccer commentator was reporting the events for one station:

'Now the CRS are charging, they're storming the barricade – oh, my God! There's a battle raging. The students are counter-attacking, you can hear the noise – the CRS are retreating . . . Now they're re-grouping, getting ready to charge again. The inhabitants are throwing things from their windows at the CRS – oh! The police are retaliating, shooting grenades into the windows of apartments . . .' At this point the radio station, which had been telling the commentator over the air not to dramatize events, interrupted him. 'This can't be true, the CRS don't do things like that!' 'I'm telling you what I'm seeing . . .' His voice went dead – they'd cut him off.

Cohn-Bendit was following the commentary on the radio; at the start of the battle he had taken shelter in a friend's apartment – everyone knew that if he were caught by the CRS he would be badly manhandled. He heard what everyone else was hearing: vivid reports of students in hand-to-hand fighting to defend their barricades, some of which were a sea of flames; the streets a choking fog of tear gas through which the black silhouettes of the CRS swirled, their clubs smashing on heads; the hail of cobbles from behind the barricades which sent them reeling; bleeding students being snatched from apartments which here and there the CRS ransacked as well; Red Cross volunteers being felled by truncheons and people dragged from stretchers and ambulances for further beating; the flames lighting up the pitched battles in the Rue Gay-Lussac where petrol from cars piled on the barricades had caught light . . .

'At dawn, when the last barricades were taken after that very tough night, I called the radio station,' Cohn-Bendit recalled. 'I said that things were now very clear, and referred to the need for a general strike. If *this* time the trade union movement did not call one, I added, it meant they were no longer on the people's side.'

In the afternoon, Geismar and Sauvageot, the UNEF leader, negotiated with the Communist-led CGT and the other unions to call a day's strike and a demonstration for Monday, 13 May – the tenth anniversary of de Gaulle's accession to power. The CGT was opposed to the timing, fearing that it would be seen, symbolically at least, as a direct challenge to the regime. But Geismar held his ground.

It was an immense demonstration. The students had touched a more profound chord in the consciousness of the nation than they themselves were aware of. Cohn-Bendit was staggered when he saw the whole avenue packed shoulder-to-shoulder with demonstrators. 'We'd thought there'd be 20,000 of us and 40,000 of the Communist Party. But there were hundreds of thousands of people there.'

A million, it was said, but no one knew for sure. This was no longer a student but a mass movement. Its sudden emergence from nowhere posed a decisive question for the future: who would lead it? The demonstration itself showed the still delicate balance of strength among the contenders. The Communist Party did not want it to be led by the far-left student groups. When Cohn-Bendit and his group had worked their way to the front of the demonstration, 'Séguy, the CGT leader, told Sauvageot and Geismar that he didn't want "that Cohn-Bendit with me".' But they replied that if Cohn-Bendit didn't come, nor would they, and so Séguy was obliged to accept his presence in the front rank.

Not without further incident between Communists and far leftists – the latter chanting, to Communist anger, Paris! Rome! Berlin! Budapest! Warsaw! One and the Same Fight! – the huge demonstration marched through Paris. The student struggles that had preceded it had changed the consciousness of a great many people; Michel Wieviorka, an unpolitical business school student, for example, who joined the march. 'I didn't give a damn about politics. But from the beginning of May I knew right away which side I was on. I suppose it came from my family background, secular Jewish, inclined to the left. On the demo my friends and I weren't part of any group. The demo happened to pass by the home of one of my aunts who did a lot of sewing. I ran up the stairs and asked her for a piece of black cloth. She gave it to me without asking questions. I ran down, went into a wood shop and bought a stick to make myself a black flag. Then I went straight back into the demo, very happy, and raised my flag aloft. Suddenly I realized I was in the middle of a group of Communist workers! They made me aware pretty quickly that I was in the wrong place! The truth is, I didn't know where my place was in the demo, but I *knew* for sure that I belonged to the movement.'

A widely-shared sentiment, as the demonstrations in most large cities throughout France showed. But when the Paris demonstration reached Denfert-Rochereau, the Communist Party called for people to go home. Cohn-Bendit was furious. 'I wanted the movement to go on, people to discuss what to do next, to organize themselves. I decided to have a meeting on the Champ de Mars, at the foot of the Eiffel Tower. I plunged into the crowd looking for groups who wanted to continue . . .'

At the meeting it was decided to call for the occupation of all French universities; but while the gathering was still in progress, the news came that the CRS was withdrawing from the Sorbonne, that the four youths were being released. The government had given in. Students flooded into the Sorbonne. In the main quadrangle a large piano was brought in and someone started to play jazz. An atmosphere of excitement and optimism reigned. The festival lasted the whole night.

In the following days the quadrangle became a hive of activity. All the groups set up tables and distributed their leaflets. Posters of Stalin and Trotsky appeared in unbelievable juxtaposition; so too did Mao and Guevara. People rushed to and fro organizing a crèche, a first aid post, a food supply centre. On all this hubbub there fell from time to time a shower of Situationist leaflets, alerting people to the dangers of left-wing bureaucrats. People from all walks of life came out of curiosity to see what was happening and often remained to participate in the organization of the occupation. Amidst all this, the Trotskyist J C R took over lecture halls and started non-stop debates on the history of the working-class movement, the place of the student movement in it, the immediate tasks ahead. Every day a general assembly was held in the main lecture hall to discuss the political situation and to vote on the next moves.

'It was fantastic,' Weber recalled. 'May was like that, like living on a constant high. Life was beautiful, the weather was lovely, the men were handsome and the women superb. Everything we did immediately belonged to History. All the hierarchies had suddenly dissolved. The student movement was threatening de Gaulle himself. As soon as we took over the Sorbonne we insisted that the movement must spread out beyond it, make links with the workers. Our goal was to topple de Gaulle.'

An illusory hope, it seemed at the time. Despite the ten-day student struggle and its culmination in the massive Paris demonstration and the one-day strike, factories were working as normal the following day. Most universities were occupied, but few showed the militancy and fervour of the Sorbonne. Cohn-Bendit returned to Nanterre to find that the students' main concern was whether final examinations should be held. 'It was a real let-down. The pressure to hold exams was very strong. We were taken aback to find the assemblies all focusing on this question. We had little to say about it, lacked a political alternative to put forward.'

And then, quite unexpectedly, came a small item of news: the workers at the Sud Aviation factory at Nantes, in western France, had gone on strike, locking the factory managers in their offices. Earlier student actions had played an important role in precipitating the strike. A small group of Situationist-inspired students had taken over the Nantes student union the previous autumn. At the beginning of May they brought the university out on strike; and during the one-day general strike of 13 May, they led a demonstration of students and workers to the Préfecture, the seat of centrally-administered power, headed by a government-appointed *préfet*.

Accompanied by trade union representatives, Jean Breteau, the student union leader, walked into the *préfet*'s office. 'I asked for the grant to the student's union which he had refused to give us the previous autumn – a ridiculous amount [equivalent to about £800] – on the pretext that we were "intolerable hoodlums". He refused once more. We went back to the demo and I announced the news. Then one of the CGT delegates whispered in my ear, "Now tell them to go home." "No, I can't do that." "Tell them!" he insisted. "No!" It wouldn't have made much difference because the crowd was determined to fight.'

The battle began: cobblestones against tear gas. But there were no CRS there that day and the local police were outnumbered. 'Soon we had the Préfecture surrounded by barricades on all sides. Finally the *préfet* agreed to see us again. The building stank of tear gas. He agreed to give us the grant. But the workers who were with us were saying, "But what have *we* workers got? Nothing. We're fools, we didn't even ask for anything."'

The next day the Sud Aviation workers came out on strike. A few hundred people; three days later, two million were out all over France; another three days, nine million. No one had called for a general strike; and yet here was the largest strike in French history, a spontaneous movement spreading over the country with incredible speed. Factories and offices, oil refineries and shipyards, transport and post offices, banks, department stores, administrative buildings, high schools, ground to a halt; all over the country a calm but massive refusal was being expressed – the refusal to continue to live and work under the authoritarian conditions of the Gaullist regime.

Pursuing a strategy of national 'grandeur', de Gaulle's policies over the past decade had involved a modernization of capitalism, a stock-piling of gold to secure independence from American economic power, and vast arms spending to gain military independence. The working class had borne the brunt of these policies. Wages were the lowest in industrialized Western Europe, work rhythms were speeded up while the average work week remained forty-eight hours. The economic policies took little account of rising unemployment, especially among the young. There had been at least two riots by young workers the previous autumn in provincial towns. The managerial class, meanwhile, was benefitting from rapid economic growth and the consumer society. In a centralized country like France, the state appeared to many as ultimately responsible for these inegalitarian policies. The employers' and state's consistent response to workers' demands was one of arrogant refusal. But this time, due to the state's repression of students, arrogance led them into a trap.

'The unthinkable had happened! The strikes were like a flame, like everything we'd been saying at Nanterre,' recalled Nelly Finkielsztejn. 'Fuck hierarchy, authority, this society with its cold, rational elitist logic! Fuck all the petty bosses and the mandarins at the top! Fuck this immutable society that refuses to consider the misery, poverty, inequality and injustice it creates, that divides people according to their origins and skills! I had never dreamt such a thing could happen! Suddenly the French were refusing the state's authority because they understood it was malevolent, evil, just as I'd always thought as a child. Suddenly they realized that they had to find a new sort of solidarity. That was what was important about May. Not the slogans like "Imagination Is Seizing Power" and the rest, not the poetry and exuberance, but this new-found solidarity. That was what May meant to me!'

Since her discovery as a youth of the Holocaust in which her relatives had died, Finkielsztejn had been in revolt against a society that could go on as though nothing had happened; at Nanterre she had become an anarchist and part of the 22 March Movement. Not everyone, without doubt, would have as much cause as she for condemning society; yet similar condemnations of the Gaullist regime were now resounding throughout France. (The most succinct and graphic illustration of this perhaps came when strikers at a lorry plant reordered the letters of their firm's name – Berliet – to call it Liberté.) Suddenly, collectively, people discovered that what they had felt, but not dared in their individual isolation to express, was shared by the vast majority: a desire for radical change, a desire for a different form of society. A society in which everyone had a say in matters that concerned them directly: a self-managed society.

The students now attempted to forge links with the striking workers. On 17 May, Sorbonne students went to the state-owned Renault automobile plant at Billancourt, a Paris suburb, which had come out on strike the previous day. Henri Weber, whose JCR had pushed strongly for the demonstration, recalled what happened when the students reached the huge factory. 'We found that all the iron gates, all the doors, had been locked by the union to "prevent provocations".' The Communist-led CGT had issued leaflets warning the workers not to fraternize with the students. 'All the same many workers came out to talk to us. They were friendly, and most of them were embarrassed by the CGT's call to keep us out. Some, when they learnt of it, turned angrily on their union officials. We had expected them to give us advice on where to lead the movement. Instead, we found that they were asking *us* for advice!'

The Communist Party feared an escalation of the movement. Since the early 1960s the party had been pursuing, not without some success, a parliamentary road to power. It believed that if the general strike turned into an insurrectionary situation, it might itself be crushed because the Gaullist regime still commanded the allegiance of the military. Fearful of the worst, the Party set out to 'contain' the strike movement, return it to 'normal' economic trade union demands that would not threaten the bourgeois state. In doing so, it reinforced rather than weakened the regime, preventing the very condition which might have led to its collapse. The fact that, despite the Communist Party, the Gaullist regime nearly fell anyway only shows the determination of the strike forces arrayed against the regime.

Contrary to the Communist Party, the Maoist UJC-ml believed that the moment was ripe for revolution. While it had scorned the student struggles as petty bourgeois in the first ten days of May, it entered the fray once the working class came out on strike. It dispatched its militants to working-class areas to mobilize support. André Liber, the high school militant, was sent to contact mechanics at the Paris bus garages; there he found a number of them who were willing to 'go all the way . . . They were former Communist Party activists or anarcho-syndicalists in the main. We formed a group, printed leaflets to firm up the strike, denounced the Communist Party . . . In the working-class suburb of Gennevilliers, the workers were preparing to fight the police. At a tar plant up on a hill, they'd got a dozen lorries loaded with stones ready to send plunging down. And they kept tar constantly boiling and the hoses ready to spray it from.'

Tiennot Grumbach, veteran of the Algerian struggles, now a UJC-ml leader, experienced May as though it were another Russian revolution. A few weeks before, in line with his group's decision that activists should become manual workers, he had started to work in a printers where many left-wing papers were printed. Among them was the UJC-ml *La Cause du Peuple* which, during the May events, had become a daily. 'I spent my days and nights in the shop, getting tremendous pleasure from seeing our paper come out. Maybe it was a kind of megalomaniac trip. I knew that in the Russian revolution, Stalin had printed *Pravda*! I kept telling myself: this time *you* are the Stalin of May 68!' he laughed. 'By the way, the shop was not sectarian; we also printed the J C R's paper.'

But apart from some Leninist groups like the UJC-ml, the revolutionary seizure of state power did not appear a widespread goal. The movement's aims were rather an attempt to change radically the power relations in work places everywhere. In factories, offices, research centres, radio and TV stations, people held general assemblies every morning where they criticized the relations of authority and the division of labour, proposing ways of reorganizing the work processes and democratizing decision-making. The general assemblies elected delegates to work-place action committees whose task – like a strike committee – was to coordinate the new initiatives. Soon the movement spread out to residential neighbourhoods, where action committees fostered self-organization and met whatever local needs were felt lacking. Their aim was essentially to mobilize ever larger numbers of people in a self-governing activity that would create new, albeit embryonic, social structures to challenge those of the existing order. In Nantes, where this self-organization reached its highest level, the city was run for more than a week by a central strike committee which interrupted the transport and distribution of food. It called on the peasants' union to sell food directly to the populace and allocated petrol coupons for emergency use. There, as elsewhere, the new committees expressed what was quintessential about May: the popularly felt need to overthrow the authoritarian and bureaucratic structures of Gaullist France in the name both of freedom and the right to manage one's own affairs.

By the last week of May there were over 450 such committees in Paris alone. While many provincial centres tended to lag behind the capital, the movement began to take root even in them; but it often required the presence of students to start it. In Angers, a conservative town in western France, for example, it was the presence of students from the Ecole Supérieure d'Agriculture which provided the initial impetus. During a demonstration which the CGT tried at the last moment to divert from passing in front of the municipal theatre, students broke away and occupied it. Among them was René Bourrigaud:

'The theatre represented the acme of bourgeois culture in the town. Some anarchists – we didn't even know there were any in Angers – were the first in through the back door and raised the black flag over the building. Then we opened the doors, occupied the theatre. It became a permanent forum of debate. Workers came and took part – it was the first time they had ever set foot in this temple of bourgeois culture. Some of them spoke about their experiences during the Popular Front occupations of 1936. We only vaguely knew about that, we lacked real knowledge of the history of the working-class movement. In that month of talking you learnt more than in the whole of your five years studying. Learnt because you could talk to anyone and everyone. It was really another world – a dream world perhaps – but that's what I'll always remember: the need and the right for everyone to speak.'

People who had never found their voice before now spoke, acted in ways that would have been inconceivable a month earlier. In Lyons, France's third largest city, two sixteen-year-old girls brought out their high school on strike. Neither had been a political activist before. One of them, Claire Auzias, had spent the previous year at school in an American college. There she had found out about Vietnam, Black Power, the counter-culture. Returning to a French lycée, with its strong discipline and arbitrary authority, had been hard to take. 'So when my own school came out on strike, oh, it was marvellous! I went to speak at a general assembly in the school playground. I wasn't afraid of anything, I was carried forward by the moment. After May '68 I've never again been able to speak at a public meeting. But then I could answer every argument, talk back to anybody. The teachers, even the headmaster of whom we'd all been afraid, were frightened now. I was carried along by this tremendous desire for revolution.'

During the strike and after, high school pupils working through their Comités d'Action Lycéens (CAL) carried their ideas on reorganizing the high school system far further than did university students. The role of the lycée in society, the need to make the teaching and subjects relevant to real life, the question of examinations and grades – could the high school exist without them? – these and many other problems were earnestly debated. In Paris alone more than three hundred reports on high school reform were drawn up in the last two weeks of May.

By releasing people from their 'normal' work and school routines, the general strike provided individuals with a unique opportunity to liberate themselves from day-to-day constraints. Time and space took on new meaning. People walked the cities in great numbers as public transport stopped and petrol became scarce; and as they walked, they struck up conversations with strangers in a way that would have been unimaginable before. For the first time, workers could tour their factories; public buildings were open to everyone; and park keepers no longer chased off young lovers lying on the grass in public gardens. Romance, sex seemed part of the air: students with rooms in the centre of towns left doors unlocked to give overnight shelter, and teenagers – following the example of some of the bolder high school youth, like Lily Métreaux during the earlier student street battles – no longer went home to sleep. 'I remember after a euphoric night of fighting the police, cars burning in the streets, I crashed out at a friend's in the Latin Quarter. My clothes were reeking of tear gas. In the morning I woke to find an unknown moustached face looking down at me. He asked me to have coffee and we became lovers: Mustapha Khayati, one of the Situationists who had written the famous tract on the *Poverty of Student Life . . .*'

Time was no longer the routine hours of a month earlier. Even the hands of some public clocks were removed in a gesture reminiscent of what had reportedly happened during the Paris Commune a century earlier. On street corners people stuck up posters expressing their criticisms of the established order. In the Gobelins, in Paris, local anarchists pasted up huge sheets of white paper on the walls. 'People would come and start writing what they had to say,' recalled André Liber, the Maoist student activist, 'and as they were writing other people would come up and disagree. Discussions flared up. A lot of funny things, a lot of bullshit, too, was said. But the point was, people were at long last expressing themselves, talking to each other. That was one of the great things about May.'

Despite the street battles and the constant denunciation of capitalism by the far-left groups, there was virtually no vandalism; very few shop windows were broken, and the crime rate dropped to an all-time low. Aggression seemed directed almost exclusively at the police; when street discussions became heated and threatened physical violence, the crowd almost always stepped in to put an end to it.

Although as a rule the far-left groups were preoccupied with liberating society as a whole and disregarded the aspect of self-liberation, there were exceptions, like Roland Castro, one of the UJC-ml leaders. From the start of the student revolt he disagreed with his group's line castigating the movement as 'petty-bourgeois'. 'I knew immediately I had to be part of this thing. I was involved in so much that even today I can't remember what happened when. I was totally happy. Besides, I fell in love – she was a Trotskyist, but who cared any more! That lovely phrase of Marx's about the Paris Commune sums it all up for me. "The only social measure of the

Commune is its very existence," he said. That's what I felt – the fullness of being alive.'

Exceptional times release unsuspected potentialities from the repressed depths of 'normal' times. The refusal of Gaullist power was lived as a liberation, an attempt to democratize power in the local workplace, for the most part. The only political organization with the strength to link these local 'powers' into a coherent attack on the regime itself – the Communist Party – was instead determined to isolate the movement. Although links between strike committees were made in a number of regional cities, the difficulty of creating an organizational structure overnight meant that these links remained tenuous. The mass strike rolled on without coalescing into a political force which could put itself forward as an alternative to the Gaullist regime.

Spontaneity, self-activity, was patently not enough. Attempts to establish these links cost tremendous personal effort. Cohn-Bendit, who went to Nantes to try to forge links with the Sud Aviation workers, recalled that he was 'completely exhausted' by all that had happened in the past weeks. 'I accepted an invitation from students to go to Berlin because I liked the idea of returning there as a leader. It was pride, of course, but also to tell the truth I didn't know how to go forward. I needed to rest. In truth, I didn't realize the importance of the moment.'

On the way back to France, he held a meeting in Holland at which he said, among other things, that the French flag was made to be ripped up and turned into a red flag. When he tried to cross the border, from Germany, he found he had been banned from France. 'The pretext was my statement about the French flag. Because I was German, they were entitled to do it. I didn't know what to do. There were a lot of journalists asking for interviews. The one from the BBC was a pretty young woman. I gave her the interview and then disappeared with her. I'd become a star, lost contact with reality.'

Paris students marched on Parliament in protest at the banning; but power, as it had always done in the Gaullist regime, plainly lay elsewhere – in de Gaulle's Elysée palace. There, a week after the strike had started, a two-pronged counter-attack was being planned: de Gaulle was to address the nation on 24 May, and a day later Prime Minister Pompidou would begin negotiations with the unions on economic demands.

Such was de Gaulle's power still in this highly centralized country that everything seemed to hang on his speech. On the day of the speech, anti-Gaullist demonstrations were held in many cities. Militants of the 22 March Movement went to factories in the Paris suburbs to bring workers to the centre for the demonstration. Anne Querrien went to a metal-working plant where she had contacts with skilled workers. 'On the way back I stopped to make myself a red flag from a piece of cloth and a broomstick. Then the few of us continued walking on into the centre of the city. By the time we got to the rallying point I was amazed to see that several thousand people had joined our group.'

Similar phenomena were happening elsewhere. In Lyons, for instance, a spontaneous demonstration by a couple of hundred students, claiming to represent the 22 March Movement, marched with black flags from the university. As soon as they crossed the river into the city, the demonstration swelled. 'In a few hundred yards it became enormous,' Françoise Routhier recalled. 'People from every walk of life were joining it, people who had nothing to do with students. With every step, the demonstration became larger. It was as if the whole city had been waiting for it.'

And then Routhier and others at the front of the demonstration heard that youth from the underprivileged housing zones on the city outskirts were joining at the rear. 'I felt a collective shiver go through the demo. It was as if people from another world, people you normally never met in the city, were joining in.'

All over France, the demonstrators stopped to listen on transistor radios to de Gaulle's speech. As the seventy-seven-year-old General's voice came over the air it was rapidly apparent that he was unsure of himself, out of touch with the mood of the country. All he was offering was to seek reconfirmation of his old sweeping powers. As the speech ended, a Paris demonstrator raised a handkerchief over his head and shouted, 'Adieu de Gaulle!' Immediately, thousands of others followed the example. Then the police fired tear gas and the fighting broke out. It was to last all night.

On orders from their leaders, student demonstrators in Paris split into small groups, forcing the police to scatter too. One group found its path to the stock exchange clear and set fire to it with cries of 'Burn down the temple of capitalism!' Others fought their way back into the Latin Quarter where they took on the police in a battle even more ferocious than the 'night of the barricades'.

In Lyons, the demonstrators marched to the only remaining seat of power – the Préfecture – but found it surrounded by the entire regional police force. The demonstrators withdrew across the river and built a huge barricade across the bridge. 'Strategically, it was nonsense,' Routhier observed, 'because there are thirty-two bridges in Lyons. But everyone wanted to do something. Soon there were long lines of people passing cobblestones up to the barricade – it was like those pictures from China where thousands of people are carrying stones to build a dam . . .' Police began firing tear gas grenades. Youngsters from the city outskirts brought up a lorry in front of the barricade, jammed down the accelerator and sent it careering into the police lines through the dense tear gas. A police officer was crushed to death. It was, despite all the preceding violence, the first fatal casualty of May. The police officer was possibly trying to contact the 'leaders' of the demonstration as occasionally happened in Paris. 'But in Lyons,' Routhier observed, 'there were none. Everyone was a "leader" and no one.'

On the morning after the fighting, 25 May, the government has lost control of several important cities. De Gaulle himself was discredited. Prime Minister Pompidou now played his last card: direct talks with the unions and employers in an historic replay of the agreements which had brought an end to the Popular Front occupations of 1936. At the same time there were rumours that tanks were taking up position around the capital for a military take-over.

The talks went on through the weekend of 25–27 May. By their end Pompidou had conceded the greatest single increase in the minimum wage – 35 per cent – since the end of World War II. But the remainder of the working-class claims were left to further negotiation. Confident nonetheless of their victory, the trade union delegates emerged smiling; all that was needed was the rank-and-file's approval. The threat of civil war was over. Georges Séguy, the C G T leader, hurried to the Renault automobile plant at Billancourt, one of the bastions of the strike, to present the agreements. The 10,000 workers listened. As he finished, whistles and boos broke out: the agreements were unacceptable. The strike would continue!

As similar reactions poured in to trade union headquarters from all over France, it was evident that the strikers were demanding not simply wage increases but more radical changes. The agreements had failed, a pre-revolutionary power-crisis had opened. Two *de facto* powers now existed: the strike movement's and the regime's. The latter seemed to have played all its cards, but the ascendant movement was still searching for a credible political alternative.

While left politicians argued about the spoils of government, without giving a decisive lead on how, finally, to remove de Gaulle from power, the student movement tried to retake the initiative. UNEF, the student union, called a mass meeting at the small Charléty stadium in Paris. Thirty thousand people attended, among them many groups of workers who disagreed with the CGT's 'back-to-work' line. They heard a succession of speakers – including some Communist Party intellectuals who had torn up their membership cards – all urging the movement on; but none of them was able to put forward a clear line of action. The movement seemed unable to translate its social strength into a political force.

At the Sorbonne, general assemblies feverishly turned on the vital question of filling the political vacuum. On the evening of 28 May, an unknown young man, with dyed black hair and dark glasses, walked to the microphone. It was Cohn-Bendit, who had returned to France clandestinely, using an old Algerian War resistance network; he felt he had to come back. 'All the way in the car to Paris I was wondering what to do, what to say, how to find a second wind ... I went up front. There was no reaction. Then I took off my glasses. After a few seconds there was a tremendous ovation. People were standing, shouting: "Les frontières on s'en fout!" ["Fuck all frontiers!"]. It went on a long time, my eyes filled with tears. But in fact I had nothing to say. The main point of my being there was to defy the government, show it was powerless. So I just said a few words, encouraging them to go on.'

On Wednesday, 29 May, the crisis reached its height. A massive, CGT-led demonstration, chanting anti-Gaullist slogans, walked peacefully through the streets of Paris. Members of the government feared it would march on the presidential palace and take it, but that was not the Communist Party's goal; its aim was rather to show Socialist politicians that any future government would have to include the Communists. Almost simultaneously news broke that the palace was empty, de Gaulle had vanished. His regime appeared lost, victory in the grasp of those who had fought it for the past month.

In barely twenty-four hours it eluded them again. The old General moved faster and more decisively than they in a single day. He flew to West Germany to assure himself of the loyalty of the French garrison there. Having received the necessary assurances, he flew back determined to make his final counter-attack.

The following day, 30 May, he broadcast to the nation. At the Sorbonne someone with a transistor radio walked into the classroom where Pierre Félix was debating proposals on university reform. '"De Gaulle is going to speak," I heard him say. The afternoon sun was streaming into the room, lighting up the words – *déjà dix jours de bonheur!* [ten days of happiness already!] – which someone had written on the wall. I felt the same. I turned to listen. The old man's authoritarian voice came loud and clear. "Eh bien, non! Je ne me retirerai pas!" "No, I shall not stand down!" And then in a voice veiled with hidden threats against any attempt to dispute his power, he barked out his new orders: parliament would be dissolved, general elections called, the armed forces mobilized under the authority of the local *préfets*. He spoke for only four minutes, his voice like thunder. We looked at each other, wondering what this upping of the political stakes meant. An east european émigré among us, who I suppose knew more about the real meaning of power than we, said quite simply: "It's all over now." As I looked at the wall the words were lost in shadow.'

Barely had de Gaulle's stentorian 'Vive la France!' faded on the radio, than Gaullist supporters swarmed into the streets of Paris for a mass rally. The shareholder and the shopkeeper, the veteran of the colonial wars, the die-hard Catholic and the heir of Vichy France poured from the apartments where they had been sheltering for the past month to be joined by Gaullist MPs and government ministers who led them, reaction triumphant, up the Champs Elysées under a storm of French flags. Some 700,000 people, intoning the 'Marseillaise' – the other face of France, the face of Gaullism and of all that students and strikers had stood against for the past month.

Inspired by the General's refound determination, the regime fought to regain the power it had lost over the preceding weeks. Its first decisive move was to restock the petrol stations for the long Whitsun weekend beginning on 1 June. The traffic jams on the roads out of all the major cities was a certain sign that 'May' for the middle classes was over. The main petrol docks for Paris were in Gennevilliers where Yves Clément, a Maoist student, had spent May and seen the workers' militancy.

'They could have stopped the tankers loading the petrol, they had the means to do so. But they were also totally disciplined, all members of the CGT. When the union leadership – and that meant the Communist Party leadership – gave the order they raised hell. But eventually they complied.'

Although June was a month of bitterness, the sense of freedom won in May was not sacrificed that easily. The strike continued. The ranks of far-leftist organizations were swollen with new recruits. The regime's pseudo-democratic mask had been torn from its face; its archaic and arbitrary power stripped momentarily from it; its hierarchies, its mandarins, its class divisions and injustices revealed in a few fulminating weeks of 'criticism through action'. Those who had experienced this liberation were not prepared to stop. The students' immediate task was to support the workers and peasants who were still resisting the regime.

In Paris, the Student-Worker-Peasant Liaison Committee (CLEOP), a Maoist initiative, now attracted some new, non-Maoist recruits. With 5,000 francs collected in the streets, Pierre Félix and fellow students bought large supplies of potatoes, bananas, powdered milk from the Paris wholesale market on CLEOP's behalf. Lorries delivered these to the courtyard of the Agronomy Institute. The students informed factory strike committees that supplies were available and they came to pick them up. Everything was sold at cost. 'Many of the strikers were as astonished as us to discover the difference between wholesale and retail prices,' Félix recalled. Although the system worked well, it was criticized by members of the 22 March Movement, who turned up one day, for copying the existing commercial distribution network. 'We should instead be helping the strike committees to help themselves, they said. That's to say, show them the way to the wholesale market and let them work it out for themselves. Not only would they learn more that way but their "exemplary action" would spread to other factories.' Convinced, the committee thereafter took workers to the wholesale market in the early mornings to show them how to buy food.

The CLEOP Maoist leadership was meanwhile devoting itself to the peasantry; it had left factory supplies in the hands of non-Maoists, as Félix discovered, after a serious 'political error'. Plans to distribute free to shantytown dwellers a lorryload of 'liberated' chicken went badly awry when the lorry was stormed and the denizens made off with as many chickens as possible. 'The comrades had "over-estimated the level of consciousness of the masses". Having made their self-criticism, they were now re-orientating their activities to the "poorest strata of the peasantry,"' Félix explained.

But the peasantry in the conservative eastern region of France where they focussed their campaign were no more accessible to their propaganda than the shantytown dwellers, as they were obliged to recognize in a report back to CLEOP. 'In one small town they had unfurled their red flags in the market place, displayed a picture of Mao and distributed leaflets,' Félix recalled. 'Peasants gathered with apparent interest round their lorry. A woman comrade took the loudspeaker and began: "Comrade peasants!" Hardly had she uttered the words when "the masses" began running in all directions, some of them shouting, "I'm going for my gun!" The Maoists had to beat a hasty retreat. "The conclusions to be drawn from this action, comrades," summed up the head of the CLEOP-political section, "is that we must absolutely revise our methods of work. As Chairman Mao Tse-tung said . . .""

Time, however, for such revisions or indeed new initiatives was running out. The movement's failure to fill the power vacuum before de Gaulle again seized the initiative opened the floodgates to reaction. The regime began sending in police to clear out the strikers in public services – a move that was initially unsuccessful. Needing a decisive victory, the government picked on the Renault factory of Flins, near Paris, where, in a surprise move, the CRS evicted the strikers. But even there they had not counted on the workers' resistance: for four days workers, aided by students who rushed out from Paris, battled the police in the surrounding countryside. It was the first time during May that workers *en masse* fought the police; and many of the students who fought by their side took their inspiration from this when, later, they created new revolutionary groups. But the CRS eventually won the battle, and this marked the beginning of the end for the general strike.

Slowly the return to work gathered pace; in some of the large plants workers received considerable pay rises, but in many smaller ones got nothing at all. Confident of its power now, the government outlawed all the far-left organizations, the JCR and UJC-ml among them, though they would soon reform under other names.

Finally, in the third week of June, the Gaullist regime won a massive victory in the general elections. Socialists and Communists lost half their former parliamentary seats. Failure to carry a movement forward rarely wins votes once the ruling order is firmly back in the saddle. Using its control of television, the Gaullist regime played blatantly on the alleged threat of a 'Communist seizure of power' during the recent events to frighten voters into a realization of where their actions might have led. Nothing could have been further from the truth, but the Communist Party had now to pay the price of its policies. Many of the radicalized youth were under the voting age of twenty-one; as many, perhaps, refused to vote in elections that they considered a fraud. The grip of ruling-class ideology had received a rude blow; but it had not been overturned. The impossibility of creating ongoing structures of self-management, new social organisms, meant that there was no realistic projection of the new forms of organization that had sprung up during May. Instead, bourgeois 'normality' returned: the sovereign general assembly in which everyone could speak gave way to the sovereign individual who, in the silence of marking his or her solitary vote, was asked to be heard from once in only every so many years.

Northern Ireland And Italy

In only two other countries in this book – Northern Ireland and Italy – did
student movements help to catalyse other social constituencies to action
that seriously challenged the existing order. The two movements and their
respective countries were very different from each other, but both challenges bore resemblances to the two phases of the French May events. In
Italy, the 'hot autumn' of 1969 attempted to democratize local powers,
notably on the shop floor; in Northern Ireland, the struggle against an
authoritarian regime from the autumn of 1968 to the summer of 1969
shook the state and led to the brink of civil war. Compared to the sudden
outburst in France, both movements took place over a longer period of
time and both began from different starting points.

Northern Ireland: The People's Democracy

As in France, it was a student movement that had barely existed a few
months before which drove events forward. The challenge came over civil
rights for the Catholic minority; like the black American movement, only
in the space of a few months, the student movement which grew out of this
challenge travelled a distance that took it from a civil rights campaign to a
socialist revolutionary movement. En route, it created an organization –
People's Democracy – which expressed the democratic aspirations
common to many other student movements; and in the course of a few
months it played a major role in the unravelling of the Northern Ireland
crisis as it confronted a state whose intransigence lay at the heart of a
conflagration which, in a very different form, continues to this day.

The underlying obduracy of the Protestant Ulster Unionist regime,
which had governed the semi-autonomous region of the United Kingdom
without interruption since its creation nearly fifty years earlier, was evident
from the start of the civil rights campaign in 1968. The Unionist Prime
Minister, Terence O'Neill, had made some cosmetic attempts from the
mid-1960s to close the rift between Protestant and Catholic communities;
but no fundamental reforms had been implemented to put an end to
the institutionalized political, social and economic discrimination of
Catholics. Since the partition of Ireland in 1921, the Protestant Ulster

regime had resorted to flagrant gerrymandering to ensure that local elections did not result in Catholic majorities, maintained an almost exclusively Protestant police force and retained a Special Powers Act that gave it sweeping powers of detention, proscription, and internment. In a region of traditionally high unemployment, the Catholic out-of-work was often twice, if not three times as high as that of Protestants, while discrimination against Catholics in the social services, most notably public housing, was common currency.

A new, moderate, non-violent organization, the Northern Ireland Civil Rights Association (NICRA) was set up in 1967 to put pressure on the regime to carry out the needed reforms. But the regime rapidly showed its hand: police prevented the first civil rights march from reaching its destination; and brutally attacked the second in Derry (or Londonderry, as the British and the Ulster Protestants call it) on 5 October 1968. It was the latter which started the student movement.

Up to that point nothing had mobilized the large mass of students. 'Our movement was very different from others,' explained Bernadette Devlin (now known under her married name of McAliskey), a politically un-affiliated Catholic student at Queen's University, Belfast. 'It didn't start from university conditions, from youth culture or Vietnam. As for what was happening with the students in Paris and London, we looked upon them to some extent as a bunch of weirdos – we didn't know what the hell was annoying them. What we related to was the American civil rights move-ment. Within the institutionalized discrimination of the state, we saw ourselves basically as blacks. Many of us weren't even aware that we lived in ghettos until we discovered the black ghettos and said, that's our position, we're all stuck here on the edge of towns with the worst social conditions. The fact that the black community in America was doing things that we had never even tried made us realize what we might be able to do. Martin Luther King's "I have a dream" speech was one of the turning points for me.'

Catholic students, like Devlin, who had played no part in politics at university, began to rally around the civil rights campaign; so, too, did the handful of radicals engaged in far-left politics at Queen's. Many of them were influenced by Trotskyism, and saw the civil rights issue as a political arena in which they had a role to play. 'NICRA's leadership was moderate, middle-class and certain, we thought, to capitulate to the regime,' noted Henry Patterson, a Protestant working-class student and member of the radical core. 'Our task was to try to point out to larger sections of the population the need for more radical change. The Ulster regime was unreformable, we thought. But until the civil rights issue was resolved, the development of any more progressive politics would be held back.'

When the police indiscriminately attacked the two thousand civil rights marchers in Derry on 5 October, injuring more than seventy people, television coverage flashed the scenes throughout Northern Ireland. 'That did the trick here where television was still quite new,' recalled Michael Farrell, one of the far-left Queen's students who was beaten by the police. 'We had seen this going on in Memphis, Tennessee, but now it was happening at home. Tennessee and Alabama were the background of my consciousness anyway, and these bastards were just the same. It had a tremendous effect on the university – we thought we'd made a really big stride forward in cracking the whole state.'

As the major centre of non-sectarian education in Northern Ireland, with Catholic students forming about one-fifth of the total, Queen's provided a fertile ground for the civil rights movement. Students began to protest immediately about the police brutality in Derry; and three days later, two thousand of them – about half the student body – marched to Belfast's city centre. There they were blocked off by the police. 'The police were standing there looking like a paramilitary group and we were sitting down looking up at them with the City Hall in the back,' remembered Paul Arthur, a postgraduate of Catholic origin from Derry. 'That's when the idea of a police state began really to fit with me.'

Three hours later, frustrated by the police, the students marched back to a meeting at Queen's. 'We were swept along by the feeling of indignation that you couldn't go and march in any part of the inner [Protestant-dominated] city in Northern Ireland without being stopped or beaten up,' remarked Henry Patterson. 'And by the determination to demonstrate that we wouldn't tolerate it, that we hated the old regime.'

'There was a tremendous amount of moral indignation expressed. Hundreds of students, including Protestants, came in. The romanticism was strong – the atmosphere was said to be like that of the Sorbonne,' Arthur recalled. 'After fifty years suddenly things had begun to happen. Everyone poured their souls out and said, "This is what we must do" and doing so, the thing took on a life of its own.'

After many hours of impassioned debate, the meeting agreed to six civil rights aims: one man, one vote; a fair drawing of electoral boundaries; houses on need; jobs on merit; freedom of speech and assembly; and repeal of the Special Powers Act. Simultaneously, it decided to constitute itself as a democratic organization in which anyone who attended its meetings had the right to speak and vote.

'We felt that any structure we created to struggle against an undemocratic regime should exemplify democracy as we understood it at the time,' commented Patterson, echoing much of the prefigurative ideas of the early SNCC and SDS in the United States. 'Basically, this meant having the weakest of possible structures that would allow the participation of the maximum number of people. For now we were dealing with hundreds of people rather than tens, and there were a lot of different political viewpoints. There was pressure for a certain openness . . .'

But to begin with, fearing that the few political activists at the university would hijack their new organization, students elected a 'faceless committee' of ten politically unaffiliated people in the hall to administer the decisions of the general meetings. Bernadette Devlin was one of the ten.

'Our job was to stay up all night when the rest went to bed and do the work for whatever decisions they'd carried out before they changed them! We were a steering committee which had no power – the ultimate in democracy! Part of our job in fact was to hold the middle ground between the small but articulate socialist group on the one hand and a Catholic group which we saw as very right-wing on the other. We had to see that this bus of ours stayed in the middle, clear of any taint of political manipulation from right, left, Catholic or Protestant, and that it remained totally non-violent. Our movement was non-political, non-sectarian, and if we got civil rights established, we could return to our books with the satisfying knowledge that we had achieved something. The vast majority of us didn't see ourselves as socialists. What we wanted was reasonable – basic rights, which we ought to have had – and all the government had to do was give them to us and we'd go away. That's certainly what I felt until January 1969. Then things changed . . .'

How they changed will be seen shortly. In the meanwhile, the new organization remained unnamed. In another piece of spontaneity by a former Queen's student who now ran a press that printed the organization's leaflets, it was endowed with one two days after the initial meeting: People's Democracy, or PD for short. Immediately, another march to City Hall was proposed. The law required that the police be given notice of all marches and an individual's name be given as the responsible organizer. No one stood up to accept the latter role.

'And then, all of a sudden, I remember this extraordinary voice with its amazing rhetorical ability came from one of the rows,' recalled Anne Devlin, sixteen-year-old high school student and daughter of a Catholic Labour politician. 'The voice went out to the roof and came back again: "Mr Chairman, I am an orphan, I have nothing to lose. I will give my name . . ." It was extraordinary because it made everyone go quiet in a meeting of extraordinary egos and extraordinary politics. Everyone turned to see who it was. And, although she had been elected to the "Faceless Committee", no one had ever come across her before. It was Bernadette. Where she got the voice and the confidence to do it, I don't know, but she grabbed her moment in history and set herself on a course for ever after.'

The daughter of a carpenter of Republican sympathies and a mother of lower middle-class origin, both of whom had died, Bernadette Devlin was born and brought up in Cookstown – one of a number of towns built in the early seventeenth century for the thousands of Presbyterians brought from Scotland for the Plantation of Ulster. The town remained essentially divided. 'At the one end was the Old Town, the original settlement which was Protestant. At the other, where the rebels once camped, stood the Catholic area where I lived . . . But it wasn't so much the communal divisions as class that I remember as a child. I was very conscious of being working class, poor working class, though not starving – and of being very much supported by the welfare state.'

As a small child, she recalled, her father told her and the other children bedtime stories of the history of Ireland. 'Naturally, he didn't attempt to be objective about it – it was Ireland's story told by an Irishman, with an Irishman's feelings. Basically, I was brought up on oral history – not only of Ireland but of my own area. I grew up, as very many of our people did, knowing who we were and being able to trace our people back seven generations and knowing what land used to belong to us before they came and took it off us. That had a much stronger impact on me, I think, than anything I read later on.'

At her 'proudly Irish' convent grammar school, the vice-principal became her heroine. 'For her everything English was suspect because most of her family had been sentenced to long prison terms by the British and ultimately gone into exile. Everything we did at school was Irish-oriented.' But she had no hesitation in openly confronting the vice-principal when, in a fit of anger, she tore from a classroom wall a chart of British history which a teacher had asked Devlin to help make for a junior class.

'Her position was unreasonable, and I told her so. If she didn't like us studying British history she should have objected to its being taught in the school – but she didn't. So why should she be allowed to get away with her arbitrariness? If something is reasonable I expect people to behave reasonably about it. That's my driving force – and also my blind spot, because they never do!'

From her convent school she went to Queen's in 1965 with 'some vague notion of being able, one day, to improve some aspect of life in Northern Ireland – such as joining the Ministry of Health and Social Services to work from within the citadel. Politically I was nothing – I wasn't interested. There were quite a few of us who lived frugally on our grants in order to help our families, who had to forgo what wages we might otherwise have earned. My father was already dead and my mother died while I was at Queen's. I had my younger siblings to look after. Working-class Catholics like me knew that our only way out was to work harder than anyone else at university, to get better degrees, so that we stood a fair chance of getting some kind of employment when we got out.'

The People's Democracy demonstration for which she had given her name as organizer was permitted to reach City Hall on 16 October by a worried police. Fifteen hundred students took part in what was to be the last anti-Unionist march allowed into the centre of Belfast.

'There was none of the "smash the bourgeoisie" rhetoric you usually got at student meetings elsewhere,' Bernadette Devlin observed. 'We spoke about ordinary simple issues like jobs, housing and involvement in the system, because we were talking to people to whom these were the issues that mattered. Moreover, we realized that, however nicely we put it, more jobs for Catholics meant less jobs for Protestants. That was a realistic fear of theirs. Understanding this, PD argued for more jobs for everyone. The slogan was, "One family, one house, one man, one job" – and for a long time no one queried the latter phrase!'

A week later, on the United Nations Declaration of Human Rights Day, some seventy PD members occupied Stormont, the Northern Ireland parliament building, and held a teach-in after the House had adjourned rather than discuss the issue of human rights. 'It was the only time in the West, I think, that students occupied a parliamentary building,' observed Paul Arthur. 'Here was the Cabinet not only with a PD sit-in at the centre of the power but sending the Minister of Education to negotiate with us. It was a clear acknowledgement of PD's potential.'

By now the orders were in fact coming from London. Constitutionally, Stormont's powers were strictly limited, and the British government retained supreme authority. Under pressure from the British Labour government, the Northern Ireland Prime Minister introduced a number of reforms which, while making no mention of 'one man, one vote', were too much for the hardliners in his party, who began to campaign for his removal. In response, the Prime Minister made an emotional television speech calling for public support; NICRA decided to call a truce on demonstrations over Christmas; PD, on the other hand, decided to continue with a planned four-day march from Belfast to Derry to start on New Year's Day.

The question of marches was not without sectarian significance in Northern Ireland, where each year the Orange Order publicly demonstrates Protestant supremacy over the Catholic minority in a series of parades and marches celebrating William of Orange's victory over the Catholic King James II at the battle of the Boyne in 1690. Now PD was planning to march through strongly Protestant areas on its way to Derry.

'The march was quite deliberately modelled on the Selma-Montgomery march of 1965, which forced the U.S. government into major reforms,' Michael Farrell, of the socialist left within PD, recalled. 'My feeling was that it would make or break the whole thing. If the regime gave us police protection, the Unionist party would fall apart. If it didn't protect us, O'Neill would be shown as a pawn in the hands of the Orange masters. Either result suited.'

The question of reforming the Northern Ireland regime was not one he posed to himself. 'I believed that if you attacked on a number of fronts the whole thing would collapse some day. If you made demands which couldn't be achieved within the existing state, if you kept on pushing those demands, the state might dissolve – and then the demands you'd been making could be achieved. But I never had the slightest perception of a Northern Ireland state which would continue to exist in some nice, reformed way. I was against discrimination and I believed that a united Ireland was the best solution to the problem. I never separated the two.'

The son of Southern Irish Catholic parents established in a small town in the North where his father was a bank clerk, Farrell had not, as an adolescent, felt personally discriminated against as a Catholic. 'But that, I suppose, was becuse I wasn't from a family that had to apply for a council house or a job with the council. Nonetheless, I and every child in the town

had a general feeling that all official posts would be held by Protestants. All
the same, it was only as the civil rights movement grew that I learnt about
segregation in Belfast and of the ghettos there, most of which I'd never
heard of. I lived in the [non-segregated] student areas around the
university.'

When PD was formed, he welcomed the participatory democracy it
embodied. 'The French May was still fresh in our minds and at that
moment mass democracy, spontaneity seemed a good thing. It was
contrary to hard Trotskyist politics but then I was never that clued up a
Trotskyist. But there came a point at which I think we should have tried to
structure PD properly to make it more democratic. Because as it was, it
ended up with a leadership like me which wasn't actually elected, and it
was unfair both to us and to the mass of students. From my point of view,
we were answerable if anything went wrong, but on the other hand the
students didn't have any real control over their leadership.'

The evidence of this came when a mass PD meeting agreed to observe
the Christmas truce on demonstrations and to call off the Belfast-Derry
march. 'The meeting,' recalled Farrell, 'was held in the Queen's science
block which was a very heavily Protestant faculty and very apolitical. So it
was like playing an away game. My feeling about it was that if this is the way
mass democracy works, then OK, let's have another meeting!' The second
meeting, held at the end of term when many students had left, agreed to go
ahead with the march. Although critical of the way the decision had been
taken, Bernadette Devlin supported the march. 'We felt we had started to
get something but hadn't got anything yet, so why should we stop? If we
had the weight of public opinion behind us, Britain would have to move
against the regime and enforce reforms. We in PD were the most
determined, the most militant, and therefore we held the struggle in our
hands. The basic weight of popular [Catholic] support went with the
students precisely because we were prepared to deal with imperialism and
blame Britain for the situation.'

The Long March, as it came to be called, turned into a watershed. It was
in many of its effects the equivalent of the 'night of the barricades' in Paris:
the supreme moment of student confrontation with the regime's violence
which, in turn, catalyzed other social forces and political organizations –
and, in so doing, finally lost the student movement its dominant role.

Some seventy marchers, most of them Young Socialists, with Farrell as
organizer, set out on New Year's Day 1969 from Belfast on the seventy-
five mile march. Recognition that the march would almost certainly

provoke violence from Protestant extremists deterred a considerable number of PDers; others were put off by the way the decision had been taken. By now large numbers of Protestants had, moreover, dropped out of PD. The civil rights issue was inevitably becoming embroiled in the country's sectarian divisions.

Continually harassed by extremist Protestants who blocked bridges and entrances to towns, the march nonetheless continued, and continued to attract more and more people. One of the few non-Catholic marchers, Paul Bew, who had just finished his first term at Cambridge, was amazed at the welcome the marchers received in the Catholic ghettos. 'Whole schools emptied out to meet us. I'd expected much the same response as I got when trying to sell the International Socialist paper in Cambridge and rarely got rid of a copy! The welcome, I thought, must be due to our intrinsic aims – after all, anybody could see we were after good things. But probably I should have been thinking, there's a problem about this, why are we quite so popular?'

Escorted by police, whom they never trusted not to lead them into a Protestant ambush, the marchers found themselves protected one night in a Catholic village by local Irish Republican Army (IRA) men. 'Had they asked us if we wanted protection, I'm sure we'd have said no,' commented Farrell, 'because we didn't want to be that closely identified with them. The Republican movement had gone quite far to the left at that time, and we were quite friendly and close to it. We wouldn't have been anti-IRA because its existence was, at the very least, a product of the nature of the Northern Ireland state. But the IRA didn't really figure for us.'

Since the failure of the last armed struggle against the Northern Ireland regime between 1956 and 1962, the IRA had renounced its exclusively militarist, politically abstentionist stance, and embraced left politics. Along with Sinn Fein, its political wing, it became involved in the civil rights movement and social and economic agitation. Republicans had, indeed, been among the founders of the Northern Ireland Civil Rights Association. But it was not so much to the Republicans as to the British Labour government that the marchers were looking for help against the Protestant extremists. Bernadette Devlin and another PDer were sent to telephone the British Prime Minister. 'We planned to ask for the Royal Ulster Constabulary [the Northern Ireland police force] to be replaced by English police who would see we got adequate protection on our perfectly legal march to Derry. Of course we knew we'd never get through to the Prime Minister, Harold Wilson, but we spoke to under-under secretaries and private secretaries and told them that it would be the Prime Minister's responsibility if someone was killed.'

Like the civil rights workers during the Mississippi Summer four years earlier, the marchers were hoping that the central government would intervene to take power out of the local state's hands. In both cases they were disappointed, for neither the American federal government nor the British government took steps to protect the civil rights activists. The marchers pressed on. On the fourth and last day their fears of an ambush came true. Only a few miles from Derry, as the marchers descended towards Burntollet Bridge, a horde of assailants burst from a hidden lane, wearing armbands and wielding cudgels. Devlin froze. 'As I stood there I saw this big lump of flat wood, like a plank, getting nearer and nearer to my face – and two large nails sticking out of it. My hand reached my face before the wood did and the nails went into the back of my hand. I fell to the ground and rolled into a ball and didn't move.'

Unlike Devlin, most of the marchers ran. 'But there was nowhere to go except down to the river or straight past our attackers,' Paul Arthur remembered. 'There were police jeeps straight ahead, too, and our people didn't trust the police. Some of them attacked our people and others wouldn't let us through . . .'

More than eighty marchers were injured; they had proffered no violence against their assailants, a large number of whom were later reported to have been off-duty B Specials, an exclusively Protestant paramilitary police reserve force. Sixteen-year-old Anne Devlin was among those hurt. 'I remember several people picking me up and carrying me to a police van to take me to hospital. The police slammed the doors, wouldn't let me in. "Don't come near us!" they shouted. They were frightened. "There's an ambulance down the road."'

The uninjured reformed and continued the march, only to be ambushed again on the outskirts of Derry; petrol bombs and stones were hurled at them. 'The police did nothing about it – in fact they took themselves off to the other side of the march. I got knocked out there,' Farrell recalled, 'and was carted off to hospital to be stitched up. I'd had my head split open. Later, when I was trying to wash all the muck, as I thought, off my arms and legs, I discovered that it wasn't dirt. I was just black and blue all over.'

That night the police rampaged through the Bogside, the Catholic ghetto of Derry, smashing windows and doors and beating up everyone in sight. The population threw up barricades, set up a 'people's militia' and declared the area 'Free Derry'. For a week they kept the police out of the Bogside. It was the beginning of a new phase in the struggle.

The Burntollet affair increased PD's reputation for militancy in the civil rights cause, and it was able to cash in on its prestige in a manner no other student movement attempted in the 1960s: by standing in the general elections for the Northern Ireland Parliament, hurriedly called in February 1969 by the Prime Minister, O'Neill, in an attempt to stave off the crisis. PD gathered over 27 per cent of the votes in the eight constituencies it contested. Bernadette Devlin was one of the candidates. 'We didn't want to get into the Stormont parliament,' she explained. 'But here was our golden opportunity to explain our policies to the people. We took on both parties, Protestant and Catholic, on a non-sectarian platform of radical policies. People laughed at us: "Whoever heard of students going to the country?" But that didn't worry us.'

In the four months since PD's formation as a student civil rights organization, it had turned itself into a socialist group. Devlin, who had been politically uncommitted at the start, thought of herself now as a socialist. 'The most effective solutions to the problems we discussed night after night in PD always turned out to be those offered by the left. Farrell was very important in this respect. We educated ourselves into socialism. The Long March contributed to our education. Previously, many of us feared that if we moved overtly to the left it would frighten people off. Now we said, What's so frightening about being on the left, if it's the only way to get justice?'

People's Democracy had now definitively broken from its original student base. In the process it became smaller. 'The more socialist and the more determined PD grew, the fewer its student numbers became,' Devlin observed. 'PD lost what it had once had – a solid movement of people who took action, and a well-attended discussion forum for the development of ideas. For a brief period, we were the leaders of the struggle and then we lost it in as many months because we didn't know what to do with it.'

From the start, one of PD's aims had been to unite the Catholic and Protestant working class. As the civil rights struggle for Catholics became sharper, and PD remained its leading edge, so this unifying aim seemed to some to grow more distant. Farrell came to recognize the problem. 'The division between the two classes was so great that there wasn't any easy way of bridging it. At that time we all had a very crude and deterministic notion

of ideology being determined by class interests which can change overnight. But, as I came to learn, the Protestant working class cannot be
approached on purely class issues because the question of their privilege
[over the Catholic minority] is sublimated into a sense of national identity,
flags and symbols etc., which are uppermost in their minds.'

People's Democracy was thus caught between having lost its student
support and being unable to find an inter-communal working-class base.
While eschewing sectarianism, it almost inevitably chose to see in the
Catholic working class the major agent of change. Catholics had indisputably voted for PD as the most advanced organization in the civil rights
movement; but it was not able to put down strong roots and attract a mass
of new members to make good the student loss. As in France, the
translation of social into political strength at a time of heightened political
tension proved very difficult. PD never again reached the heights of the
Long March and the elections.

Before events finally started to unravel in August 1969, Bernadette
Devlin achieved one of the most spectacular victories of an individual
student in those years: her election, almost despite herself, to Westminster
in a by-election for Northern Ireland's largest constituency, Mid-Ulster.
Aged twenty-one, she was the youngest member of a British Parliament
for nearly two hundred years.

'I didn't want to stand. I didn't know anything about Parliament or about
formal politics. I didn't even respect the system. My whole experience
in Northern Ireland showed that politicians elected to Parliament lost
honesty, integrity ... But I was selected when both the Republican-
and Nationalist- [Catholic-] backed candidates withdrew.'

Standing as a Unity candidate of the political forces opposed to the
Ulster Unionists, she adopted the PD's non-sectarian radical socialist
platform, and was elected with the biggest anti-Unionist majority since the
seat's creation. The next day violence erupted in Derry after a civil rights
march from Burntollet bridge, scene of the Long March ambush, to the
city. Police again rampaged through the Catholic Bogside, and Devlin,
who happened to be there, encouraged the defenders to build barricades.
The next day Derry was on the brink of open war; rioting spread to Belfast,
and the Prime Minister took the only step remaining which he hoped could
defuse the situation: he accepted the principle of one man, one vote. A
week later he was out of office, resigning rather than accept defeat by his
party hardliners.

'The riots in April were the beginning of the road that ended four months later,' Devlin, who now rushed to London to take her seat and speak in an emergency parliamentary debate on Northern Ireland, maintained. Arriving only a few hours before the debate was to start, she was met by hordes of photographers and pressmen. Overnight, she had become the biggest media attraction in Britain. 'As far as they were concerned, I was a mass of flesh which had become public property. None of them wanted to ask the basic questions to find out why the situation in Northern Ireland had produced the "baby" of Parliament.'

Her maiden speech to the House warned that the time for Westminster's discussion and action had almost passed. '"There can be no justice while there is a Unionist party," I said, warning them, too, of the danger of sending British troops in. And they all said "Hear! Hear!" and thought it was delightful stuff, which showed the House up for what it was.'

In August, four months after her election, communal strife exploded into virtual civil war. The summer is usually a dangerous period, with July and August the Loyalists' marching time when they demonstrate their 'ascendancy' over Catholics. It was one of these marches in Derry which led to the outbreak of fighting there – fighting which rapidly spread to Belfast. The British army was called in, and for a month the Catholic ghettos of Derry and the Falls Road in Belfast virtually seceded, becoming behind their barricades 'no-go' areas even for British troops.

The fighting in Bogside, Derry's Catholic ghetto, lasted for over forty-eight hours before the British army appeared. Again Bernadette Devlin was at the heart of the defence; to her anger, the leaders of a recently created Citizens' Defence Committee were not in their place behind the barricades when the fighting broke out. 'It was left to hooligans like myself and other political activists to organize the defence against the police, who were going to settle the Bogside once and for all.

'It was youths who did most of the fighting. As long as something I suggested made sense to them they'd do it. In moments of crisis like that it doesn't matter whether you're right or wrong, it's whether you can issue short, sharp, clear instructions that give the impression that you know what you're doing. You've got to be able to put the world in slow motion and seem to have thirty minutes in what is actually thirty seconds to see what's got to be done. You've got to have an instinct for mass movements, an ability to see where the gap in the hedge is, and how to drive through it . . . All the same, if something didn't make sense, some kid would point it out and come up with a better idea. And I'd say, "That sounds good, who'll do it?"'

As youths rained down petrol bombs from the roof of a high-rise block of flats that she had seen provided a strategic vantage point, the police retaliated with CS gas for the first time in Northern Ireland. 'The gas made you vomit. But I believed you could vomit just as well going forward as back. I kept telling people, "If you don't breathe through your nose, the gas won't do you any harm." I may have even believed it myself for a time! But it was the kids who showed us the only thing that worked. With a bit of rag or blanket in their hand, they'd pounce on the cannisters the moment they landed and throw them back. It was unbelievable! And although it didn't stop them choking, at least it made the police choke as well.'

After forty-eight hours of battle, the police, Devlin was convinced, were on the point of winning. 'And then suddenly, just as we were about to be overwhelmed, we saw them pulling right back to their lines. People thought we had beaten back the police and won! It seemed illogical to me. What had happened was that the British army had appeared.'

Hoisted on to a commandeered post-office van, she listened as the Defence Committee leaders – 'the only clean shirts in the Bogside' – told the crowd that the army, which did not attempt to enter the area, had come to protect them. 'Then a kid, who had been on the roof of the block of High Flats for the whole battle, shouted up at me: "Will we fight the British army, Bernadette?" And I said, "Not yet, let's see what's going to happen . . ." But my words were lost as I landed in the street. Terrified that I was going to say yes, the leaders pushed me off.'

For the next couple of days, at street corner meetings, she argued strongly that the British army should not be made welcome, that it had not intervened to help the Catholic minority. She knew that she was going against the grain of opinion, which welcomed the army as having delivered Catholics from the tyranny of the Ulster police forces. 'I could see that the people were going to have to learn for themselves. It was hard to persuade them intellectually that an army which had been sent in to shore up the state would inevitably have to take issue with the people who were causing the state to shake. And, indeed, the honeymoon period lasted for a very short time.'

Four months later, Devlin was convicted of 'incitement to riot' for her part in the Bogside defence and sentenced to six months prison, a sentence she started to serve in June 1970.

As the fighting was ending in Derry, it was beginning in Belfast on an even more serious and deadly scale. After rioting at a police station in the

Catholic Falls Road area, Loyalists launched a fierce attack on Catholic ghettos, shooting and burning houses as they went. That night, 14–15 August, five Catholics and a Protestant were killed – the heaviest death toll in a single night in Northern Ireland's history till then. There was fear of a massive pogrom, and the Catholics barricaded their streets.

'It was amazing,' recalled Michael Farrell, who was in the Falls Road area. 'We'd read about barricades in Paris in the nineteenth century, and Russia in 1905, but here they were going up in the working-class streets of the Falls. It was a Belfast Republican tradition from the 1920s and obviously it had been handed down and people just came out and did it.'

As in Derry, British troops took up position without breaching the barricades, behind which 'Free Belfast' had been declared. A handful of PDers set up a radio transmitter and started the *Citizens' Press*, a duplicated paper which sold as many as 25,000 copies for a penny each. John Grey, a Protestant PDer, was active on both paper and radio. 'The station was, I think, the best form of free radio – a mixture of politics, by and large non-sectarian, and satire. My own speciality was doing nightly sermons purporting to be the Reverend Ian Paisley [the extremist Protestant leader] on such matters as the duty of all Protestants to paint every blade of grass in Ireland orange or on the dangers of British troops accepting a cup of tea from a Catholic . . .' As a Protestant himself he had no problems in Catholic 'Free Belfast'. 'Not only that, but I've always held that a Protestant who shows any vestige of sympathy with the Catholic situation is by and large perfectly safe in Catholic areas. That is a tremendous contrast to the situation the other way round.'

When the British army moved in on the other side of the barricades, he had felt a sense of relief. 'Quite honestly, if they hadn't turned up, the pogrom could have gone very much further. It was common knowledge that the area had been left defenceless at the time, that the Republicans had been caught napping and were unprepared militarily for the situation. It shows, I think, how little people had conceived of an armed struggle at the time. But at the same time I was convinced that bringing in the army without any resolution of the longer term problems was creating a new problem on the horizon.'

As, indeed, it did. Unprepared and unable to defend the area, the Republicans rapidly attempted to reassert some sort of control. PD now shared the experience of the French movement with the Communist party and found its path blocked by an older challenger to the established order.

Admittedly thin on the ground, PD was excluded immediately from the non-elected Central Citizens' Defence Committee, in which Republicans were solidly represented; and the latter were openly hostile to popularly-elected committees in the zone.

'After about a week or so this Republican guru turned up from Dublin,' recalled Grey, 'dressed in a suit and carrying a briefcase. Almost the first thing that happened was that he got himself arrested because he went in the wrong direction! The Republicans, who were at the time pursuing a quasi-Communist line politically, wanted everything under their direct control. They were totally averse to popularising any concept of armed struggle, to politicizing the situation. A PDer who brought in a poster of Che Guevara and put it up on the wall of the radio station was hauled before them and told he'd be declared *persona non grata* if he ever brought in anything like that again.'

Young women PD members like Anne Devlin, a Catholic, also felt the weight of Republicanism in 'Free Belfast'. 'One day I was told off by the Republican commandant because I was wearing a dress. An order had been given out that girls had to wear trousers. Apparently Republican women had complained about me. It was all very trivial, but it made me think of personal freedoms that I wasn't willing to give up. There was a feeling that the line was hardening. And since I had never supported Republicanism I had no faith in it.'

Nonetheless, behind the barricades the situation seemed revolutionary to many. 'People's control, barricades, committees, clandestine radios and power politics going on outside. I really thought I was a revolutionary!' recalled Jeff Dudgeon, another Protestant PDer. 'My dominant memory is of sitting on the barricades at night with a cup of tea talking to the locals. The talk was very mature, sensible, unsectarian. The people showed a sense of relief that they'd got the Unionists off their back, but there was no feeling that they wanted to dominate the Protestants.'

Despite the failure – due to Republican hostility – to set up popularly elected political institutions where the state's power was no longer oper-ative, Michael Farrell saw 'Free Belfast' as an extraordinary manifestation of a revolutionary force seizing part of the state's power. 'To find ourselves in a situation of dual power like that, where the British army and police wouldn't come into our streets, was an amazing development. You'd read about things like this happening in Russia in 1917 but this was happening in our own streets. It wasn't as politically explosive as it could have been because of the failure to set up popular assemblies, street committees and the like. But if you didn't make the best use of the occasion the first time – so what? You learn for the next time.'

After a month, despite PD opposition, the barricades were dismantled, largely due to the intervention of local politicians and the Catholic clergy. Four months later, the IRA split. Anger and frustration at the lack of defence preparations for the ghettos in August – attributed to the Republican movement's turn to left-wing politics in the previous years – led to a walkout by dissidents. The Provisional IRA (better known as Provos) was born. Believing in the power of the gun, they went into action for the first time in June 1970, and the British army was soon involved in trying to eliminate them. The rest is unfinished history.

In the year between the first civil rights march and the barricades of Free Derry and Belfast everything had changed: what had begun as non-violent protest had ended in laying the ground for armed struggle. Was the end result inevitable?

'Communal defence would have provided self-defence,' argued Bernadette Devlin, who was re-elected to Westminster in 1970. 'There was no need for armed struggle. Everybody will defend a barricade but not everybody will shoulder a rifle. Armed defence took away from the people themselves the responsibility of their own defence and put it in the hands of somebody – inevitably "somebody" whom they didn't know what they were doing – who was supposed to be looking after them. That militated against democracy when the basic need was for the democratic political organizing of people to understand where the struggle was going . . . But at that stage we couldn't win the argument for political defence, because between August 1969 and the introduction of internment two years later, people instinctively felt that we were already into a fight to get rid of the state. And in people's psychology here that's where armed struggle belongs. It's hard for people outside Ireland to understand that, because of our history, armed struggle is not a big step to envisage.' (Twelve years later, in 1981, she was herself narrowly to survive a Protestant extremist assassination attempt; gunmen shot her and her husband, wounding both.)

There were numbers of rank-and-file PD members who felt after August 1969 that their own organization's 'irresponsibility' had started something that had been allowed to get out of control. Jeff Dudgeon, the Protestant PDer who had thought of himself as a revolutionary behind the Belfast barricades, felt 'personally responsible and guilty for the monster we had created.' Though later he would come to see that the break-up of a fossilized state was bound to be violent, he would not have joined PD – 'an organization that maintained a Trotskyist style of exacerbating minorities, driving up and onward in order to destabilize things' – had he foreseen the consequences.

'We had never really come to terms with sectarianism, we failed to recognize that there were actual divisions between both communities which were important to both sides,' noted Carmel Roulson, a Catholic PD student who had been in at the organization's founding. 'And we had some very confused ideas that civil rights were the first step towards socialism – if you pressed on without stopping, in the framework of a [Trotskyist] theory of permanent revolution, you would achieve socialism. That was a mistake. Neither the Catholic nor obviously the Loyalist community was particularly interested in socialism or non-sectarianism. Most of us felt there wasn't much we could do. We stayed in and around PD but we gradually became less involved in politics.'

After August, PD declared itself a revolutionary socialist party and, in a further attempt to bridge the sectarian divide, devoted its energies for the following year to social campaigns aimed at both communities. They met with limited success. Although by late 1971 PD was giving 'critical support' to the Provos, Farrell, the PD leader, believed that even at that time quite a large proportion of the Protestant population 'was prepared to admit that things had been wrong and were going to have to change'. The armed struggle, he felt, need not have begun.

As in other countries, the transition from anti-authoritarian and civil rights struggles to socialist revolution was readily made by student activists but not by the constituencies which their initial militancy had helped rouse to action. Even in insurrectionary situations like France and Northern Ireland, the established order's ideological hegemony over these constituencies was not easily broken. The expansion of democratic rights within the existing order, rather than the overthrow of the order itself, appeared as the immediately galvanizing force; the struggle for socialism was for the long haul.

Italy's Hot Autumn, 1969

The situation in Italy was very different from either Northern Ireland or France. To begin with, the Italian state lacked the authoritarian features that characterized the Gaullist and Unionist regimes. Indeed, there was a traditional separation between Italian society and state which in part was filled by a large bureaucracy, in part by strong regional and local loyalties. The country's political regime could be in crisis – had in fact been for a number of years – without causing unduly threatening tremors to the system. In these circumstances, the challenge to the established order did not arise in reaction to state oppression, nor did it have the same repercussions on the political regime as in the other two countries. It arose rather against the power exercised by those in authority in factories, offices and schools.

While in France the movement was compressed into the space of eight weeks, and in Northern Ireland into the same number of months, the Italian movement continued for several years. Beginning in the spring of 1969, the movement swelled into the 'hot autumn' of the same year – the third largest strike in Western Europe since the French May and the British General Strike of 1926 – and then flowed on through the capillaries of Italian society until the mid-Seventies. It was a revolt, of wage labour in particular, which revealed links with the Turin student movement's earlier struggles against the 'feudal' structures of the university.

Indeed, it was in Turin that the movement began. The student rebellion there awoke a sympathetic response from a large sector of the new Turin working class, created by the expansion of the Fiat automobile complex. Recruited mainly from the impoverished South, these new, largely young workers were mobilized into action by high-speed assembly-line work, to which they were not used, and by the extreme shortage of housing in the city. Neither Fiat, local nor central government had made any plans for accommodating the sixty thousand migrants who had arrived in 1967 alone. Living in miserable conditions in a city that was hostile to them, un-unionized and unskilled, it was these Fiat assembly-line workers who led the strike wave. It was not the first time in modern capitalism that a new working class of rural origin was to become the leading edge of an insurrectionary movement.

But it was their alliance with students which gave the movement a new tonic. The student rebellion itself had climaxed in the wave of university struggles before the French May, and by the autumn of 1968 was in a state of flux. 'Even in the university the movement was no longer there, I don't know why,' commented Luigi Bobbio, the Turin student leader. 'The movement had produced militants who didn't know what to do – over-produced political activists who saw in politics the realization of their own lives. Meanwhile the workers' struggles were continuing . . .'

It was at this point that the Student-Worker League, formed in Turin in the spring of 1968, argued ever more insistently in student assemblies for the movement to link up with the working class. This, in the very bastion of 'student autonomy', was anathema to many of the student veterans; they had always argued that their struggle must concentrate on their own emancipation as students, and had repudiated traditional political forms of waging their battles.

Laura Derossi, one of these veterans, expressed her hostility to this 'turn to the working class' in the assemblies. 'I was totally against it because I was convinced of the value of the sort of exemplary actions we had undertaken in the past. The student movement, I thought, was finished, we'd expressed all we had to say. I didn't now want to be transformed into an intellectual preaching to the working class. I had terrible fights in the assemblies with the Student-Worker League which argued that the working class was the central agency of change and students peripheral to it. I believed that as students we could relate to the working class as one social stratum to another.'

Very shortly even she would be obliged to change her view. In the meanwhile, the Student-Worker League made headway – among students, at least. Peppino Ortoleva, who in the past had argued the case for student autonomy, joined the League. 'There was this huge force accumulated at the university which couldn't find an outlet. Then a series of strikes began at Fiat in May for a forty-hour week – they were still working on Saturday mornings – and for three Saturdays there was a huge student presence at the factory gates.'

The two movements, students and workers, did not yet make an organic link. There were considerable distances between them, as Ortoleva discovered some months later when, in response to a police slaying of two workers in the south, he and other students broke down the gates of a Fiat factory. 'The place was deserted because the workers were in the canteen. They weren't of the new working class like at the car body shops, but the old type of worker who mistrusted the students. It was a ships' engine plant, and there we were amidst these huge engines, having to climb on each others' shoulders to write our Che Guevara slogans on the walls. That was all we could do. But the story goes that as we were doing this, a solitary worker arrived from the canteen to find a mass of students surrounding him. "Excuse me, are you a worker?" a young student asks. The man looks at him and says, "Why, yes." "Well . . . you are exploited!" The story, which became a joke, gives you a sense of the total distance between them and us.'

But the distance from the new working class, which lived its exploitation much more directly, was less great than even the most optimistic might have supposed. Unsuspected, the link which the students were searching for was on their very doorstep. And when it appeared, even those who had argued against the 'turn to the working class', like Laura Derossi, were convinced.

'In the autumn of '68, the unbelievable happened. The student movement called for a general assembly of workers at the university. And they came in their hundreds!' Derossi recalled. 'The hall was full, packed – it was amazing! Most of them were migrants. And they didn't only pack the hall, they took the microphone and spoke out about their living conditions. "We've had enough," they said. "We live in miserable conditions in the slums and pensions, sometimes able only to rent a bed for the night, half a dozen in a room. And during the day our beds are rented to workers on the night shift . . . We support what you're doing, you students are right." What could one say after that?'

As a result of the student-workers link – decided as much by the workers as by the students – large numbers of students started to picket the huge Fiat Mirafiori assembly-line shops when spontaneous strikes broke out in the spring of 1969; their presence gave a new sense of strength to the workers and isolated the blacklegs.

'We went to the factory gates for every change of shift. The workers told us what had happened. Then we went to the local cafés with them and wrote leaflets based on what they were telling us. It was extraordinary,' recalled Elsa Gili, who had just returned to Turin after eighteen months spent working with African liberation movements. 'Extraordinary to see a grassroots movement springing up, extraordinary for workers and students to be together like that. We felt that we belonged to a powerful movement that was changing the relations of power, changing history. I didn't go back to Africa as planned because I believed I was challenging world capitalist relations of power more directly in Turin. I felt we were living through a pre-revolutionary situation.'

Even those, like Bobbio, who had opposed the link-up, found the new situation incredible. 'We couldn't believe it ourselves. We immediately found we had a role to play that was unquestioned. So we ended up doing in '69 what we'd refused to do in '68. And it led slowly, of course, towards professional militancy, the formation of the political party, all the things we'd fought against in '68. But now we were on the other side.'

The centre of student activity through 1969 – a year when the collective wage agreements in the metalworking and other industrial sectors were due for renegotiation – was now not the university but Fiat Mirafiori. Small meetings were held at the gates, while assemblies took place every night in a nearby hospital, made available by sympathetic doctors. The struggle had historic overtones of the 1920 Turin factory occupations and the intervention of Antonio Gramsci, the Marxist theoretician; but now the students were attacking as reformist the present-day Communist party which he had helped to found. For the new struggles were not confined to wage demands but directly challenged the organization of work and the system of authority within the factory – in a sense the same struggle the students had waged in the university. Shortly, the students would coin a new slogan: 'Fiat is our university!'

Leaflets informing other factories and workplaces of the Fiat demands were signed Assemblea Operai-Studenti (Worker-Student Assembly – a new body distinct from the Student-Worker League which disbanded at the end of 1968) and La Lotta Continua (The Struggle Continues). They put forward egalitarian demands for equal pay rises for all and for unskilled workers to be granted semi-skilled status – the latter inevitably seen as scandalous by older, skilled workers – and in one important point rallied to the positions held by the Turin student movement. 'We are all delegates', the Assembly's leaflets proclaimed – meaning that on the shop floor, as in the university, only direct and constant democracy should apply. Everyone was his or her own representative – no one, neither trade union official nor shop steward, could represent the individual worker, any more than any elected representative had in the student movement.

To some young workers, even those critical of the trade unions, like Rocco Papandrea, a Trotskyist, this was carrying things too far. A twenty-year-old worker, originally from the South, he had started at Fiat Mirafiori in 1969; the previous year, while at night school, he had followed the student movement's development and now attended the Assembly meetings.

'This call for self-representation was a ferocious spontaneism. They didn't just want to change the trade unions, they thought they shouldn't exist. My experience showed the opposite. I became a shop steward very soon after starting at Mirafiori and I went on strike. Alone, the only one of my team. It was in part because I was a shop steward that I was able to bring the others out. And once we started to struggle together, that's when there was democracy on the shop floor. That's when workers at Fiat started to change their lives, when they no longer felt like pariahs but began, with pride, to realize that their problems were common to all and could only be resolved by common action. People freed themselves, life in the factory changed in a radical way. But shop stewards were essential to the process as far as I was concerned.'

The constant and massive presence of students at the Fiat gates had a deep effect on the workers, as Guido Viale, the student leader, recalled. 'It wasn't just the great numbers – although that of course gave them a feeling of physical strength – but, as I discovered later, the sense of finding themselves in a situation where they were supported by students: why were the students there? To answer that question led them to communicate with us, to find a voice to say to the world outside what they wanted. Here were those who had been silenced discovering themselves as the protagonists of their own lives, expressing their needs in a new language. Their descriptions of the assembly line or their emigrant pasts – the language of shepherds mixed with an industrial idiom – were a thousand times more expressive than anything one could imagine. To us it was important that a social stratum that had been silenced should finally speak, for as always it requires a great effort to redefine reality.'

Viale listened to the workers talking. Every day, every night he and many others transcribed their demands into an idiom that would be instantly understood by the other workers, writing leaflets which were then duplicated; up to 50,000 copies would be distributed outside the gates. He believed that the intellectual's role was to become the 'channel' between workers, that the written word had to retain something of the vernacular to make its full impact.

After two months of wildcat strikes, the Worker-Student Assembly called an illegal demonstration 'to carry the struggle beyond the factory'. The demonstration was organized outside and against the official trade union organizations which had called a strike over rents for the same day, 3 July. Thousands of workers and students gathered outside the Fiat Mirafiori gates. 'The head of the police was there with a megaphone insulting the comrades as they arrived. "Sons of bitches," he yelled, "go home and see who your sisters are screwing!" Immediately after that,' recalled Marco Revelli, a Turin student, 'the *carabinieri* charged. The people fought back, inhabitants threw flower pots and other objects from the roofs of their houses. The place was swarming with police. Rumours arrived of another rally starting, of the town hall in a working-class neighbourhood being seized. A truck was used to make a barricade. Then a student arrived on a motorbike carrying a trophy – a policeman's plastic riot shield. I felt I was in the midst of a mass insurrection.'

The demonstration reformed and started off along the Corso Traiano, a wide boulevard running from the main Mirafiori entrance. Elsa Gili was in the front ranks. 'There we were, a line of women and workers, marching towards the police ranks blocking our way. The boulevard in front was black with them. We were unarmed, just chanting slogans. As we reached them they charged . . .'

Under the weight of the police attack, the demonstrators, Gili and Revelli among them, fled into the fields around. 'We could run faster than the police with all their gear. All the same there was a taste of battle. I ran into a working-class block of flats guarded by workers who kept the police out,' Revelli recalled. As night fell, news came that clashes with the police had started again outside Mirafiori and that people were blocking the streets near the railway station. 'When I returned home I felt I was leaving a city in the throes of a civil war. Columns of smoke were rising into the sky, helicopters were whirling back and forth . . .'

These were astonishing events, but they were not repeated elsewhere. Nonetheless, the press, which had so far ignored the Fiat struggles, gave the battle front page coverage next day; and the government, coincidentally, fell yet again. The Worker-Student Assembly called a national conference of working-class militants under the theme: 'From Fiat to Turin, from Turin to all Italy'. Agitation began spreading to other factories in the industrial North and, although on a much more limited scale, southwards as well.

Piero Bernocchi, a Rome University student, was active in the student-worker alliance which set out to mobilize workers in the capital's relatively small industrial sector for the new contracts to be negotiated in the autumn. 'We chose the three largest factories, which had several thousand workers between them, and a number of smaller ones. In the space of three to four months, we'd got rank-and-file committees or factory councils, directly elected by the workers, going in most of them. It seemed as though the worker-student alliance was a means of widening the student movement, which in fact was dying.'

In Naples, engineering and medical students formed a safety and health commission to investigate conditions in a local Olivetti plant. 'Eight hundred workers came out of the factory to open a passage through security guards to bring us in,' recalled Giuseppe Di Gennaro. 'It was beautiful! They really believed that not only could we measure the health hazards but eliminate them. We were brought to trial for going into the factory, but the judge decided in our favour and allowed us to continue studying conditions in the plant. Then we clashed with the trade unions who believed that these matters were their sole concern. But we stuck to our line: no money, no increase in wages, can compensate for health hazards. We were aiming at the sky!'

It was becoming rapidly clear that the trade unions and political parties were being left behind by the gathering movement. In the summer of 1969, strains began to show in the Communist party when a group of dissident party intellectuals and parliamentarians began publishing a monthly called *Manifesto*. Stressing the importance of the student movement, workers' councils or soviets, the Chinese Cultural Revolution and the worker-student alliance, it brought support from a new quarter for workers who were organizing independently of their traditional forms of representation and resorting to forms of direct action. Moreover, just as in France during the May events, technicians and clerical workers were now beginning to mobilize alongside manual workers; it was a new phenomenon that was to widen the strike movement beyond the traditional working class.

Adding to the increasing sense of social tension, hundreds of thousands of high school students across the country began occupying their schools, demonstrating and picketing outside factory gates. Their movement, which started in 1968, gathered pace during the following year around a number of radical demands: the right of self-government in school, the right to study in groups and to select courses outside the official curriculum, the raising of the school-leaving age for all to eighteen. Underlying their agitation was the political position that high school selection was based on class discrimination, and that students were being prepared for a life of exploitation which resembled the workers' condition. These were themes which university student leaders disseminated in the high schools when their own movement appeared to be stagnating in 1968; and when the link with the working class arose, high school students followed the example set by university students and picketed outside factory gates.

The high school movement illustrated the deepening anti-authoritarian mood that was sweeping across the country. Federico De Luca Comandini was a sixteen-year-old student at one of the elite Rome high schools, the Liceo Mamiani, in 1968; although both his lawyer parents had been in the Resistance, he did not think of himself as political. 'I read Nietzsche and Sartre, but the only things that interested me were girls and my own reflections on life. And then one day I got a phone call: "Come quickly, the school is being occupied." I went and very soon I found myself in the front line . . .'

The occupation, the second of a high school in Italy, had been started by a couple of hundred left-wingers among the 1,500 students. In retaliation, the principal ordered the school closed. De Luca Comandini was suddenly seized by an idea: ' "If the principal won't come to us, we shall go to him," I said to the assembly. It was a real inspiration! Between eight hundred and one thousand of us set out and went to his house. He was obliged to re-open the school and to recognize the assembly in a signed document, the first time it had happened. A document that wasn't even legal because he had no power to recognize the assembly!

'But it wasn't the document that mattered or even the recognition. What was important was the anti-authoritarianism we were expressing, the right to say no to an institution. Out of it came a change in the relations between students and teachers, a change in the relations between the generations, a practical and psychological change in one's life. Because we were adolescents we were more likely, perhaps, to have our lives changed by an act of refusal, by an occupation. For a student to go on a Vietnam demonstration was an affirmation of personal freedom, a way to do something for Vietnam. But his or her own Vietnam was the possibility of self-expression, of saying: "Now I am organizing on my own behalf, now it's I who count." And that is what was important to me about the occupation and about '68.'

After months of wildcat strikes and agitation – 250 million working hours had been lost in stoppages in industry and public services by the autumn of 1969 – the three trade unions went on the offensive. Having followed rather than led the movement so far, they feared that it might escape their control, and accepted many of the new demands that were being made. Factory councils and assemblies; equal wage increases for all workers, irrespective of grade; the elimination of regional wage disparities for the same work; the forty-hour week. With more than a million metal- and building-workers' pay settlements due for renegotiation in the autumn of 1969, the unions' traditional role was reinforced. These two factors enabled them to monopolize the pay negotiations during the 'hot autumn' and to re-establish a measure of control on the shop floor. Due in large part to the pressures the movement had created, the unions were able to negotiate an agreement in the metalworking industry which included many of the demands.

The agreements satisfied some of the workers' immediate demands but not the many more profound demands for power in the workplace. The movement continued in factories and high schools, spread out to government and corporate offices, and to such public services as transport and mail, and affected the professional classes, especially lawyers. 'Society became so polarized,' commented Elsa Gili in Turin, 'that it felt as though we were on the brink of civil war.'

The established order in workplaces and schools was certainly being challenged but Italy was not on the brink of civil war. Turin was not Paris, the capital of a highly centralized nation where unrest was immediately reflected on the political regime. But the feeling of civil war was understandably reinforced when, in December 1969, a massive bomb blast in a Milan bank killed seventeen people and wounded eighty-eight. Originally blamed by the government on anarchists, one of whom the police maintained 'threw himself' to his death from a window during interrogation, the bombing was in fact the work of the extreme right.

'For the first time there was suddenly a feeling of having to defend the left from the state apparatus itself,' Gili continued. 'It contributed to the idea of building political organizations.' From the end of 1969 student activists began to form political groups, and from the summer of 1970 the Red Brigades (as will be seen subsequently) started a bombing campaign.

But the grass-roots movement in workplaces and schools continued into the early 1970s. Women university students found themselves playing a new role at the factory gates. Franca Fossati, a member of Lotta Continua, one of the new political groups formed by students, volunteered with her girlfriend to 'intervene' at the Autobianchi car works forty kilometres from Milan. There they ran up against the strength of the Communist trade union.

'Nobody else wanted to go, so we said, "All right, we're going alone." Me and Silvia and four thousand workers! It was an incredible life. Driving from Milan in my little Fiat 500, we were outside the works at 6 a.m., at 1 p.m., and again at midnight as the shifts changed. In every sort of weather. At the start it was very hard, the tyres of my car were slashed, a *dazebao* [a Chinese Cultural Revolution wall poster] I was holding aloft with the news of what was going on at Fiat in Turin was set fire to in my hands – these were the union people doing these things.'

When the Communist Party secretary of a nearby village who worked in the plant put out the story that the two women were whores, they confronted him in his Party office. 'We, twenty-year-olds, opened the door to see all these male Communist workers in their fifties sitting there. "Is it true that you go around saying that we're whores?" "No, it's not true!" We had a real set-to with them. "Look," we said, "You're going to pay for this. We'll never move from the factory, we have the right to stay here."'

And stay they did, for several months. 'Once we'd got it clear that we weren't whores, a collective relationship built up between us two women at the factory gates and the workers. We were the women they didn't have in their environment and that had a huge fascination for them. We became a myth, a habit, someone to whom they opened their heart over a glass of wine. When Silvia got pregnant – she married my brother – workers who had hardly spoken to us expressed their jealousy, it was very strange . . .'

In the small-town high school where Elsa Gili was now teaching she took part in mobilizing the students. 'During a student assembly over the right to study subjects not on the official curriculum, I stood in the corridor shouting through a megaphone, inciting the students to claim their right to study what they wanted. I turned part of my own geography lessons on the Mediterranean into a study of the Palestinian questions . . . Well, as a result of my intervention in the student assembly I received a letter from the school's principal telling me that my behaviour was "an act of patent and ostentatious insubordination". The fact that I ignored the letter showed that I felt our power was strong enough not to be overthrown by the authorities. And this was true in many workplaces. It was all part of a huge wave of insubordination which was spreading throughout the country.'

This wave began to spread in a small way even to the army, where an organization called Proletarians in Uniform organized by Lotta Continua mobilized conscripts against abuses of military power, and for the right to hold political ideas and to take part in political demonstrations off base. Marco Revelli, a former Turin student and a full-time Lotta Continua militant, staged a virtual mutiny among his fellow-conscripts.

'There was a tradition that after you'd been in the army a certain length of time you didn't have to stand to attention when reveille sounded in the morning. But our company captain ordered me and three others who'd done our time to spring to attention by our beds. We organized a campaign round the issue. When the captain came in with the bugler no one in the whole company got up. Nor did the company go out on parade for the flag-raising ceremony in front of the colonel that morning. It was an act of insubordination, mutiny. We gambled that the captain wouldn't dare tell the colonel – and we were right. He pretended that he'd put the whole company on fatigues because the sleeping quarters were dirty. After that, we went to talk to him, made him understand that he couldn't run the company unless he gave us self-management. Thereafter, we had assemblies each week to decide who was to have passes to go home, who would do guard duties and the like. We'd discuss the political situation, the threat of a right-wing coup d'etat and plans to put it down. It was a great institution – a soviet, a soldiers' soviet, in fact.'

It was not an isolated case. In military as in civilian life, the students' and workers' movements raised demands for democratic self-management. But the link between the two movements could also prove disillusioning, as Piero Bernocchi noted in Rome. Having worked for months to get rank-and-file committees and workers' councils established in the capital's largest factories, his belief in working-class leadership of the revolution was disabused. 'At the personal level it was great to have a relationship with workers, but the longer you went on the more you realized that they were interested only in their immediate economic and political demands. Their alliance with students was really aimed at giving more weight to their own struggles or even to secure advantages for the Communist Party. They weren't open to the liberating demands that we were trying to make.'

The strength of the workers' movement was vitiated, moreover, by the failure to link up its different demands into a coherent challenge to power at all levels. Strength in the factories won the workers significant gains; but their struggles to change social policies – public housing, transport, health – were, with the exception of the latter, less successful. And, overall, state power remained unaffected by their struggles.

But for many, like Elsa Gili, the movement, even if often confined simply to acts of insubordination, had a deeper significance. 'It changed for a time, though not everywhere, that deferential attitude to authority which had existed in Italian society for so long in the past. It changed the way power was exercised on the shop floor and in offices, schools and cultural institutions. Italian society was never quite the same again.'

Starting as a movement to democratize the university, the Italian movement aligned itself with a sector of the working class and seriously challenged the established order. Without this alignment, the impact of the student movement would not have run so deep. This, too, was the lesson of France and Northern Ireland. Articulating grievances and needs that the traditional left parties and organizations did not address, these student movements found resonances in other constituencies, crystallized the many ways in which oppression affected people's lives directly. Before a serious challenge to the existing order could be mounted, it was necessary for these constituencies – blue- and white-collar workers as well as sectors of the professional classes – to want, and be prepared to struggle for, profound change. But once these other sectors of society took up the struggle, the students' role as major protagonists began to diminish; and when the political crisis became acute, as in France and Northern Ireland, the student movements found no way of regaining the political initiative. Under the state's counter-offensive and the shadow of civil war, their untried and untested organizations lost ground to the traditional organizations – trade unions, Communist Party, Republican movement – which offered a time-tested bulwark.

Although in West Germany, Britain and the United States, movement struggles mobilized increasing numbers of people, especially youth, they did not mobilize any significant sector of the working class. The movements' grievances found no ready echo in the organized labour movements which retained their faith in a broad alignment with the status quo. The Vietnam War, for example, evoked little or no resonance amongst the American, German or British working classes. While these difficulties did not dampen student militancy in any of these countries, they did make the immediate challenge to the social order significantly different from that in either France, Northern Ireland or Italy.

6

The Established Order
Challenges the Movements

West Germany and Britain: 1968–69

As the leading West German and British organizations appeared to be gathering strength they suffered reverses which brought about their virtual collapse: by the end of 1968 the West German S D S and Britain's Vietnam Solidarity Campaign (V S C) existed in name only. The failure to evoke a decisive response from the working class, in the German case, and the difficulty of where to take a single-issue campaign, in the British instance, were largely responsible. Although this was by no means the end of student mobilization, or of new forms of struggle and organization, these setbacks, amidst escalating counter-offensives, began to reduce the political space in which students could operate. Thrown back on the university, both movements met further rebuffs. New notions of violence began to emerge. Hopes placed in an imminent French 'revolution' had been dashed; and, in August, hopes of a revolutionary transformation of the Eastern bloc were extinguished by the Soviet invasion of Czechoslovakia. In the same month, a brutal police attack on protesters at the Democratic National Convention in Chicago, and the Convention's failure to nominate an anti-war presidential candidate, dampened hopes of change through the American democratic process. It was increasingly evident to student activists in West Germany and Britain that their struggle was long-term and would have to be waged by new means.

West Germany: The demise of SDS

In their first real political trial of strength, just as French students were throwing de Gaulle's regime into confusion, German students attempted and failed to shake their own government. Here, unlike France, it was not a student movement that had barely existed six months before that was taking on the regime, but a movement with long training and theoretical preparation. Moreover, in the past year, since the police shooting of a student in West Berlin, SDS had become a mass student movement; and in the past month, since the attempted assassination of Rudi Dutschke, it had grown into an Extra-Parliamentary Opposition, attracting many young workers as well as new middle-class recruits. It had achieved its new position in large part by its militancy in battling police in the streets in the bitterest fighting of the post-war era. And yet, when it mounted its challenge to the government it found, in contradistinction to France, that the working class was not there to support it.

The issue was the Emergency Powers Act which the Grand Coalition of Christian and Social Democrats was pushing through parliament. SDS had mobilized against the proposed Act for a number of years, seeing in it the increasing authoritarianism of the state, and in 1966 it had rallied a number of trade union leaders, including the head of the Metal Workers' Union, West Germany's largest, to its cause. On 11 May, as Paris student leaders were calling on the trade unions to demonstrate and strike against the police violence of the 'night of the barricades', a large protest demonstration against the Emergency Laws was held in Bonn. 'It was supposed to be a show of the combined student and workers' strength,' recalled Jürgen Seifert, a long-time SDS activist. 'But the unions copped out beforehand and called a separate demonstration in Dortmund for the same day.' The major reason was that the unions had won a compromise on the Act – the conditions under which strikers could be forced back to work had been eased.

Seventy thousand students and workers nonetheless turned out in Bonn for a peaceful demonstration. In the following two weeks the French general strike heightened a sense in the SDS rank-and-file of the possibility of an 'imminent revolution' in West Germany; under pressure for more radical action, the student organization – or more correctly the Extra-Parliamentary Opposition – called on the trade union movement for a general strike over the Emergency Laws. The call was refused. 'The unions, which have never been a revolutionary force in Germany, found alien to them the role of political counterweight to the Grand Coalition in power,' continued Seifert. Thus the student movement was driven back not by the repressive forces of the bourgeois state but by the refusal of the trade unions to break their post-war consensus with that state.

The sense of disappointment among radical students went deep. 'Democracy in Germany is at an end,' Hans-Jürgen Krahl, the Frankfurt anti-authoritarian leader, proclaimed to 5,000 demonstrators outside the Paulskirche in Frankfurt – the place where the first German parliament after the 1848 revolution had met. His words were shared by great numbers of students, who responded to the events with strikes and occupations in almost every university. Their strategy now was to intensify the struggle within the university in the hope of drawing new recruits into the movement and then to 'carry the struggle into the cities'.

In Frankfurt, the Chancellor closed the university for a week; when it re-opened the students occupied the main building and renamed it 'Karl Marx University'. 'We felt under terrible pressure to do something radical,' recalled Detlev Claussen. 'During the previous semester we'd interrupted lectures to hold debates on the Emergency Laws. The tactic was successful but we had to have something bigger now. We couldn't let the support we'd mobilized during the street battles after Dutschke's attempted assassination melt away.

'The greatest thing of all was that 15,000 people, mainly workers, demonstrated in Frankfurt against the Emergency Laws on the day we took over the University. We'd been agitating permanently at the factory gates, had put the union leadership under a lot of pressure. They even called a half-day strike, which was a lot more than in the rest of the country. I believe there was a readiness to act among the rank-and-file unionists . . .'

Barbara Köster, who had only recently joined SDS and still felt an outsider, went to the Chancellor's office when the occupation started. 'The comrades were all standing in front of the glass doors doubtful about the legality of breaking in. I smashed the glass and opened the door. For the first time I really felt part of the movement – then and later, because I was involved in action. During the occupation I helped to print leaflets, distribute them at factory gates, was on guard at university entrances. After a couple of days, I wasn't allowed in the Chancellor's office, it had been taken over by the strike committee. Shit, I thought, that can't be true! Since I'd smashed the door I felt it was "my" university now, "my" Chancellor's office. I and others who felt the same went in and sat down. "Come on," we said, "you can't do this." They started to talk – they were much better at talking than us – so we just said, "You can go on talking but we're going to stay." The dispute didn't last long but it was an important experience for me to be able to say, "You won't take the occupation away from me."'

It wasn't long – two and a half days – before the occupation was brought to an end by the police; but in that time the students got their Karl Marx University going. It was conceived in part as a direct challenge to the West Berlin Critical University, which had been set up the previous year. 'Those Berliners with their reformist parallel university! Ours was going to be something better, a true "political university". And for two days it really worked,' Claussen recalled.

Two days in which students also sat at the Chancellor's desk and smoked his cigars. Even an old S D Ser like Oskar Negt was impressed by the 'very liberated atmosphere. They were having a lot of fun, answering the phones, giggling. They put on the Chancellor's ceremonial robes and cycled through the main shopping street. I don't think those robes were ever used again after that irreverent treatment!'

During the strike and occupation students went out to factories to try to mobilize workers in support. Claussen's previous optimism about the willingness of rank-and-file unionists to demonstrate their opposition to the Emergency Laws now received a cold shower. 'It was a disaster. Everything we had to say about the proposed laws they knew already. Our arguments about anti-authoritarian education were greeted with a marked lack of enthusiasm. And even Vietnam aroused only an apolitical hostility or a defensive reaction of, "Well, yes, we understand but that's how things are . . . Those in power . . ."'

After files in the Chancellor's office were broken into, the police were called in and ended the occupation. Claussen felt he was living a bitter defeat. 'It was impossible to mobilize any working-class or student support against the police action – there was a terrible sense of powerlessness. I had a physical feeling of defeat that went to the tips of my toes. With the means we'd used up to the present it was clear that we were going to suffer one defeat after another. We'd meant the occupation to be symbolic, and they took it as a real seizure of their seat of power. We realized then that they were forcing us into civil war. It was the only resort left. None of us at that stage wanted it. Out of that defeat, the cult of violence, new forms of action, grew. "A punch to the head is worth more than an argument." And it ended finally with the Red Army Faction [an underground armed struggle group known, in police parlance, as the Baader-Meinhof group] being formed – many of the same people were involved.'

The defeat was more than a political defeat; it was the death knell of

SDS itself as the leading student organization, and by the winter of 1968 it was functioning only in name. But it was not the end of a new radical student thrust. Realizing that their aims could be achieved only by mobilizing social groups outside the university as well as students inside, SDS activists initiated 'base groups' in neighbourhoods to agitate and organize around issues of direct concern to people's lives. Students radicalized by the past year's events became the driving force of these groups. Their action harked back, though with different political perspectives, to the forms of organizing that the American SDS had undertaken in its early days.

'We wanted to contact workers and youth at large to carry on what Dutschke had stressed was the way forward. To draw on the lessons from the attempt on his life,' recalled Michael von Engelhardt, newly radicalized from his right-wing background by the Easter riots. 'We had some working-class apprentices and high school kids in our group, and we took part in a lot of actions. Absurd things, sometimes, like breaking up a Protestant youth club's film show. I was furious at the church trying to seduce young people with Godard movies instead of talking about fascism! We went in and yelled, creating a bit of havoc. Strangely enough, the young people seemed to like it when we came round and stirred things up! . . .'

Even in small, sober provincial towns, youth was 'stirring things up' by now. In Sobernheim, in the Hunsrück region of the Rhineland, the traditional Remembrance Day ceremony for the dead of two world wars turned into something totally unexpected. 'I and others of the Extra-Parliamentary Opposition were going to lay a wreath to the Viet Cong and distribute leaflets,' recollected Thomas Hofmann, a high school student. 'But as I approached the memorial I saw that the bronze statue had a strange shiny look. Others in the group had painted it red overnight and the fire brigade had had to use solvent to get it off! Pistol shaking in his hands, the local cop stopped us and said that "something terrible would happen" if we went to the square. He wasn't so wrong. Practically every local Christian Democrat member was waiting for us with sawn-off broomsticks and attacked us furiously. Girls were beaten up and pulled across the street by their hair. We retreated and got to the square by another route. There the priest, who was also a military padre, was making a speech against people like us who called the red flag our own – "the flag of blood and genocide". A real anti-Communist fervour was being whipped up when suddenly the two soldiers standing to attention in their helmets by the memorial fell to the ground. They'd passed out from inhaling the paint solvent! That was the limit, the town's notables and citizens agreed! Poison must have been mixed with the paint!'

On 20 August, Soviet tanks entered Czechoslovakia to put an end to the reforms initiated by the Dubcek regime during the 'Prague Spring' of 1968. The news of the Russian invasion, which put an end to hopes that a Communist regime could be liberalized from within, came as a blow to student movements everywhere; but nowhere more so than in West Germany, where SDS members had been closely following Czech events for a number of years. Students staged protest actions in many German cities, and SDS, along with other student organizations, issued an open letter to the Warsaw Pact nations – the Soviet Union, Poland, Hungary, Bulgaria and East Germany – which had participated in the invasion of their fellow-pact country.

The letter noted that the American war of extermination against Vietnam had not sufficed to set the Warsaw Pact countries on the march, yet the 'shabbiest of reasons' had been enough to provoke the invasion. 'Through their intervention, based on the danger of a peaceful return to capitalism, these countries have cut off all chances of a truly communist development there. This military intervention makes it clear yet again to all forces of proletarian internationalism how necessary it is to fight against all forms of bureaucratic domination in the different social systems.'

While supporting the reforming Dubcek regime in its attempts to break down the congealed bureaucratic structures of the society and Communist Party, SDS had also been critical of the regime's economic reforms which it perceived as a return to Social Democratic reformism and capitalist structures. Nonetheless, the open letter noted that the 'objective possibility' had existed for workers' self-management and power to 'grow into a new stage of socialist development'.

A few days after the invasion, Peter Tautfest, the American-born SDSer, set off from Berlin for Prague by car with three fellow members. The spontaneous trip was in keeping with the revolutionary internationalism of the time, as Anna Pam who also wanted to go, but was unable to, explained. 'In all extraordinary situations, and none is more extraordinary than a revolutionary situation, the world seems open all of a sudden. The traditional barriers between "home" and "abroad" break down to some degree. It becomes a matter of course to take part in unknown people's activities, whether at home or in a foreign country. It's not only the revolutionary's "extraordinary" state of mind, but the fact that the outside world changes, too. For example, even normal, traditional people suddenly open their doors to strangers. That all this happened in '68 and the few following years indicates that there was at least a revolutionary climate, if not a "revolutionary situation".'

Tautfest and his friends reached Prague without difficulty. None of them spoke Czech. They had with them the mimeograph matrix of a leaflet which a Czech SDSer in Berlin had translated. As a matter of course, they went to the student union to duplicate their leaflet. Suddenly, a Russian tank stopped at the entrance. 'That's it! we thought. But we went on with the job, I don't know why. Either you become naive in dangerous situations or we were just silly. When we had finished, we walked out with our leaflets under our arm, past the tank, and went on our way.

'We distributed the leaflets in the streets. Nobody seemed scared during the week we were there. It was a cultural revolution: wall newspapers everywhere, petitions demanding "neutrality" for Czechoslovakia being openly signed on the streets, a man with a megaphone announcing the petition under the eyes of Russian soldiers. We went to a factory and said we wanted to talk to the workers. After a while we were received by a very impressive, embittered, distressed and tired-looking man. We told him we wanted to convey the total support of the Socialist German Students' Association, we condemned the invasion and wanted to know what we could do for them. He found it difficult to answer, but he told us a bit about the resistance in the factory and that we should tell people at home what we had seen.'

They had no difficulty leaving the country. But two Czech journalists they tried to get out were stopped at the border. 'They had a lot to fear from the re-establishment of the old regime. And they had to stay behind and bear the brunt. I got back to Berlin completely shattered from seeing the Russians' naked display of force, the people's powerlessness against it, the human suffering and the daily life which went on all the same.'

SDS's attempt to set up neighbourhood base groups was a failure. The adult population remained hostile, working-class youth tended to drift in and out, and the radicals found themselves isolated. Their most fertile ground turned out yet again to be the university where base groups were started later in the year. Although as a rule set up by SDS activists, the new base groups did not rally students to SDS; many of the groups' members resented the activists' attempt to dominate their groups, and did not join the student organization. The old anti-authoritarian SDS leaders began to find themselves confronted increasingly by a new wave of student anti-authoritarianism; and the students themselves by university administrations which were reacting strongly to protest: police evictions on the one hand, the carrot of reform on the other, as Claussen recalled.

'After the summer of '68, we were suddenly confined to this goddam university and its reform. The latter was much too little for us after all that had happened before. The one-third student representation they were offering us on administrative bodies wasn't good enough for us. We wanted "self-determination", one person, one vote, the same as we were demanding for South Africa. Even people who called for fifty-fifty representation were regarded as reformists. Any realistic politics was considered bad, if not worse. And that led to a complete incapacity to act politically at all, which in turn led to the continuous self-destruction of SDS in factional fights.'

'Before Christmas 1968, we were evicted from the sociology institute we'd occupied to protest the university reform,' Barbara Köster remembered. 'SDS had proposed that we occupy it. Although I had joined SDS, I was very angry because the longer-standing members wanted to take the initiative away from us in the base group. They called us "base worms". But we wanted all political actions to come from and be led by the base group, and it was we who, in fact, organized the occupation. We had a great time, reading and learning collectively.

'Then we were thrown out. Coming back after the vacation was terribly depressing: the occupation over, the base group dissolved, a girlfriend committed suicide and I was close to it, too. It was the end, the absolute end. And no other action in sight. The only thing left was to go "straight" and study for exams. Then somehow we in SDS decided to occupy the Adorno Institute . . .'

To take over the Institute of Social Research, seat of the so-called Frankfurt School, from which SDS had gathered so many of its early ideas, was an act of desperation that indicated SDS's disarray – and, effectively, marked its demise. Even academics friendly to the student movement were now coming under attack. Adorno called in the police to evict the occupiers; and the liberal and conservative university establishment gloated at the sight.

Despite this, Köster did not lose faith in the anti-authoritarian struggle in the university. She organized a boycott among sociology students of important examinations which decided a student's future. Half the candidates agreed to support her. 'What we wanted was emancipation through collective learning. We were against individual competition and the pressure on performance. It was stupid, we argued, to test this kind of learned stuff – exams are nothing but initiation rituals, and we didn't want to be initiated by this type of repressive institution.'

After the exams had been disrupted several times, professors threatened that students would not be allowed to sit their finals, and support crumbled. Köster now resorted to a tactic that was to boomerang badly: she called in the 'leather jacket faction' – SDS rank-and-filers who were prepared for violence – to disrupt the exams with stink bombs. Three members of her own communal apartment, among others, denounced the 'troublemakers' to their professors; and the 'leather jacket faction' retaliated by smashing up the apartment. It was the first use of physical violence in the factional fights within SDS and the student movement, and it was not the last. As Detlev Claussen recalled, he and other SDSers started going to meetings in groups because of the danger of being beaten up.

'Essentially, it was an anti-authoritarian revolt against the anti-authoritarian theoreticians, against us . . .' A revolt that now also came from a new source: women. In May 1968, a Women's Action Council was formed in Berlin which heralded the re-emergence in Germany of the women's movement.

'At the time we weren't thinking of setting up a separate women's movement, but to make SDS and the movement deal with issues of direct concern to women,' Anna Pam, an SDS member, recalled. 'It began with a rather aggressive rebellion of SDS women against the male patterns of leadership. We also felt uneasy about the theories of sexual liberation, without being able to pinpoint it concretely. And finally, we were angry about the behaviour of the men in the movement – today you'd say their male chauvinism. The last was so obvious that we immediately got a large following of women.'

In September 1968, the Women's Action Council sent a delegation to the SDS delegates conference to make an attacking speech. 'Comrades, your meetings are unbearable and aggressive . . . Why don't you finally admit, after what has happened this past year, that you're "kaput", that you can't take the physical and intellectual stress of political actions any longer? . . . Why do you talk about class struggle here and about the problem of having orgasms at home? Isn't the latter worthy of discussion by SDS?'

'The speech was greeted with nasty remarks and laughter, which reduced our speaker, Helke Sander, to tears,' Pam continued. 'None of the SDS delegates even bothered to deal with the questions raised.

Thereupon, Sigrid Rüger, a prominent Berlin SDSer who was often pointed to as proof that women were not oppressed in the organization, pelted Krahl [one of the leading old-guard anti-authoritarians] with tomatoes. The women's action – the tomatoes more than the speech – was naturally picked up by the press and became *the* issue of the conference. And as a result of that, many women's groups came into existence within the movement.'

By the following meeting of the suspended delegates' conference two months later, eight SDS women's groups had been founded. The Frankfurt group produced a leaflet for the occasion on which was depicted a woman with an axe and above her, each bearing a leader's name and mounted like hunting trophies, a series of penises. The slogan read: 'Liberate the socialist eminences from their bourgeois pricks!' This time the women refused to engage in debate at all.

The SDS women's revolt – paralleling a similar rebellion in the American SDS – was both a factor and a sign of the German student organization's disintegration, as it was of its U.S. counterpart. The re-emergence of a women's movement, one of the most notable of the 1968 phenomena, would shortly occur in other countries also.

In the midst of these strains, the West German SDS collapsed, its ten-year history as an independent socialist student organization played out. But its collapse meant not less but more militancy, though of a different sort from the past, as the battle of the Tegeler Weg in Berlin in early November 1968 demonstrated. This was the most violent street battle to date between the Extra-Parliamentary Opposition and the police and reaffirmed some of the strategies of violence which had begun to be discussed after the fighting that followed on Dutschke's assassination attempt seven months earlier.

The battle began while Horst Mahler, the movement's lawyer, was appearing before a law tribunal in the Tegeler Weg, which threatened to disbar him for his activities. Students, many of whom had come prepared in helmets and boots, assembled in protest. The police overreacted, trying to disperse the crowd with horses and tear gas. 'Then "Rockers" [motorcycle gang members of a mainly working-class youth cult] started throwing stones at them,' recalled Peter Tautfest, an SDSer who was present. 'That was something new. Other people soon joined in. We weren't willing to take this stuff from the police any more. Under a hail of stones, the police ran like rabbits. It was a lovely sight – the first time students weren't doing the running and complaining afterwards how badly they'd been treated. We kept them off for a couple of hours. Then we withdrew to celebrate our victory. Mahler had been acquitted in the meantime. Afterwards, as usual, the battle was immediately worked up into a theory.'

An SDS leaflet a couple of days later articulated something of this theory, though by this stage of the organization's disintegration it could not be called an official SDS theory. 'Any leftist organization which labels as "adventurist" an action resisting the police declares its bankruptcy,' the leaflet declared. 'There is no such thing as militancy in itself. All militancy in the class struggle is progressive or reactionary depending on the aim it serves.'

What this signalled was a change from the anti-authoritarian position that actions breaking the law, even if symbolically, were both liberating for those who participated and mobilizing for sectors of the wider society. Now, it appeared, violence could be justified differently – by the goals it sought to attain. This was to have important consequences for the subsequent turn to violence as a means of struggle. A mass meeting after the Tegeler Weg battle to decide whether to break up the Christian Democratic party convention in Berlin – influenced perhaps by the August events in Chicago – revealed, meanwhile, the tensions that the use of violence was creating in the movement.

'It was a terrible debate,' Tautfest recalled. 'Half the meeting thought the Tegeler Weg was great and wanted more of it, and the other half – especially SHB [the Social Democratic student organization] – was totally opposed because they found the violence destructive. I got up and said that I stood wholeheartedly behind the Tegeler Weg action but that it would be foolish to feel pressured into escalating the violence by this great battle. Because everything had to be derived from some revolutionary theory, I quoted Mao: "If we can be victorious we shall fight, but if we feel we cannot, we shall withdraw." My speech, I think, was decisive for calling off the action.'

As he admitted, the belief in revolution often entered into contradiction with common sense. 'Our theory of revolutionary change was a bit like a religion. It often clashed with common sense, so sometimes the one, sometimes the other prevailed. We all were convinced that there would be no change without violence. We had read Lenin's *State and Revolution*, Marx's writings on the Paris Commune. Even Marcuse said that "repressive tolerance" had to be met not only with civil disobedience but violence. But as to our revolutionary strategies – well, they were more or less conscious fantasies which we didn't take seriously ourselves. Common sense told us that the Tegeler Weg sort of violence was not going to shake the bourgeois state. Bloodshed it might mean, but not revolutionary change. In spite of our revolutionary euphoria, we knew that a revolution could not happen tomorrow or the day after through a straightforward confrontation. So we went into 1969 beginning to think about a long-term struggle . . .'

The Tegeler Weg battle revealed a change of mood in the more radical sectors of the movement. Unlike the earlier SDS, which had attempted to mobilize people through exemplary actions, what remained of the organization now came to believe that it could confront and defeat state power in certain areas when the balance of forces was favourable – as Tautfest's quote from Mao indicated. But before there could be any overall victory a long struggle would be necessary. An organization like SDS was not the appropriate instrument to wage such a struggle – as the few remaining members who officially disbanded it in early 1970 recognized. What was needed, it seemed, were authentic revolutionary parties or – the opposite side of the coin – underground revolutionary groups devoted to armed struggle. And it was these which emerged in Germany in 1970 as they did simultaneously almost everywhere.

Britain: Successes and Setbacks

There was never any serious doubt in the minds of British student leaders that revolution was not an immediate prospect in Britain. A relatively liberal state – in terms of its resort to coercion by violence, more liberal then than any on either side of the Atlantic – did not create the conditions for major confrontations with the state. Nor did a labour movement which, despite discontent with the Labour government, appeared no more prepared than the West German working class to break the post-war consensus with the state. Although since 1966 disaffection with the government had fuelled the rise of student militancy – a militancy which was given a new impetus by the French May – the many differences between the British and French situation in 1968 were clear enough to most student activists.

'As we listened to the news from Paris,' remembered Pete Gowan, a Trotskyist student leader at Birmingham University, 'we were aware that what was going on there was worlds away from the everyday realities of the British student movement. The British state, the whole political system in this country, had immensely more ideological authority amongst students than was the case on the Continent. British universities were fairly flexible, tough institutions that didn't have a great deal of difficulty in absorbing and containing radical impulses. We believed that students represented the rebirth of the revolutionary movement in Britain, but we knew only too well that we had to make an impact on the labour movement if we were to have any serious political impact here.'

Impressed, nonetheless, by the example of France and the German SDS, student radicals decided to create a revolutionary student organization to mobilize the discontent with the Labour government. The decision was precipitated by the shocked realization that the discontent, rather than further left-wing aims, appeared suddenly more likely to provide the cause for a right-wing backlash. Only days before the French May began, London dockers, traditionally among the more militant sectors of the working class, marched with meat market porters on parliament in support of a Conservative Shadow Cabinet member, Enoch Powell, who had bitterly denounced what he saw as the coming inundation of Britain by black immigrants.

'That was a real eye-opener to us,' recalled David Widgery. 'Here were workers doing what we International Socialists were recommending: rank-and-file activity, political struggle on an industrial basis – only they were doing it the other way round. So it was all blowing up in our faces . . .'

Before the new revolutionary student organization could take shape, a wave of occupations hit British universities, adding hope that the time was ripe for its creation. Essex University set the ball rolling at the height of the May events. Originating in protests over racism and Vietnam, the twin issues that most rapidly mobilized students in Britain, the Essex occupation was sparked off by an American-style factor: war-related recruitment on campus by a scientist from the government's germ warfare establishment. David Triesman was selected by the student union's executive to open the attack on the scientist.

'We decided – and it was entirely in line with what we had been doing over Vietnam,' Triesman recalled, 'that we would engage him in a discussion of what he was doing and why rather than simply allowing him to make his speech. Using the format of the Nuremburg indictment, we prepared an indictment which we were going to ask him to respond to . . .' The scientist refused to answer any questions, however, a row broke out, and suddenly the local police appeared with a couple of dogs which got loose. 'The police, who said they'd come to rescue the scientist, were pushing through to try to recapture the dogs, a student leapt forward and emptied a packet of mustard powder over the scientist to the cry of "Ban mustard gas!" or something equally erudite, and one or two fist fights broke out. What we had imagined would be a rather prosaic affair, like a law court, turned into pandemonium! We all got out and milled around, thinking it had been a curious outcome, with an element of fun about it, but no great disaster.'

The next day Triesman and two other students were banned from the campus by the university authorities. In Triesman's case it meant he would not be able to sit his final exams. 'I thought, Christ, that's blown it! In between the political stuff I'd been working quite hard, looking forward to getting a good degree.' His parents, of Jewish working-class origin and Communist background, were 'devastated' by the news; a garment worker uncle and Communist Party member was 'delighted', on the other hand. 'He regarded it all as being in the family tradition. "Fantastic, fight them, occupy, smash the bastards!" he'd say on the phone. But before I had time to think too much about the consequences, I was swept into a mass student meeting. Nearly every one of the twelve hundred students – and a large proportion of the staff – ordered that I and the two others were not to leave the campus.' The occupation started immediately; Triesman played a central role in its three-week course.

Radicalized as a teenager by Youth CND, a Labour Party member until 1964, when disillusionment with the newly elected Labour government set in, he became an unaffiliated Maoist at Essex where he went in 1965. 'Chinese Communism had a good deal going for it, I thought, because it seemed capable of embodying conflicting trends of socialist opinion to produce a unity of practice and did not lead to the eradication of people who held different views. The notion of cultural revolution which pre-existed the Cultural Revolution seemed quite exciting and dynamic to me.'

Destined originally by his parents to become a doctor, he had rejected the idea at the end of his grammar school years and done a variety of jobs – building labourer, lorry driver, warehouseman, journalist – before going to Essex as a 'mature' student, aged twenty-two. His decision to go to university came after working as a reporter covering society events and debutantes' coming-out balls for a mass-circulation London evening paper. 'I wrote stuff that the paper thought was funny. But after a time I came to see that being witty and derisive wasn't enough. I had no intellectual grasp of what produced people of that class – and nothing in the Labour Party instructed me on questions like that. So I decided I wanted to go to university to study sociology and economics. I chose Essex because it was supposed to be more democratic than the traditional universities which I felt were class-ridden, comprised of people who had a tremendous and undisguised contempt for people of my class.'

One of eight new universities opened in the 1960s, Essex offered a large number of places to 'mature' students from non-middle-class backgrounds who were several years older than the average. 'But when we got there and found it was still a building site with hardly any facilities, we were doubly resentful,' Triesman continued. 'It produced an atmosphere in which radical progressive thinking spilled over into all sorts of other things: the film and theatre societies, for example, became socialist societies that happened to show films and put on plays.'

The student progressives, however, he found by and large a 'humourless lot' who totally failed to understand his passion for soccer. 'There was a strong belief among the left there that playing football was consorting with those who were seeking to dupe the working class, at the very least. So, I used to have to tell people that I was going off to a political meeting when in fact I was going to play semi-professional football for a team that was just far enough away and suitably anonymous for it never to be picked up. At that stage the left was absolutely intolerant of anything that didn't reflect a total commitment to political work. I don't think people spent much time laughing or playing or engaged in any other activities than dancing to rock at Saturday night parties.'

During the occupation, he helped to set up a 'free university' on the model of those created by students elsewhere: courses on alternative views of the British economy and its relationship with imperialism, on Vietnam, on the Third World were started. Students also went out and leafleted the nearby town of Colchester, inviting everyone to come in. 'Don't believe what the newspapers say, come and see for yourselves! The place has never been open before! Large numbers of inquisitive middle-class people as well as working-class kids came,' Triesman recollected. 'A consultant psychiatrist at the local mental hospital sent a letter saying he thought we were all mad. We replied, Come in and discuss it . . . We got R. D. Laing and David Cooper [radical psychiatrists] down to argue with him. One of the military garrison commanders said the occupation cast a slur on the town. Rubbish, we replied. If you believe in something you fight for it. Indeed, the military is even paid to do it. Come in and talk about the nature of fighting for belief – and he turned up . . .'

Brought to an end by a technical academic device which reinstated the three students, the occupation concluded amidst student euphoria. 'At a spontaneous outdoor party at the university that night, I thought, there really are important periods in people's lives when all the verities of their culture and ideology are shaken, and what they find underneath isn't terrifying but exciting,' Triesman recalled. 'And then, that other thing, the thing that brought me most joy in politics, the experience of being the author of successful events. No one has done it for you or to you, but you've done it with others. That's a seminal experience, it certainly was for me.'

Most of the occupations which burst over British universities in 1968 were led by students who had been radicalized for a number of years, many of whom belonged to far-left groups. In the 'lower tier' of Britain's class-demarcated higher educational system, however, far-left politics did not necessarily dominate. This was notably the case of the rebellions in art colleges, like Hornsey, in London, which staged Britain's longest occupation, lasting six weeks. Precipitated in large part by government reforms enforcing specialization and academic qualifications on art students, the Hornsey occupation rejected the domination of political groups, and tried to concern itself with new ways of creative teaching and the place of art in society.

Kim Howells, from a Communist background in a South Wales mining village, was one of the prime movers of the Hornsey occupation. But when he ran up a red flag over the art college, there was a storm of protest. 'The occupation wasn't about red flags but about creativity. I was very keen on storming buildings, really saw myself as a Red Guard when I went in and told the Principal he had to leave his office because the student body had decided we needed it. But, in fact, the debate about creativity was in many ways even more fundamental to me than the directly political debate. For some time I'd been asking myself what I was doing art for. To put it on display in a bloody gallery, owned by some upper-class toff who'd sell it to one of his friends? That wasn't what it should be about. The occupation was the only time during that whole period when people actually talked not just about art and creativity and the quality of life, but about work – the usefulness of work.'

The occupation took over the administrative building and ran it. Partitions dividing student and staff sections in the canteen were torn down, the cooking, cleaning, food purchases taken over by students. 'Nobody told anybody what to do,' recalled Val Remy, a previously unradicalized student of working-class origin, 'people discovered talents they'd never known they had. We wanted to prove we could run the college without bureaucratic administration. It was absolutely exhilarating, liberating. There was a sudden and new-found sense of solidarity. You really felt you loved people, they were no longer just fellow students, but comrades-in-arms.'

Seminars and general assemblies put forward new proposals for art education to end the enforced specialization, and demanded the abolition of academic qualifications and compulsory examinations. The flood of speech from students who had been previously silent impressed Howells as it did student leaders elsewhere. 'People began to talk about things which previously hadn't been talked about. Communal living, for example. You didn't feel the need for privacy any more, which was something none of us had experienced before. There was a definite sense of personal liberation. It's something that left-wingers elsewhere, who were perhaps much more politically radical than I, who understood the whole thing in its historical context, missed completely.'

Before the occupation was finally ended some thirty other art colleges staged occupations or went on strike. But the Hornsey defeat was bitter: staff members who had sided with the students' demands were purged and a number of students left of their own volition, Howells among them. 'My ideas about what constituted creativity had been strongly reinforced by the occupation and all that led up to it. Painting pictures and making sculptures was just bourgeois individualism! I stopped drawing and painting, and I've never done either since, although until then that was all I had ever wanted to do.' Returning to his origins, he found a job first in a steel works and later in the coal mines.

Hornsey's rejection of the far-left groups was exceptional. When the new student organization, the Revolutionary Socialist Students' Federation (RSSF) was formed in June 1968, in an attempt to further radical students, the far-left groups dominated its proceedings. They were able to agree on a founding statement opposing imperialism, racism and ruling-class control of education, and expressing support for national liberation struggles and workers' power as the only alternative to capitalism. But the organization was hamstrung in trying to mobilize a larger student base, in part because of the infighting between political sects who had different visions of where a revolutionary student organization should head.

'The model I had in mind was the German SDS,' recalled Michael Thomas, an independent Marxist. 'An organization which was not tied to any of the existing left organizations, that would be open to political debate and would have a clear idea of its priorities. It should create a student power consciousness to expose and destroy the authoritarian structure of education as a means of creating revolutionary consciousness. British students were still largely hostile to the left and largely ignorant of Marxism.'

At the opposite pole, some libertarians felt it was unimportant to have an organization at all. 'I just couldn't see the point of putting an official umbrella organization on top of the bush telegraph type of coordination among students that worked well enough,' recalled Alan Hayling, a Cambridge libertarian. 'I believed in popular power type revolution. But my opposition to organization didn't go as far as some Cambridge anarchists who proposed a blank piece of paper as the RSSF manifesto in opposition to what they called its trivial set of slogans.'

RSSF wavered somewhere between these different visions. Organizationally, it did briefly provide a network of information and contacts between left-wing students, and mobilized the first large British student presence in Northern Ireland in support of a People's Democracy march between Belfast and Dublin at Easter 1969. But in general, the far-left groups saw RSSF less as a specifically student organization than as the means of mobilizing students, with greater or less rapidity, for working-class and anti-imperialist politics mainly outside the university. For those students who subscribed to such aims, it was soon apparent that their place was in the political group itself rather than in a bitterly divided student organization. For those who wanted an organization independent of the groups, it became equally clear that the sectarian divisions within it were not likely to produce the mass base of new recruits which, alone, could perhaps swamp the divisions. Like its predecessor, the Radical Student Alliance, the new organization lasted a bare eighteen months.

'The real reason it failed was, logically, because the majority of students didn't support it,' continued Thomas. 'The mass of students were not won over to Marxism. I never believed they would be. Effectively, we were caught between the left groups who let a thing grow until they could asset strip it, and the conservatism and insularity of the mass of students. With only three years of university, you've got no more than half that time for political activity if you want to get a degree. So a radical university one year could change completely by the following year. We socialist students were a happy, colourful carnival, but nevertheless a very clear minority.'

Uncommented on by most student leftists was another factor: the National Union of Students, hitherto run largely by right-wing Labour members, was itself becoming more radical. Jack Straw, a left Labour student, who was elected to the NUS presidency in April 1969, had argued for several years that students should work to radicalize their own union 'rather than be diverted into small left-wing sects . . . We'd had our fights with the Labour government, and it looked as if we'd have an even bigger fight with the Conservative government that was probably going to replace it.'

In 1968, however, the movement, in the American or German sense of the word, arose in Britain around the single-issue campaign of Vietnam, organized by the Vietnam Solidarity Campaign. Although a national organization, local groups were free to engage in their own activities; and the Campaign itself was both an example of left-wing unity and the mobilizing power of Vietnam. It was given focus by the appearance in May of a new radical paper, *Black Dwarf*, which had been planned for well over a year but was rapidly transformed by the French May events under the editorship of Tariq Ali. It concentrated on the anti-imperialist struggle, notably Vietnam, encouraged student militancy, raised the new issue of feminism, and attempted to speak to the cultural dissidents: John Lennon debated in its pages, Mick Jagger sent in the hand-written version of his song 'Street Fighting Man', David Hockney, Jim Dine and other artists contributed paintings.

As 100,000 demonstrators gathered in London in October 1968, for the biggest ever Vietnam march in Britain, few believed that this was to be both the zenith and nadir of the movement. The problem of how to keep up the momentum of a single-issue campaign and where to go next were to prove insuperable. As elsewhere, the establishment played its part by mounting an hysterical media campaign about the threat of violence and even revolution.

'Never at any stage did anyone seriously involved in V S C imagine that the October demonstrations would be anything more than a show of the anti-imperialist left's strength,' commented Tariq Ali. 'But the establishment embarked on a campaign of black propaganda and disinformation. They did it for two reasons: to isolate the march from the bulk of the population by raising the fear of violence – an old trick – and because they over-reacted, panicked after May. France shook the ruling classes throughout Europe, and the British decided to take no chances that the disease would spread. Hence their ferocious attacks on V S C – *The Times* put its crime reporters onto covering it – and on me personally. I was the foreigner, the black, the evil in our midst.'

Under the impact of the French May, the tone of revolutionary rhetoric had all the same risen a notch or two. In a television programme to which the BBC invited student leaders from East and West shortly after the May events, Ali called for the expropriation of private property, all power to the soviets or workers' councils, and for the abolition of money. 'We were always being attacked as "Soviet agents" or "utopian dreamers", so I wanted to show that we weren't either,' Ali recalled. 'The Prague Spring had given us a very good idea of the society we wanted. At the same time we refused to come up with a blueprint for a future society, believed that it was impossible to foresee what shape this would take. But the abolition of money – that was a totally utopian and anarcho-syndicalist demand!'

Despite VSC's denials that it was planning anything more than a peaceful march, there were those who thought that the Vietnam demonstration might lead to violence if not more. LSE students, who had shortly before begun the new academic year with an 'unlimited revolutionary meeting' to welcome new students, occupied the school to create a base for the demonstration: among many other things, they set up a medical centre with a team of doctors and nurses.

'None of us knew for sure what might happen,' recalled John Rose at LSE. 'But we thought the revolution was going to start then – *The Times* was even predicting the possibility. If there was fierce fighting with the police, the thing could escalate in ways we couldn't predict. We would have welcomed a major confrontation which would have raised the stakes and drawn the workers into the struggle. Not, it has to be said, that most workers gave a damn about Vietnam. But had there been fighting, with serious injuries, possibly even a killing, I'm quite sure a major student rising across the country would have taken place, and the thing would have exploded.'

As events showed, the British state and its police forces were too sophisticated to provoke violence – 'indeed, much more sophisticated than we gave them credit for, and they contained the thing very effectively,' Rose recalled. In ensuring an absence of violence, they were in part helped by VSC itself which decided that the risk of serious confrontation was too great to allow it to lead the demonstration to the United States embassy, previously considered the natural target; it went instead to Hyde Park. There several thousand demonstrators, led by Maoists, broke away for the embassy where they were effectively held back by serried ranks of police; as a result the media was able to boast that the 'violence and revolution' it had alone been predicting had been skilfully contained.

The demonstration showed that the movement had mobilized support in new social groupings. According to a survey published subsequently by a London weekly, only half the marchers were students (and of these 10 per cent were still in secondary education), while 12 per cent were non-student manual workers under twenty-five. Nearly 70 per cent of the demonstrators had turned out to protest not only about Vietnam but about capitalism and the structure of British society.

But there were some who, in a clear indication of a changing mood, refused to turn out at all. 'These demos were organized as ego-trips by men who wanted to be at the front, get their pictures in the paper, and prove they were "prolier" [more proletarian] than thou,' maintained Elisabeth Tailor. 'The arrogance of a small elite, thinking they were leading the revolution and telling the working class what to do! They controlled the language – their Marxism was always better than yours – and made women feel like idiots. A group of us students believed that demonstrations, sit-ins couldn't change anything, and that most of these leftists hadn't even read Marx. So we started a *Kapital* reading group – a group which at least was prepared to admit in advance that it didn't know everything.'

In the event, V S C's refusal to go beyond the issue of Vietnam and place concrete demands on the Labour government left it unable to capitalize on the mass mobilization and led the demonstrators politically nowhere. 'We ran out of steam,' admitted Ali. 'It was, I think, the end of the phase where a single issue movement could do the trick. It was a tragedy because large numbers had been radicalized and now didn't see anything with which to identify as they would have, for example, in Germany and the U.S., with the two S D Ss. Lots of people who were interested in doing more joined political groups.'

The idea of ending the march with a call for creating a unified socialist youth, along the lines of the French Jeunesse Communiste Révolution-naire (J C R), had been mooted by the International Socialists, and Ali was tempted to agree. But it never got off the ground because the organization he had just joined, the International Marxist Group (the Trotskyist Fourth International's British section), turned it down.

Some of the momentum that had gathered went into solidarity with the Northern Ireland struggle. In Lond, David Widgery and other I S members organized a Northern Irish Solidarity Campaign. 'At that early stage there was a lot of emotional solidarity with the People's Democracy because they were people of our age who were showing what seemed phenomenal bravery in just asking for things which, by right, they should have had fifty years ago and were being brutally bashed down for it. Later on, we helped raise money for things like a radio transmitter which we got made and sent to them.'

In the main, however, students were thrown back on the university: occupations took place at a number of them, but it was the London School of Economics which witnessed the most dramatic events. After the School's occupation for the Vietnam demonstration, the authorities erected internal steel gates to prevent further occupations; at the same time they proposed regulations for maintaining 'order' which included staff reporting on students. On 24 January 1969, of LSE's 3,000 students, 500 voted by a small majority to take down the gates.

'I remember walking to that first gate fairly slowly and yet finding myself almost the first person there,' recalled Paul Hoch, an American graduate student. 'Many of us felt a certain dread that we'd trapped ourselves into this, a dread of the consequences, even though I believed in direct action. As an American, it seemed to me very characteristic of the British left to talk Marxist ideology but remain in many other ways entirely encapsulated within the system and its ways of doing business.'

Despite his fears, other students with sledgehammers and picks soon joined him and began to knock the gates off their fixings; a number of academics, one of whom clung to the structure itself, tried unsuccessfully to prevent their removal. 'It was a euphoric feeling, I felt a great sense of power,' remembered Rachel Dyne, a Marxist student. 'We were doing something authentic, we resented the gates, felt they were transforming the place more or less into a prison. Taking them down was a way of challenging authority.'

Two hours later, the authorities responded by calling in the police and closing the School; the students were to remain locked out for nearly four weeks. It was clear to most students that, as in Germany, the initiative had passed to the other side. Disillusioned, there were those who fantasized about resorting to arms to regain entry to LSE. 'We were very frustrated,' recalled John Rose, who had become one of the leading International Socialist activists at LSE. 'I could feel it in myself, the wanting to pick up a gun. Without a proper and practical orientation towards the working class, as we in IS had, the natural outcome of the student movement was to armed struggle . . .'

In fact, the worst that happened was that some anarchists broke into the refectory and swimming pool of the University of London Union, which the LSE students had occupied. 'There'd been these constant reminders that we had to respect property,' remembered Rod Burgess, a member of the occupation's executive committee, 'so I went to see what had happened. I soon found out that it wasn't only anarchists who had broken into the pool but Marxists, too. The anarchists were swimming with no clothes on and the Marxists were wearing their underpants!'

In the face of attacks by the Labour government, injunctions on students, including Rose and Hoch, and serious media distortion, nearly 2,000 LSE students voted at a mass meeting to reject a motion condemning the taking down of the gates, and called for the School to be reopened without police or victimization. It reopened without the former but quite soon with the latter: Robin Blackburn, a former LSE student and subsequently a sociology lecturer at the School, and another young lecturer were fired after a couple of months for siding with the students. The latter went on strike and took the struggle to the very heart of their own academic world – the Senior Common Room – where they harangued professors. On one occasion they were led by Paul Hoch.

'He just went in with a big megaphone and announced that the place was now occupied,' recalled Burgess, who was among the many students present. 'There was no response. The professors all looked at him. Then he walked across to the wall where a picture of the Chairman of the LSE Court of Governors was hanging and took it off . . .'

'I guess it just came into my head,' remarked Hoch. 'I thought it was very important to try to get a reaction out of these people whose colleagues were being sacked. The portrait symbolized authority to many of the academics there. So I moved it about two feet off the wall and put it on the floor. Within a second I was grabbed by about five people – it was almost as though I'd shot the Queen! Academics were erupting from their seats, yelling and screaming. The place was in an absolute uproar. It was what I intended really – it made clear what the authority relationships were to everyone there.'

Attempting to have Hoch committed to prison for breaking his injunction, LSE charged him with removing the portrait – a charge the judge laughed out of court. 'All the same, I hadn't realized how bitter the situation could become. I guess we'd had an idealistic view in 1968 when everything seemed to be changing so rapidly,' commented Hoch, who a year later was sentenced to nine months imprisonment and deportation for 'unlawful assembly' for his part in a student demonstration. A number of Cambridge students were also sent to prison or borstal after a demonstration protesting against the Greek military junta which seized power in 1967; the 'idealistic' phase was indeed over, even in Britain.

'That's when I began to realize what it was all about,' recalled Paul Ginsborg, a newly radicalized Cambridge researcher. 'The state had mobilized. It taught me two lessons. First, that students by themselves would never get anywhere. Secondly, that the contribution of student activism, intelligence, humour and organization had to go into the workers' movement in some way.'

Although it was unable to mount a challenge to the established order, the British movement had mobilized more people than ever before. But, like the West German and French movements, it had not found a way to translate this new-found strength into a political force. Given the relative dominance of far-left groups in the movement, it was not surprising that radicalized students should attempt to carry their vision of revolutionary politics to the working class. But the same response was to come from all the student movements. Anti-authoritarian revolt no longer seemed sufficient against an established order which, sooner or later, was prepared to launch a counter-offensive. To achieve the goals which the perceived possibility of revolution in France had placed on the historical agenda, radical students felt they had to pursue new means and new goals. As they finally converged, the movements on both sides of the Atlantic broke up into different factions, each convinced that it was pursuing the 'royal road' to revolution. It meant, among other things, the demise of the two oldest student organizations, the West German and American S D Ss.

The United States: 1968–70

As the British and German movements were pushed back, the American movement was growing in size, militancy, diversity – and divergency. In its most turbulent years ever, 1969–70, it activated new constituencies, momentarily revived inter-racial coalitions, fuelled new revolutionary aspirations, and mustered some of the largest mobilizations ever. At the same time it confronted a mounting state counter-offensive on a scale far more massive than in Western Europe. But it was less the latter than the movement's success in mobilizing a diversity of constituencies which proved to be its ultimate weakness, for it did not seek to define a strategy to focus their divergent goals into a coherent challenge to the established order.

Instead, SDS added to the divergencies by focussing on other, 'revolutionary' constituencies – the working class, the black proletariat, youth culture – which failed to respond. The 'turn to revolution' split the organization. The mass of students were not prepared to follow any of the roads to revolution which emerged from the split. Just as surely as it had in West Germany, SDS's ultra-leftism heralded its demise, leaving the American student movement at one of its most critical moments without even the loose organizational ligaments that had led it forward throughout the 1960s.

The movement's diversity, militancy, divergencies, the turn to revolution and state repression were apparent in microcosm from as far back as the Columbia occupation of April 1968. From then on these different strands were never far from the surface; the assassination in June 1968 of Robert Kennedy, the leading Democratic presidential candidate of the anti-war forces, and the watershed of the Democratic party's National Convention in Chicago in August of the same year reinforced them.

Kennedy's assassination at the hands of a disgruntled Palestinian in Los Angeles signalled for many students the end of the still widespread hopes of an electoral solution to the Vietnam War. As Carl Oglesby, a former SDS president, asked:

'And what do you do with that? Martin Luther King dead in April and just a couple of months later Kennedy. What do you do? Go get a new hero and spend years teaching him and having the debates and doing the sit-ins and pushing people at him and pushing him at people – do it all over again while the people are dying in Vietnam and how many other countries? That's why people started talking about revolution, because reform had been made to seem like a dead-end street. How many times do you climb that tree just to have it chopped down beneath you?'

Rejecting any further attempt at liberal reform, SDS answered by electing a new leadership which promptly proclaimed itself revolutionary, and refused to participate formally in any of the actions planned around the Democratic Convention in Chicago. The diversity and divergency of the movement now became apparent. Those who prepared to demonstrate at Chicago were more divided in their aims than at almost any other moment in the movement's history. Many students came to show support for Senator Eugene McCarthy, the leading peace contender, for whom they had worked by the thousands in the primaries; many SDSers responded to the call from various movement leaders to engage in confrontation, without being clear whether this meant street fighting or non-violent direct action in the civil rights' tradition; others came to witness in the tradition of the pacifist peace movement. Meanwhile, the Youth International Party, a new organization formed by Jerry Rubin, Berkeley anti-war activist, and Abbie Hoffman, who had made his name as a CORE activist in New York's Lower East Side, was also trying to make its mark on the situation.

Never a real party, the Yippies, as they called themselves, were a small group around Rubin and Hoffman who hoped to draw the growing numbers of counter-cultural youth into the radical movement. Enthused by the Oakland and Pentagon confrontations of the previous year, the Yippies hoped to replay them with a more counter-cultural flavour in the context of the convention. Proposing to nominate a pig for president, they promised a 'Festival of Life' complete with rock 'n roll, poetry, a nude grope-in for peace, holy men, free food and lots of excitement. 'We demand the Politics of Ecstasy!' they cried. 'Rise Up and Abandon the Creeping Meatball!'

While concerted, coordinated action between these different tendencies proved impossible, events were soon taken out of the protesters' hands by the police forces under the command of Mayor Richard Daley, Chicago's Democratic political boss. Several days of widespread police violence culminated in a brutal police attack on a street demonstration during the vote nominating Hubert Humphrey for president. Seen live on television by millions across the nation, this attack, together with the Democrats' refusal to nominate an anti-war candidate, destroyed many American students' last hopes of winning reform through the electoral process.

The police attack began when a 'demonstrator', who was in fact a police provocateur, attempted to remove the American flag from a pole in Grant Park where 10,000 protesters had gathered. Immediately the police started beating up demonstrators. 'They had riot gear on and they just came after us,' recalled Bob Hall. 'As they came plowing through, people were running back – the crowd just got jammed up and couldn't move back far enough, so they went slam, slam, slam! I got hit on the head with a club and blood was all over my face . . .'

'I saw a cop hit a guy over the head and the club break. I turned to my left and saw another cop jab a guy right in the kidneys. And then I turned round,' remembered Josh Brown, 'and the cop behind me was saying, "Move, move!" and I took off and kept going.' But he found, as did all those trying to escape, that the exits and bridges over railroad tracks had been taken by police and National Guardsmen. The single bridge open was the one nearest to the hotels where convention delegates were quartered. 'And it was there,' Brown continued, 'that people really got beaten up and right full out for the T V cameras to see, and the T V camera people got beaten themselves. That began the whole wave of violence that night.'

The police attack further polarized America. Chicago became for the white student movement what Atlantic City had been for S N C C four years before: the moment of disillusionment in the Democratic Party as a force for change, of disabusal of electoral politics. With the model of the Black Panthers before them, greater numbers of students than ever turned to revolution as the only way forward. Aware now of the West European student movements, and under the growing influence of Maoism, these new revolutionaries began to speak of themselves as Marxists, something new in the movement. As Oglesby recognized, there was a certain inevitability in the process.

'The attraction of Marxism was based on the fact that it was the only coherent philosophy of revolution on the shelf. Nobody else had tried to systematically think about where revolution came from, where it had headed, what was the ideology of this process that seemed to dominate history for the last two centuries or more. The movement as such hadn't worried much about revolution until around 1967–68. And really, one talked about revolution to begin with because the Vietnamese were having a revolution, or because the Cubans had had one. And then it became something to blast people with, via an analogy which may not have been sound but was certainly strong, like: how do we think about the black movement in the U.S. in terms of revolutionary models? . . . Then there was May '68 in Paris, which made people think that it wasn't at all so crazy to think there could be a revolution in a modern developed industrial country. It had come within a whisker of happening in France. Who was to say that if events kept developing as they were in 1968 that the same thing couldn't happen here? So after 1968, it became somehow suddenly a plausible idea – revolution in the mother countries of the world, revolution in the West. And revolution in which, somehow, a leading role would be played by students.'

Vietnam, the Chinese Cultural Revolution, Cuba, the Paris May events, and American activists' own experience of successfully forcing reform through mass mobilization – all these combined, as Frank Bardacke in California recalled, to make the turn to revolution plausible. 'We had the experience of a mass movement and that was transforming. People could feel, if this is an authentic mass movement that has changed so much, why can't we just go a bit further?' This combination of factors led significant numbers of people 'to develop revolutionary hopes in a non-revolutionary situation. Looking back, that was the beginning of the end for the movement. Boy, was that a mistake!'

By the fall of 1968, 368,000 enrolled students considered themselves revolutionaries, according to a survey by *Fortune* magazine – a figure that would rocket to over one million by 1970. Student radicals raced to read Lenin, Trotsky, Mao. David Gilbert, one of a small group of S D Sers who had studied Marxism seriously over a number of years, observed that S D S 'went from being students with a moral vision to realizing that we were up against the heaviest power structure in the world. We were seeing blacks that we associated with killed by the government. It was life and death serious. There was a sense that either we get some sort of power base or we have to retreat. So people looked around for almost magical solutions, and within the left, in S D S in 1968–69, the magical answer became a regurgitation of the Marxist formulation of the working class.'

The power structure which Gilbert pointed to was now in the hands of a group of arch-conservatives under the new Republican president, Richard Nixon. Determined to crush the radical movement, Nixon stepped up the counter-offensive begun by his predecessor, mixing concessions and direct repression. Although never acknowledging that the movement had any effect on his policies, his concessions included the gradual reduction of U.S. forces in Vietnam, thus ending the massive draft calls that had brought the war home to so many young men; a continuation of various government programs designed to ensure equal rights for blacks and other minorities; the reduction of the voting age from twenty-one to eighteen, and the opening of diplomatic relations with China.

But it was direct repression which most marked the movement: two dozen federal agencies, including the FBI and CIA, engaged in surveillance and infiltration activities, the FBI alone fielding 2,000 agents and informants to 'expose, disrupt, misdirect or otherwise neutralize' both the black and white movements. Conspiracy charges were brought against various movement leaders, such as 'the Chicago 8' – eight men, including former SDSer Tom Hayden, Yippie Abbie Hoffman and Black Panther Bobby Seale, who were accused of being the cause of the Chicago police attack during the Democratic Party convention in August 1968. The single most shocking facet of the Nixon era's political repression was the nationwide campaign to crush the Black Panther Party. From coast to coast, wherever a Panther group appeared, the police moved quickly to force it out of existence. Hundreds of Panthers were jailed on charges ranging from illegal use of sound equipment to resisting arrest to attempted murder. Police raided Panther headquarters, shot up the walls, smashed typewriters and furniture and destroyed the food destined for the Panthers' food program for children. Gun battles between police and Panthers erupted in many cities. At least ten Panthers were killed, and another ten wounded by police, between 1967 and early 1969. Estimates run as high as forty-four Panthers murdered in the decade. In one case, twenty-one-year-old Illinois Panther leader Fred Hampton was murdered in his bed by a team of Chicago police and FBI agents.

Many government and police activities were blatantly unconstitutional. In the late 1970s a court awarded damages to thousands of activists who were illegally arrested in one Washington, DC, anti-war march. Most of the federal conspiracy charges brought against activists were eventually thrown out of court. And the evidence suggests that many police informants and FBI infiltrators themselves repeatedly broke the law by acting as provocateurs – urging activists toward violence, provoking violence themselves during demonstrations, and sometimes providing people with weapons and explosives. In one case, after infiltrating the Northern Illinois University SDS chapter, a Chicago police agent physically attacked the University president and threw him off a stage, thus creating a pretext for official action against the chapter. In another case, Larry Ward, a decorated but later disillusioned Vietnam veteran, was lured into planting a bomb in Seattle, Washington, in May 1970. An FBI informant offered Ward $75 to do the bombing, gave him a bomb and drove him to the site. When the police surprised the unarmed Ward, he tried to run, but was shot and killed. The FBI informant justified his actions, saying, 'The police wanted a bomber, and I got them one.'

In no other nation, except perhaps Northern Ireland, was the police and state reaction so complete. Many movement activists were arrested on various bogus charges. Karen Duncanwood spent eighteen months before an Arizona grand jury, refusing to answer their questions, because she happened to be in the same house with some former students suspected of transporting explosives. Steve Fraser was set up by the Philadelphia police, in a case that was later thrown out of court. However, it forced him into an eleven-months' defense, and costly legal fees. At the same time, through-out the country there was a wave of expulsions of activists from colleges and universities, and numerous firings of activist faculty, or denial of tenure to supporters of the students.

Government subversion and infiltration also made it more difficult for white movement activists to act politically, as Josh Brown recalled. 'I remember when one of the people who hung around the Peace Parade office turned out to be one of the police informants in the Chicago 8 conspiracy trial. Everybody was just totally thrown for a loop.' Given the movement's loose democratic structure and the personal openness it encouraged, police infiltration was particularly disturbing: 'Anybody who wasn't well-known, you couldn't treat as trustworthy. That cuts down on a lot of political activity.'

Nonetheless, federal government repression did little to stop veteran activists and drove many of them to even greater militancy. Nor did it appear to discourage new recruits from joining the movement, and the spread of movement activism to campuses heretofore unaffected, such as UCLA and Harvard.

In the spring of 1969, the SDS chapter at long quiescent UCLA led a series of protests over University racial policies and its treatment of student dissenters. Mike Balter was one of the organizers. 'People were always saying, "you'll never organize anything at UCLA,"' he remem-bered. But then the campus mood began to change, he added, for many reasons: increased militance of the national anti-war movement, heightened government repression directed at the movement, and the emergence of a new militancy among black and Chicano students. 'The very aggressive putting forward of the grievances of black people in white society had a tremendous influence on white students. It had a dramatic effect on the campus.'

This new mood erupted in several confrontations. The largest occurred when then Governor Ronald Reagan and the entire University of California Board of Regents came to UCLA to hold a meeting and angry students turned out to protest. 'There was a demonstration estimated at about 3,000 people, and there was a lot going on. People were just wild, they did everything they could get away with. On the side of the Faculty Center (where the Regents were meeting) there were people using some kind of implements to try to burrow into the building. I kid you not. I saw it with my own eyes. There was a real fury that had built up over People's Park, and Vietnam. There was a *Herald Examiner* truck which drove through and got trapped. There was a strike at the *Herald Examiner*, and that truck was turned over. At the Faculty Center students were throwing rocks which broke almost all the windows. The Faculty Center was surrounded, with the Governor inside. They couldn't get out. Finally 200 highway patrolmen and LAPD officers swooped onto the campus. They pushed the crowd not more than five hundred feet away . . . Ronald Reagan came out the front door smiling and waving and the TV cameras moved in. On TV that night the TV station I watched said, "The Governor was unperturbed by the demonstrations." The cameras did not show that a hundred feet away there was a howling mob of 3,000 people.'

The Harvard strike began in April of 1969 when after a series of fruitless negotiations over issues such as ROTC, university expansion and black studies, 300 students led by PL/SDS stormed the administration building and ejected nine deans. Unlike earlier takeovers, such as Columbia, police were called fairly soon to retake the building. Removing their badges they clubbed and trashed the occupying students, as well as newsmen and bystanders. One hundred ninety-six students were arrested and forty-one students and seven policemen were treated for injuries. The actions of the police so infuriated students and faculty that in a mass meeting of 10,000 people they voted to strike in support of the heretofore isolated SDS. The strike manifesto called upon students to 'Strike because you hate cops. Strike because your roommate was clubbed. Strike to stop expansion. Strike to seize control of your life. Strike to become more human. Strike because there's no poetry in your lectures. Strike because classes are a bore. Strike for power. Strike to smash the Corporation. Strike to make yourself free. Strike to abolish ROTC. Strike because they are trying to squeeze the life out of you. Strike.'

Deborah Levenson, who was then an SDS traveller for the New England region, recalled the process of confrontation and growth at Harvard. 'SDS at Harvard was, really, probably one hundred and twenty active people, which for SDS was huge. Meetings would run bigger. The Worker-Student Alliance (PL) was almost sixty people. There was a big mass meeting of about one thousand people to debate the question of whether or not to seize University Hall. It got voted down but PL went and did it anyway, and a lot of people were forced to join. PL didn't feel that a meeting of a thousand people had the right to decide that issue because it was a transient – all kinds of people were at that meeting, not just SDS.' Once the police were called, any questions about the leadership of SDS were submerged, but the actions at Harvard reveal how far the erosion of the call for 'participatory democracy' had gone since Berkeley.

Although racked by internal splits, SDS claimed between eighty and one hundred thousand members in 1968–69, an unprecedented high; anti-war demonstrations mobilized half a million people nationwide, and the number of campus demonstrations rose to over 9,000 compared to only 400 three years earlier. One-fifth of these demonstrations now involved violence of some sort – from bombs to fires in university buildings; but SDS (along with other national New Left organizations) was responsible for leading only one-quarter of the total campus protests. The movement was simply exploding on its own.

As it exploded, so it fissured into new but divergent sectors and constituencies, which were unable to establish any true organizational links. Working-class community colleges and high schools saw protests break out for the first time; organizing against the war among GIs became widespread; the counter-culture grew vastly, as seen in the giant Woodstock rock festival, and one sector of it became increasingly politicized; Mexican-American students organized themselves into a Chicano movement that scored a number of notable successes; struggles for ethnic minority studies on Northern campuses saw black activism make a major comeback; women in the re-emergent women's movement began to stage actions: the ultra-left Weather student revolutionaries started setting off bombs across the country ... But all that seemed to unite these diverse movements was a generalized opposition and hostility to 'the establishment'.

Such was the diversity of the movement that it is possible here to give only an overview of its depth and multiplicity. For example, two of the more important new developments were anti-war organizing among white working-class students and among G Is.

Robbie Skeist, a Triton Community College student and anti-draft organizer, began speaking at working-class community colleges in the Chicago area. 'It's ironic that the anti-war protests are happening at the university and not out here,' he recalled telling his audience at Triton, 'because here is where all the guys are being pulled out of school and drafted and getting killed. Is this fine with you? Or do you think this is wrong?' A few years earlier, he might have been harassed by the students; now they responded by forming the Triton Peace Union which, in the fall of 1969, organized a 'speakout' on Vietnam.

'We drew some hostile response, especially from some Vietnam veterans,' Skeist recalled. 'But we let them come up and take the mike, and I don't know if we were lucky or what, but by the end of it their anger was no longer directed at us. It was directed at the whole experience they had gone through. And it was very powerful for people to hear veterans – their fellow-students – talk about going over there supposedly to fight for democracy and seeing people rounded up and brutalized, and seeing their friends killed for nothing.'

This type of organizing, which illustrated that participatory democracy was still a powerful and viable force, was repeated in hundreds of community colleges around the country. There was no room within it for the revolutionary rhetoric that was now becoming common in S DS, for the organizers were breaking new ground and had to tread with care. So too did those engaged in anti-war organizing among G Is.

Isolated acts of resistance by G Is had occurred since 1964 – most notably the refusal of the 'Fort Hood Three' to go to Vietnam in 1965; but by 1968 an increasing number of draftees were prepared to face court martial in protest against the war. In Vietnam itself there was a notable decline in morale, as the effects of the counter-culture and black power began to make themselves felt: the use of drugs, refusal to obey commands and 'fragging' – the killing of officers with grenades – were widely reported. At home, students supported the resisters in a variety of ways. One of these was the G I coffee house movement, begun by a former Harvard student, which rapidly spread throughout the country. Located off base, the coffee houses were placed where G Is could congregate, share resentments away from the watchful eyes of their officers, and have access to movement publications and people.

Barbara Garson, who worked in the GI coffee house near Fort Lewis, Washington, helped in the publication of a base newspaper and provided, along with her co-workers, psychic support for acts of resistance. 'We tried to foster self-confidence. Giving somebody confidence was what we were about. Make him feel good about himself and feel he had a right to have an opinion. When a person felt he was an organizer, then he had a purpose in the army.'

It was the sense of empowerment typical of the early days of SNCC, FSM and SDS which was again being given expression here. By 1968, some of the far-left political organizations, Progressive Labor (PL) among them, were arguing that college students should not take advantage of their special deferred status when a class-biased draft was sending mainly working-class youth – especially black and brown young men – to Vietnam. At a time when millions of Americans were expressing their revulsion against the war, PL urged students to join the army to organize dissent and revolution within its ranks. Mike Balter, a PL-SDS member, accepted this line. 'I went in to the army with a mixture of motivations. I did believe it was the right thing to do. But it also had something to do with my own sense of myself, whether I was a brave or a cowardly person. I was afraid to go in, and I wanted to overcome that fear.'

Classified as a G-2, a security investigatee, he spent seventeen months at Fort Ord, California, organizing anti-war actions at the base with other PLers and disaffected GIs stationed there. 'We concentrated upon what was going on at the Fort. It wasn't difficult to organize because everybody hated the army, especially black and Latino GIs. Nobody really understood what the war was all about, and people were very, very receptive to any point of view that argued against the war. Their lives were on the line. They were on their way or getting ready to go to Vietnam eventually.'

He was hauled up on charges five times and court-martialled twice for his activities in distributing anti-war literature on the base, mounting defenses of GIs hailed before courts martial, protesting when a Latino GI was run to his death during basic training. Although convicted by his second court martial, he was not sentenced to jail. 'I don't think they wanted me in the stockade. There was a lot of rebellion there. But also, their powers were not infinite. They were dealing with a pretty disaffected bunch of people. They just physically didn't have that kind of control. I have my army file. It seems as though, when I was in, they were trying the strategy of tolerating us. They didn't want people to get the idea that simply by being an opponent of the war you could stay out or get out.'

By the early 1970s, the creation of the Vietnam Veterans Against the War became an incontrovertible sign of the cumulative effects of the war and the movement's success in mobilizing against it.

As state repression became ever more violent, and hippies were lumped in with the radicals, many in the counter-culture became more explicitly political, until the boundaries between them and the student movement almost vanished. Rock 'n roll bands performed at rallies and movement militants took LSD. The new mood in the counter-culture was reflected by John Sinclair, drop-out graduate student and hipster:

'After the carnage in Chicago [at the 1968 Democratic convention], it became absolutely clear to us that in order to preserve and develop our culture we couldn't ignore the political aspect of the revolution any more. We realized, or began to realize, that there was a lot more to it than we had anticipated, that the cultural revolution was only part of the social revolution, and that in order to make the cultural revolution we would have to make a political revolution first.'

Sinclair and his commune of radical hippies and rock 'n rollers in Detroit formed the White Panther party, loosely modelled on and linked to the Black Panthers. Their combination of rock 'n roll and angry rebellious posturing touched a powerful nerve among the city's working-class youth. 'It spoke directly to them, it wasn't abstract like someone from college talking to them. It was dope fiends, rock 'n rollers, people they looked up to. People they wanted to be like who said, "The Black Panther Party, End the War, Smoke Dope, Burn your Bras, Kill Your Parents, Tear Your School Down. Fuck 'em! Smash the TV set! Fuck 'em!"'

The White Panther party was still growing in July 1969, when it was crushed. First Sinclair, then half-a-dozen other leaders, were imprisoned – Sinclair to an extraordinary term of nine-and-a-half to ten years for smoking two marijuana cigarettes in the presence of an undercover agent. Beatle John Lennon, who was increasingly politicized during these years, wrote a song about Sinclair in 1971 and performed at benefits on his behalf.

Both the conjunction of the counter-culture with the radical student movement and the state's monopoly of armed repression was again in evidence over People's Park; this was a small plot of University of California land in the city of Berkeley that a group of hippies had turned into a park with flowers, a vegetable garden and children's playground. In the middle of negotiations, the university sent squads of men to destroy it at night so that it could be turned into a parking lot. A violent confrontation developed, involving thousands of Berkeley students and residents and massive numbers of police and National Guardsmen. One student protester was killed and another blinded by the National Guard.

Frank Bardacke, who was facing trial as one of the 'Oakland Seven' for his part in Stop the Draft Week in the fall of 1967, was active in the campaign to defend the park. 'We had this theory around this time that actually, historically, political revolutions take place after the social revolutions have been won . . . That's the way capitalism replaced feudalism in Europe. And if you apply that to the present situation, what we really had to do was build this whole counter-culture, build different ways of living, different ways of being with each other, a whole different economic base. So the excitement about People's Park is easy to see. What have you got there? You've got a parking lot versus a park. The conflict is over private, or state property that we took over and said, "It's ours!". It sounds like a revolutionary demand: "We don't care who owns the country on paper. Our claim to ownership is that we can treat it better than you can. Besides, your claim to ownership is just brute force. It originally belonged to the Indians, who had some kind of view closer to ours. Then the church took it from the Indians, and the Mexicans took it from the church, and the Americans took it from the Mexicans, and it was all just who had the most guns. That's all the land title means: who had the most guns. Well, we don't have any guns, but we're willing to fight you for it!"'

And it was the power of guns that again defended the existing order. After the blinding and the fatal shooting, things changed dramatically, the protesters no longer controlled the streets. 'From then on, a very small number of cops could control a crowd just by pumping their shot guns.'

Throughout the American Southwest, Mexican-American students had organized themselves into a Chicano movement with its own identity. Raised in the barrios of the cities of California and Texas, or in the countryside of rural New Mexico and Colorado, by 1960 they were the second largest ethnic minority in the country, and in some places faced hostility and discrimination as great as that faced by blacks. Drawing upon a long tradition of revolutionary nationalism derived from the Mexican revolution, almost from the start they won a number of resounding victories. In 1967 and 1968, a student-led community movement in Crystal City, Texas, won control of the local government as a response to a campaign against school discrimination. At the same time, various

Mexican-American student organizations began to emerge throughout the area; the most important were: the United Mexican-American Students (UMAS) in California, and the Mexican-American Youth Organization (MAYO) in Texas. By the end of the year chapters had been established on almost all of the campuses of those states. From 1966 to 1969 Chicano students were deeply involved in the unionization campaigns of the United Farm Workers, led by Ceasar Chavez. And, in the spring of 1968 tens of thousands of high school students walked out of the Los Angeles schools in a protest over segregation and discrimination starting a wave of similar 'blow-outs' throughout the Southwest.

These successes reflected the fact that the Chicano student movement, right from its inception, had deep ties to the Mexican-American community. As Juan Gomez Quinones, one of the founders of UMAS, a native of Los Angeles, and UCLA student, noted, 'The role of the student in the Mexican-American community is a little sharper than in other areas. They bring a set of skills and self-confidence, a style, that is not prevalent or available. Because the community is a cultural minority, intensely segregated from the larger society, what a student group could do on behalf of the community is remarkable, when compared to a group of white students in the white community. It is the hermetic nature of the Mexican-American community.'

The 'blow-outs' had a deep effect upon the Chicano student movement. Not only did it mean that students arriving on college campuses in the fall of 1968 and 1969 had this experience behind them, they also brought college students back into the community in the roles of advisors, and observers. The 'blow-outs' were, Carlos Vasquez recalled, 'a way of making connections in the community between issues. Missing classes, spending days in the community, speaking over and over to different groups, not only gets you to believe it, but to see other connections. You can't just talk about one issue. Pretty soon you're looking for links, for a context, other things that might put things in a context: the black struggle, Vietnam, war industries. It unfolds. As with blacks, Chicano students became radicalized when they asked, "Why are our schools like they are?"'

In October 1968, hundreds of Mexican students and workers were shot by the army and police during a mass demonstration in Mexico City to protest against government spending on the Olympic Games, which were about to open there, when the bulk of the population lived in poverty. It was the largest single massacre of students in the Western Hemisphere in the 1960s, and it shook the Chicano movement as it did student movements everywhere. The exact number of deaths was never known, and skeletons were still being discovered years later. As Vasquez recalled from his visits to Mexico in the early 1970s, when the repression continued unabated, the government forces 'were very sadistic. They took people out over the Pacific and just threw them out of planes . . . But I also saw the widespread worker input into the Mexican student movement. They had a really accessible tradition of Communist and anarchist movements to draw on. Down there I realized how isolated and limited we were in the U.S.'

In March 1969, Chicano activists from across the country met in Denver to elaborate a vision of revolutionary nationalism in the light of what appeared to be a revolutionary situation. 'A lot of us felt that social upheaval and armed struggle were imminent – that's how naive I think we really were,' continued Vasquez. 'But by then, blacks had already burned down a number of American cities. It looked like a cycle that was speeding up. You were seeing these transformations before your eyes. You were seeing tactics being made out of nothing, out of nowhere, at meetings, and then working. And you perceived the terror and confusion in the eyes and faces of bureaucrats who didn't know how to deal with this thing. It seemed clearly that the system was corrupt. It *was* decadent. We thought, my goodness! This thing is going to fall. The power of disruption was heady stuff.'

The meeting adopted a program which accented the historic identity of brown people on the American continent, self-defense 'against the occupiers', community control of Chicano neighbourhoods, Spanish language equality with English, support for the working class at home and for anti-imperialist struggles abroad. But the extreme nationalism of the new movement was illustrated when the conference refused to admit blacks, and the Puerto Rican contingent withdrew. Once again, new-found militancy resulted in divergency of goals.

Another important militant constituency came from the reemergent women's liberation movement, which began to take a number of militant actions. From the earliest days of the movement, women, especially organizers, had felt dissatisfaction at the way their views and concerns were relegated by men; but they were either too timid to express their resentment, or felt it necessary to submerge their concerns within the larger struggle. Cathy Wilkerson recalled the process through which the concerns of women were relegated to minor issues in Swarthmore SDS in the early Sixties, and how women failed to challenge that process. Intimidated by the men in the chapter, she had withdrawn from attending meetings. 'I don't think I was aware that when I didn't go to meetings it was because it was all men talking, but I think in retrospect that it had a tremendous effect on me.' Later, when ERAP was founded, she was 'uncomfortable' because of the 'male–female stuff.' 'If you lived with one of the male leaders, then you were accepted as his mate. And that's how most of the women who were involved in the projects were accepted. Basically, you had to sleep with them. It sounds gross, but it was true.'

For Fay Bellamy, who worked in SNCC's Atlanta office and later in Selma, Alabama, the question was one of priorities. 'Chauvinism carried over. It had to. We were all from the same environment. We all had the same bad lessons we had learned, male and female, about how to treat one another. I can't speak for all women but I always got the feeling that we were always putting women's struggles aside for later, because once again it's prioritizing your movement. We didn't feel that the movement could stand it at that time for black men and black women to be dealing with this on that level.'

In 1965, two white SNCC organizers, Casey Hayden and Mary King, produced an informal memo, 'Sex and Caste', which they circulated through the movement. At the end of the same year, SDS held a workshop on women as part of a conference to 'rethink' its general aims. A group of women decided to hold their own meeting. Seeing the meeting as yet another part of the broad movement in which black and white students were defining themselves and their needs, Heather Booth joined them. 'My reaction was that it was the right thing to do. There were some people who were upset about it, or thought, what did this imply, would it break up the organization – but we can't make progress if we're all sitting and talking. There's more that has to be done.'

Barbara Haber, on the other hand, initially resisted the walk-out, seeing it as a potential break with the movement. Instead, she joined an informal discussion of men and women SDSers who were talking about 'what was going on with "our women" ... I heard men talking and I suddenly understood that they had a point of view about the world, about human-hood, manhood, that was totally wrong. I found myself saying things I didn't have any idea that I knew, thought or felt. Within an hour I discovered that I was a feminist. *Bohngg!* A woman friend put forth the view that it was natural for a woman to wear a wedding ring, to do the dishes, and a man not, because of the nature of her genitalia. I got angry, and put forth a counter-notion of myself as a sexual being, a being that acted. The meeting went on for eight hours. It was one of the six great evenings of my life. I just felt I could see the light, and that I was telling it without any self-consciousness.'

Feminist consciousness did not come easily to all women. Teresa Meade recalled her initial hesitation in being called a *woman*. While an undergraduate at the University of Wisconsin in 1969, she attended a meeting about door-to-door organizing. 'We were going to go out to talk to people, and the woman running the meeting said, "I don't want any of the women to go alone." I remember sitting there and looking around, "We don't have any women here." I had never heard a girl called a woman before. I was twenty-one years old, but I was not a woman! My *mother* was a woman! This was a very hard thing for me to get used to. We forget that for many of us who first became involved in the women's movement, the idea of calling ourselves – juniors in college – "women," was very strange.'

Over the following years as more and more women mobilized, they began to initiate their own actions on their own concerns. Rayna Rapp recalled how she and a number of other SDS women from the University of Michigan followed the lead of WITCH (Women's International Terrorist Conspiracy from Hell) in pressuring the Michigan state legislature, which was considering a new abortion law. 'We hexed the legislative committee. We flew in as WITCH and we hexed these old men with a chant about how they were going to die because they were all men and they were controlling women's bodies. Then we flew out again.'

Rapp had been active in SDS in Michigan since 1964 but made her first contacts with the women's movement in 1968, and found herself transformed by it. 'Once I let feminism in, I reorganized everything I understood about the world. That was my conversion experience – it was natural and it was quick. Afterwards I was so angry about the number of mimeograph machines I had turned and the number of phone calls I had made, and the number of cups of coffee I had brought for other people.' Like many women activists, Rapp focused that anger on the movement as well as on society. The two themes were inextricably merged. 'At first we saw it to be a problem of the left. Later, we understood it to be a problem of the entire culture, maybe the culture of humanity.'

But at that time, she remembered, 'I couldn't understand it as being anything but a critique of the left because the left was supposed to be accountable on the question of equality. We believed in democracy, so how had they [male activists] pulled the wool over our eyes for all these years.

They had all this empathy for the Vietnamese, and for black Americans, but they didn't have much empathy for the women in their lives; not the women they slept with, not the women they shared office space with, not the women they fought at demonstrations with. So our first anger and anguish and fury was directed against the men of the left. They should have known better, as far as we were concerned. And we should have known better, too. A lot of it was self-anger, that we had allowed ourselves to be put in such a secondary role.'

As in West Germany, the new women's movement not only criticized the student movement but began to break away from it, adding to the divergency and fragmentation of the American SDS. 'The men have said that, by leaving, the women rent the movement asunder, which is a way of accepting the maleness of the movement as a fixed given, as a planet, and seeing the women as a moon that went out of orbit,' commented Haber. 'I would say the intransigence of the men and their inability to move at all on this issue drove out the women who would otherwise have been much happier staying in a mixed leftist movement centered around the war. SDS was absolutely the most sexist place I've ever been.'

In the fall of 1968 several hundred radical young women staged the first public feminist protest, disrupting the annual Miss America contest in New York. Throwing bras, girdles, false eyelashes and other 'instruments of female oppression' into a large trash can, they held a ceremony at which a live sheep was crowned 'the real Miss America'. At the same time they issued a statement listing their principles, the first of which read: 'We take the women's side in everything. We ask not if something is "reformist", "radical", "revolutionary" or "moral". We ask: is it good for women or bad for women?'

Yet another and important sign of the movement's diversity was a new wave of black student activism; it erupted this time not on black Southern campuses, but on white campuses such as Harvard, Michigan and Cornell in the North where, as a result of the civil rights movement, the number of blacks was increasing. At these three universities, as well as at many others, there were important strikes by massive numbers of students aimed at increasing minority enrolment and getting the curriculum changed to include Afro-American studies. At Cornell this campaign climaxed in the *armed* occupation of a major campus building. Although, as at Columbia's Hamilton Hall during the occupation, blacks did not allow whites to make any decisions, SDS enthusiastically organized support among white students, took over other buildings and formed a human barrier to prevent a police or right-wing attack on the black students.

'Perhaps that doesn't sound very heroic, but I think it was an important thing,' Sarah Elbert, a Cornell SDSer, avowed. 'It was a physical realization in terms of racism and radicalism, that that's what you had to do. You had to become a "voluntary nigger".' She summed up the whole experience in terms that recalled the FSM and the early Sixties. 'It still seems to me to be a terribly significant thing. I think there's been a strong attempt on the part of a lot of my friends to devalue the whole thing and not to look at the process that took place. The process that took place was the seizing of power over our lives. It wasn't that we got anything for the blacks – they probably would have gotten the Afro-American Center themselves. It isn't that we changed the structure of the university or university investments. We didn't smash the state and end capitalism. What we did do – all of us – was to teach ourselves something. For a very brief time we created a real community of our own, a real community in which we supplied our own needs. We fed each other – and we fed each other not only food, but knowledge and support and comfort. And we understood for the first time that there was something else possible that wasn't competitive, that wasn't ridden with power and ego . . . I remember people I had barely known who said things that struck me as remarkably intelligent and correct. It was a moment of saying, to the whole university, to the whole country, OK I may not have put it all together, but I know what time it is – and you don't. And that's very very important.'

Three of the crucial 'moments' of the period – the established order's repression, inter-racial coalitions and the turn to revolution – intersected particularly dramatically on one campus: San Francisco State College. There, a black-led student coalition, which included white radicals and newly mobilized Asian-American and Chicano students, clashed head on with the fully aroused forces of the state, led by Governor Reagan, over student demands for the right to hire whomever they chose, even revolutionaries, as their teachers. The outcome was a strike that lasted five months and was attended by more state violence than had been used at Berkeley or even Columbia.

San Francisco State was one of the most ethnically mixed of the major colleges in the country; its 26,000 students were also more predominantly working-class and older than, for example, at Berkeley. Since the mid-1960s, student radicals there had been quietly using student funds to reshape the university to address larger social issues. Influenced by the early SNCC's sit-ins and Mississippi Summer of 1964, they initiated tutorial programs for the city's blacks and a community involvement program. In 1965, responding to the same reservations about the nature of education as the Berkeley Free Speech Movement, they established an experimental college where students could design their own course, hire their own teachers and, with faculty approval, earn credits towards graduation.

'I thought of us as creating a new society and a new culture in microcosm in San Francisco,' commented Jim Nixon, who is generally credited with being one of the chief architects of the new system. A former Lutheran seminarian and ex-member of the Young People's Socialist League and the Trotskyist Socialist Workers Party, he didn't consciously identify with the New Left; and yet his concerns seemed to fit the latter's categories exactly. 'I was very militant that we needed to figure out a uniquely American way of going about this. Essentially it was a bringing together of a white political movement, a white hippie cultural movement and black power on the basis of working together for mutual interests. The other thing was taking the techniques of community organizing and consciously, conscientiously applying them in order to create an organization or an institution which would ultimately clear away some territory for us in the guerrilla warfare context, rather than using it to identify an enemy and bring about a confrontation.'

Sharon Gold remembered, 'We had organizers in every rent strike, every welfare rights organization, every women's group. Every single organizing project in the whole city by the spring of '68 had a SF State student as their organizer. Each program spun another program. It grew and grew. The capacity to provide academic credit for students complemented our control of the student government so that we dispensed all work-study jobs. Plus, the fact that the leadership of these programs, the graduate students, also had part-time instructorships in the college gave us control of the TA union. And we were making contact with the radical wing of the AFT [American Federation of Teachers] and we knew almost every secretary in every department, and we knew what every administrator was doing before they did. We had a network that went as far as Sacramento [the central offices of the state college system]. We had political power, and it grew quietly. We had a power base that touched every single ghetto and barrio in the city, and every nook and cranny of the campus, except the math department and ROTC, the reactionary section of the campus.'

By 1968, revolutionary students had considerable power on campus. The blacks and Chicanos among them argued that more minority students must be admitted to the college, but that their education would be meaningless if they did not return to their communities to struggle for change. Therefore they had to be educated in black and other ethnic study programs by radical teachers; the only way to ensure both aims was if the students themselves had the power to determine the curriculum and to hire and fire faculty. As Roberto Vargas, a poet and revolutionary student leader of the Chicano Brown Berets, put it, these demands were an attempt to 'extend the revolution into the educational side. The campus was going to be a community resource.'

The main student revolutionary forces on campus were the Black Student Union (BSU), closely linked to the Black Panthers, the Third World Liberation Front (TWLF), created by a Chicano professor to promote Latino admissions to the College, and the Maoist PL, which dominated the local SDS chapter. When Reagan and conservative faculty members blocked their attempt to set up a black studies program, the BSU called a strike; the initial intention was not to shut the school down, but to get black students to boycott classes. The TWLF, however, rapidly joined the BSU's strike call, and white students were then asked to take part, although forbidden to add any of their own demands. The strike began on 6 November 1968. The state soon revealed that it was not prepared to allow the students to expand their territory but would attempt to crush them and roll back their gains.

'They brought the police out. It was going to be a strike for a few days, then go back to school, right?' explained Terry Collins, a BSU member. 'But when I saw a woman who was on the student council whom we considered conservative throw a rock at the police I knew we were in for a long battle.'

Early on in the strike the College president was fired by Reagan and his allies on the board of trustees for attempting to find a compromise, and replaced by a hardliner, S. I. Hayakawa, who forbade all campus demonstrations. The strike now turned into a war of attrition with constant skirmishing, marches, demonstrations and picketing. Until January, when the nature of the conflict was changed by the teachers' union joining the strike, most of the campus was effectively shut.

'Every day you'd come out to the campus, have a shot of good strong coffee and work your courage up, knowing there was a good chance you were going to come home with bones broken,' recalled Peter Shapiro, a radical white student. 'One day I saw a student who happened to be going into the library when the police were making a charge and they clobbered him, right round the kidneys. He made it to the third floor and collapsed. The police wouldn't let a medic from the Medical Committee for Human Rights get to him. Finally, after lying there for an hour bleeding internally, they drove him to the hospital. His spleen had been ruptured. He went without medical attention for two hours at the hospital because the police wouldn't let anyone near him.'

Hari Dillon, a TWLF steering committee member and also a PL-SDSer, was picketing one day when he made the 'mistake' of going into a campus building which was thought not to be occupied by the police to use the rest rooms. 'By that time most of us had bodyguards, but I went in without one. Two cops came around the corner. They put their .327 Magnums up to my head and cocked the hammers. It was raining and I had my hands in my trench coat. We were armed at different times, but I wasn't armed then. They said, "take your hands out of your pockets real slow." I was a goner if I did, I knew they'd say you were going for your gun. I couldn't make my hands come up. I kept telling them I didn't have one. What was racing through my mind was that it would be really stupid for the ruling class to do this right now, at the height of the strike. And then another part of my mind was saying that these two cops had probably never heard of the ruling class. They're just going to kill the straight-haired nigger, as the tactical squad called me. "You can take my hands out of my pockets," I said, and gradually they did.'

As in most campus strikes much of the students' energies went into spontaneous organization. A strike newsletter was published, support groups organized, art students produced posters, some of the most flamboyant and colorful of the American movement. Community support – a crucial factor from as far back as the original SNCC sit-ins and successfully used by the black students during the Columbia occupation – was again a vital factor in keeping the strike going, especially after the police violence.

'When Hayakawa came in and the whole strategy was Reagan's of crushing the strike by force and thousands of police were mobilized – that generated tremendous community support for the students,' continued Dillon. The earlier community links forged by the students, the fact that they were struggling for ethnic studies programs and open admissions, helped to ensure this support.

Just before the Christmas break, the TWLF organized a Third World community day march as a challenge to Hayakawa. Blacks, Chicanos, Latinos, representatives of the Chinese, Japanese and Filipino community groups announced that they would attend, as Dillon recalled. 'We were elated. It was one of the biggest highs of my life. Hayakawa closed the campus the day before the march. So in December we marched off campus and had a big rally of several thousand at City Hall. When we came back in January we had rallies of hundreds of people from the community and thousands of students.'

The students also attempted to generate support from local trade unions, not without some success. Some came from PL contacts in various unions, some by students volunteering for picket duty in various local struggles.

Two events in January fundamentally changed the nature of the conflict. Early in the month, the teachers' union joined the strike but without endorsing its demands, succeeding thereby in turning it into a regular labor dispute, limited to picketing, which allowed Hayakawa to reopen the college. But just as serious for the students was a mass police arrest later in the month in which 450 students were charged with a series of offenses, some of which carried jail terms of two to three years. In past rallies, when the police broke them up, only leaders had been arrested; but this time the police adopted a new tactic. 'They drove a wedge and surrounded the 400 people,' remembered Dillon, who was one of those arrested. 'We tried to break out, but they had too many police.' The arrests broke the back of the strike.

'It was a mistake,' Terry Collins of the BSU recalled, 'one of the biggest we ever made. Before that we had had about one hundred people arrested, mostly for speaking out. But 450 more was too much. The bail was enormous, three charges each. Fifteen hundred dollars per person. Out of 2,000 at the rally that day, 450 arrested. They shouldn't have been . . .'

In court, many students, under the leadership of PL, attempted to make the trial a political statement, and sentences were stiff. Most of the strike leadership eventually served over a year in jail. John Levin, the PL leader who was jailed for almost a year, believed that these tactics had been another mistake. 'We could have cut a deal, but we dragged it out through these endless trials. A powerful mistake in that people who otherwise would have remained active were worn down. People were still in jail two and a half years later.'

When the faculty settled in April, the defeat was consummated. Although ethnic studies were subsequently introduced, many nontenured militant faculty leaders were fired, and most of the hard-won student gains of the earlier years were lost.

The long strike demonstrated a number of things, both positive and negative. Among the former was the reforging of an inter-racial unity which had not existed since the civil rights movement. As Dillon put it, since the rise of Black Power and the ghetto uprisings there had been no such unity – 'no major struggle where you demonstrated the unity of black and white and Third World people. And San Francisco State was that. For three and a half bloody months thousands of students – ten to twelve thousand people at rallies by *their* figures, 90 per cent of these white students – stood out there with us, fought the cops and got arrested.'

But in general, given black and other nationalisms and the growing sectarianism of sectors of the white movement – during the San Francisco strike, PL suddenly came out with a new political line condemning nationalism – this unity was short-lived. The exclusion of whites from formulating their own demands and from the leadership of inter-racial coalitions did not help, nor did police provocateurs who played on racial tensions. In the absence of any national black student organization, alliances remained local and could be generated only over local issues. Moreover, the very success of the considerable number of strikes over black and ethnic studies programs throughout the country itself removed many minority student dissidents from the struggle by turning them into faculty members, administrators or supervisors of such programs.

The San Francisco strike also showed that a single campus, however united, could not defeat an established order which was determined to crush rebellion. The strike, as Peter Shapiro saw, 'raised issues that, in challenging the forces of the state, could only be challenged in the context of the whole state. You were talking about how the state budget is arrived at, about state policies concerning access to higher education, challenging the board of trustees and the state legislature. The BSU and TWLF did pretty well in making the strike an issue in their communities. But to win, we would have had to rally significant political forces that were not connected with higher education at all, some unions or at least some kind of working-class organizations which really saw a stake in the issues of who had access to college.'

It was the same problem as always. Without support from sectors of society critical to the functioning and legitimacy of the established order, a student movement could cause considerable disruption, even present the state with considerable problems of subduing the rebellion; but it would not profoundly challenge the ruling order.

In this maelstrom of diverse and divergent movements, with only their opposition to 'the establishment' in common, what hope was there of finding a set of goals around which they could cohere? Could movements as disparate as the anti-war mobilizations, the women's movement, black and other minority student campus revolts, GI organizing, and the counter-cultural White Panthers be linked in a way that their individual strengths would be combined? With which of these groups should the student movement ally to achieve the maximum leverage on 'the establishment'? It was, for sure, an unprecedented situation for any student organization to confront – and it was not perhaps surprising that the new SDS leadership, searching for the revolutionary constituency, was unable to envisage the wider goals needed to weld this massive movement into a coherent force.

Which was the revolutionary constituency? The working class, the black proletariat, youth culture? Each had its partisans: Progressive Labor, the working class; the Black Panthers, the black proletariat; the White Panthers or Yippies, youth culture. Conflicts over the correct constituency first drove a wedge into and then split SDS in 1969. The new leadership saw the way forward as building a revolutionary movement among white, and increasingly counter-cultural, working-class youth. Heavily influenced by the counter-culture and the black and anti-war movements, it saw the Black Panthers as the only valid leaders of the American revolution and the function of the white working-class youth movement as supporting them, and the heroic war of the Vietnamese. It called itself first the Revolutionary Youth Movement (RYM), and then Weatherman, after a line from a Bob Dylan song, 'You Don't Need a Weatherman to Know Which Way the Wind Blows', which it used as the title of one of its strategy papers.

A contributing factor to the emergence of the RYM/Weatherman positions was the fear that the Maoist PL, whose strength in SDS had grown since joining the organization in 1966, was going to take over the SDS leadership. To combat it, new Marxist strategies had to be found; what emerged could hardly have been further from PL's positions, for the latter believed that the student movement should direct its energies towards the industrial working class, the classic Marxist agent of revolution. Moroever, it was hostile to the counter-culture, black nationalism, women's liberation and the North Vietnamese, whom it now stigmatized as 'Moscow's lackeys'. But the leading role it had played in the most visible campus uprisings of the spring of 1969 had increased its prestige.

Beneath the differences, however, both factions shared a number of things: lack of interest in the wider constituencies that had been mobilized since the Chicago Democratic Convention, especially white college students who made up the bulk of the movement; lack of interest in the democratic concerns which had always mobilized the majority of students; a Marxist jargon that made their publications virtually inaccessible to those students, and a commitment to the vision of a vanguard Leninist party.

Leninism did not involve a radical shift for PL, but it was a nearly 180-degree turn for the RYM/Weatherman faction. The American student movement had long prided itself on its combination of ends and means, participatory democracy as a goal and a form of organization. The demands of revolution, however, seemed to dictate a different structure and different principles. 'I had read some Marx and Lenin in 1969,' Jeff Jones recalled, 'and once you read Lenin's *What Is to Be Done?* you realize that if you're serious about making a revolution, then all your energy has to be geared toward creating the Leninist party.' As David Gilbert noted, one of Lenin's 'fundamental contributions to revolutionary theory' was to point out that 'the bourgeoisie, the imperialists are very well organized. And I wish it weren't so but it is, they have a lot of power and force. They use it systematically. There is no example of a peaceful road to fundamental social change. You need a well organized, disciplined, combat party. That's the model of how to deal with their power, their military intervention, their ability to infiltrate and disrupt.'

By definition, a Leninist party limits disagreement and diversity, the toleration of which had long characterized the American movement. Consequently it became increasingly difficult for PL and the RYM/Weatherman factions (and later the various RYM factions) with their conflicting lines, to exist in the same organization. Throughout 1968–69 the two factions turned SDS national and regional meetings into a series of running battles, which climaxed at the June 1969 National Convention. There, representatives of the Black Panther Party, aligned with the RYM faction, after clumsily insulting SDS women with a set of sexist remarks, announced that the PL line on nationalism was counter-revolutionary and that SDS must expel PL or face dire consequences. Bedlam erupted, and when all the shouting ceased, there were two separate organizations;

PL/SDS which actually won a majority of the delegates, and RYM/Weatherman which held the national offices and the allegiances of most students throughout the country. When RYM/Weatherman split again, it became clear that a disaster had occurred in Chicago.

Gilbert, a strong supporter of the RYM/Weatherman position, still justifies the expulsion of PL. They 'came to the convention very well organized, bringing a lot of people, to the point where they could control the votes, control the direction of the convention. One position they had was that black nationalism was reactionary. They had a position condemning the Vietnamese for negotiating. So, there was tremendous feeling that the most fundamental principles that SDS had grown and formed around were being violated – the SDS that I had put all my life into building for the last five years.'

PL member Hari Dillon is somewhat more muted. 'Basically, it was PL's line versus RYM's line,' he says. Today he is critical of the PL line, particularly their positions on black nationalism and the NLF – and he notes that he and other San Francisco State activists were uncomfortable with them when they were announced in the spring of 1969, but he had no say in shaping them. 'You know these democratic centralist groups – there's no democracy, only centralism. So we got to the culmination of this whole period here in June, and here we are saddled with a line that none of us agreed with, a line the total opposite of everything we fought for all these years.' Ironically enough, the reason PL had such a substantial following at the convention was their leadership of two of the major strikes of that spring – San Francisco State and Harvard – both in support of black and ethnic studies programs which they were now condemning as 'reactionary'.

Dillon is also critical of the RYM/Weatherman faction. 'The self-destruction of SDS can only be 50 per cent blamed on PL. The RYM forces were very ultra-left. At the convention we ended up with a slim majority, simply because the RYM leaders were viewed as dangerous adventurists, which many turned out to be, or do-nothing bureaucrats – the kind who put out New Left Notes but weren't really leading the struggles on campus.' The real problem was the attempt to turn SDS into a tight, revolutionary vanguard organization. 'The idea for SDS should have been to build a mass anti-racist, anti-imperialist organization, not a Marxist-Leninist organization. That was the original idea, but we got away from it,' Dillon concludes.

To get a full picture of the convention, one needs to see it through the eyes of someone not committed to either faction. Barbara Joye attended the convention as part of a contingent from Atlanta. She had been active since the early Sixties as a member of SDS and the Southern Student Organizing Committee, and her memories convey the flavor of the convention. 'I went to Chicago because I hadn't been to an SDS convention in a long time – it sounded exciting, and I'd find out what was going on,' she explained. But the convention was not what she expected. 'God! the whole thing was so confusing.'

'It was in this really ugly barn-like warehouse structure. And there were the serried ranks of the American left, with factions like in a high school football game. There were the PL people, and here were the RYM people, and then the rest of us just sort of sat anyplace. And up on the podium most of the time seemed to be either a Black Panther or Bernardine Dohrn wearing a leather mini-skirt, and I think high heeled boots. And she was kind of amazing. She and the other Weather leadership were always yelling various positions at us, mostly having to do with which faction was going to be most accepted by the Panthers.

'So, there was this struggle about alignment with the Panthers, and there was this whole thing about whether women should form a separate caucus, or have a separate movement. And the PL people were trying to break up both the pro-Panther activities and the feminist activities – very aggressively invading meetings and so on. When the debates got really heated, these different choral groups would wave Red Books and shout slogans at each other, which I found absolutely mind-boggling. If I'm not giving a coherent explanation of the agenda, it's because I don't have the faintest idea of what was going on. I mean, not the faintest. I got the position papers – they were unintelligible. The Weatherman position paper was completely mysterious. It had nothing in it that gave me the slightest clue, except that they were more interested in youth culture than the other side.' When the split came, Joye went with the Weatherman faction 'because they seemed to have more of a sense of humor', but she was far from happy with the outcome. 'I was sort of buttonholing people and asking them: what the hell is going on?'

After the split, Gilbert, who was deeply committed to the anti-racist, anti-imperialist program of SDS, 'was mind-blown. SDS had existed when I got conscious and active. I felt it as a sense of identity – if somebody asked me who I was, I could say I was an SDS organizer, and that stood for something morally, politically, culturally . . . and all of a sudden, *chhoofff*, it blew apart. I felt very positive about how we dealt with it, but it was still emotionally – shattering is too strong a word – but it was very powerful emotionally, very shaky!'

As word of what had happened in Chicago spread through the movement, thousands of other people felt even shakier than Gilbert. Andrea and Richard Eagan, veterans of the Columbia strike, had gone to the Chicago convention, but left early. After the convention she went to some Weatherman meetings and heard one Weather leader put forward the line that black people could make the revolution by themselves, and that white students were irrelevant. 'I remember feeling like it was a complete disaster, and that it meant the end of the movement,' Andrea recalled.

Jim Jacobs, who had been active since 1965, was by the summer of 1969 teaching and organizing at a working-class community college near Detroit. 'I remember reading about the convention and just feeling terrible because I wasn't there, helpless, because I'd spent two years totally into this organization – reading every word of *New Left Notes*, really believing that this was going to be *the* organization of the Seventies – this organization was being smashed to pieces.'

Neither of the two factional SDSs proved capable of mobilizing the constituencies it aimed for nor of carrying the mass of students with it. PL's strident Maoism, strict democratic centralism and dogmatic positions on the black movement and the war appealed to only a narrow spectrum of students; and the Weatherman-SDS, supported at first, if reluctantly, by most rank-and-file SDSers, soon lost its credibility by a wild ultra-leftism. In the six months or so of their above-ground activities, Weatherman projected a violent, aggressive image in order to attract working-class youth and to try to build a Red Army of the streets.

'Part of the theory was that we would get respect by fighting – they would see we were tough,' recalled Weatherman leader Jeff Jones. 'We did a terrible job of organizing ... We weren't really organizing, we were confronting, and the line was, either you're with us – and we're with the people of the world – or you're against us. And if you're against us, and against the people of the world, then you're the enemy and we're going to fight you.'

'It was trying to reach white youth on the basis of their most reactionary macho instinct, intellectuals playing at working-class toughs,' observed Cathy Wilkerson, an SDS activist since the early 1960s who joined the Weatherman collective. She believed that the leadership were 'the only people to have understood the importance of black nationalism. I think a lot of people joined for that reason. However, there was this kind of moralistic furor that if you didn't understand black nationalism or the leadership's terms and you don't get it tomorrow, forget it. If you missed it you were a dummy, and you created a mortal sin that would stain history forever. You were part of the fascist backwash of history.

'I was acting out of emotion around Vietnam, too. As a response to what was going on – the saturation bombing of Hanoi – ours was the very sane response, one of total outrage. Not to be outraged was more insane than to be outraged and go bananas. External reality continued to make our emotional response historically on target. But from the standpoint of rational politics and organization, we had no plan, no program, therefore our rage quickly became ineffective.'

In order to join the collective, Wilkerson had to go through a two-day self-criticism of her women's politics which she had argued in a *New Left Notes* publication. It was, she reflected, a 'male ego exercise designed to destroy independent thinking and unity among the women.' In the Weatherman ideology, the liberated woman was a woman who knew how to fight in the streets. Both male and female members had initiated an intense process of collective self-transformation in which every aspect of personal life, from eating habits to family relationships, was subjected to intense scrutiny. They met questions about the role of women in society and in the movement with programs of forced sexual rotation – 'smashing monogamy', it was called – and teaching women karate and the use of weapons.

Throughout the summer, Weatherman moved into urban collectives to transform its members from 'bourgeois' students to revolutionary warriors. At the same time they attempted to mobilize working-class youth for their planned 'Days of Rage' in Chicago in October. Their failure was revealed when, instead of the tens of thousands of youth they hoped would rally to 'tear apart Pig City', six hundred people turned out, perhaps half of them committed to Weatherman. Wearing helmets, gas masks and goggles, and carrying sticks, lead pipes and similar weapons, they stormed at night into the city's affluent Gold Coast sector, smashing the windows of apartments and cars to the chants of 'Ho! Ho! Ho-Chi-Minh! Dare to Struggle, Dare to Win!'

'The slogan was, "Bring the war home",' recalled Jeff Jones, who led part of the first night's action. 'The point of it was that if they're going to continue to attack the Vietnamese and to kill the Panthers, then we as young white people are going to attack them behind the lines, at the center of their bourgeois power. That's why we went to the Gold Coast. What the

U.S. was doing was so grave that we had to take extreme measures to stop it ... Thank God the Vietnamese weren't depending on us – mounting a national effort with six hundred people!'

Jones was one of the first to be arrested; the Chicago police, as they had shown the previous year, were pitiless in their repression. In the hour the rampage lasted, six Weathermen were shot, an unknown number injured and sixty-eight arrested.

Actions like this did nothing to mobilize those, like Carol Brightman, an anti-war activist and founder-editor of *Viet Report*, who shared the Weatherman's anger but couldn't join their campaign of destruction. She attended the Weatherman war council in the fall of 1969 at which Weather decided to go underground. 'They were at their worst phase. . . . It was grotesque, but it was like theatre, because it didn't seem to be related to anything real. There was a huge gun on the wall with a big sign over it saying P-I-E-C-E NOW!'

Having failed in its effort to build a revolutionary movement among white working-class youth and alienated from the existing radical student movement – the entire Wisconsin SDS chapter physically turned their backs on Weatherman speakers who came to address their chapter – Weatherman's response was to go into clandestine armed struggle. Two months after the Days of Rage, its leaders and about three hundred followers went underground. Not long afterwards, it officially disbanded SDS.

Before SDS was buried, one last attempt was made to hold the movement together and give it new impetus. The initiative, he claims, came from Carl Oglesby, a member of the SDS leadership who was opposed to the new line. On behalf of the organization, he attended the tenth anniversary celebrations of the Cuban revolution in February 1969, and heard Fidel Castro announce the mobilization of the Cuban population to achieve a sugar harvest of ten million tons that year – 25 per cent more than ever before. Deeply concerned about American ignorance in general about Cuba, and the American movement's inability to think of 'where to go next, how to intensify the struggle without going deep into illegal action', Oglesby saw in the harvest a solution to both problems. Thousands of ordinary Americans could go to Cuba to help bring in the harvest.

His plan was scaled down by the SDS leadership to sending students, chosen by a committee representing all movement factions, to Cuba. Numbers of non-students, especially Third World revolutionaries, and

some old left-wingers, also joined. The Venceremos ('We Shall Win')
Brigades were born. The first group of just over two hundred people left
for Cuba in November 1969, followed by another Brigade three times as
large in February 1970.

Despite many problems, the Brigadistas were deeply affected by the
experience, their personal contacts with Cubans and their sense of
involvement in an international revolutionary movement. 'It was a terrific
experience,' recalled Karen Duncanwood, who was on the first Brigade.
'The energy of the county was very high and you just got this feeling that
you were part of this country creating its future, in that the democracy of
the country was really amazing. Mississippi made me a radical, Cuba made
me a socialist. Cuba gave me the experience that there was a better way to
organize society, and that people who were very poor and very hungry
could create their own future.'

On the second Brigade, Teresa Meade found the Cubans' 'exceedingly
exuberant happiness and genuine support for the revolution a fantastic
experience.' At the same time, however, she noted 'an enormous number
of problems. The major contradiction that was never resolved was racial.
There was a lot of hostility and distrust between blacks and whites. What
most sabotaged the Brigade was the planting of racial tension by provocateurs and agents. Nobody could cause more problems than an FBI
agent who was a Third World person. There were also attacks on the gay
men in the group. The Cubans weren't great on gays, but they didn't think
they needed to have their mosquito netting cut or be beaten up. Most of the
whites supported the gays, who were also white, and got upset at the
hostility coming from the Third World men. White guilt was running high.
The women's movement had begun and was really taking force. There
were some people who weren't able to handle the work – it was back-
breaking, and very, very hot. There were some people who only wanted to
smoke dope – and the Cubans never understood dope and this counter-
culture stuff . . .'

Thus, while many of the Brigadistas found it heartening to be working in
a revolutionary country, the experience did little, if anything, to ease the
tensions in the American movement. Oglesby's hope of giving the latter a
new impetus and direction was unsuccessful; perhaps, indeed, such was
impossible by this time. Although the Brigades continued into the 1970s,
they were organized then by the American Communist Party and ceased to
be part of the movement as such.

SDS had come to the end of its ten-year history. With it went the last organizational possibility of coordinating the student movement. For this Weatherman bore the main responsibility. Until it dissolved SDS, Weatherman remained in the eyes of many Americans, even students, a symbol of the student movement in its entirety. Massive governmental repression, massive media coverage – in the year that it was part of SDS, Weatherman received more coverage than the former SDS had received in its entire existence – forced many activists to defend its actions, albeit critically. There seemed no other immediately accessible political space in which to operate. But in going undergound, in burying SDS, Weatherman destroyed the important network for communication, debate and coordination that the student organization had provided through its publications, national office and regional travellers. But something of perhaps even greater importance was lost. Although SDS had never been able to offer a coherent strategy for taking on the state over Vietnam, it had always been a leading voice in merging the race issue and the war; this explained in part the student organization's concern to work with the Black Panthers. With SDS's collapse, this voice was lost, and with it went one of the major common goals that could link different sectors of the movement. For so long one of the main driving forces behind much movement protest, the race issue became increasingly isolated from movement concerns, most notably the war. From 1970, this left the field open for the takeover of the peace movement by Democratic Party liberals who believed in separating the issues of the war and race.

In this their task was made easier by the Trotskyist Socialist Workers' Party, a leading component of the anti-war movement, which had consistently argued in favour of making the war a single-issue campaign. Arguing that all the elements of dissent must be mobilized around a single issue – the war – the liberals maintained that the blacks' problems would be solved within the programs of the Great Society, initiated by President Johnson, and kept in place by Nixon. Most of the moderate black leadership accepted this line – a line which the Black Panthers refused. But without SDS, the possibility of uniting the white movement simultaneously around anti-racist and anti-imperialist goals vanished.

SDS's demise – even the loss of its name which had made it prestigious among newly radicalized students – was not then lamented by Weatherman. 'Who needed it? We saw it as a bourgeois, not a revolutionary organization,' explained Jeff Jones. 'But, looking back, it was a profoundly serious error which had tragic consequences.'

Despite the setbacks inflicted by Weatherman, the movement's strength still remained enormous. On 15 October 1969, less than a week after the failed Days of Rage, millions of Americans took part in a nation-wide, peaceful protest, or 'moratorium', organized by anti-war moderates; and a month later up to three quarters of a million people gathered in Washington to call for peace in the largest single demonstration of the decade. Then, in April 1970, President Nixon ordered American troops into Cambodia, which the U.S. had been clandestinely bombing for some time. The escalation of the war at a time when it appeared that the U.S. was beginning slowly to withdraw its forces from Vietnam, and the invasion of neighbouring Cambodia in defiance of international law, caused a massive outburst of protest on American campuses.

At one of them, Kent State in Ohio, where students had already burned down the ROTC building, National Guardsmen shot into a crowd of protesting students, killing four of them. In the following days over four million students and one million others walked out on strike in protest over Cambodia and Kent State. Almost 900 campuses were shut down. The National Guard was called in to 21 different universities. There were over 2,000 political arrests, 35,000 National Guardsmen and troops were called up, 100 people were either killed or wounded and there were 169 bombings of buildings. These actions combined with massive nationwide marches the next week marked the largest mobilization of the American anti-war movement. It was also the most violent moment of the movement.

By far the largest number of violent incidents were triggered by, or directed by, the agencies of the state, local police forces, agents pro-vocateurs, or by the urging of political figures, such as Richard Nixon's applauding of an attack on student demonstrators by two hundred con-struction workers in New York City – workers who were paid their day's wages to beat up the students at Wall Street. But at many universities, frustration over a seemingly unending war and the blatant hypocrisy of the invasion, combined to move students to violent confrontation. Teresa Meade remembered the reaction at the University of Wisconsin. 'I went to the Student Union to watch Nixon on TV. There was dead silence in the room. Everybody was very quiet and watched the whole thing. At the end of it people began to scream, and there were some demonstrations that occurred spontaneously, people went out in the streets just to throw rocks.' But the shock of Kent State set the campus in motion. 'A demonstration was called that night and we marched toward the administration building, and some trashing began.' Students then marched on the town of Madison, attacking banks and local merchants identified with the pro-war Nixon administration. 'It went on for days,' Meade noted. Police and National Guardsmen were called in, and street fighting broke out. 'The campus was closed down. There was nothing there. It was completely filled with tear gas. You could not go into any of the buildings, or onto the campus without a handkerchief over your face. At night there would be big demonstrations and each side would escalate more. The police at one point cornered people in the union building. They were on the top floor and there was gassing outside. People didn't know what to do. Then all hell broke loose in the dorms on the other side of campus. Students started fires in garbage cans, threw stuff out of windows, and hundreds of people poured out of the dorms and caused this diversionary tactic. The police went there and left the union. The people in the union were scared. They thought they were going to die in there.'

In Berkeley, where the news of Kent State hit a community which had been the scene of violent street fighting since May 1968, the outpouring was less spontaneous and more organized. Andor Skotnes remembered, 'They burned cars and stuff. The most remarkable thing was the high school students involved in this. Little kids running around throwing rocks at cops and turning over trash and burning it, and busting windows. I could not believe the Berkeley High students, and the younger college students. They just wanted to fight. And they dug it. They really enjoyed busting windows.'

So widespread were the protests in California that Governor Reagan was forced to close the entire university and state college systems. On many campuses across the nation, spontaneous demonstrations and marches moved out into the community, where the growing division between the anti-war movement and students on the one side and the state and its conservative adherents on the other was symbolized in the con- frontation. The same division was observed on a national scale: while a large proportion of the American population was reported to believe that the Kent State students had 'got what they deserved', the movement showed the wide popular support it commanded by mobilizing a day of massive, nationwide marches on May 9. Over 100,000 marched in Washington, 60,000 in Chicago, 50,000 in Boston, 20,000 in Austin, Texas.

'It was the largest demonstration I ever saw in Austin,' remembered Jose Limon, at the University of Texas. 'It went from the main mall of the

University through the city. People camped there overnight. It was really a moving sight. The thing reached its climax at that point.'

Reached its climax and lost its momentum at the same time. The marches marked the end of something, as Jeremy Brecher, a veteran SDSer who took part in the Washington march, observed. There was a failure everywhere to drive the movement forward, and nowhere more than in the capital itself. 'Basically, we had a nationwide upheaval with conflict on probably one hundred campuses, and thousands of people arriving and marching. But the administration totally outfoxed the movement in Washington. They set it up as if it was going to be a confrontation, so that people who wanted confrontation had their plans all set. Then at the last moment, the administration just pulled off the police and let the demonstrators come into the city. As a result it turned into a picnic.

'Now, in hindsight, I can see that we should have done something to escalate the whole situation. The Peace Corps volunteers, for example, went and occupied the Peace Corps building. There were 10,000 people in Washington that weekend who would have been ready to occupy government buildings. We could have occupied ten buildings, it would have created an entirely different situation. Nobody was set up to think that way. Even after years of confrontation politics.'

The failure to strike, even symbolically, at the heart of a state whose violence was responsible for the murder of students – by May 1970, at least fourteen had been shot dead – revealed the radicals' inability to put forward common goals and strategies for the bulk of the movement. Despite its long history of stimulating protest and upheaval, the American movement proved, at a time of heightened political tension, to be no different in this from student movements on the other side of the Atlantic. As in West Germany and Britain, the American movement had not catalyzed social layers, notably the working class, which would pose a serious challenge to the power structures of the established order. Nonetheless, it achieved more in influencing federal government policies than the movements in either of those two countries because its massive protests and campus actions put pressure on Nixon to withdraw U.S. troops from Cambodia, just as earlier it had contributed to his announcement of America's gradual disengagement from Vietnam.

But the reaction to the Kent State killings did not lead to further action. When two black students at Jackson State in Mississippi were shot a few weeks later, the student response was notably muted. The inter-racial student alliance had been short-lived. The failure to find a way of uniting the diverse constituencies mobilized by the movement was most graphically illustrated in the racial arena. The white American movement had always been at its strongest when it linked, in their impingement on students' lives, the dominant contradiction of the epoch – Vietnam – with the major domestic contradiction – racism. This had happened in 1965 – 67, briefly again in 1968 at Columbia, and in the black upheavals on Northern campuses in 1969. But thereafter, due in great part to SDS's collapse, the movements bifurcated again, leaving the white movement without one of its most important constituencies.

The killing of an innocent student – the first fatal casualty caused by the movement – in the New Year Gang's bombing of the Army Mathematics Research Center at Wisconsin in August, added to the sense of disintegration. (The Gang, without connection to or sanction from Weather Underground, laid claim to being a Weather cell.) 'Apart from the horror of the bombing itself, the reaction on campus was that the movement wasn't going anywhere,' recalled Teresa Meade, and this feeling was shared by many students elsewhere.

In place of a movement, there were now in fact a host of movements: white middle-class student anti-war demonstrators, politicized hippies, working-class Vietnam veterans, Chicano revolutionaries, women's movement activists, GI organizers, black revolutionaries . . . No organization sprang up that could encompass this diversity. Weatherman destroyed the only one that might have been up to the task, and government repression severely limited the space available for the growth of another. Instead, each of the movements focused on a single issue, none of them mounted a fundamental challenge to the structure of power in America.

By the fall of 1970, the levels of campus protest dropped sharply. The next few years saw occasional large protests, but overall the student movement went into a decline from which it was not to recover. 'It's interesting', Michael Frisch mused in retrospective reflection, 'the universal assumption in the summer of 1970 was, "Boy things are going to blow the minute the students get back. The clock ran out, but boy! Wait till we get back! Everything's going to blow completely, totally." And then, of course, nothing happened. Partly because everybody expected everything to happen, but things don't happen that way. They need a whole process.' It was the process that had come to an end.

7

The 1970s

Postscript

As the burial of both S D Ss graphically illustrated, the student movements had run their course. Though capable here and there of a sudden re-emergence in the 1970s, they were generally succeeded by other forms of struggle – revolutionary party building, clandestine armed struggle, the formation and consolidation of new movements, most notably the women's movement, and collectivist or communitarian challenges to the established order. The history of these organizations and movements is distinct from, but related to, the student movements; it is with their connections to the latter rather than their separate histories that this postscript is concerned.

The established order's mounting counter-offensive to the student movements made it rapidly evident to most radicalized students that their loosely-knit, campus-based organizations were inadequate to sustain the assault, let alone to realize the often unformulated but nonetheless strongly held vision of a radically different society which the preceding years had opened up to them. Instead, it appeared to many that new types of organization were needed, capable of attracting other sectors of society, in particular the working class, in a long-term offensive on the power structures of capitalist society. The student movements had been without historic models: now, as student radicals confronted the escalating power of the ruling order, many turned increasingly to Leninism or Maoism as historic models for overthrowing the state, while others took the road into clandestine armed struggle; both these options can be related to the perceived lessons of what had happened during the French May events.

The French students' seeming success in having 'sparked off' a large-scale revolt of the working class, and the containment of that revolt by a reformist French Communist Party, were interpreted in two different ways. On the one hand, a small minority of activists came to believe that armed violence would reveal to the oppressed layers of society the violent nature of the capitalist state, could be the 'spark' that set them in motion. On the other, a much larger number of activists saw their task as building an 'authentic' revolutionary party that, unlike the reformist Communist parties, would be the vanguard of the coming mass struggle to overthrow capitalism. In both cases, activists definitely abandoned campus politics, the final step, paradoxically, on their slowly convergent paths over the previous decade.

The activists' revolutionary hopes were fuelled by a new labour militancy in Western Europe and the U.S. Growing unemployment as the West's economies began to slacken, the ruling orders' counter-offensive which was directed also at the labour movements, and the impact of the previous years' radicalization, on young workers especially, were among some of the factors accounting for this militancy. In West Germany, the largest spontaneous strikes in the Federal Republic's history took place in September 1969, with 200,000 workers laying down tools. The following year saw the revival in Britain of mass struggle which culminated in the miners' strike of 1974 and the downfall of the Conservative government. In 1971, strikes in the U.S. resulted in the largest number of hours lost since 1946. Black workers, in revolt against their unions, set up the League of Revolutionary Black Workers; and in 1972, young workers' grievances against both industry and unions were highlighted in the Lordstown, Ohio, wildcat auto strike and the systematic sabotage of the assembly line. Social unrest continued in France and Italy; and in Northern Ireland, the Provisional IRA started armed struggle.

'It sounded like something was shaking out there,' commented Paul Buhle in the United States. 'To the extent that we thought the movement was going to keep rolling right on, that it had just suffered a couple of blows, it had to take some form. The logical form was where these mass strikes were breaking out.'

In the founding fever of party-building, a host of new Maoist groups, aspiring to become vanguard revolutionary parties, sprang up. Maoism had always been one element within the student movements; its increased attraction in the 1970s arose not only for its 'organizational model' but because it seemed to provide a ready revolutionary answer to the deformations of Russian-style Communism and Western Communist parties. Since the Sino-Soviet split of the early 1960s, China came to provide an alternative revolutionary model which, for many students, was given additional weight by the Cultural Revolution of 1965–69.

Other new organizations, however, retained the anti-authoritarian positions that had marked the student movements. 'We believed in spontaneity in the sense that we didn't allow ourselves to be guided by what was ideologically right or wrong,' recalled Dany Cohn-Bendit, who was now a member of the new Revolutionärer Kampf (Revolutionary Struggle) in Frankfurt. 'The Maoists said "The housing problem can't be solved under capitalism – Engels, volumes one to five" – and we said "What do you mean, the housing problem? Here are empty houses, here are people who need houses, let's occupy them so that we can solve the problem."'

Yet again others attempted to avoid being drawn into party-building or armed struggle by developing new strategies. Such was the case of the major post-1968 French organization, Gauche Prolétarienne (GP). Formed by a small group of Maoists and 22 March Movement activists, GP developed a strategy of 'exemplary' but non-violent actions – the 'expropriation' of luxury food from a fashionable Paris shop, the invasion of millionaires' private property, industrial sabotage in response to re-pression of its activists – which made newspaper headlines and attracted to the group radicalized young workers. As the government began to attack GP's newspaper, *La Cause du Peuple*, intellectuals such as Jean-Paul Sartre, Simone de Beauvoir, the playwright Jean Genet and others came out in support of the group's right to publish and sell its newspaper, although not necessarily backing its political line. As will be seen, the government counter-offensive also increased pressures within the group to move towards clandestine armed struggle.

By and large, students who threw themselves into the building of revolutionary groups saw their new activity less as a rupture with their past movement experience than as a necessary continuation of it. 'During the [American] invasion of Cambodia in 1970, when all the campuses went on strike, we realized that this was powerful, but also that you could put every campus in the U.S. on strike and not change the war policy that much,' recalled Karen Duncanwood. 'The need was go out and reach people who had not been reached.' She joined some friends in a Maoist-influenced group which went into Los Angeles factories to work, as did activists from many of the new revolutionary organizations – mainly but not exclusively those influenced by Maoism.

Few, however, questioned the basic premise of winning the working class to revolutionary ideas. To Michael Thomas, an independent British

Marxist, the premise was 'highly problematic', however. 'Societies that guarantee political freedom and a considerable amount of material satisfaction – even with several million unemployed – are a long way from turning to revolution. The far left exaggerated the militancy of the early 1970s in order to vindicate an underlying model that is much more problematic than it will ever admit.'

In their commitment to revolutionary politics many former student activists remained undaunted by such thoughts; their new work often brought them a sense of unity of purpose and a new-found comradeship. Paul Ginsborg, for example, who had been radicalized in Britain in 1968, joined the International Socialists (IS) and as a young lecturer plunged into organizing tenants' groups and supporting working-class struggles. Soon a number of workers joined his IS branch in York. 'That attempt to live together, people like me and people who came from such completely different work and life experiences, was the most important political experience of my life. It was my ideal of politics, where everything seemed very equal, where no one was talking down to anyone else, where we were doing everything together on a basis of deep friendship. Everything, including planning to build a revolutionary party. We really thought we were getting somewhere then, though in the end we didn't.'

Nadia Lacroix felt not only the comradeship of being in Gauche Prolétarienne, but also the need 'to serve the people'. Coming from a strongly Catholic middle-class family, she was radicalized by the May events and started to read Marx. 'After that, I began to reject as bourgeois everything except Marxist culture. I stopped playing music, I stopped studying. I became almost a professional militant. We went to the factories, to the working-class suburbs. That's where I discovered reality – the life of the immigrants, factory life. I lived in a commune with immigrant workers and party comrades. Never before had I experienced such solidarity and comradeship. We lived poorly, didn't care about comfort or earning money. People sacrificed everything to help others. That was the importance of Maoism to me – not so much as an economic theory but as paving the way for a new type of humanity. Reconciling intellectual and manual work, on the Chinese model, and in the spirit of serving the people – it's a good way of reworking one's bourgeois individuality and struggling against egoism. I still look back with nostalgia on those times.'

For four years Guido Viale worked in the Rome newspaper office of Lotta Continua, the major Italian anti-authoritarian organization to arise in the 1970s, putting in fourteen to sixteen hours a day without pay. He lived with a woman he had met in the movement who was also a member of the editorial board. 'We lived in total poverty. At the time we thought it was a very good thing, it was a source of extreme pride that stressed our Franciscan character. In fact, it was an extreme form of voluntarism. For ten years I never bought any clothes or shoes, just wore what I could find around. We had a child – wanted, mutually decided – in this situation where we had nothing, where we faced the constant threat of arrest . . . It has taken me years subsequently to get it into my head that one can spend money on oneself for books or a pair of shoes.'

While this party-building was going on, in West Germany and Britain student militancy suddenly took on renewed vigour. In the former, a long battle against government witch-hunting of the left, in the latter a struggle to prevent the Conservative government shackling student unions and in support of striking miners, saw university mobilizations bigger than any in the 1960s.

In West Germany, the Social Democratic government's *Berufsverbot* (employment ban) – a 1972 measure to purge state employees ranging from dustmen through civil servants to professors who belonged to any organization pursuing 'anti-constitutional aims' – provoked massive student resistance. 'For the first time since 1968, the different factions of the left rediscovered a unity,' commented Helmi Karst, a West Berlin student who was active in the campaign. 'And that was thanks to this repressive measure.' Demonstrations by thousands upon thousands of students for years on end, and sympathy strikes which closed down universities, did not, however, get the measure repealed. 'We realized we needed international support,' continued Karst, 'so we called on the Bertrand Russell Peace Foundation [an organization founded by the British philosopher which, in the mid 1960s, set up an International War Crimes Tribunal on the Vietnam War] and in 1978 it set up a tribunal in Frankfurt on the *Berufsverbot*.' A few months after the tribunal found that the measure constituted a 'grave danger to human rights', the Social Democratic Party leadership in power admitted that the *Berufsverbot* had been mistaken and allowed it to lapse. For Karst, who was the tribunal's secretary, 'the continuing mobilizations, the tribunal and the press publicity that went with it put considerable pressure on the SPD which saw its position as the leading force of the Socialist International come under fire.'

But it was local movements against the building of nuclear power stations and on environmental issues that were to have the longest-lasting impact in West Germany. Although the Green movement did not originate directly from the student movement, and a conservative element within it attempted at the beginning to reduce the influence of radicals, the movement's development nonetheless owed much to both former student activists and to the forms and style that the anti-authoritarian student movement took in the mid-1960s. Rudi Dutschke, the former SDS leader, and Dany Cohn-Bendit were the major student movement figures to support the Greens, and the new movement began to attract many rank-and-file student militants who were disillusioned with party-building. Soon, the Greens began to put up candidates in local elections and scored a number of successes. Convinced that the movement must shift from single-issue campaigns to take in the democratic and socialist-oriented issues posed by the women's movement, the peace movement and the ecological movement, Dutschke helped to found the Green Party shortly before his death in 1979. Four years later, the party scored its first major national electoral success by winning over 5 per cent of the total votes cast and securing representation in the Bundestag. Today, after the 1987 general elections when it increased its percentage of the vote to over 8 per cent, it is the fourth largest party in the Federal Republic. Many of today's party staff members were politicized by the student movement or the political parties which sprang from it; and the party's decentralized structure and participatory democracy owe much to the 1960s movement.

In Britain, a new Conservative government from 1970 on launched an assault on the trade unions. The next four years saw the greatest continuous strike wave of the post-war period as the organized working class fought back. 'There was a feeling now that this was for real,' commented David Widgery. 'Parts of 1968 had been as serious as your life and other parts had been a good joke, and I'd never been sure which was which. But now unions that hadn't been on strike for fifty years were coming out.' Students radicalized by the earlier events, and by renewed struggles in a number of universities, joined the International Socialists and, to a lesser extent, the Trotskyist International Marxist Group (IMG). As part of the government's anti-union offensive, Margaret Thatcher, then Education Minister, attempted to restrict the autonomy of student unions. In December 1971, the National Union of Students, dominated by the left as a result of 1968, brought out 400,000 students in a day of action. A month later, coinciding with a miners' strike, 40,000 students assembled to protest against government policies, a sizeable number of whom went on to demonstrate in support of the miners. Some student unions offered facilities and accommodation to miners who moved out of the coalfields to picket power stations, where students joined them. Confronted with this militancy – and more importantly with the fact that the strike was causing power cuts in part of the country – the government withdrew its student union proposals. And finally, in 1974, a second miners' strike led to the Conservative government's electoral defeat and the victory of the Labour party.

Before this, two events in Northern Ireland – the British Conservative government's introduction of internment in 1971, and the massacre of thirteen unarmed civilians by British paratroopers in Derry on Sunday, 30 January 1972 – led to mass protest. When internment was brought in, Michael Farrell, the PD leader, was one of those immediately rounded up by the British army and held for five weeks.

'They screened us, played games with us. A number of internees were taken out in helicopters, blindfolded and thrown out – the helicopter was only about a foot off the ground. I missed that fortunately. Then, in batches, we were made to run into the jail between soldiers who batoned and kicked us. But the scariest part of all was being in a cell on my own, not knowing what they were going to do, hearing shooting outside . . .'

In Britain, the Anti-Internment League was set up. John Grey, a People's Democracy activist who was now working in London, was one of the founders. 'In a short time it had a remarkable impact. Our biggest demo quite early on involved four marches into Hyde Park and something like 30,000 people turned out. The Conservative government's policies were so obviously outrageous that people were actually pouring into the streets.'

After the second event, 'Bloody Sunday', which occurred during the first civil rights demonstration in Derry since internment, Catholic Ireland exploded; in the North there were riots, mass protests, roadblocks and hijackings. In Dublin, 30,000 demonstrators burnt the British embassy to the ground. Bernadette Devlin, the only Westminster MP who had witnessed the Derry massacre, attempted to speak in an emergency debate in the House of Commons in which the Conservative Minister of Home Affairs, Reginald Maudling, defended the government. When the debate ended without her being called, she strode across to the Tory front bench. 'As I had been sitting there I'd been planning what to do. I meant to get hold of Maudling by the throat. Just for one second he'd think his time was up! But I allowed myself to get angry as I walked across the floor and instead of grabbing his tie I hit him.' The outcry in Parliament and the press was tremendous. 'This terrible deed of striking someone in the

House of Commons created more furore than the fact that the British army had killed thirteen people.'

Eighteen months after 'Bloody Sunday', in 1973, Farrell was imprisoned for PD's part in demonstrating against internment and went on a thirty-five-day hunger strike for political status. By then Britain had imposed direct rule on Northern Ireland and was negotiating with both Belfast and Dublin to end the crisis. As a result, Farrell was released and returned to the struggle.

Although by the mid-1970s student protest had diminished in Britain, one last, and successful, attempt to revive a 1960s-style movement came in 1976 after the sudden growth of votes for fascist parties in local elections in a number of cities. The Anti-Nazi League, inspired by the Socialist Workers' Party (SWP) – into which the International Socialist group had transformed itself – mobilized thousands of people, including 'sixty-eighters', newly radicalized students and young people. One of the means used was music, organized by the League's cultural counterpart, Rock Against Racism (RAR). 'We wanted to kick the politics of anti-racism into the vernacular of working-class youth by using the route of pop music,' Widgery, one of the SWP organizers recalled. 'And it brought in the young punks who didn't know or didn't care about 1968. The reggae musicians would come and shake hands with them, they could see they had a common cause. All the people involved at the core of RAR were "sixty-eighters", though mostly they weren't former students.'

In France, the movement was occasionally capable of rediscovering its earlier mobilizing strength as when, in 1973, several thousand people gathered at Larzac, in the southwest, to support peasants struggling to prevent Defence Ministry expropriation of their land to build a military base. Larzac became a symbol of anti-militarism, defence of the weak against the powers that be, of a nascent ecological concern. In the same year, the takeover by workers of a micro-mechanics factory threatened with closure and, under self-management, their production of watches, evoked memories of May 1968, and gathered large-scale support. Although the Lip factory in Besançon, eastern France, continued under workers' management for the best part of a year, it remained an isolated event.

In Italy, the wave of anti-authoritarianism which had begun before the 'hot autumn' of 1969 continued through into the early 1970s, as has been seen. In the United States, despite the movement's decline after 1970, protests against the Vietnam War went on until January 1973, when the

Nixon government signed a series of accords with the North Vietnamese and NLF to withdraw American forces and 'Vietnamize' the war. One of the most dramatic of these protests took place in April 1971, when over one thousand Vietnam veterans, organized by the Vietnam Veterans Against the War, turned in their medals on the steps of the nation's Capitol. Meanwhile, young people were turning from anti-war protest and counter-cultural exploration to environmental activism, revitalizing the traditional conservation movement with the passion, tactics and organizational style of the New Left. Although the ecology movement was one of the largest and most durable outcomes of the 1960s in the U.S., most radical activists saw it as a 'cop-out', a way of avoiding the tough issues of class, race and revolutionary commitment.

A more hard-hitting vision of a radically different order was kept alive throughout the 1970s by a range of other organizing efforts, the largest of which – community organization – had always been an important aspect of the New Left agenda. Many former student radicals moved into small towns and cities and started various local organizations. For example, Charles Sherrod, one of the SNCC founders, built up a cooperative farm in Albany, Georgia, to 'provide an economic base for the movement'; the farm, which still existed in 1986, was for a time the 'largest piece of land owned by blacks anywhere in the country in a single tract ... It's an attempt to become self-sustaining in this regional area by acting as a production, educational and marketing unit. It's an effort that, as black people and as poor people, we've got to make. I keep saying black and poor because white folk some day are going to see that they have the same stake in it that we have, that we're fighting, for different reasons, the same power structure that keeps us subjugated.'

In some instances, these organizing efforts were overtly revolutionary. In California, Bruce Franklin, former SDS activist, helped found a locally-based organization to 'bring people into alliance with liberation movements.' Venceremos ran candidates for local office on openly socialist programs, and mounted various community education and organizing programs, including a college and a people's medical center. 'The model we were trying to develop was one in which Third World people would be in leadership at every level. We never claimed to be a party, but hopefully a model showing that multinational organization could work, that you could actually have white working-class people and black and Chicano people working together in the same organization.

Few of the new revolutionary organizations, nor some of the old, lasted beyond the mid-1970s. By then, the hoped-for revolution had failed to materialize. Although the new organizations often gathered some working-class support, helped on occasion to organize wildcat walk-outs and mobilized in support of strikes, the working-class militancy of the early 1970s continued only sporadically. The Western recession, which began in earnest with the oil crisis of 1973, played its part; so, too, did the ruling order's counter-offensive. On the international level the scales seemed similarly to be turning: the Popular Unity government of Salvador Allende in Chile was overthrown by Pinochet's military coup in 1973; and the only post-1968 revolution in Western Europe – the Portuguese, which began in 1974 – was being turned back.

In general, the far left had been able to do little to open up a new revolutionary space in either Western Europe or the United States. Disillusionment began to set in, a disillusionment that had its roots not only in the lack of working-class response but in the very nature of the attempt to emulate a Leninist or Marxist-Leninist model in the context of advanced bourgeois democracies. Even without going to the extreme of trying to replicate the Chinese Cultural Revolution, as some did, or directly borrowing the terminology of Chinese publications, as did others, there were problems enough, as Karen Duncanwood remembered from her time in a Los Angeles factory. 'The kinds of things we were talking about and studying were so different from people's consciousness in the plant,' she recalled. 'How to bridge that gap was real unclear. We were doing a lot of studying of Maoism at the time, and Maoism concentrates, I think, on ideological questions, ideological transformations . . .'

For others, like Guido Viale of Lotta Continua – to whom the articulation of hitherto silenced needs, 'the collective process of liberation', had always been an important part of the 1960s movements – even non-Maoist party-forming soon appeared to have its negative side. 'Influenced by the traditional labour movement, and the example of the Third International, we turned ourselves into little parties or organizations. It was inevitable, but it was also very counter-productive. The movement became institutionalized. A process of conformism settled on us, a certain political orthodoxy crept in. The process of creating a new language seized up, for me, my organization and in general. It was only with the advent of feminism in the mid-1970s in Italy that it returned.'

Similar lacks were felt by former student radicals in other revolutionary organizations. 'As the years passed,' recalled Paul Ginsborg in Britain, 'I got less and less happy about IS because it became less libertarian, the old-guard leadership never seemed to change. The organization's internal democracy contracted as it began to turn itself into a fully-fledged Leninist party. By 1977 I was beginning to have very serious doubts about it.'

And finally, the rigid democratic centralism of some of the new Maoist groups came to be seen as the antithesis of the revolutionary society they were attempting to create. 'We slowly came to realize,' commented Peter Weinreich of his experience in one of the major new West German Maoist parties, the Kommunistische Partei Deutschland (KPD), 'that we had been members of an organization that – were it actually to exercise state power – would definitely result in a cynical dictatorship. We now had to admit what we, in our anti-authoritarian days, had so peremptorily demanded that our parents admit: that they – like us – had devoted years of their life to a bad cause, that our well-intentioned revolutionary enthusiasm had got bogged down in a backward and undemocratic process.'

It was not only the new revolutionary groups but some of the parties formed in the 1960s – most notably Progressive Labor and the Black Panther Party in the United States – which went into decline. PL's total abandonment of national struggles, sectarian sniping at the Cubans, Vietnamese and, eventually, the Chinese, as well as the organization's authoritarian nature, spelled its doom; while the Black Panther Party disintegrated between 1970 and 1975. Police attacks, which left forty-four Panthers dead in five years, infiltration and costly trials brought disarray, internal dissension and even personal violence. 'They were a movement under siege, beleaguered, isolated,' recalled Steve Fraser, member of the Labor Committee (a PL split), who went to the party's headquarters in Oakland, California, to discuss possible political alliances. 'The whole house was armed, they had people posted at windows and doors. They were ready to be attacked at any moment . . . I understood the necessity of guns for self-defence, they'd always said that's what they had guns for, but it was clear that they'd lost their ability to function in any other way. If self-defence was the only political option they had left, it meant the government had got the upper hand.'

In France, the two major post-1968 organizations, Vive La Révolution (VLR) and Gauche Prolétarienne (GP) were dissolved by their respective leaders because of their fear of escalating violence. The increasing government offensive had led GP to consider going underground. A military branch was organized under strict political control, and engaged in a number of actions, including two kidnappings, one of which was in response to the shooting of a GP militant. But unknown to most was the fact that, though armed, the military branch could not kill. 'The arms weren't loaded,' explained Béni Lévy, the organization's clandestine head, 'we had trained them in the idea that they could not kill.' But increasingly there was pressure to 'go the whole way'. Having come to have doubts about the concept of revolution itself, and seeing the possibility of GP turning to armed struggle, Lévy decided to disband GP; the military branch threatened to secede, and it took a year before he prevailed. 'I'm as proud now of having dissolved GP as I am of having founded it. We prevented the birth of a terrorist group that would have had the strength and legitimacy of stemming from GP and thus from May 1968.'

At around the same time in 1972, Roland Castro, the VLR leader, dissolved his organization overnight because he thought there was a risk of its members fetishizing violence and also because he could see no revolutionary way forward.

As organizations and causes vanished, there were many instances of personal disillusionment, despair, breakdowns and even suicides among former student radicals. For example, Nadia Lacroix, whose life had been changed by becoming an activist in Gauche Prolétarienne, was one of those who felt on the edge of suicide. 'I felt I'd given my life for a cause that no longer had any point. I was still on the left, but I couldn't see any longer where Marxism, Maoism could lead. Everything was so black that I wanted to kill myself. If I hadn't returned to the Catholicism in which I was brought up, I would have committed suicide because everything that had made my life worthwhile had collapsed.'

The future costs were also high. Years spent militating in groups cut activists off from personal and career opportunities they might otherwise have pursued. 'Politics didn't pay,' observed Franca Fossati, a former Lotta Continua militant in Italy. 'The only work my husband and I can find now is in journalism, and neither of us have got permanent jobs. And there have been even higher personal costs. I'd like to have another child. I had my first one late because of all the political work. And yet those years in the movement seem to both of us to have been so rich – full of problems and confusions, too – but so rich that we say, "It's all right, despite it all we're OK."'

The student movements everywhere had shared a generic and abstract theory of violence: exaltation of Third World liberation wars, the need for armed struggle, the idea that political power is born from the barrel of a gun werecommon to all. China, Vietnam, Cuba . . . But the theory had remained at an abstract level. The violence in which students had been involved in response to police repression had certainly, on occasion, been bitter; but in most cases it was a form of protest, of existential anger which was not aimed at directly revolutionary goals. They had never taken up arms. This was what changed in the 1970s. Violence, especially armed violence, came to be seen by a number of small groups as a means to an end: the 'spark' that would set the working classes and oppressed sectors of society in motion.

Weatherman in the United States, the Red Army Faction in West Germany, Red Brigades and Front Line in Italy, were the leading protagonists of armed struggle. The connection between Weatherman – or Weather Underground as it called itself now – and SDS has already been seen. Hoping to mobilize disaffected white youth in support of black and Third World struggles, Weather Underground restricted its actions to armed propaganda: the bombing of buildings – including the U.S. Capitol and the Pentagon in Washington – and attacks on property in retaliation for specific American government actions of repression; it killed no one except three of its own members who, in March 1970, were blown up in a New York townhouse where they were making bombs. In 1973 it ended its bombing campaign, and the group began to convert itself into a clandestine Leninist party with an above-ground organization. By 1975, this, too, had failed. 'The impact and strength of internal national liberation struggles was not as strong as it had been. The radical impulse in our own movement had dissipated a lot with the ending of the massive draft calls, and then the peace treaty in Vietnam in 1973,' explained David Gilbert, a Weather member.

When, in 1976, Weather Underground disbanded and its members began surfacing, it was surprising, given the government's concern about the group, how relatively mild the charges against most of them were. The majority were sentenced for offences committed in student strikes or the Days of Rage prior to going underground. Having served their sentences, most of them stayed above ground; but a few, Gilbert among them, returned underground where they joined forces with groups of blacks, most of them the remnants of previous organizations, the Black Panthers included. Gilbert was arrested in 1981 for his part in an armed robbery in which two policemen and a Brink's guard were killed; he and another accused conducted a political trial, arguing that they were revolutionaries helping to end American imperialism by carrying out 'expropriations'. They each received three life sentences to be served consecutively, which they are currently serving.

In West Germany, the Red Army Faction (RAF, or Baader-Meinhof group, in police and media terminology) was formed in 1970 by a small group, among them a number of long-standing SDSers, including Horst Mahler, the movement's lawyer, and the well-known left-wing columnist, Ulrike Meinhof. The discussion among a handful of SDSers about violence after the 1968 Easter street fighting, and the much larger debates after the Tegeler Weg battle in November of the same year, led a number of individuals to believe that a separate guerrilla-style organization was needed by the Extra-Parliamentary Opposition to carry out exemplary actions around which revolutionary struggle would develop. In May 1970, the RAF fired the first rounds of a war that continues to this day. In a shoot-out, Andreas Baader, one of the RAF leaders who was serving a prison sentence on charges unrelated to any RAF activities, was freed from a library of West Berlin's Free University where, under guard, he had been allowed to continue his studies. Meinhof, who had been pretending to be writing a book with Baader in the library, fled with him. A prison officer and a university employee were severely wounded in the shoot-out.

The RAF's armed struggle has claimed more than fifty victims to this day. Industrialists, members of the judiciary and American servicemen have been assassinated; police officers have been killed in gunfights, and innocent citizens who got in the way of RAF operations or the police hunt have been shot dead. RAF members have been killed by the police, blown up by their own bombs, died on hunger strike, or committed suicide in prison (Baader among them, although many still believe that he and three others – Meinhof, Enslin and Raspe – were murdered by the state).

To what extent had the fascist past played a role in this readiness to take life for political ends? 'Without doubt, there was a connection,' maintained Peter Weinreich, the former Maoist student. 'How could one expect a generation of fathers, whose mystified ethics and religion had allowed them to sacrifice everything, including their own lives, to their cause – how could one expect them to personify to their children a self-evident respect for human life? The propensities which, for instance, made Auschwitz possible in Germany can't be eradicated from a people's soul within one generation, either by denazification or a new constitution.'

But it was not the fascist past, Elsa Gili believed, which gave rise to groups like the Red Brigades in Italy. 'For one thing, the example of the wartime Resistance had a powerful influence on political imagination. Secondly, the absence in the mid-1970s of any form of radical politics after the hopes raised by the movements of the late 1960s and early 1970s, coupled with the Communist Party's "historic compromise" with the Christian Democratic Party in the later period, was another important factor. That said, it's impossible to draw a direct cause-and-effect link in the Italian case.'

The Red Brigades originated in a student-worker group, the Collettivo Politico Metropolitano (Metropolitan Political Collective) formed in Milan during the 'hot autumn' of 1969. Renato Curcio, student leader at Trento, and subsequently the Red Brigades' leader, was one of the driving forces behind the Colletivo which, like others formed at the time, attempted to mobilize support for factory and high school struggles. By the summer of 1970 it had taken to armed struggle. Initially justifying the move as a defence against a military coup d'etat (one such attempted coup was, in fact, aborted by the government in the same year, and the extreme right had earlier begun a violent bombing campaign), the Red Brigades subsequently claimed to be alerting the working class to the dangers of reforms which would inevitably be 'reabsorbed' by capitalist development.

Like Weather Underground, the Red Brigades began by attacking property; but in 1972 there came the first kidnapping and then an escalation of violence against the state which culminated in 1978 in the kidnapping and later execution of Aldo Moro, president of the Christian Democratic Party.

Prima Linea (Front Line), which arose in Italy in the mid-1970s, did not share the Red Brigades' rigid, party-like organization, but carried on some of the student movement's informal, breezy way of being to begin with; and, although it saw itself as the nucleus of a 'future liberation army', it did not immediately adopt a hard line on violence. This, however, changed by the second half of the 1970s when it, too, embarked on assassinations and woundings. Something of the mentality of those prepared to kill can be seen through the recollections of Silveria Russo, who was in at the start of Prima Linea. The daughter of an ex-army officer and a housewife, she took part in the Fiat student-worker mobilizations while at Turin University, later joining Lotta Continua and becoming a feminist. By 1977, she was part of Prima Linea's *gruppo di fuoco* or firing group.

'I found myself killing people, yes. I'm one of the two who fired at policeman Lo Russo. I killed him, I remember it as though it were now. It was my first direct killing. He was a prison policeman, known as a torturer. For me it was like a work routine. For us, there were friends on one side and on the other enemies – and enemies are a category, symbols, not human beings – so that our relationship to their death was an absolutely abstract one. That was our ideology. If I had been a white-collar employee, instead of a murderer, it would have been the same thing for me. An incredible split. I'd leave home in the morning and go out to trail people, to prepare operations, if I wasn't myself going out to kill. Then I'd go home quietly, lead my life as an ordinary housewife, cook a meal, take care of my things, live with my man, look after my dog – moments of joy and love . . .'

In 1980, she was arrested and is currently serving two life sentences. Between 1969 and 1980, terrorism claimed 362 lives in Italy; the extreme right was responsible for 178, of whom 135 were in bomb massacres; the extreme left killed 119. A further 65 people died in clashes with the police or in unknown circumstances.

Britain saw a short-lived and relatively minor wave of bombings, carried out by a group, comprising a handful of people, called the Angry Brigade, which shook a number of prominent establishment and industrial targets in and around London in 1970; two of the explosions coincided with mass trade union demonstrations protesting the Conservative government's anti-union legislation. A further two were aimed at explicitly sexist targets, wrecking a trendy boutique and damaging a BBC TV broadcast van. None of the bombings caused casualties.

Kathy May, a libertarian socialist, supported the bombings. Though her reasons were related specifically to British society, they give an insight into the rationale for this sort of commitment that transcends the national context. There was, she felt, 'a need for direct action, violent or non-violent. Violence in itself wasn't the issue. We felt violence was being constantly perpetuated by the state, that it was built into its operations. Britain's wealth historically had been accumulated through violent means, the state was involved in direct violence in Northern Ireland. Moreover, we saw state violence being perpetuated through administrative means, through the way the system worked, keeping some individuals in a miserable state of poverty and whole sections oppressed. The Angry Brigade's bombings were largely symbolic. We saw them as a rather dramatic way of pointing the finger and defining things which should be challenged – not just by the working class but by all oppressed groups, women and black people, in particular. We felt we were part of a force that could move things forward and bring about total revolutionary change.'

In 1972, at the end of a seven-month trial, four students were sentenced to ten year's imprisonment for conspiracy in the Angry Brigade case.

Armed struggle, even if only symbolic, was the ultimate abrogation of everything that the student movements had originally stood for. From the expansion of democratic rights through anti-authoritarian struggle to Marxism, these movements had in their different ways always attempted to work within a concept of democracy, whether participatory or socialist, had always refused the idea of isolating themselves from broader masses of people, whether students or other sectors of society. The party-forming of the 1970s in some countries, the more rigidly doctrinaire positions of existing far-left groups in others, made serious inroads on those initial stances. But nothing was further from the original thrust than the small self-constituted armed groups which, as Bernadette Devlin observed in Northern Ireland, removed democratic responsibility from people and 'put it in the hands of "somebody" who was supposed to be looking after them and whom they didn't know what they were doing'.

In the mind of Henri Weber, the Trotskyist student leader in Paris, there was similarly no doubt. 'Marxism was constructed against anarchism, Leninism against terrorism. The latter was the heresy of all heresies for us.' And for Jeff Jones, a Weather Underground leader, there was, on looking back, also no doubt. 'You give up an awful lot when you voluntarily take yourself out of mainstream organizing, you give up contact with the masses. I've come to the conclusion that you should never give up your democratic rights until they're taken from you at the point of a gun, and then, if you survive that moment, you go underground to continue the struggle. What we were doing was premature, or just not necessary to be doing.'

The classic revolutionary perspective of a vanguard party engaged in the struggle for state power mobilized considerable numbers of students; but as many others believed equally firmly in the constant undermining of the established order by revolutionizing day-to-day life, beginning with their own. Self-activity showed people that they could take their destiny into their own hands, shake themselves loose from the reigning ideology and its personal, repressive affects, and change them into the agents, rather than the objects, of history. In the course of this struggle people transformed their own lives in an attempt to begin transforming society.

The commune and squatters' movements were among the most visible of the attempts to create an alternative society within the context of the existing order. Deriving their impetus from the counter-culture which started in the United States and Britain in the second half of the 1960s and spread in the following years to the Continent, they reached their maximum growth at the beginning of the next decade. In the United States, for example, there were claimed to be over 10,000 communal households and some 3,000 rural communes by 1970, their growth in part a reflection of the demise of the wider movement and a sign of retreat into purely personal rather than social transformation. But in Britain, where at the time there were at least fifty rural collectives and a much higher number of urban communes, many of these had directly political objectives, as Kathy May, who took part in forming a London commune, explained.

'It was a central premise that the nuclear family was the cornerstone of capitalism. Living collectively, therefore, was a political act in itself, presenting an alternative way of life ultimately incompatible with capitalism, and which would eventually lead to its collapse.' Moving into an empty house without beds, she and the others slept on double mattresses on the floor. 'The mattresses belonged to no one. If you came in late you just crawled into one and woke up in the morning wondering who had been sleeping next to you. There was no private property – everything was shared. All the clothes were bunged into a big cupboard. Extraordinary as it may sound today, it seemed absolutely right to me at the time.' Nonetheless, the experience was fraught with conflicts and contradictions, as May recognized. 'For a start, there was a sort of sexual purity not in keeping with the times. Free love was seen as reducing sex to sex, while deep caring couple relationships were seen as a step on the road to the nuclear family. Every relationship was scrutinized to ensure that they weren't either exclusive or exploitative. People were tearing themselves inside out really – and yet there was very strong support and sometimes real solidarity. More equality between men and women than I had ever experienced – and yet I felt quite intimidated about speaking because every word was significant.'

In West Germany, the attempt to establish 'ideological' communes on the lines of West Berlin's Kommune 1 failed fairly rapidly. In their place, communal living arrangements, *Wohngemeinschaften*, became – and remain to this day – an important feature of post-adolescent socialization. These shared apartments replaced the former single rented rooms that most students had lived in, often under the eye of a landlady. 'A communal apartment was something I could really tune in to,' recalled Ottfried Jensen. 'It gave me a lot. Sure, it took its toll, too, one relationship after another blew a fuse, each would have their new guy or woman move in. But the great thing was you were never alone, you were socially integrated. You attended the same courses at university, shared the work a bit and that was very productive. And then you'd all go to demonstrations together. The *Wohngemeinschaft* from down the block would ring at the door, you'd smoke a cigarette or a joint, and then off you'd go.'

'Squatting' – the occupation of empty houses – was another widespread phenomenon in Western Europe, London becoming an early centre for this type of activity. In 1969 the London Street Commune, whose aim was to 'return the streets to the people' and to provide a viable way out of the family and other 'repressive' institutions for young people, squatted in a mansion in Piccadilly, the fashionable centre. It aroused press hysteria and a rapid reaction from the local authorities. But other squatting groups began moving homeless families into empty housing in protest against the fact that 100,000 people were homeless when over half a million houses stood empty in London. A similar movement started in West Germany and Italy; in Frankfurt, Revolutionärer Kampf (Revolutionary Struggle), the group to which Cohn-Bendit belonged, began to move immigrant workers into empty houses; while in Italy by the mid-1970s between five and ten thousand squatters had taken over and were living in about one thousand occupied houses in Milan.

Eventually, the squatting of some empty municipal housing in London was officially tolerated under certain conditions, thereby 'institutionalizing' to some extent what had begun as a direct action campaign. The commune movement began to decline in the latter half of the 1970s, the victim of some of the problems that Kathy May indicated. The counter-culture also started to die. 'Illusory thinking, a dearth of common sense, that's what killed it,' commented Gurney Norman in the U.S. 'It was thought that you could lead a life separate from the society, that you could actually create your own culture as if the larger culture was no longer affecting you. This was an illusion. There was no real analysis of what drugs were about. The people who first took drugs had good experiences and developed this attitude that drugs are good automatically and everybody should take them. There was no maturity, too little understanding of tradition. We thought we could make time begin now, that we could willfully ignore history and create a tradition – but life doesn't work like that. We had very little sense of how the counter-culture connected to other counter-cultures back in history. Nobody read any books. We had no scholarship, no guidance.'

The single most enduring movement to arise from the late 1960s and early 1970s was the women's liberation movement. While the history of the latter's re-emergence goes far beyond the limits of what can be described here, it seems undeniable that, in many countries, women radicalized by their involvement in the student movements brought a new cutting edge to the women's movement, and in some instances were among the instigators of its resurgence. Male chauvinism was common to all the student movements. In the United States and West Germany, women challenged the male-dominated structures of both SDSs, and the latters' refusal to reform contributed to their disintegration. Experience of the movements' sexism was undoubtedly one of the causes that led many women students to organize; so, too, was the highly ambivalent nature of the sexual liberation which accompanied much of the revolution of everyday life. Some of these influences can be seen through the experiences of a number of women in different student movements.

Like many other women, especially organizers in the American student movement, Sue Thrasher, first Executive Secretary of the Southern Student Organizing Committee (SSOC), experienced sexism early on. 'I came to consciousness of it pretty rapidly because the officers in SSOC were all men except me. It became clear to me that I was doing all the shit work, holding the office together, keeping the mailings and stuff like that going on. I likedwhat I was doing, so it took me a while to get angry about it. A lot of my anger about the position of women came later, part of it from seeing women in the organization. The boys would sleep around with different ones and that caused frictions at different times.'

Throughout the movement, women found themselves ignored or relegated to tradition roles. Barbara Haber recalled meetings of SDS's Radical Education Project at which all the ideas she suggested were ignored until some man in the meeting restated them. Then they were discussed. Sarah Elbert, in 1969, during the Cornell strike agreed to arrange a meeting to forge contacts between the male leadership of the SDS chapter, to which she belonged, and her friends among the striking black students. 'I said, "Why don't you all come to my house and we'll have lunch." Boy! Talk about sexism! I remember making the hamburgers and getting the beer in the refrigerator, setting the table, all that. I was the only woman there and it was clear that I was cooking the hamburgers in every sense. It didn't occur to anyone else that, tactically, I might have a contribution to make other than smoothing over the points of disagreement.'

Gayle Rubin, a Michigan activist who helped lead women out of the student movement and into the independent women's movement, recalled her anger at male radicals who claimed that women's liberation was secondary to national liberation, ending the war, or the class struggle. 'It was sort of like what Lenin said to Clara Zetkin: personal problems must be transcended. We reacted against this. We got more and more staunch about defending our autonomy and our right to just forget about these guys who were giving us such a hard time, and began to relate to other women. We were arguing for the right of women to be in separate political organizations and to develop an analysis of the oppression of women irrespective of what was going on in the rest of the world.'

Separatism and anger were common themes of the women's movement in the early 1970s. Carol Brightman, who had been active in anti-war work as the founder of *Viet Report* since 1965, found herself growing increasingly irritated with what she saw as the sexist behavior of her male comrades and their refusal to take her seriously as a woman. As her interest in women's issues grew, she made contact with a group of younger women who were militant feminists. 'There was a genuine sort of excitement about these young women. They were all in karate class and sometimes one woman would have a problem with a boyfriend or a landlord, and we'd go in and take care of the situation, mostly using the threat of force rather than actual force.'

'Why were we women militants always bringing up the rear? Always,' Lily Métreaux, a militant in the French Vive La Révolution (VLR), asked. 'And then came the day when some of us women got together and started to talk. It was extraordinary, an initiation for me. A wind of revolt rose in that room. It was splendid. We locked the door. The men were banging on it, shouting "Open up, you bitches!" And we just laughed at them. It was a marvellous period when suddenly we started not to give a damn about men, when we started to demand political responsibilities. Later, a group of us VLR women chained ourselves to La Roquette [a women's prison in Paris] to demonstrate that all women were in chains.'

For Sheila Rowbotham, a British left-wing activist, 'the only way you could be accepted, as a politically active woman, was if you became like a man. I refused to become this sort of asexual political cardboard person. And yet I noticed that it was almost impossible for me to get any of my ideas accepted by men. To begin with, I didn't think it was because they were *men*. And then an American, whose wife was involved in the women's movement, pointed out to me after a meeting in 1968 that it was the men who constantly blocked my proposals. Suddenly the scales fell from my eyes.'

A year earlier, at the Dialectics of Liberation Congress in London, Rowbotham had been shocked to hear Stokely Carmichael, the American Black Power leader, answer a question on women's position in the revolution with a single word: 'prone'. 'As a socialist, I obviously supported the black movement in America. Now here was the person I thought I was supporting sneering at this person who was actually like me.'

There could be no ambiguity about experiences like these. Sexual liberation, which the increasing availability of the contraceptive pill was facilitating, was not quite as clear-cut, however: emancipating on the one hand, it reinforced male sexual exploitation on the other. 'The men were experiencing the height of the sexual revolution,' recalled Bettina Berch during the Columbia University occupation in 1968. 'I mean, they could really sleep with whoever they pleased. For most of us women, frankly, it was like you could basically choose which future revolutionary you felt like sleeping with. At the time it looked like a real treat. So, on a scale of what you were interested in at that point in your life, the concept of sexual liberation was clearly very promising.'

But a double-edged liberation, as Michele Ryan in Britain saw. 'It came in with the hippie thing, that we're all free, men and women, there should be no inhibitions. You could make love as and when you felt like it. As a woman one really believed that at the time. And for a while it *was* liberating to feel you no longer had to obey any conventions or inhibitions, that you could sleep with anyone because you were on the pill. If you fell in love or felt desire, you could actually say it. But the other side of the coin was that, having said it, it was used totally to the man's satisfaction. Nothing seemed to have changed very much.'

Indeed, to take a very extreme and isolated case, things sometimes had changed for the worse. Barbara Köster recalled living in a *Wohngemein-schaft* in Frankfurt which, with the idea that they would be open to revolutionary ideas, sheltered young boys and girls who had run away from state welfare institutions. 'That was one thing, but on top of that, I'll never forget it, we women in the *Wohngemeinschaft* were supposed to fuck with these kids. Andreas Baader, who was one of those living there, said to me one day, "Well, honey, it's your turn tonight". When I came home in the evening there were two kids lying on my bed with a crate of beer bottles –

they'd been promised a "birthday party". I couldn't do it. And then I was accused of not being an emancipated, liberated woman like the other comrades who did it.'

While the male dominance of both the student movements and sexual liberation contributed ineluctably to the resurgence of the women's movement, so, too, did the politics of the 1960s, especially the revolution of everyday life; its emphasis on the confluence of the personal and the political affected, and was in turn affected by, feminism. Another element from the American movement that women were able to put to use was consciousness-raising, which harkened directly back to the insistence of the American civil rights movement, early SDS, and the FSM on personal transformation as a means of collective mobilization for change.

The first groups were tentative, and their very existence was a part of that transformation. Cathy Cade's experience was typical. The first meeting of a consciousness raising group she attended in New Orleans was composed of women who had been active in the civil rights movement. 'It was all or mostly white women who had been in Mississippi.' The holding of the meeting itself became an issue. 'We were all kind of nervous and embarrassed. We weren't really sure that, with all of our rights and privileges, that we should be having this meeting, that we deserved it. We had gotten Casey Hayden's and Mary King's letter, and we thought about it and talked about it, and we knew there was something there. After the meeting we were sitting around and, one by one, everybody started talking about the ridicule that they had to go through from the men in their lives to come to this one meeting. And the evidence began to mount. Finally, we thought, if we had to go through this much shit just to come to a meeting to talk about being women, there must be something there.'

Such groups gave women new strength. Sue Thrasher, for example, recalled joining a weekly meeting of women staff members of *The Great Speckled Bird*, an Atlanta underground newspaper. 'It was a process of getting confidence that you're in a group of people where you can say what you want and voice anything you want to voice, and people are not going to respond in horror. There's going to be some sort of response based upon the honesty of what you've said. And then you grow. The first time I experienced that was in women's groups where you were able to talk about yourself personally, and how you feel, and what you're angry about that day. The basic lesson I learned was the need for your own organized power group. As long as you were together and organized as a group you could make some changes and you could have a voice.'

Or, as Sheila Rowbotham saw it, 'the formation of small women's groups was a rebellion against large, student meetings where the men flaunted how revolutionary they were. We were rejecting that. We wanted a politics which would be acceptable to women who weren't like that. The idea that by sitting round and talking about your experience you could reach a social understanding of something wider was very important. At the same time, the fact that we were talking about oppressive relations connected up with the student movement which was concerned with relationships of authority between students and teachers.'

To some extent then, the student movements' anti-authoritarian spirit helped to open a space in which the oppressions at the very heart of the movements could be challenged by women. Indeed for some, like Heather Booth, one of the American SDS activists who joined the first separate women's meeting at an SDS conference in 1965, it was the experience of women organizing around their own concerns, rather than SDS's sexism, which gave the major impetus to the women's movement. 'The main force behind the movement was that your whole life was being freed, you were finding expression. It was this that motivated us at a deeper level. We were all in this together. We were changing our lives, we were changing the world. The future lay open. It was very exciting.'

By the mid-1970s, the American women's movement had become a very broadly based movement, with its own publications and its own agenda. Despite many internal differences, the agenda became more and more thoroughgoing throughout the decade, from support of a constitutional amendment on women's rights, to support for welfare mothers, equal pay for women and a more aggressive assertion of rights for women in the family, the society, the polity and within the university. New recruits flocked to the banners of various women's organizations which had already been formed and infused them with new life and new concerns, or created hundreds of new groups to put forward women's demands over a wide range of issues.

The sense of liberation and excitement expressed by American women were echoed everywhere. 'The only time I felt really free to talk was not in SDS but in the women's groups,' recalled Barbara Brick, a West German activist. From September 1968, SDS women had initiated courses for women only at West Berlin's Critical University on Freud and Reich. 'What we were trying to do with these courses,' recalled Anna Pam of the West Berlin SDS, 'was to attempt to reformulate Freud's and Reich's theories for a liberation of women. It was a truly herculean task if you remember that the first feminist critique of psychoanalytic concepts – the oedipal complex, penis envy etc. – came only two years later in the U.S.'

Soon afterwards, the first meeting of what was to become the Action Council for the Liberation of Women was held in West Berlin. The response was immediate, drawing in a number of women whose major concern was not sexual liberation but to create support groups for raising their children while they worked or studied. They created the first day-nurseries, known as *Kinderläden* (children's shops) because the first was situated in a former shop – an example which was soon followed by others and spread through West Germany. In the 1970s, these day-nurseries were formally state-supported, and continue to this day. From its first national convention at Easter 1971, the West German women's movement, which consisted of some thirty autonomous groups, mobilized principally around the question of abortion, which was still illegal at the time. The campaign was successful in getting abortion legalized, though with certain restrictions.

Early in 1970, the first Women's Liberation Conference in Britain, organized largely by women students, was held at Oxford; nearly double the three hundred women expected turned up. 'It was incredibly exciting,' recalled Sheila Rowbotham. 'I'd never seen women in that mood before. Hearing people speak who'd never spoken before, seeing people inspired to do things they wouldn't have done in the past – the atmosphere was very much, any woman who wants to do anything must do it, and it was really exciting.' Another participant, Hilary Wainwright, who until then had 'not really connected' with the incipient women's movement, was similarly impressed. In the student movement she had always had the feeling that as a woman 'you were only partly there. You could never be quite whole-hearted because not all your needs were being expressed politically.' The conference, she recalled, brought home views that she hadn't thought about. 'It expressed many things to do with women's experience in the family. I remember very vividly one women's long description of house-work and child care which – although it was outside my experience and was something I wanted to avoid – was obviously the fate of large numbers of women. I felt moved by that. And then there was the more explicit discussion of women's sexuality and that made an impact, too.'

The conference led to the setting up of a national coordinating commit-tee, a loose network of women, which put forward four demands: free twenty-four-hour nurseries; equal pay now; equal education and job opportunities; and free contraception and abortion on demand.

In Northern Ireland, the complaints voiced by women everywhere about the male-dominated student organizations extended, in the case of some People's Democracy women members, to the slogans adopted. 'Shouting, "One Man, One Vote" just didn't sound right,' recalled Margaret Ward, then a teenage PD member. 'But I didn't know why it didn't sound right. In retrospect, I can see that the maleness of that demand is one of the things that I felt uneasy about. And when I think about a lot of the meetings, I can remember men talking, but not many women.' It was only in the early 1970s, when she helped to found a socialist-feminist group in Belfast, that she felt 'for the first time in control of my political destiny'. She and her group in Belfast went on to campaign for the British legislation on divorce and abortion, passed in the 1960s, and the sex-discrimination laws of the 1970s, to be applied to Northern Ireland.

In France, the movement was formed in 1970; soon afterwards, police prevented feminists from laying a wreath 'To the Unknown Woman' at the tomb of the Unknown Soldier at the Arc de Triomphe in Paris. On the wreath were the words: 'One Man in Two is a Woman' and 'More Unknown than the Soldier is his Wife'. As elsewhere, many women students felt that in the women's movement they were, for the first time, fighting for a cause with which they fully identified. Brigitte Ballet, a medical student, had never felt totally at home in the Maoist groups of which she had been a member. 'But women's liberation interested me enormously, almost in inverse proportion to my previous political activities. I felt that here was a huge intellectual mobilization which could reflect on women's position in society, which was engaged on a discourse that was much more authentic than the groups I'd been in.'

In the Paris Faculty of Medicine, she and other women decided to get up a group to militate in favour of abortion. 'We organized meetings, were physically attacked by men. I showed a lot more courage then than I did during May 1968, because I was more worked up. It seems strange to think that we were militating for abortion, but it was illegal at the time. I also took part in a consciousness-raising group, a sort of introspection on ourselves as women.'

Joining the early women's movement was an exhilarating experience for many women. But the 'women's community' was not always perfectly harmonious, as revealed by the experience of Devra Weber. The Women's Liberation Front, which Weber helped organize at UCLA, 'divided fairly quickly between what we later described as radical feminists and socialist feminists. The radical feminists were opposed to patriarchy, but were not necessarily opposed to capitalism. And, in our group at least, they opposed so-called male dominated national liberation struggles. We had a meeting at the house of the spokeswoman for this faction – Anne for Freedom, she had renamed herself. She had this huge painting of a pioneer woman with a rifle shooting Indians. She made some statement about this woman fighting off these men, these beasts of the wilderness. The other women brought up the fact that this woman was killing off people whose land had been taken from them.' Unable to contain such differences, the group disintegrated.

Nevertheless, many female activists found that, at least at the time, they were most comfortable in a women's movement, focusing on women's concerns. When, in 1973, Elsa Gili, an Italian activist, plunged into radical feminism, she felt a great relief. 'Finally, I didn't feel obliged to play a leading role, even to talk at meetings. We didn't believe in handing out leaflets, propagandizing, talking to others – not even women. We were concerned no longer with the world out there but with ourselves. Think what Italy was still like at the time. A dozen of us women would go out to a restaurant and the waiter would welcome us with the words, "Are you alone?" He meant no insult, he was simply saying, "Are there no men with you tonight?" So the group engaged in learning how to live with one another as women, consciousness-raising, homosexuality in a metaphorical and real sense. All this caused a great scandal.'

Gili had been one of a number of women who formed feminist groups in the early 1970s; but the Italian women's movement did not really explode until the mid-1970s, when the generation of women directly formed by 1968, often while still at high school, and who subsequently went into one or other of the small left-wing groups, came to form the mass base of the women's movement. The contrast between the groups and the women's movement was very great, as Irene Palumbo noted in Naples. 'In the groups, the men were much better at talking, were stronger, had power. A woman counted only if she were the companion of an important man or was capable of doing things in competition with men. With women you didn't have to compete, be good at everything at all cost. I felt a new sense of solidarity and democracy, of being myself. In that respect, there was, I believe, a continuity between 1968 and feminism, the same sense of solidarity and democracy, of anti-authoritarianism. But in the women's movement, the relationship between women and men was totally different.'

Women's oppression within the student movements and subsequent political groups thus contributed an important element to the development of the women's liberation movement. The same can be said of lesbians and gays who, when it came to their sexuality, found themselves silenced within the student movements and groups. Lesbians discovered in the women's movement a significant intermediate step in their growing sexual awareness and political development. In the United States, for example, Cathy Cade, who had taken part in consciousness-raising groups, traced the roots of her involvement in the lesbian community to the movement. In San Francisco in 1969, she went to a women's conference. 'In this workshop on sexuality there were these lesbians talking, and they just seemed so free and independent and together. They were standing around kind of cuddling while they talked to one another and that was very appealing.' Two years later, Cade 'came out' and started to speak on lesbian platforms. 'In my life there's been a steady progression: Unitarian to civil rights to women's movement. They have just built on one another. I haven't gone through an identity crisis of repudiating something, which is nice and comfy.'

Lacking the supportive network that lesbians found in the women's movement, student radical gays tended often to experience a greater lack of continuity with their past when the new Gay Liberation Fronts formed from 1969 on. The first of these, in the United States, was created after the Stonewall riot in New York in that year, when police raided a gay bar and homosexuals fought back; indeed, some of the credit for triggering gay awareness was attributed to the student movement itself. 'A lot of the people that all of a sudden seemed to appear out of the woodwork after Stonewall and who formed GLF came primarily from the anti-war movement,' commented Craig Rodwell, a gay activist. 'They were radical politically. Some were Marxists and socialists, some were anarchists, a few Democrats and Republicans even.'

Something of the repressive silence which gays had felt obliged to maintain in the student movements and subsequent political groups can be judged from a number of witnesses. Holger Klotzbach, a West German SDS activist, would have preferred 'the earth to swallow me up rather than be known as the gay chairman of the Tübingen University student council in 1967–68. Such matters were not discussed in SDS.' Nor, indeed, were they in the Berlin *Wohngemeinschaft* he subsequently lived in. 'There just wasn't such a thing as coming out, as it was called later.' Homosexuality remained a crime in West Germany until the late 1960s;

and it was only when the gay movement got off the ground there in the mid-1970s that left-wing organizations became willing to discuss it.

From the age of fifteen, Jeff Dudgeon, who was brought up in Belfast, had known he was gay. 'I was totally happy about it, but totally afraid to mention it to anyone. The anger of virtually being silent and too paranoid to speak, and therefore to make any other relationships or to find any other gay people, has affected me to this day. I think you have to be gay to know this inability to speak.' Things were no better when he joined People's Democracy. 'The silence was there, few people would have known. On the very few occasions I mentioned it, people weren't willing to accept me as a gay person. I just knew it mustn't come out.'

In Italy, where a gay liberation organization was set up by an older generation in 1973, it was still not until 1978 that Paolo Hutter, a high school activist ten years earlier, felt sufficiently confident to state publicly that he was gay. 'I couldn't do it before because of my work as a militant and journalist in Lotta Continua and later for a free radio station in Milan . . . But ten years before, when I was sixteen and taking part in demonstrations and occupations, I felt something changing, something that allowed me to accept falling in love as a homosexual. Although such things were never mentioned in our assemblies, I didn't feel guilty for having fallen in love with a boy. I felt I was living an expanded form of freedom, although not as a homosexual in the strict sense of the word. Today, I share the feminist view of the 1968 movement. It was a phase of great sexual emancipation, but not of liberation, and its major protagonists were male.'

Although Britain decriminalized homosexuality between consenting adults in 1967, as a student activist at the London School of Economics David Fernbach still found that he could not say publicly that he was gay. 'I was fortunate in that – unlike most other gays in that milieu – I was able to combine a private life, in which I was gay, with a political public life where such a question was only brought up behind my back, as I later heard, by my political opponents as a bludgeon against me. But I never thought that being gay impinged in any way on politics and the problems of the wider society.'

In joining gay liberation movements, former student activists usually experienced a profound sense of liberation; but it did not necessarily dispel a sense of isolation and rupture with the past, as Robbie Skeist, a veteran American anti-war activist, discovered. 'Joining the Gay Liberation Front radically changed my life, but it was an abrupt thing. For the most part it meant I was in a totally different group of friends in a totally different neighbourhood of Chicago, and working in a political context where suddenly a lot of my friends I'd gone through a lot of political experiences with before thought, Why are you doing this? For the first time I cut off communications with my family. This, I knew, was going to be really different.'

'Although I was both gay and radical, I had to re-think a lot of my politics before I could take part in the movement which held its founding meeting at the LSE in 1970,' recalled Fernbach. 'And that was because orthodox Marxism basically assumes that men are hunters and women nurturers by nature. Once that is put in question, once you explore the ways in which male and female are socially constructed into men and women, and how this is relevant to the total organization of society, then new possibilities are opened up for the way in which social change may take place.

'As gays we learned by struggling around our own oppression. All this opened up a whole new dimension in terms of politics and society for me, and linked up in some ways with elements of student politics. I didn't have to reject my past politics, but I had to put them on the back burner until I could find ways of integrating them with the new dimensions which had become important.'

Like the women's movement, gay liberation set off on a path totally independent of the student movements in the 1970s. Nonetheless, both owed something to the struggle to overcome personal oppression, and the attempt to make new connections between the political and the personal which the student movements re-initiated in the late 1960s, even if they were particularly blind to the important oppressions they contained within them.

It was not, however, the student radicals but those whose political views were formed in opposition to them who were the main beneficiaries of the earlier upheavals and the changing economic situation of the 1970s. The realities of the world recession – high inflation, high unemployment, lowering of real wages – brought back a pervasive sense of crisis in the West in which the often utopian demands of the 1960s movements seemed out of place. The recession favoured the new right's ideological and political backlash, most graphically expressed in the electoral victories of Thatcher in Britain and Reagan in the U.S. in 1979 and 1980, respectively. But the way was also paved in these two countries by the readiness of Carter's Democratic administration and the British Labour government to make their own constituencies – the labour movements and less economically favoured sectors of society – bear the major brunt of the recession.

The assault on the post-war consensus initiated by the student movements was, in a diametrically opposed form and content, pursued by the New Right. In doing so, the latter put to use some of the anti-bureaucratic, anti-statist, libertarian discourse of the 1960s and, standing it on its head, attempted to turn it into a populist-style capitalist politics. Self-improvement became a substitute for social transformation; freeing society from the constraints of the state now meant more free enterprise instead of democratic self-management, less rather than more social welfare, lower taxes instead of state spending to reduce unemployment. Appeals to the values of a mythical past replaced those addressed to a utopian future, the Protestant strains of the 'beloved community' became the puritanical sectarianism of the Moral Majority. Hand-in-hand with these transformations went a frontal assault on the values of the 1960s' 'permissive society': 'law and order', defence of the family, racist legislation, attacks on civil rights – not least a backlash in the U.S. against the civil rights movement and affirmative action programmes; even AIDS has been used as a weapon to bludgeon the past. The external enemy again became Communism, and the Cold War and the arms race started again. In many of these aspects the 1980s resembles the 1950s, in reaction to which the student movements began. It is not altogether surprising therefore that students should again be on the move: in the U.S. and France, as well as in Spain, Mexico and China, 1986 and the beginning of 1987 saw the largest student mobilizations since the late 1960s. These movements, however, were in many important ways significantly different from 1968. History does not repeat itself, but the past offers instruction for the future. What lessons can be drawn from the 1960s? The gains, the losses, the experiences, repeatable or better not repeated? The attempt to answer some of these questions concludes this book.

8

Retrospect

Summing Up

The students asked the right questions – but they couldn't find the
right answers – *John Rose*

The historical significance of past events can be fully appreciated only
when their contribution to shaping the future becomes clear. The present
– only two decades on from 1968 – is not yet that future; the intervening
timespan is too short to know what, if any, long-lasting contribution the
student rebellion has yet to make. The conjectural nature of an assessment
today is rendered even greater by two further factors: the need in this case
to distinguish between the overall impact of a decade and the precise role
of the student movement within it; and the very intangibility of many of the
movements' achievements.

A start might be made, however, by asking whether things would not
have changed without the student rebellion? Undoubtedly, Western
societies would have 'modernized' to some extent anyway. To take one
example: the major social reforms of the 1960s in Britain – the abolition of
capital punishment, divorce and abortion reform, the decriminalization of
adult homosexuality – did not come about thanks to the student movement
but to a reforming Labour Home Secretary and a number of backbench
MPs. Social and cultural change would inevitably have come elsewhere.
But, as will be clear from the preceding pages, the student movements did
not set out to 'modernize' society, even if in some cases that appears to have
been one of their unexpected effects.

The same question can be posed another way: what, concretely, did the
student upheavals change in terms of government policies? Undoubtedly

SNCC played a significant role – as part of a much broader civil rights movement – in helping to end legal segregation in the U.S. South; and the American SDS – if not as a national organization then through its local chapters – became the leading edge of the anti-Vietnam War movement. The latter indisputably made it more difficult for the American government to pursue the war, bringing down a President *en route*, but it was the Vietnamese who ultimately defeated the U.S. and brought the war to an end. Nonetheless, it is in these two areas – civil rights and Vietnam – that American students had the greatest success in contributing to changes of official policies. A further success on both sides of the Atlantic was the democratization – to a greater or lesser degree – of the university. In Italy, for example, the student movement's demands led to government reforms opening the university to all those with high school diplomas in place of the previous restricted access; in the U.S. more minority students were admitted to higher education than before, while everywhere students won a greater say in the running of their places of education, curricula were reformed and new courses developed. Sexual segregation on residential campuses, dress codes and *in loco parentis* regulations were abandoned.

Important as these successes were, they seem on the face of it limited returns for a decade of struggle and years of often violent confrontations. But to restrict 1968 to its impact on official policies is to deny its real significance. In historical terms alone, the anti-war movements represented an international left-wing mobilization on a scale not seen in the West since the 1930s and the Spanish Civil War; while not since the early 1920s had politics and culture found so many common causes. As for the wave of anti-authoritarianism, the culture of insubordination which arose in the student movements, this was totally unprecedented in the twentieth-century West.

It is in these areas that the meanings of 1968 must be sought. To begin with, the anti-authoritarianism challenged almost every shibboleth of Western society. Parliamentary democracy, the authority of presidents and prime ministers, the right of governments to further racism, conduct imperialist wars or oppress sectors of the population at home, the rule of capital and the fiats of factory bosses, the diktats of university administrations, the sacredness of the family, sexuality, bourgeois culture – nothing was in principle sacrosanct. The reason for this outburst can perhaps be ascribed to the uneven development of post-war Western societies in which the actual and ideological authority structures were out of synchronization with the rising expectations seemingly afforded by rapid economic growth; and to the increasing awareness on the part of a new generation, conscious for the first time of its weight in society, that these structures were blocking its development and would continue to do so for as long as they were defended by those whom they served.

This sweeping challenge posed questions that are as relevant today as they were twenty years ago: imperialism; racism and sexism; authority and power in society; the definition of 'politics'; democracy and revolution; ecological issues. Some of the answers proposed, like the anti-war movements, showed that within very clear limits mobilization in the developed countries could do something about the powerful, hierarchical world of imperialism; and, to some extent, the effects of this have lasted until now because the West's dominant power, the U.S., has not again mounted a massive armed intervention in the Third World. The internationalism of the movements was another strength, an exemplary re-evocation of an old socialist ideal, and a decisive rejoinder to the national parochialisms of the 1950s. The extent and definition of politics itself was redefined to include the cultural and personal in ways that will be hard to reverse on the left; and some gains have been made in the fields of racism and sexism. Overall, one of the major effects of the student rebellion has been a generalized disrespect for arbitrary and exploitative authority among the 1968 and succeeding generations in the West, a lack of deference towards institutions and values that demean people and a concomitant awareness of people's rights.

Undeniably though, many of these gains have an intangible feel, but that is because they are part of a still disputed political and cultural terrain; they are not irreversible, have constantly to be struggled for and defended against the counter-offensive waged by the right. Something of this can be felt in the way Charles Sherrod looks back on the achievements of SNCC: 'What we've done in America is to lift some weight off the backs of our people – black and white. We've done nothing to change the system which is as entrenched as ever it was – but the freedom that we feel, and the freedom that our children feel, is real. The process through which people are educated in this country – we've changed it somewhat. We've changed the airwaves . . . Our children or our children's children will get together and say, "Enough of this!"'

In some ways, then, 1968's impact was as intangible and yet as important as a change of the airwaves; a generation of students learned that it was possible to confront the established order not just in the streets but socially, politically, culturally, and in its most intimate manifestations in the human personality. It anchored large sectors of that generation on the left, even if that term today can have very diverse meanings for them. At the same time, it revealed the difficulties of trying to defeat the ruling orders of the West, which offer political and cultural rights and a considerable amount of material well-being, and which historically have put down deep social and ideological roots, as well as maintaining a monopoly of repressive agencies. But 1968 also showed that, from small beginnings and scattered hopes, social movements can arise, and arise very rapidly, to challenge the established order. It is this that a generation barely reaching forty today has experienced and remembers.

Significantly, one of the moments that remains most vividly engraved in many students' memories is the sense of personal engagement and freedom they felt when they took their lives into their hands, occupying their small spaces of liberated territory, democratically managing and deciding their own affairs. Participatory democracy – a direct challenge to the established hierarchical norms of authority – had its drawbacks without doubt: it could be manipulated by interested groups, infiltrated by provocateurs, throw up leaders who were not subject to democratic control and prove an inadequate instrument when it came to taking on the repressive agencies of government. But for all that, it expressed an ideal, that is neither new nor outmoded, which is the essence of any democratic type of socialism: the aspiration of people to have the power and the resources to manage their own affairs. However briefly, 1968 restored this to the political agenda of the West, even if students failed to solve its practical forms or even, perhaps, to grasp its mobilizing potential beyond their own circles.

No left-wing thinkers in the post-war period had been able to elaborate a concrete or plausible strategy for a transition beyond capitalist democracy to socialist democracy in the West. To expect the student movements to do so was no doubt asking a great deal; but their inability to develop even an enduring organizational form and strategies to encompass participatory democracy, spontaneity *and* programmatic planning was particularly striking. For three years, from 1965 and the takeover by the young guard to 1968 and Chicago, the American student movement, for example, was able to contain in a dynamic tension anti-imperialist and anti-racist struggles, the counter-culture, student syndicalism, the emerging women's movement, attempts to redefine the relationship between students, intellectuals and the labour movement, the first student analysis of imperialism and so on. This was the movement's high point: radical democratic demands, the politics of identity, intersected with Marxist analysis; but no consistent synthesis or lasting organization ensued from it.

This failure marked almost all the movements and was due in part to the fact that students are a transitory sector of society. The escalating confrontations and the ruling order's counter-offensive certainly compressed the political space for such possibilities. And yet the two strands of radical democracy and Marxism which, in different dosages and at different times, existed in most of the movements presented a striking opportunity for evolving new strategies and organizations. Demands for the expansion of democratic rights, at the individual as much as at the social and political level, could be integrated into the Marxist analysis of the unaccountable social power of capital as the ultimate source of the lack of democracy. But such syntheses were rarely made, and even more rarely embodied in new forms of organization that almost inevitably would have had to extend beyond students. Here, it might be argued, the evidence that students (or, at the most, large sectors of the post-war young) appeared the only immediate constituency for challenging the ruling order seemed to justify an absence of strategic thinking about how to project the movements' values and aims to other sectors of society, and of creating organizations for the long haul that programmatically embodied these aims.

Perhaps the nearest approach to a new type of strategy came from SNCC. Personal transformation through participation in a democratically self-managed organization was combined with the projection of goals to the racially (and economically) oppressed to help them secure their democratic rights *as a step towards* transforming American society, black and white. That this emancipating project rejected a synthesis of its own radical democratic vision with the Marxist analysis of the cause of inegalitarian power structures, and that it ultimately failed, does not detract from its exemplary attempt as a student movement to evolve a new strategy of social transformation.

That students were not the only constituency of change was revealed by the French May. So, too, was the deep pull of radical democracy: the millions on strike seemed mobilized less by the idea of a revolutionary seizure of power, or even of removing de Gaulle from power, than of taking power over their own affairs in factory and office. Participatory democracy and self-management suddenly flowered, presenting a challenge not only to the Gaullist regime but more seriously to the entire hierarchical relations of production. The radical impulse was here umbilically linked to a socialist perspective. Though the French student movement participated keenly in these experiments, it could not lay claim to having initiated them. During Italy's 'hot autumn' of 1969 and the following years, and to a lesser extent in the other countries, similar local experiments took place, demonstrating the democratic potential that the student movements had evoked in their own midst without theorizing its political or organizational projection.

This lack perhaps explains why students were able to make so easy a transition from direct, decentralized democracy to a Leninist-style democratic centralism in the post-1968 period. They had founded nothing that they themselves could see as of value in the coming struggles; nor in the end did they leave anything very tangible behind, as Bernd Rabehl in West Germany comments. 'The '68 movement didn't found a tradition like that of the 1848 revolution or the German revolution of 1918. We weren't prepared for the role we had to play in 1968. We didn't know enough, weren't radical enough. We politicized a situation but had no perspectives on how to carry it further. And after '68 we fell back into traditional politics, traditional ways of thinking.'

The movements' undisputed vigour and vitality was certainly a function of youth. But the inability to see beyond a specific age group and student experience led to more than organizational failure. Lack of a discourse which took in the real (as distinct from the theoretically assumed) experience of other social strata left the movements bereft of a valuable political and historical corrective. Thus at times it became possible for movements, or sectors within them, to conflate 'repressive tolerance' with repression full stop, parliamentary democracy with bourgeois dictatorship if not fascism, democratic rights with forms of coercion; and eventually to reach an emotional over-identification with (as distinct from militant support for) the Vietnamese revolutionaries. Though the student onslaught shed light on important areas of ideological domination, it left unilluminated the significance to other social strata of democratic rights and parliamentary institutions. And in the more extreme cases, it led to grandiosity, arrogance and sometimes downright silliness by sections of the movements. Rayna Rapp in the United States expresses this well. 'I think all our flamboyant "politics and culture" and "politics as confrontation" and "politics as theater" stretched the boundaries in the U.S. and was useful – but it wasn't a strategy for reaching people who were different from us, who were either older or more ensconced in working-class or even middle-class jobs. That was a tremendous mistake. You can't presume that the experiences of one group – be they left students, blacks or women – can speak for the whole of society.'

Indeed, some of this politics as theatre and confrontation can be seen as a carnival-like outburst which, as in medieval times, appeared sometimes to pose a serious threat to power by developing, beneath the play in the streets, a subversive mass force; but which at the end of the day left power untouched (and, some claim, even stronger than ever because it had survived this subjective and symbolic challenge). This is certainly what has happened: the ruling orders survived and have strengthened their coercive powers. 1968 may perhaps come to be seen as a watershed in that respect.

It is in part a recognition of these factors that makes the new generation of student protest in France and the U.S. different from that of 1968. French students demonstrating against government reforms restricting access to the university in late 1986 rejected any connection with 1968, the failure of which they attributed to sectarian left-wing dispute and to having stood out for 'revolution'. In their widescale and coordinated protests from 1986 on against U.S. policy towards South Africa and university investments in American companies with major ties to the racist South African government, American students rejected what they called the 'violent' movements of the 1960s. In their concentration on single issues, the new movements turned against the way the 1960s movements were able to link a wider critique of contemporary Western society to the particular interests and demands of students.

Nonetheless, in avoiding many of the pitfalls which befell the 1960s movements, the new movements' strategy of limited aims achieved considerable success: massive and peaceful student demonstrations and the popular support they received led to the French government's retreat; having achieved its goal, the movement dissolved. French workers, whose unofficial strikes paralyzed the country for a couple of weeks after the student protests, similarly refused to allow their movement to be captured for directly political ends and called off their attacks on the government once they had won limited gains. In the U.S., students succeeded in forcing disinvestment by many private universities and by the systems in California, New Jersey, Wisconsin and Michigan. (A similar student movement at the London School of Economics was underway at the time of writing, early in 1987.)

The contemporary student movements' 'new realism' should not allow certain affinities with the 1960s movements to be obscured. To begin with, the issues which mobilized students in 1986 were among those around

which they rallied twenty years earlier: racism and, in France, governmental reform of the university which would restrict the number of
students. Beyond this, there were organizational similarities: participatory
democracy was again put to use and there was a profound anti-
authoritarianism, although the word itself might not be used. There were
occupations of university buildings in the U.S., and mass demonstrations
in the streets of Paris. But it was the authorities' reactions that, as in the
1960s, again led students to a sharper understanding of the relations of
power under the established order. University authorities' resistance to
demands over South Africa once more raised the issue of how, and for
what ends, the university is governed in the U.S.; while in France police
brutality even worse than in 1968 – one student was killed and two severely
wounded in 1986 – led many students who, initially, had called themselves
apolitical to move towards democratic left-wing positions, although remaining clearly distrustful of political party or trade union apparatuses. In
both countries, old 'sixty-eighters' joined the new protests. At Columbia
University, students who were occupying Hamilton Hall held a special day
when those who had taken it over in 1968 came to express their support;
and at the University of Massachusetts, the alliance was expressed by the
arrest during a sit-in of Abbie Hoffman, the 1960s Yippie leader, and Amy
Carter, the former president's student daughter. Initially French 1968
veterans – many of them the parents of those in the streets – stayed aloof
from the demonstrations; but after the student killing by the police great
numbers came out to act as marshals to prevent further violence on the last
protest march, held under the single slogan of 'Plus Jamais Ça!' ('Let it
never happen again!').

In some senses then, the new student generation has delivered its
judgement on the 1960s movements, a judgement shaped, of course, by a
different set of circumstances to those of twenty years ago. The under-
standable determination not to repeat the political errors of the past may,
however, underestimate some of the changed airwaves brought about by
the politics of the 1960s, starting with the right to protest. But in each
country the frequency of the wavelengths are different, reflecting specific
national characteristics. It is also important therefore to hear the views of
those who participated in the 1960s movements on what some of these
national changes have been, the lessons to be drawn. This selection of
opinions, gathered like all the others in this book in 1984–85, makes no
pretence of being an historical analysis of the impact in each country

which, for reasons stated at the beginning, it is still impossible to do. The fact that those who hold these views are still young enough to play an active role in future developments is one of the reasons why this is still unfinished history.

West Germany

The student movement was Germany's first really democratic upheaval since the 1848 revolution. Democratic in a modern sense, in all its anti-authoritarian and cultural dimensions. It founded a radical democratic tradition. A society which claimed to be democratic was made to confront its authoritarian structures, the authoritarian personality was challenged, society's smooth running profoundly shaken. The repercussions can still be felt today. Certain things just aren't accepted any more as they were before 1968. I defend the procedures of formal (parliamentary) democracy now, but I want an extension of democracy, decentralization. – *Dany Cohn-Bendit*

The student revolt broke the century-old hegemony of the right-wing nationalist and conservative-to-fascist influence on German higher education and the teachers in it. Apart from their commitment to social justice, democracy, individual liberty, students rebelled because they felt like alienated cogs in the academic process which in turn was part of a gigantic and confusing industrial or state machine. That's why the revolt spread to the Soviet bloc. The idea of self-management in academia and work had no place in modern industrial societies either East or West. – *Siegward Lönnendonker*

One the most negative things, as I know from personal experience, is to allow yourself to be persuaded – by others, by vanity – of your own self-importance. It's not a coincidence that it was intellectuals in revolt who so grossly over-estimated themselves. As a result, I've become sceptical of their practical influence, react strongly against the kind of Marxism and jargon which emerged at the time. – *Niels Kadritzke*

Italy

It seems paradoxical but, like many a subversive movement, this one ended up contributing in some respects to the modernization of the existing system, becoming integrated in it. Perhaps this integration is only provisional and contains such contradictions within it that the present power structure will again be threatened though at different levels. Take the university for example. Access has been democratized, yes, but there's no corresponding democratization of the job market. Students, especially in the humanities, get degrees that are practically worthless in terms of finding a job. And the university is still ruled by a series of corporations that have simply been enlarged to admit more people into their ranks. – *Elsa Gili*

Political activity in the student movement has been very fruitful to many people, not only personally but from a professional point of view. If you look at those who were cadres like me, you'll find that in whatever work they're doing today they've almost always found some new way of doing it – starting cooperatives, innovative means of marketing, re-thinking the professions. And those who remain in politics have evolved types of activity that go beyond political parties. – *Pedro Humbert*

The critique of roles – leadership, gender – begun by the 1960s movements has had such a deep and lasting impact on me that I've never wanted to make a profession of my political activity. I'm a Member of Parliament now for Democrazia Proletaria, but when my term expires I'll go back to my part-time job in a publishing house. There's a continuity for me between 1968 and being – or rather making oneself – a communist. – *Franco Russo*

France

To achieve reforms you have sometimes to try to make the revolution. Much has changed in French society since 1968, even if things are by no means perfect. Authority in factories and schools is less strong than it was, women's place and role in society is no longer what it was, contraception and abortion have been legalized, the death penalty abolished. We've finally escaped from the leaden weight of Gaullism which stifled life and freedom. And all that, I believe, is as a result of May '68. – *Nelly Finkielsztejn*

For a moment, the time of a smile, May '68 made it possible to get a glimpse of what relations between people could be like. It was one of those exceptional moments when power seemed to have collapsed. But you can't live on mythology – the left has got to have policies. We have to reinvigorate parliamentary democracy – a type of democracy I have finally come to terms with. – *Roland Castro*

The French '68 was a great illusion, and it's difficult to remain faithful to it. The illusion in our ranks, Trotskyists and Maoists alike, was the seizure of power. No one believes in that any more. All the same, May '68 changed a lot of things, especially in the relationship between intellectuals and the working class: today you'll find many more intellectuals working in the trade unions than before. The working-class world isn't as closed as it was in the past. – *Robert Linhart*

Northern Ireland

There was a time when I thought that if we'd done things differently in People's Democracy, the reaction would have been different. But I think subsequent events have made clear that it wasn't the way we did things but what we did that mattered. We demanded something of the Northern Ireland state which that state was created to prevent happening, and it didn't matter how nicely we did it, we would simply have prolonged the essentially inevitable outcome. Once people challenge authority, it runs on – and it's run through the whole social fibre here. People who challenged state repression gradually came to challenge repression within the family, Women Against Violence Against Women was set up. Once you dispose of the notion that you do something simply because somebody in authority says you must, it's very difficult to stop that. – *Bernadette (Devlin) McAliskey*

Oh yes, we got lots of things wrong. The main thing in terms of political activity, I think, was to underestimate the Catholic population's interest in physical defence. If the civil rights movement had been more prepared itself to provide that defence then the IRA's military campaign might not have got off the ground. I thought then, and I still think, that political means, defensive means – mass mobilizations, civil resistance, barricading areas and defending them – could have achieved everything that's been achieved. – *Michael Farrell*

Britain

The movement encouraged the growth of a radical, anti-capitalist current of thought, brought an interest in theory and ideas – look at the number of radical and Marxist sociological, economic and philosophical journals that have come into being since then – which went against the grain of the philistine anti-intellectualism of British society in general and the British left and Labour movement in particular. But, the movement's populist strain, the idea of controlling one's own life, which in 1968 was subsumed into hopes of a complete change of society, showed its negative side when it no longer appeared that society was going to change. Then Margaret Thatcher was able to give a neo-conservative twist to this radical individual appeal: instead of controlling your own place of work it became a question of owning your own house. Common to both was anti-statism. – *Robin Blackburn*

The ideas developed in the student movement have fed their way into challenges towards the established structures of the Labour party. An awful lot of people involved in the party over the last decade or so were active in student politics. Going to a Labour party conference now is like a throw-back to a National Union of Students conference in the late 1960s and early 1970s – people I knew then are people I know in the party now. – *Jack Straw*

1968 led us to see that power comes through building organizations at the base rather than restricting our political paths to the established institutions. The sort of social transformations that working-class people, women, black people need can't come through a purely parliamentary route to power – a power which turns out to be illusory – not even from an extra-parliamentary process that's finally consumated in parliamentary fashion. It needs new forms of political power. – *Hilary Wainwright*

United States

Current wisdom is that all we produced was reaction, a law-and-order President. That's the way the bourgeoisie has tried to re-write history, and it's been fuelled by people who developed revolutionary hopes in a non-revolutionary situation and so ignored or denounced the real things that were accomplished. We helped put a stop to the Vietnam War. As crazy as it sounds, the tactic of threatening chaos in the mother country if the war continued worked. What a fantastic victory! – and it's been hidden from the people. The second thing we did was help create space for the civil rights movement, the Black Power movement and all the stepped-up social programs of the Great Society. We also made gains in terms of educational reform, bringing more Third World people into the universities, for example. A lot of these victories have been taken away, but not all. What we won will sustain me in passing out leaflets at canneries where people don't pay attention for years. Because I passed out leaflets on campus for years without anybody paying attention. And then, all of a sudden, BOOM! it changed. – *Frank Bardacke*

The fact that we've got a pro-war, anti-civil rights President who makes women the focus of attack, and attempts to constitute a certain kind of family life, means that, for the time being, we've lost. We called forth a super reaction – because we made a super challenge. We were unprepared and naive about what we were challenging, but it wasn't a mistake to make the challenge. We've lost a round but it's not over. – *Rayna Rapp*

We're not all dead. We're here, and somehow we're invisible, and I don't quite understand why. I feel that I'm part of a community, that I can call on, talk to, people with whom I share a history and the sense of possibilities that we had, even if you were in California and I was in New York. Real changes have occurred. We were responsible for those, we're part of that. It's what gives me a sense that it's worth going on because it is possible to change things. I grew up believing that, and I'm forty-one years old and I was supposed to get over this and I haven't. – *Andrea Eagan*

Afterword

What has become, professionally and politically, of the 175 participants in this book? Before attempting to answer the question, it is necessary to stress that the participants were chosen for their roles in the movement and not as a statistically representative sample; what follows, in consequence, is a 'profile' not of the 1968 generation at large but of those 'sixty-eighters' who appear in this book.

Occupationally, they fall into four broad categories: just under one-half are today in teaching – both secondary and tertiary – and research; slightly over one-quarter are in media and communications (publishers, free-lance writers, film-makers etc); about one in seven are in social or trade union work; just under one in eleven are professionals; while other categories account for about one in thirty. The major departures from the overall averages are in the U.S. and Britain; in the former, there are more people in social and trade union work (nearly 20 per cent); while in the latter the proportion between teachers and media/communicators is reversed.

The fact that the large majority of participants work in the same two fields as the collaborators responsible for the interviews in this book casts an immediate doubt on the validity of generalizing from these figures. Nonetheless, the high proportion of teachers/researchers can also be taken to illustrate how the expansion of education in the 1960s and early 1970s provided career opportunities for many of the brightest students who were often also leading movement activists. To a lesser but still significant extent the same appears true of the media; here the speaking and writing skills which activists learnt, and their exposure to the media, have probably stood them in good stead. The relatively low percentages in the two remaining broad categories, social and trade union work, and professionals, is striking, but it is difficult to know whether they represent anything more than the distortions of interview selection. Finally, despite the working-class origins of a number of participants, only a handful today are in working-class jobs.

Political categorization is a more difficult task. Although each partici-pant was asked to define his or her current political position in a few words, the outcome (see the List of Contributors) was not immediately illuminating. To begin with, 75 per cent of American participants declined to identify themselves in political categories, explaining that their politics were described by their activities in community organizations or reform and radical movements. In Italy and West Germany, the majority referred to themselves as 'independent leftists', which on closer examination turn out to have significantly different meanings in each country, while in France the current, and indeterminate, phrase was 'on the left'. In Britain and Northern Ireland, on the other hand, more specific and self-defining political affiliations were generally given.

Despite these difficulties, three points are immediately clear: very few of the participants in this book today belong to any political party; very few describe themselves as Marxists or revolutionaries (Britain is the major exception on these first two points); and none declares support in any shape for a right-wing party. (The common assumption that many have shared the trajectory of a few famous names who have become right-wing supporters is not borne out here.) Thereafter, it is a question of distinguishing different political definitions within their own national contexts.

The lack of active left organizations in the United States is adduced as the major reason why American participants are unable or unwilling to define themselves in terms of specific political affiliations. (When they do, however, they fall into categories that are generally quite self-defining – more so, indeed, than most of their Continental European counterparts. Marxists, radicals, liberal pacifists, revolutionary nationalists, anarcho-socialists, make up the bulk of the 25 per cent who responded.) Nonetheless, among the majority who refuse to respond, many consider themselves deeply involved in political action or think of themselves as political while strenuously rejecting any political identification other than that conferred on them by what they are doing. The long American history of community-organizing and reform movements undoubtedly plays a role here; and the fact that the U.S. shows the highest proportion of 'sixty-eighters' engaged in social and trade union work is no doubt a reflection of this commitment to action.

In describing the current political positions of Continental European 'sixty-eighters' it is necessary again to make some broad generalizations for each country. In France, 'on the left' can be taken to stand for a non-revolutionary, non-Communist stance, combined with support, albeit disappointed, for the Socialist Party, and acceptance of parliamentary democracy as a prerequisite for any political and social advance, and a reluctant acceptance of the market economy. It is here that the reaction to the politics of 1968 has been sharpest, a reaction which can be explained by a number of factors: the bitter deception of revolutionary hopes in what – despite the luminous appearance of May – was a non-revolutionary situation; the sense of the French Communist Party's 'betrayal'; and the subsequent inroads of Maoism and its virulent anti-Soviet stance which, for some, could turn to straightforward anti-Communism. Two further setbacks – of Eurocommunism and the Socialist government's subsequent inability from 1981 to 1983 to transform massive nationalizations into real social reforms – have more recently added to the deception.

Although the reaction has also been severe in Italy, the other Continental country where the 1968 movement appeared most immediately set to leave the deepest impact, it is somewhat less so than in France. 'Independent leftist' is taken there to mean a non-party, radical-democratic stance to the left of the Italian Communist Party that focusses its politics on greater social justice and egalitarianism. It is in many ways a reprise of the New Left positions of the 1960s. ('Progressive', the other term used, is a more moderate version of the same thing.) A general acceptance of parliamentary democracy is accompanied by an anti-Communist, anti-Soviet posture.

In Germany, 'independent leftist' must be read quite differently. It stands for opposition to capitalism – and the growing power of state bureaucracy. While concepts of an 'alternative' or socialist society vary greatly, self-management, the autonomy of the shop-floor collective, is usually a common strand. Though critical of parliamentary democracy, most would now see it as the road through which direct democracy can be attained, not by increasing the powers of elected representatives to confront the bureaucracy, but by its enlargement to include means of directly expressing the popular will, as well as by expanding civil rights. Reflecting the student movement's own trajectory in the 1960s, these positions can be premised on a traditional Marxist outlook inflected by libertarian and feminist ideas or on an anti-authoritarian, populist and anarchist base informed by elements of Marxism.

Britain is exceptional in the high proportion – just under one half – who belong to political parties; of these about 50 per cent are Labour Party members. As such, their positions can vary from support of the present reformist leadership to Marxist perspectives by way of a politics that stresses self-management or cooperative industrial strategies. The remaining 50 per cent of party members belong, in equal numbers, to the Communist Party, the Socialist Workers' Party (Trotskyist) and the recently formed Green Party. Perhaps because Britain was spared the expectation and consequent disappointment of a 'revolution that never happened', it is also exceptional in the number – about one-third of non-affiliated participants – who continue to define themselves as independent Marxists or revolutionary socialists.

Northern Ireland is akin to Britain in this latter respect. Party membership at about one-third is not as high, however; the fact that the British Labour Party does not exist in Northern Ireland means that participants who might join have to define themselves as 'Labour supporters'. In fact, party membership among the former 'sixty-eighters' in this book is confined to two small left-wing parties: the Irish Workers' Party, a formation whose origins lie in the official Sinn Fein, and People's Democracy, now a member of the Trotskyist Fourth International.

Finally, it should be noted, over half of the women 'sixty-eighters' in West Germany and Italy, and the majority of those in Britain and Northern Ireland, describe themselves as feminists today. (The absence of any reference to feminism among the American women participants can be explained on the grounds that they took their feminism for granted.)

If the most immediate characteristic of the 'sixty-eighters' political profile appears its heterogeneity, marked by national specificities whose importance was notable in the 1960s and has become more so since then, some common underlying traits can nonetheless be discerned. The exaggerated revolutionary optimism of those years has, not surprisingly, vanished and with it confidence in Leninist-type strategies for the seizure of power. The past twenty years have no more produced a viable strategy for a transformation of parliamentary to a more progressive form of democracy than did the previous two decades. Nor has a socialist democracy tangibly superior to parliamentary democracy emerged elsewhere to serve as a referential model. The easy scorn poured by the student movements on parliamentary democracy has been revised because, despite its clearly perceived limits, it is now seen to retain widescale credibility as the ultimate, if not only, institutional source of self-determination; and because, as a political practice, it offers, some have come to believe, an avenue to the expansion of democracy. Whether social transformation can come through parliamentary democracy or not remains, as it always has, the major line of division.

The setbacks and defeats of the years since 1975 should not allow the major legacy of 1968 to be obscured: the concept that social transformation in the West can no longer be divorced from the goal of more democracy, greater civil rights, more freedoms for the vast majority of people than they are presently afforded. And similarly, that any movement, party or alliance that proposes such a political and cultural transformation will itself have to be democratic and include the demands of women, ecologists, ethnic and cultural minorities and others if it is to entertain any hope of success.

List of Organizations

BSU	Black Student Union (US)
CADRE	Chicago Area Draft Resistance Effort
CAL	Comité d'Action Lycéen (France)
CFDT	Confédération Française Démocratique du Travail (Communist, France)
CGT	Confédération Générale du Travail (Communist-led, France)
CLEOP	Student Worker Peasant Liaison Committee (Maoist, France)
CND	Campaign for Nuclear Disarmament (Britain)
CORE	Congress of Racial Equality (US)
CPGB	Communist Party of Great Britain
CRS	Compagnie Républicaine de Sécurité (France)
ERAP	Economic Research and Action Project (US)
FDJ	Freie Deutsche Jugend (Communist youth organization, East Germany)
FER	Fédération des Etudiants Révolutionnaires (Trotskyist, France)
FLN	Algerian National Liberation Front
FSM	Free Speech Movement (Berkeley, US)
GLF	Gay Liberation Front
GP	Gauche Prolétarienne (Maoist, France)
GS	Gioventù Studentesca (non-conformist Italian catholic youth organization)
LID	League for Industrial Democracy (US)
IMG	International Marxist Group (Trotskyist, Britain)
INS	Immigration and Naturalization Service (US)
IRA	Irish Republican Army
IS	International Socialists (far left organization, Britain)
JCR	Jeunesse Communiste Révolutionnaire (Trotskyist, France)
KPD	Kommunistische Partei Deutschland (Maoist, Germany)
LC	Lotta Continua (far left organization, Italy)
LSD	Liberaler Studentenbund Deutschland (Liberal Party's student organization)
MFDP	Mississippi Freedom Democratic Party (US)
NICRA	Northern Ireland Civil Rights Association
NLF	National Liberation Front (Vietnam)
NUS	National Union of Students (Britain)
PCI	Partito Comunista Italiano

P C (m-l) d'I   Partito Comunista marxista-leninista d'Italia
PD   People's Democracy (Northern Ireland)
PL   Progressive Labor Party (Maoist, US)
PLPI   Proletarische Linke-Partei Initiative (Spontaneist-Maoist,
                Germany)
PSIUP   Partito Socialista Italiano di Unità Proletaria
RAF   Red Army Faction (Germany)
RSA   Radical Student Alliance (Britain)
RSSF   Revolutionary Socialist Students Federation
RYM   Revolutionary Youth Movement (US)
SAS   Students' Afro-American Society (US)
SB   Sozialistisches Bürer (association of Socialists and Marxists,
                Germany)
SDS   Students for a Democratic Society (US)
SDS   Sozialistiche Deutsche Studentenbund (radical student
                association, Germany)
SHB   Sozialdemokratischer Hochschulbund (Social Democratic Party's
                student organization, Germany)
SNCC   Student Nonviolent Coordinating Committee (US)
'SocSocs'   Socialist Societies (Britain)
SPD   Sozialdemokratische Partei Deutschland (Social Democratic
                Party, Germany)
SPUR   Munich Counter-Cultural Group
SSOC   Southern Student Organizing Committee (US)
SWP   Socialist Workers' Party (Britain)
TWLF   Third World Liberation Front (US)
UEC   Union des Etudiants Communistes (France)
UGI   Unione Goliardica Italiana
UJC-ml   Union des Jeunesses Communistes, marxistes-léninistes (Maoist,
                France)
UNEF   Union Nationale des Etudiants Français
VDC   Vietnam Day Committee (US)
VLR   Vive La Révolution (France)
VSC   Vietnam Solidarity Campaign
WLM   Women's Liberation Movement
YCND   Youth Campaign for Nuclear Disarmament
YS   Young Socialists (Ireland)

Chronology

	BRITAIN & N. IRELAND	FRANCE	ITALY	W. GERMANY	USA	OTHERS
1945	Labour government elected	Communist-Socialist moderate government under de Gaulle	END OF WORLD WAR II 20 per cent of economy destroyed by war	over 30 per cent of economy destroyed		
1946		De Gaulle resigns	START OF COLD WAR			
1947		Communists ejected from government	Communists ejected from government: Christian-Democratic government formed			Independence of India
1948					Marshall Plan for Western European reconstruction	
1949						Victory of Chinese revolution

	BRITAIN & N. IRELAND	FRANCE	ITALY	W. GERMANY	USA	OTHERS
				NATO CREATED		
1950				Federal Republic created		
				KOREAN WAR (ended 1953)		
					Senator McCarthy's witchhunting	
1951	Conservative government elected					
1953			Mass firings of left-wing factory workers (1952–3)			Death of Stalin Workers' rising in East Germany
1954	End of food rationing	Beginning of Algerian War			Army-McCarthy hearings – end of McCarthy Segregated education ruled illegal	French forces defeated at Dien Bien Phu, Vietnam

	BRITAIN & N. IRELAND	FRANCE	ITALY	W. GERMANY	USA	OTHERS
1955					Murder of Emmett Till	
					Beginning of Montgomery Bus Boycott led by Martin Luther King	
1956	Look back in Anger – John Osborne's play			Communist Party declared illegal	Howl published	Khrushchev's denunciation of Stalin's crimes
	Anglo-French invasion of Egypt after Nasser's nationalization of the Suez Canal				Elvis Presley top of the charts	Uprising in Hungary crushed by Soviet forces
	N. Ireland: IRA begins campaign against Unionist régime: ends in 1962					
1957	Prime Minister Macmillan says Britons 'Never had it so good'	Battle of Algiers systematic use of torture by French paratroopers			Little Rock Central High School desegregation	Russians launch Sputnik
	Angry Young Men declare against Establishment values				Southern Christian Leadership Conference organized	Ghana, first British black African colony, gains independence
	Beginning of New Left				On The Road by Kerouac published	

	BRITAIN & N. IRELAND	FRANCE	ITALY	W. GERMANY	USA	OTHERS
1958	First CND Aldermaston March	De Gaulle returns to power; Fifth Republic instituted	Pope John XXIII opens era of better relations with Communists Internal migration from South to North intensifies			Independence of French black colonial Africa
1959	Conservatives third successive general election victory	Start of 'Salut les copains' pop radio programme			Krushchev tours US *Studies on the Left* begins publication	Victory of Cuban revolution
1960	Labour Party Conference votes for unilateral disarmament: vote reversed following year	Intellectuals' manifesto declaring conscripts' right to desert rather than fight in Algeria	Fascist Party national congress leads to clashes with dead and wounded	SPD expels SDS	Black students begin sit-in in Woolworths, Greensboro, N.C. SNCC founded Anti-HUAC demonstrations in San Francisco Kennedy elected President	Independence of Belgian Congo Sino-Soviet split

	BRITAIN & N. IRELAND	FRANCE	ITALY	W. GERMANY	USA	OTHERS
1961	Mass arrest of Committee of 100 in Trafalgar Square	French generals' putsch in Algeria crushed	*Quaderni Rossi* starts publication		Freedom Riders attacked First US military lands in Vietnam	Berlin Wall built Invasion of Cuba at Bay of Pigs beaten back Lumumba, radical Congolese leader, murdered Gagarin first man in space
1962	Unknown Beatles get first record – 'Love Me Do' – in charts	Eight killed in anti-Algerian war demonstration (Charonne) End of Algerian war	First centre-left government School-leaving age raised to 14 Fiat strike, violent demonstrations in Turin Vatican Council II	Easter marches against nuclear weapons mobilize 50,000 Youth riots in Munich	SDS: Port Huron Statement Integration of University of Mississippi after two nights of rioting	Cuban missile crisis
1963	Beatles four new records go to top of charts CND enters decline	First pop concert, Paris	Start of Economic Crisis (1963–5)		Birmingham bombings and riot Medgar Evans, NAACP, assassinated	Fall of Ngo Dinh Diem in Saigon Test Ban Treaty, easing of Cold War

BRITAIN & N. IRELAND	FRANCE	ITALY	W. GERMANY	USA	OTHERS
Robbins report on Higher Education				Massive civil rights march on Washington: 'I have a dream' – Martin Luther King	
				Kennedy assassinated	
1964 Labour wins general election after 13 years of Conservative rule	University of Nanterre, Paris, opened	Threatened military coup	SDS, left-wing groups demonstrate in Berlin against Tshombe, Prime Minister of Zaire	Bob Dylan rockets to popularity	Krushchev falls, replaced by Kosygin and Brezhnev
Pop boom reaches height			Subversive Aktion joins SDS	Mississipi Summer	
Major financial crisis				Civil Rights Act signed	
Mod–Rocker clashes				Riots in New York, Rochester, Newark, Chicago etc	
				Atlantic City Democratic Convention refuses seats to Mississippi Freedom Democratic Party	

	BRITAIN & N. IRELAND	FRANCE	ITALY	W. GERMANY	USA	OTHERS
1964— contd.					FSM Berkeley President Johnson elected Herbert Marcuse's *One Dimensional Man* Betty Friedan's *The Feminine Mystique*	
1965	Wilson reiterates support for US in Vietnam Rolling Stones in charts 'Swinging London' Economic sanctions against all-white Rhodesian government's unilateral declaration of independence	De Gaulle re-elected with reduced majority of popular vote		Left students organize a congress against proposed Emergency Powers Act	Escalation of Vietnam War Malcolm X assassinated Teach-in on Vietnam at University of Michigan Selma March SDS anti-war march, Washington National teach-in broadcast to 100 colleges	Cultural revolution begins in China

	BRITAIN & N. IRELAND	FRANCE	ITALY	W. GERMANY	USA	OTHERS
					SDS national meeting chooses ERAP over war as major focus of actions	
					Uprising in Watts ghetto, Los Angeles	
					International Days of Protest, anti-war rallies initiated by Berkeley Vietnam Day Committee	
1966	Labour wins general election with increased majority	JCR formed	Trento Institute of Social Sciences occupied	West Berlin student demonstration against war	Rise of Black Power, Stokely Carmichael elected chair of SNCC	
	Massive financial crisis	UJC-ml formed	Death of Paolo Rossi at hands of fascists	Free University of West Berlin sit-in		
	VSC founded	Situationist students takeover Students Association at Strasbourg, publish 'On Student poverty'	Rome and other universities occupied	Marcuse's essay on 'repressive tolerance' published in Germany	Mobilization to End the War in Vietnam (MOBE) founded	
	RSA founded					
	Seaman's strike – state of emergency declared			SPD agrees to join Christian	Black Panther Party founded	

	BRITAIN & N. IRELAND	FRANCE	ITALY	W. GERMANY	USA	OTHERS
1966–contd.	Government announces increases in foreign students' fees – massive student protests			Democratic party in Grand Coalition Rudi Dutschke calls for extra parliamentary opposition		
1967	Dialectics of Liberation Congress, London 100,000 students demonstrate against foreign students' fee increases First student occupation at LSE, lasts 9 days First VSC demonstration brings out 10,000 Formation of Northern Ireland Civil Rights Association (NICRA)	Student strike starts at Nanterre spreads to Sorbonne	First large wave of university occupations (spring) Milani's *Lettera a una professoressa* published Second wave of university occupations (autumn)	Police arrest 11 Kommune I members accused of planning attack on US vice-President Humphrey Police kill Benno Ohnesorg during anti-Shah demonstrations Student movement becomes mass movement Critical University set up	Largest anti-war demonstrations to date 'Summer of love' in San Francisco Haight-Ashbury Black uprisings in Newark, Detroit, riots in 27 cities The Resistance formed Oakland Draft actions Dow Chemical demonstration at University of Wisconsin March on the Pentagon	Colonels' coup in Greece Che Guevara killed in Bolivia

	BRITAIN & N. IRELAND	FRANCE	ITALY	W. GERMANY	USA	OTHERS
1968	2nd VSC demonstration: violence in Grosvenor Square (March)	Incident between Cohn-Bendit and Interior Minister (Jan.)	Half of all universities occupied	International Vietnam Congress, West Berlin (Feb.)	Anti-Rusk demonstration ends in street fighting in New York	Tet offensive
	'Rivers of Blood' speech by Enoch Powell (April)	Nanterre occupation – formation of 22 March Movement (March)	Battle of Valle Giulia, Rome (March)	Counter-demonstration organized by political parties and trade unions	COINTELPRO in effect	Students overthrow Belgian government
	London dockers demonstrate in favour of Powell (April)	May events: May 3–mid-June	Workers collectives expanding	Dutschke shot – heavy street fighting follows, 2 killed, hundreds injured (Easter)	Johnson announces will not run again (March)	Prague spring
	Occupation of many universities and colleges (May–July)	Sweeping Gaullist victory in general election (end June)	The left gains ground in general elections	Demonstrations against Emergency Powers Act which is passed by Bundestag (May)	Martin Luther King assassinated; riots in 126 cities (April)	Warsaw student riots
	Black Dwarf published (May)		2,700 students facing police charges	Demonstrations against Soviet	Columbia University occupation (April)	Gold Crisis
	RSSF founded (June)				Robert Kennedy assassinated (June)	Tokyo–Narita student/police battles
					Chicago Democratic Convention riots (Aug.)	Soviet invasion of Czechoslovakia
						Massacre of 300 Mexican students by police and army

	BRITAIN & N. IRELAND	FRANCE	ITALY	W. GERMANY	USA	OTHERS
1968 – contd.	3rd VSC demonstration (Oct.) N. Ireland: Derry civil rights march attacked by police (Oct.) PD formed (Oct.)			invasion of Czechoslovakia (August) Women SDSers revolt against the student organization (Sept.) Collapse of SDS Violent street battle – Tegeler Weg – in West Berlin (Nov.)	San Francisco State strike begins – lasts 5 months (Nov.–April) 550,000 US troops in Vietnam	
1969	LSE closed after students take down gates (Jan.) Government attempts to outlaw 'unofficial strikes' Counter-culture growing; Rolling Stones free concert attracts 250,000 in Hyde Park (June) Jack Straw (moderate left)	Student agitation in Paris, national day of action against repression in university	High school students mobilize throughout year	Willy Brandt elected first Social Democratic Chancellor (Oct.) Last attempt to re-organize Extra Parliamentary Opposition in West Berlin fails (Dec.)	Nixon President Secret bombing of Cambodia starts (March) Los Angeles school 'blow-outs' – 10,000 Chicano students strike (March) Stonewall riot, NY City (June) SDS Chicago convention,	Paris Peace talks on Vietnam open Phased withdrawal of US troops from Vietnam announced End of Chinese Cultural Revolution US puts man on moon

BRITAIN & N. IRELAND	FRANCE	ITALY	W. GERMANY	USA	OTHERS
ousts right-wing president of NUS (April)				effective destruction of student organization (July)	
N. Ireland: PD's Belfast–Derry 'Long March' ambushed at Burntollet (Jan.)				Woodstock music festival, 500,000 gather (Aug.)	
PD gains 27 per cent of votes in constituencies contested in general elections (Feb.)				Weatherman Days of Rage in Chicago (Oct.)	
Bernadette Devlin elected to Westminster (April)				Millions demonstrate in home towns against war (Oct.)	
Premier O'Neill resigns (April)				300,000 demonstrate in Washington, teargassed, mass arrests (Nov.)	
Major sectarian riot in Derry (April)				Chicago Black Panther leader, Fred Hampton shot: 25 Panthers killed in 1970 (Dec.)	
Heavy riots in Derry, Belfast: Britain sends in troops (Aug.)					

	BRITAIN & N. IRELAND	FRANCE	ITALY	W. GERMANY	USA	OTHERS
1969 – contd.	Bernadette Devlin sentenced to 6 months for 'incitement to riot' (Dec.)					
1970	Conservatives win general elections (June) Anti-union legislation leads to highest number of working days lost since General Strike Beatles split up 1st National Women's Conference (Feb.) RSSF ceases to exist 'Angry Brigade' begins bombing campaign N. Ireland: Provisional IRA formed	Maoist militants 'expropriate' luxury Paris food shop (May) Government outlaws Gauche Prolétarienne (GP), brings action against party paper (May) Creation of Red Help by ex-GP leaders backed by J.-P. Sartre A. Geismar and other GP militants stage hunger strike in prison (Sept. 1–25) Geismar sentenced to 18 months (Nov.)	Law recognizing a series of workers' and trade union rights approved Divorce law approved by Parliament Red Brigades' first actions against property	SDS officially disbanded (March) Red Army Fractions first action, freeing Andreas Baader from police custody (May)	Weatherman goes underground (Jan.) Chicago Seven convicted of conspiracy, later overturned (Feb.) Invasion of Cambodia (April) Kent State Killings, nationwide 4 million strong student strike (May) Jackson State Killings (May) Chicano Moratorium, 3 killed, 20,000 march in East Los Angeles (Aug.)	

	BRITAIN & N. IRELAND	FRANCE	ITALY	W. GERMANY	USA	OTHERS
	Provisional committees go into action (June)	De Gaulle dies (Nov.)			2nd Chicano Moratorium, police and marchers in pitched battle (Sept.)	
	Bernadette Devlin jailed (June)					
	All marches banned for 6 months (July)					
1973	1½ million workers strike against Government pay policy	*Libération* newspaper founded by ex-Maoists and libertarians under J.-P. Sartre (Jan.)	Abortion law in parliament (Feb.)		American-Indian movement occupies Wounded Knee (Feb.)	Vietnam ceasefire US troops withdrawn (Jan.).
	Broad-left CP leadership asserts NUS 'is a student union as real as the NUM is the miners union'	Abortion liberalized (May)	'Historic Compromise' with Christian Democratic Party proposed by Communist Party (Oct.)		Senate Watergate hearings begin (May)	Military Coup in Chile, Allende killed (Sept.)
	Miners strike – government orders 3-day working week to conserve electricity (Dec.–Feb. '74)	Workers at Lip take over their bankrupt factory (June)			Vice-President Agnew resigns as a result of tax evasion (Oct.)	Yom Kippur War (Oct.)
						Oil Crisis

	BRITAIN & N. IRELAND	FRANCE	ITALY	W. GERMANY	USA	OTHERS
1973 – contd.	N. Ireland: Referendum in favour of remaining part of UK (March)					
	34-day hunger strike by Farrell and Canavan for political prisoner status (July)					
	Britain, Irish Republic, N. Ireland agree to power-sharing for N. Ireland (Dec.)					
1974	Labour returned to power with slender majority over Conservatives (Oct.)	Death of Georges Pompidou (April) Election of Valéry Giscard d'Estaing as President (May)	Red Brigades' first kidnapping of a magistrate, later released (April) Referendum approves divorce bill (May) Fascist massacre in Brescia (May)		Continuing exposure of Nixon abuses in Watergate investigation (Jan) House Committee votes articles of impeachment (July) Nixon resigns, pardoned by Ford	Portuguese Revolution begins (April)
	2nd general election: Labour increases majority to 43 over Conservatives					

	BRITAIN & N. IRELAND	FRANCE	ITALY	W. GERMANY	USA	OTHERS
	N. Ireland: Strike by Protestant workers leads to end of power-sharing plan for N. Ireland (May)					
1975	Thatcher elected Conservative Party leader (Feb.)		800,000 sign petition demanding a referendum on the abolition of fascist abortion laws (July)		Watergate trial ends with conviction of 4 major ex-administration officials (Jan.) US withdraws from Cambodia (April)	Saigon captured by NLF – end of Vietnam War (April) US total dead in Vietnam 56,555 Vietnamese dead, over 1,250,000

Select Bibliography

The following is a brief list of books for further reading in each country.

Britain

Stuart Hall *et al.*, *Policing the Crisis* (Chapters 8 & 9), London, 1978.

Nigel Young, *An Infantile Disorder? The crisis and decline of the New Left*, London, 1977.

David Widgery, *The Left in Britain 1956–1968*, London, 1976.

Alexander Cockburn and Robin Blackburn, eds, *Student Power*, London, 1969.

Lynne Segal, ed., *What is to be done about the Family?* (Chapter 2: 'Smash the Family?' Recalling the 1960s), London, 1983.

Peter Stansill and David Z. Mairowitz, eds, *BAMN: outlaw manifestos and ephemera*, London, 1971.

Jeff Nuttall, *Bomb Culture*, London, 1970.

Students and Staff of Hornsey College of Art, *The Hornsey Affair*, London, 1969.

Paul Hoch and Vic Schoenbach, *LSE: The Natives are Restless*, London, 1969.

Tariq Ali, *1968 and After*, London, 1978.

Avishai Zvi Ehrlich, PhD thesis, LSE (unpublished), 'The Leninist Organizations in Britain and the Student Movement 1966–1972', 1981.

Northern Ireland

Michael Farrell, *Northern Ireland: The Orange State*, London, 1976.

Paul Bew, Peter Gibbon and Henry Patterson, *The State in Northern Ireland 1921–72*, Manchester, 1979.

Paul Arthur, *The People's Democracy*, Belfast 1974.

Eamonn McCann, *War and an Irish Town*, London, 1974.

Bernadette Devlin, *The Price of My Soul*, London, 1969.

USA

Judith C. and Stewart E. Albert, *The Sixties Papers: Documents of a Rebellious Decade*, New York, 1984.

Wini Breines, *Community & Organization in the New Left, 1962–1968: The Great Refusal*, New York, 1982.

Clayborne Carson, *In Struggle: SNCC and the Black Awakening of the 1960s*, Cambridge, Mass, 1981.
Morris Dickstein, *Gates of Eden: American Culture in the Sixties*, New York, 1977.
Sara Evans, *Personal Politics: The Roots of Women's Liberation in the Civil Rights Movement and the New Left*, New York, 1979.
Todd Gitlin, *The Whole World is Watching: The Mass Media in the Making and Un-making of the New Left*, Berkeley, 1980.
Fred Halstead, *Out Now! A Participant's Account of the Movement Against the American War in Vietnam*, New York, 1978.
Harold Jacobs, ed., *Weatherman*, Berkeley, 1970.
James Miller, *Democracy is in the Streets: From Port Huron to Chicago 1968*, New York, 1987.
Abe Peck, *Uncovering The Sixties: The Life & Times of the Underground Press*, New York, 1985.
Kirkpatrick Sale, *SDS*, New York, 1973.

Germany

Uwe Bergmann, Rudi Dutschke, Wolfgang Lefevre und Bernd Rabehl, *Rebellion der Studenten oder Die neue Opposition*, Reinbek bei Hamburg, 1968.
Rainer Langhans und Fritz Teufel, *Klau mich*, Frankfurt/Main u. Berlin, 1968.
Hans-Jürgen Krahl, *Konstitution und Klassenkampf*, Frankfurt/Main, 1971.
Jürgen Miermeister und Jochen Staadt, *Provokationen. Die Studenten- und Jugendrevolte in ihren Flugblättern 1965–1971*, Darmstadt-Neuwied, 1980.
Siegward Lönnendonker und Tilman Fichter, *Freie Universität Berlin 1948–1973, Hochschule im Umbruch*, Teil IV. Berlin, 1975.
Siegward Lönnendonker, Tilman Fichter und Jochen Staadt, *Freie Universität Berlin 1948–1973, Hochschule im Umbruch*, Teil V. Berlin, 1983.
Jürgen Miermeister, *Rudi Dutschke*, Reinbek bei Hamburg, 1986.

Italy

Carlo Donolo, *Mutamento o transizione?*, Bologna, 1977.
Norman Kogan, *Storia politica dell'Italia repubblicana*, Bari, 1982.
Carlo Oliva e Aloisio Rendi, *Il movimento studentesco e le sue lotte*, Milano, 1969.
Gianni Statera, *Death of a Utopia: The Development and Decline of Student Movements in Europe*, New York, 1974.
Massimo Teodori, *Storia delle nuove sinistre in Europa (1956–1976)*, Bologna, 1976.
Guido Viale, *Il sessantotto tra rivoluzione e restaurazione*, Milano, 1978.

Two unpublished theses:
Marco Grazioli, *Il movimento studentesco in Italia nell' anno accademico 1967–68:*

ricostruzione e analisi, Università degli Studi di Milano, anno accademico, 1979–80.

Robert Lumley, *Social Movements in Italy, 1968–69*, Centre for Contemporary Cultural Studies, University of Birmingham, 1983.

France

Edgar Morin, Claude Lefort et Jean-Marc Coudray, *Mai 1968: La brèche. Premières réflexions sur les événements*, Paris, 1968.

Daniel Bensaid et Henri Weber, *La répétition générale*, Paris, 1968.

Alain Schnapp et Pierre Vidal Naquet, *Journal de la Commune étudiante. Textes et documents novembre 1967–juin 1968*, Paris, 1969.

Michèle Manceaux, *Les maos en France*, Paris, 1972. Préface de Jean-Paul Sartre.

Daniel Cohn-Bendit, *Le grand bazar*, Paris, 1975.

Alain Delage et Gilles Ragache, *La France de 68*, Paris, 1978.

Hervé Hamon et Patrick Rotman, *Génération*, Paris, 1987.

List of Contributors

Note: The place name indicates the participant's university or place of higher education; it is followed by student and political affiliation in the 1960s (for meaning of initials see List of Organizations); the remaining two categories are today's situation and self-defined political position.

ALI, Tariq: Oxford; VSC, IMG; broadcaster-writer; editorial board, *New Left Review*; 'independent Marxist'. 11, 129, 132–3, 171, 179–80, 185, 186, 195, 279, 280, 281

ARTHUR, Paul: Queen's University, Belfast; YS, PD; senior university lecturer in politics; 'Labour party supporter'. 233, 236, 240

AUZIAS, Claire: Lyons; high-school student; freelance sociologist; 'left libertarian'. 221

BACHELET, Prisca: worker in cultural affairs dept., Nanterre Town Hall, Paris; 22 March Movement; school teacher 'on the left'. 188–9

BALLET, Brigitte: Paris medical school; UJC-ml; psychiatrist; 'feminist on the left'. 210, 346

BALTER, Michael: UCLA; SDS, PL; investigative journalist/oral historian; 'independent radical'. 118, 119, 120, 290, 294

BARDACKE, Frank: Harvard; University of California, Berkeley; People's Park; Oakland Seven; organizer, Teamsters for a Democratic Union. 151–2, 158, 288, 296, 364–5

BARNETT, Anthony: Cambridge/ Leicester; RSSF, editorial board, *New Left Review*; freelance university lecturer and writer; 'independent Marxist'. 12, 19, 100

BELLAMY, Fay: SNCC; writer/photographer, hostess and interviewer on jazz program, Radio Free Atlanta; 'working to pass on the traditions of the movement.' 40, 44, 299

BERLAND, Carol: University of Chicago; CADRE; mathematics teacher Chicago inner city; Amnesty International; 'liberal and pacifist'. 110

BERNOCCHI, Piero: Rome Polytechnic and University; Nuclei Comunisti Rivoluzionari, Avanguardia Operaia; teacher; 'independent leftist'. 140–1, 182, 254, 259

BEW, Paul: Cambridge; PD, IS; university lecturer in politics; 'member of left-wing Socialist Irish Worker's Party'. 239

BLACKBURN, Robin: Oxford/LSE; university lecturer, RSSF, editor, *New Left Review*; 'independent Marxist'. 168–9, 180, 283, 363–4

BOBBIO, Luigi: Turin; PSIUP, LC; teacher; 'independent leftist'. 22, 70, 71, 79, 96, 141, 165, 167–8, 184, 185, 249, 251

BOOTH, Heather: University of Chicago; SDS, WLM; founding director Midwest Academy; co-director Citizen Action, a national progressive citizen's organization. 110, 299, 344

BOURRIGAUD, René: Ecole Supérieure d'Agriculture, Angers; Young Catholic Farmers; rural sociologist, CFDT. 9, 220

BRECHER, Jeremy: Reed College; Student Peace Union, SDS; community historian; peace activist. 62, 78, 143, 319

BRETEAU, Jean: Nantes; Situationist; high-school teacher. 217

BRICK, Barbara: Humboldt University, East Berlin/Munich/Frankfurt; SDS; archivist of Herbert Marcuse's literary estate; 'feminist and independent leftist'. 13, 191, 194, 344

BRIER, Pam: Berkeley; FSM; senior vice president for administration, New York City Health and Hospitals Corporation. 91, 95, 106

HAMILTON, Steve: Berkeley; FSM, PL; Bay Area Revolutionary Union; Oakland Seven; marriage and family counselor, Oakland, California; North Star Network, an association of Bay Area socialists. 91, 92, 94, 95, 152, 155, 190

HAMLIN, Mike: League of Revolutionary Black Workers; factory worker, Detroit. 46, 47

HARDING, Susan: Michigan; SDS; Women's Liberation; anthropologist, University of Michigan; 'smouldering'. 102

HARRIS, McCree: Albany State College; SNCC; teacher, Albany, Georgia. 42

HARRIS, Rutha: Albany State College; SNCC; teacher, Albany, Georgia. 42

HAYLING, Alan: Cambridge; UN Students Association, Shilling Paper; ex-chief executive News on Sunday; 'unaligned anti-authoritarian socialist'. 278

HOCH, Paul: City College, New York/ Brown/Toronto/LSE; head of science policy research unit, Warwick University (UK); 'Freudian-Marxist (inactive)'. 282, 283

HOFMANN, Thomas: high-school student; SPD, KPD; PhD candidate in history, Hamburg; 'independent leftist cooperating with the Green Party'. 265

HOUSE, Gloria: Berkeley; SNCC; Republic of New Africa; poet and faculty member, Wayne State University; 'revolutionary nationalist'. 43, 54, 103

HOWELLS, Kim: Hornsey College of Art, London; RSSF; researcher/editor, National Union of Miners, South Wales Area; Labour Party member. 276–7

HUMBERT, Pedro: Milan State University; trade unionist; manager; 'progressive'. 26, 362

HUTTER, Paolo: high-school student; LC, GLF; journalist and Milan local government officer; 'elected as independent on PCI ticket'. 349

JACOBS, Jim: Harpur College; SDS; History Department, McComb Community College; organizer of campaign to eliminate anti-'red squad' campaign, Michigan. 12, 63, 312

JACQUES, Martin: Manchester/Cambridge; CP; editor, Marxism Today; Communist party member. 168

JENSEN, Ottfried: sailor, conscientious objector; Free University of Berlin; social worker; 'independent leftist'. 25–6, 148, 339

JOHNSON, Genie: TransLove Energies, White Panther Party; video arts documentarian, Detroit. 114–5

JONES, Jeff: Antioch; SDS, Weather Underground; writer/journalist, The Guardian: An Independent Radical Weekly; active in Central American solidarity movement. 12, 16, 120, 157, 195, 198, 200, 309, 312, 313, 316, 337

JOYE, Barbara: Vassar; SDS, SSOC, Great Speckled Bird; member department of English, Atlanta University; staff, Radio Free Atlanta. 311

KADRITZKE, Niels: Tübingen/Free University of Berlin; SHB; translator; 'independent socialist'. 20, 59, 124, 149, 178, 361

KARST, Helmi: high-school student; German Black Panther solidarity committee, secretary of Third International Russell Tribunal; teacher. 325

KERNER, Karin: journalist; Free University of Berlin; social worker; 'independent leftist'. 100, 147

KLOTZBACH, Holger: Tübingen; SDS, PLPI; cabaret clown; 'anarcho-socialist'. 148, 348

KOEPKE, Paula: Michigan; physical therapist, San Francisco; 'unaffiliated radical'. 157–8

KÖHLER, Michael: locksmith; assistant TV camera person; 'independent socialist'. 145, 192

KÖHLER, Suse: nursing school, Hannover; cabaret. 20

KÖSTER, Barbara: Munich/Frankfurt; LSD, SDS, Revolutionärer Kampf; instructor at the 'Women's School' in Frankfurt; 'feminist cooperating with the Green Party'. 144–5, 178, 180, 263, 268, 269, 342

KROVOZA, Alfred: Frankfurt/Hannover; SDS; university professor; 'independent leftist'. 20

nomics/Heidelberg; SDS; social scientist at Institute of Social Research, Frankfurt; 'independent leftist'. 80, 127

SINCLAIR, John: Creative Artists Workshop; TransLove Energies; White Panther Party; jazz promoter/poet, Detroit. 12, 75, 113, 114, 116, 295

SKEIST, Robbie: University of Chicago; Chicago Area Draft Resistance Effort, The Resistance, Venceremos Brigades; Chutzpah, Peace Now; director, community health center; active with senior citizens, progressive Jewish movements, and in reform electoral campaigns in Chicago. 106, 293, 349

SKOTNES, Andor: Long Beach State College; SDS, Organizing Comittee for an Ideological Center; assistant director, Oral History Research Office, Columbia University; 'Marxist-democrat'. 318

SMITH, David: Lancaster; freelance writer; 'independent socialist'. 187

STARK, Joann: has requested anonymity. 117

STRAW, Jack: Leeds; Labour Party, NUS; Labour Party MP, shadow education minister. 130, 278–9, 364

TAILOR, Elisabeth: Kent (UK); IS sympathizer, WLM; writer and film-maker; 'non-aligned Marxist-feminist'. 76, 79, 80, 281

TAUTFEST, Peter: Free University, West Berlin; SDS, PLPI, Liga gegen den, Imperialismus; editor geographical teacher's journal. 177, 266–7, 270, 271, 272

THOMAS, Michael: London; RSSF; commentator on current affairs; Labour party member, 'independent Marxist'. 130, 161–2, 177, 277–8, 323–4

THRASHER, Sue: Scaritt College; SSOC, SNCC, Vietnam Summer; coordinator, Residential Education, Highlander; 'radical educator'. 104, 105, 340, 343

TRAUTTEUR, Anna: Turin; teacher; 'progressive'. 166

TRIESMAN, David: Essex/Cambridge; YCND, RSA, RSSF; one of two deputy secretaries, National Association of Teachers in Further and Higher Education;

'centre-left member of Labour Party'. 35, 73, 79, 131, 132, 135, 273–7

VARGAS, Roberto: San Francisco State; TWLF, Brown Berets; poet; cultural attaché, Republic of Nicaragua. 304

VASQUEZ, Carlos: UCLA; United Mexican American Students; General Brotherhood of Workers (CASA); editor, *Sin Fronteras*; coordinator, Academic Relations, UCLA Chicano Studies Research Center; 'independent'. 46, 47, 297–8

VESTER, Michael: Frankfurt; SDS; university professor; 'independent socialist', SB. 59, 66, 124–5

VIALE, Guido: Turin; LC; freelance researcher; 'independent leftist'. 96, 140, 159, 165, 185, 252, 324, 330

WAINWRIGHT, Hilary: Oxford; Young Liberals, RSSF, WLM; political economist and freelance journalist; 'socialist-feminist, member of Socialist Society'. 28, 81, 345, 364

WALLACE, Mike: Columbia; SDS, Mid-Atlantic Radical Historians Organization; historian, John Jay College; editorial board, *Radical History Review*. 10, 200

WARD, Margaret: Belfast high-school student; PD, WLM; writer; 'socialist-feminist'. 346

WEBER, Devra: UCLA; historian, California State University, Long Beach. 118, 346–7

WEBER, Henri: Sorbonne, Paris; UEC, JCR; associate professor; member of the Socialist party. 67, 69, 97, 135–6, 162, 206, 209, 210–11, 216, 218, 337

WEINREICH, Peter: Free University of Berlin; KPD; 'independent leftist'. 331–4

WIDGERY, David: Royal Free Hospital Medical School, London; RSA, RSSF, IS; general practitioner, London's East End; co-chair, North East Thames Branch of the Medical Practitioners Union; member of Socialist Workers' Party. 27, 35, 79, 169–71, 186–7, 273, 281, 326, 328

WIEVIORKA, Michel: Paris; associate professor; 'left liberal'. 215

WILKERSON, Cathy: Swarthmore; SDS, Weather Underground; mathematics teacher, continuing education program for women; raises children, does Attica support work, Brooklyn, NY; 'still political'. 17, 64, 111, 118, 298, 312, 313

WILLIAMSON, Carol: independent peace activist; doctor of medicine; New York City. 151

YOUNG, Marilyn: Harvard, Michigan; EPIC, Teach-in movement, women's lib-eration, historian, New York University, feminist and socialist. 46, 47

ZAMORA, Emilio: Texas A and I; United Mexican American Students, La Raza Unida; historian, Chicano Studies Program, University of Texas. 30

ZEITLIN, Maurice: Wayne State, Wisconsin; sociologist, UCLA; director, Committee for Economic Democracy, Santa Monica, California. 17, 153, 154

Index

abortion laws, reform of, 345, 346, 353
Action Council for the Liberation of Women, 345
Action Faction, 197–8, 200
Adenauer, Konrad, 86
Adorno, Theodor, 59, 268
Albany, Georgia: bus station sit-ins, 42; Sherrod's cooperative farm, 329
Aldermaston marches, 34, 35, 186. *See also* Campaign for Nuclear Disarmament
Algerian National Liberation Front *see* FLN
Algerian War (1954–62), 33, 36–8, 66, 67
Althusser, Louis, 68
American Bandstand, 29–30
Angers, France: demonstration, 220–1
Angry Brigade, the, 336–7
'Angry Young Men', 34
Anti-Internment League, 327
Anti-Nazi League, 328
Antioch College, Ohio, 114–5
Argument, Das (magazine), 60
Assemblea Operai-Studenti, *see* Worker-Student Assembly
Atlantic City, New Jersey: Democratic National Convention (1964), 52
Austin, Texas: demonstration, 318
Autobianchi car factory, 257

Baader, Andreas, 334, 342
Baader-Meinhof group, *see* Red Army Faction
'baby-boom', 4, 76, 113. *See also* demographic growth; population growth
BBC (British Broadcasting Corporation), 129–30, 208, 223, 280, 336
Beatles, the, 77, 79, 115, 131, 202
Beats, the (poets and writers), 23, 61, 82, 113, 131
Beauvoir, Simone de, 323
Belfast, Northern Ireland: Queen's University, 72, 232, 233–4, 238; uprising (August 1969), 14, 244–6
Berch, Bettina, 342
Berkeley, University of California: 1964 campaign, 87, 88, 89–95, 97, 99, 164, 166, 199; defense of People's Park, 295–6
Berlin, West: occupation of Free University

(1966), 125; 'Critical University', 165–6, 174, 264, 344; Congress on Vietnam, 177–81; battle of the Tegeler Weg, 270–2
Berry, Chuck, 77
Bertrand Russell Peace Foundation, 325
Berufsverbot (employment ban) (1972), 325
Black Dwarf (newspaper), 279
Black Panther Party, 55, 103–4, 150, 189, 289, 308, 309, 311, 316, 331
Black Power slogan, 53, 54
black student movements, American, *see* Black Student Union; Student Nonviolent Coordinating Committee
Black Student Union (BSU), 304, 306, 307
Bloch, Ernst, 83
'Bloody Sunday' (1972), 327
'Bloody Tuesday' (1967), 155–6
Bonn: demonstration against Emergency Powers Act, 262
Bourdet, Claude, 33
Britain: in the 1950s, 18, 19, 26–7; 1960s youth culture, 76, 77–9, 131; and the Vietnam War, 128, 129, 132, 135, 185–7, 279; university occupations, 133–5, 272–84; women's movement, 345. *See also* Angry Brigade; Campaign for Nuclear Disarmament; International Socialists; National Union of Students; New Left; Radical Student Alliance; Vietnam Solidarity Campaign
British Army in Northern Ireland, 243, 244, 245, 246, 247
Brown Berets, the, 304
B Specials, 31, 240
BSU, *see* Black Student Union
Burntollet Bridge, Northern Ireland, 240, 241, 242

CADRE, *see* Chicago Area Draft Resistance Effort
CAL, *see* Comité d'Action Lycéen
Cambodia, invasion of, 317, 319, 323
Cambridge University, 98; imprisonment of students, 283
Campaign for Nuclear Disarmament (CND), 33, 34–6, 73, 132, 169, 186, 195
Camus, Albert, 46, 82

Mexican-American community, *see* Chicano movement
MFDP, *see* Mississippi Freedom Democratic Party
Michigan University: black student activism, 301; teach-in (1965), 102
Milan: occupation of architectural faculty (1963), 69; occupations of Private Catholic University (1967, 1968), 165, 183; right-wing bomb attack, 257
Milani, Lorenzo: *Lettera a una professoressa*, 140
miners' strikes, British, 322, 326–7
Mississippi Freedom Democratic Party (MFDP), 52
Mississippi Freedom Summer (1964), 41, 48–52, 89, 93, 111
Mitscherlich: *Medizin ohne Menschlichkeit*, 86–7
Mobilization Committee, 151, 156
Montgomery, Alabama: segregated bus system, 39
Moro, Aldo, 335
Moses, Bob, 44, 48, 49, 50
Munich Counter-Cultural Group, *see* SPUR
Musatti (Freudian analyst), 166
music, pop, 77, 79, 80–1, 328

NAACP (National Association for the Advancement of Colored People), 39
Nanterre University, 171–2; 1967 strike, 171–2, 173–4; May 1968 events, 9–10, 203–4, 216. *See also* 22 March Movement
Nantes, France: Sud Aviation factory strike, 216–7, 220, 223
Naples University, 99, 254–5; 1967 occupations of, 139, 166–7
National Defense Education Act (1958), 98
National Union of Students (NUS), 278–9, 326–7
NATO, 18, 178
Nazis, campaigns against, 21, 146, 328
Neue Kritik (magazine), 66
New Left: British, 33–4, 35, 57, 59, 73, 130–1; *Out of Apathy*, 59; American, 62, 102, 105, 106, 116, 117, 201, 292
New Left Notes (SDS paper), 111, 310, 312
New Left Review, 33, 161
Newton, Huey P., 55
New Working-Class Theory, 159–60
New Year Gang, 320
NICRA, *see* Northern Ireland Civil Rights Association
Nixon, President Richard, 288–9, 316, 318, 319, 329

NLF, *see* Vietnamese National Liberation Front
Northern Ireland: in the 1950s, 27, 31–2; early radical students, 72; civil rights demonstrations, 233, 237–40, 241, 242–3, 327–8; internment introduced, 327; women's movement, 346, 347. *See also* IRA; Northern Ireland Civil Rights Association; People's Democracy
Northern Ireland Civil Rights Association (NICRA), 232, 237, 239
Northern Irish Solidarity Campaign, 281–2
nuclear power stations, movements against building, 325. *See also* Campaign for Nuclear Disarmament
Nuclear Test Ban Treaty (1963), 85
NUS, *see* National Union of Students

Oakland, California: demonstrations at Induction Center (1967), 154–5
'Oakland Seven', the, 296
Ohnesorg, Benno, 143–4, 145, 178
Open Process (underground newspaper), 121
O'Neill, Terence, Unionist Prime Minister, 231, 237, 241, 242
Oracle (underground newspaper), 121
Orange Order, 237
Ortoleva, Peppino, 18, 138–9, 184, 250
overseas students' fees, protests against (1967), 130, 132

Paisley, Reverend Ian, 245
Palumbo, Irene, 347
Papandrea, Rocco, 252
Paris: May–June 1968 events, 203, 204–17, 218–24, 225–9
Pearse, Padraig, 81–2
Pentagon, march on the, 156–8, 190
People's Democracy (PD), 14, 231, 234, 236, 237–40, 241–5, 245–8, 278, 281, 363
People's Park (Berkeley), defense of, 295–6
Pham Van Dong, Premier, 133
pill, the, 79, 118–9, 342. *See also* sexual mores
Pisa, Scuola Normale di: sexual discrimination, 71
Pisa University: 1967 occupations, 139, 168; 1968 sit-in, 183
PL, *see* Progressive Labor Party
Pompidou, Georges, 223, 225
population growth, 4, 76. *See also* 'baby boom'; demographic growth
Port Huron Statement (1962), 62–3
Potter, Paul, 103
Powell, Enoch, 273
'Prairie Power Faction', 105, 109
'Praxis-Action' group, 197–8